The Computer-Animated Film
Industry, Style and Genre

Christopher Holliday

EDINBURGH
University Press

Edinburgh University Press is one of the leading university presses in the UK. We publish academic books and journals in our selected subject areas across the humanities and social sciences, combining cutting-edge scholarship with high editorial and production values to produce academic works of lasting importance. For more information visit our website: edinburghuniversitypress.com

Edinburgh University Press Ltd
The Tun – Holyrood Road
12 (2f) Jackson's Entry
Edinburgh EH8 8PJ

Typeset in Monotype Ehrhardt by
Servis Filmsetting Ltd, Stockport, Cheshire,
and printed and bound in Great Britain by
CPI Group (UK) Ltd, Croydon, CR0 4YY

A CIP record for this book is available from the British Library

ISBN 978 1 4744 2788 3 (hardback)
ISBN 978 1 4744 2790 6 (webready PDF)
ISBN 978 1 4744 2791 3 (epub)

Contents

Figures

Acknowledgements

This book grew out of a doctoral thesis undertaken within the Film Studies department at King's College London, and funded by the Arts and Humanities Research Council. I thank both for giving me the opportunity to study the computer-animated film. Deepest gratitude is reserved for my superlative PhD supervisor Michele Pierson, whose unwavering intellectual generosity and care for the project (as well as her trusty blue ink pen) made the work much better than it ought to have been, and the whole experience even more so. The seeds of this book were first sown whilst studying as an undergraduate student at the University of Warwick. I would therefore like to give wholehearted thanks to my very first film and television teachers José Arroyo, James Bennett, Charlotte Brunsdon, Stella Bruzzi, Richard Dyer, Ed Gallafent, Iris Kleinecke-Bates, Rachel Moseley, Amy Sargeant, Ginette Vincendeau and Helen Wheatley and for creating such an inspirational and encouraging environment all around me, and to V. F. Perkins for showing me first-hand the sheer enjoyment of it all. Though he won't know it, Steve Allen's last-minute decision to screen *Toy Story* instead of *Jurassic Park* on a first-year film history course caused a small lightbulb to turn on somewhere in the back of my mind that is luckily still burning bright. My thanks must also go to Tom Brown, another influential film teacher at Warwick and friend, and Jon Burrows, whose words of reassurance and supervision greatly shaped both the BA and then MA dissertations at Warwick that helped to further cultivate something of my animated enthusiasms.

I continue to benefit immensely from the intellectual support of numerous teachers, colleagues and friends at King's College and beyond, many of whom have delivered welcome moments of scholarly inspiration and clarity as this book came to fruition. Alice Haylett Bryan, Malcolm Cook, Amy M. Davis, Ivan Girina, Annabelle Honess Roe, Chris Pallant, Luke Robinson, Martha Shearer, Ben Tyrer and James Whitfield all offered their time, friendship, advice, honesty, recommendations and encouragement when I needed them most. I also wish to acknowledge the following people for their guidance and support that has come in many forms: Mark Betz, Jinhee Choi, Sarah Cooper, Victor Fan, Rosalind Galt, Hannah Hamad, Lawrence Napper, Mark Shiel, Belén Vidal and Catherine Wheatley. In addition to these names, I must add three people in particular. Edward Lamberti and Alexander Sergeant have been a constant source of friendship, and I am enormously grateful to them both for contributing conversation, offering passionate defences of some of my early ideas that otherwise might have fallen by the wayside, keeping me focused, and then taking my mind off it all at just the right times. Sincere thanks also goes to Lilly Husbands, who provided unbeatable intellectual support during the turbulent emotions of writing and rewriting, and who continues to offer treasured friendship and characteristically excellent scholarly advice delivered with precision and humour.

The opportunity to test out ideas at multiple conferences and in class-rooms has been vital in seeing this project to its completion. I would like to thank in particular the many undergraduate and postgraduate students at King's College London, London South Bank University, University of Kent and University of Surrey who have given me so much to think on and to question – their input and insights have been integral to the shape of my research. Gillian Leslie at Edinburgh University Press has been hugely supportive and enthusiastic about the project right from the start, and I thank too the reviewers for their comments on a previous draft of the manuscript. Earlier versions of Chapters 3 and 4 were previously published as 'Notes on a Luxo world', *Animation Practice, Process & Production* 4: 1 (December 2014), pp. 67–95, and '"I'm not a real boy, I'm a puppet': Computer-Animated Films and Anthropomorphic Subjectivity', *animation: an interdisciplinary journal* 11: 3 (November 2016), pp. 246–62, respectively. Some of the arguments in Chapter 6 appear in 'Toying with performance: *Toy Story*, Virtual Puppetry and Computer-Animated Film Acting' in Noel Brown, Susan Smith and Sam Summers (eds.), *Toy Story* (Animation: Key Films/Filmmakers) (London: Bloomsbury Academic, an imprint of Bloomsbury Publishing Plc., 2018), pp. 87–104. I am tremen-dously grateful to the anonymous reviewers for their comments on these articles and chapters, and to the editors and publishers for the opportunity to further develop my thoughts around the computer-animated film. In addition, Barry Langford and Paul Wells were extremely forthcoming in the project's early stages, with highly constructive feedback and advice when I was trying to mould everything into something that resembled a book on animation. I would also like to thank Anna Robertson, whose patience and encouragement during the writing made me believe that what I had to say might be worthwhile.

Finally, I wish to make a special dedication to my parents, Frances and Robert, the best people I know. Their decision in the winter of 1992 to take me to see Walt Disney's *Aladdin* as my very first film at the cinema probably explains a lot of what was to follow.

To my siblings Doug, Emmajo and Louisa, for the love and laughter, I am grateful to each of you for allowing me to take over small parts of our childhood (and then even larger bits of our adulthood) with all things animation. Here are the results of my passions.

Introduction

Emerging at the intersection of feature-length animated cinema and computer-generated imagery (CGI), and preceded by a cycle of preparatory shorts made by the Pixar Animation Studios during the 1980s, feature-length computer-animated films have become the dominant form of mainstream animation. The rapid ascendency of computer-animated filmmaking and the reinvention of animation as a computer-generated medium has been widely recognised for its positive contribution to the fortunes of the US animation industry. Paul Grainge has argued that the first wave of computer-animated blockbusters released during the 1990s and early 2000s inspired a 'revival' (2008: 119) of animation across millennial Hollywood cinema. Terms such as 'revitalization' (Krämer 2006: 168), 'revivifying' (Willis 2008: 47), 'renewed' (Dobson 2009: xlix), 'rebirth' (Sickels 2011: 95), 'resurrection' (Ghez 2011: 595), 'resurgence' (Brown 2012: 183) and 'revolution' (Sperb 2016: 86) all boldly announce the substantial impact of digital technology upon popular animated film in America.

The Computer-Animated Film: Industry, Style and Genre traces the expansion of the computer-animated film as a global phenomenon of mainstream Hollywood filmmaking and across a variety of other national cinemas. This book seeks to theorise the place of computer-animated films within film and animation history and digital media culture, arguing that their visual currencies and formal attributes can be organised as a framework that supports their study as a new genre of contemporary cinema. This book therefore seeks to sharpen and develop the critical discussion of computer-animated films' defining industrial, technological, historical and textual features. It proposes a set of stylistic relationships between over 200 films released over more than a twenty-year period, and produced by a variety of animation studios. Drawing such distinctions offers a more robust account of their visual style within the multifarious fields of popular animation and digitally assisted filmmaking. However, to talk about computer-animated films is to talk about the very recent history of Hollywood, and a group of films caught up in (if not fundamental to) the rapid computerisation of popular North American cinema during the mid-1990s. This introduction therefore begins by outlining the shape of an increasingly competitive and stable computer-animated film industry, one that began during the first decade of the new millennium, and evidenced the growing importance of computer graphics to mainstream Hollywood production.

Reanimating an Industry

Taken together with the late-1980s 'renaissance' of Disney Feature Animation and the almost simultaneous 'artistic revitalization' (Pallant 2011: 90) of the cartoon format on US television, the arrival of computer-animated films plotted an immediate upward trajectory for popular animation in America. Following the release of Pixar's *Toy Story* (John Lasseter, 1995) on 22 November 1995, an exponential growth in the volume of studios invested in the production of feature-length computer-animated films reflected the industry's direct reaction to the possibilities of three-dimensional computer graphics. The market response to Pixar's debut feature was, as Scott Kirsner points out, the expansion of an animation industry almost immediately populated by copycat studios and 'would-be Pixars' (2008: 74). A number of companies, facilities, divisions and subsidiaries rapidly emerged, many of which made the transition from visual effects companies offering 'customized services on a contractual basis to major clients' (Scott 2005: 96) to specialising in computer-animated feature film production. With Pixar themselves having usurped the Walt Disney Studio 'atop the proverbial heap in the cartoon world' (Goldmark 2013: 214) through its computer-animated films, their new station at the head of the global animation market was soon challenged as technical innovation, software availability, workforce expertise and augmented computer power enabled computer-animated films to be produced more efficiently and cost-effectively.

Several film studios during the early 2000s established independent animation units as a way of integrating computer-animated films into pre-existing production hierarchies. In 2003, the San Francisco-based Lucasfilm founded Lucasfilm Animation; renowned visual effects company Industrial Light & Magic (ILM) moved into full computer-animated film production with *Rango* (Gore Verbinski, 2011); and in 2007 filmmaker Robert Zemeckis' ImageMovers studio founded a separate animation facility with Walt Disney Pictures under the banner of ImageMovers Digital. Paramount Pictures announced the founding of Paramount Animation that same year, their own in-house animation studio (their first since Paramount Cartoon Studios was dissolved in 1967) intended to challenge Pixar's market dominance. Paramount was not the only studio to return to feature animation after a period of dormancy. Following a decade-long hiatus from theatrical cartoons (producing only television series and shorts for The WB and Cartoon Network), Warner Brothers announced in 2013 that it was resuming feature animation as the newly formed Warner Animation Group (WAG), the successor to Warner Bros. Feature Animation that had shut down in 2004. WAG's inaugural feature was the computer-animated film *The LEGO Movie* (Phil Lord and Christopher Miller, 2014), animated by Australian visual effects studio Animal Logic, who had produced their own computer-animated feature films *Happy Feet* (George Miller, 2006) and *Legend of the Guardians: The Owls of Ga'Hoole* (Zack Snyder, 2010) a few years earlier.

The restructuring of many other US studios with longer animated histories resulted in the progressive phasing out of traditional cel-animation methods, with digital technologies firmly dislodging hand-drawn practices as the animated film's principal language. Crest Animation Productions, Arc Productions (formerly Starz Animation) and DNA Productions all converted from cel-animated features to exclusively computer-animated filmmaking. In 2000, DreamWorks Animation (initially a division of DreamWorks SKG, though now a subsidiary of NBCUniversal) purchased digital effects company Pacific Data Images, and the two merged to become DreamWorks Animation, which was spun out as a separate company in 2004 (DreamWorks would purchase another computer animation unit in 2012, Big Idea Productions). As DreamWorks co-founder and ex-Disney Chief Executive Jeffrey Katzenberg proclaimed, 'traditional animation is a thing of the past' (in Sito 2006: 339). Among the many animation units shifting production from traditional techniques to become exclusively all-digital animation studios, most seismic of these was Disney. The Disney studio's fluctuating commercial and critical fortunes (particularly during the 1970s and 1980s, and then again in the early 2000s) have been used to graph the historical rise and fall of American animation as an industrial art form. In response to the force of the marketplace, Disney announced that it was ceasing traditional methods after its forty-fifth (and, at that time, final) cel-animated feature *Home on the Range* (Will Finn and John Sanford, 2004). Disney's decision to jettison its hand-drawn heritage in favour of computer-animated filmmaking for its next feature, *Chicken Little* (Mark Dindal, 2005), signalled what John

Canemaker (2005) called the end of an 'indigenously American contribution to the international art form of animation'.

The sheer volume of computer-animated films and the rapid growth of Hollywood animation over the last twenty years has, however, prompted occasional moments of uncertainty. As early as 2006, several journalists in the US were suggesting that the computer-animated film market may have reached its saturation point, only twenty years after the first computer-animated short, Pixar's *Luxo Jr.* (John Lasseter, 1986), and a little over a decade since *Toy Story*. This unexpected congestion was widely noted in the Hollywood trade press, including cautionary pieces that made their way into the pages of *Screen International* and the *Hollywood Reporter*.[1] In *Variety*, Ben Fritz and Dave McNary pointed out that the thirteen computer-animated films due for release in the US during 2006 was a 'record so out of proportion to recent years that marketers are wondering if the business has the capacity to absorb them all' (2006: 1). Between 2007 and 2008, another 'mass of features' were released across America including *Shrek the Third* (Chris Miller and Raman Hui, 2007), *Ratatouille* (Brad Bird, 2007), *Bee Movie* (Simon J. Smith and Steve Hickner, 2007) and *Kung Fu Panda* (John Stevenson and Mark Osborne, 2008), all of which were 'big-exposure' computer-animated films replete with 'exorbitant budgets' (Goldmark 2013: 214) and sustained marketing campaigns. More recently, in 2016, Hollywood's sixteen major computer-animated film releases (three up on the total for 2015) that premiered between Walt Disney's *Zootopia* (Byron Howard and Rich Moore, 2016) in March and DreamWorks Animation's *Trolls* (Mike Mitchell, 2016) in November once again surfaced popular and industry fears around another potential bumper year in which supply would outweigh demand.

The question of market capacity is not far from the production of computer-animated films, particularly as American studios remain increasingly susceptible to the lure of animation. However, any caution expressed by the Hollywood trade press against industry surplus has typically been a readymade response to box office under-performance. In an earlier *Variety* piece from 2004, for example, Fritz had noted that for investors there was 'no downside in CGI-animated pics – at least not yet', and speculated that their financial security 'will inevitably hit a bump in the road' (2004: 6). Just two years later, Fritz and McNary's scepticism at market saturation was in response to one such 'bump', namely the critical and commercial disappointment of Pixar's *Cars* (John Lasseter, 2006). In 2013, Richard Verrier warned again that the 'abundance' of computer-animated films might be once again 'nearing a saturation point' (2013). Verrier not only identified the eleven films readied for theatrical release in the summer of 2013, but the thirteen slated for 2014 and the total of seventy-five computer-animated films produced since 2008. Yet his counsel of a congestion in computer-animated film production was likewise cued by the poor critical and commercial performance of DreamWorks' *Rise of the Guardians* (Peter Ramsey 2012) and *Turbo* (David Soren, 2013), two films described by Verrier as 'high-profile stumbles' and 'unexpected misfire[s]' (ibid.) at odds with the high ticket sales normally expected of computer-animated feature films.

The generally positive critical and commercial reception of computer-animated films has certainly alleviated any concern over their projected over-supply within the Hollywood entertainment industry. Highly profitable family-oriented computer-animated films have consistently attracted strong audiences and – since *Toy Story* and *A Bug's Life* (John Lasseter, 1998) became the top grossing films of 1995 and 1998 respectively – have continued to perform successfully at both the US and global box offices. In 2012, the London-based IHS Markit analysis group reported that the 'booming popularity' of computer-animated films between 2001 and 2011 had doubled the US total box office for animated features. Their revenue within the American theatrical market is a clear indication that computer-animated films lie at the heart of today's Hollywood film industry. It comes as little surprise, then, that Kristin Thompson suggested back in 2006 the anxieties expressed by studio executives and critical commentators over that year's surge were 'bizarre' given their box office successes and typically favourable reviews. Thompson argued that computer-animated films remained among the 'best work' (2011: 159) being produced by mainstream Hollywood, and described them as one of the most popular, commercially successful and critically lauded cinematic forms currently circulating within the global film market.

The healthy commercial reputation of computer-animated films has certainly made them increasingly desirable investments, sustaining studio interest in the production of feature-length animation. Shilo T. McClean has specifically attributed the economic viability of computer-animated films (especially those made at Pixar) to a 'new willingness for studios to back long-form animation', previously considered to be 'too expensive and of a limited market' (2007: 99–100). Produced at Mac Guff – a French visual effects studio founded in 1988, but purchased in 2011 by California-based production company Illumination Entertainment – the computer-animated film *Despicable Me 2* (Pierre Coffin and Chris Renaud, 2013) is the most profitable film in the 101-year history of the Universal studio. Disney's blockbuster *Frozen* (Chris Buck and Jennifer Lee, 2013) holds the distinction of being the top grossing animated film of all time, with only one film in the current top ten not computer-animated (Disney's *The Lion King* [Roger Allers and Rob Minkoff, 1994]). McClean, as well as Pat Brereton (2012), have noted how the ongoing achievements of the computer-animated film in the post-exhibition arenas of DVD/home video entertainment have only extended their lucrative commercial and consumer value. In a 2015 list of best-selling DVDs of the past decade, the top position was once again held by *Frozen*, which has sold 4.26 million copies since its release in March 2014, with another computer-animated film, the original *Despicable Me* (Pierre Coffin and Chris Renaud, 2010), currently ranked at number four. Pixar's *Finding Nemo* (Andrew Stanton, 2003) remains the best-selling DVD of all time, symbolically replacing previous number one, Disney's cel-animated musical *The Lion King*.

To Hollywood and Beyond

Just as Silicon Valley's proximity to Hollywood contributed to the area's 'preeminence as the locus of digital cinema' during the late 1980s (Brown 2013: 13), *Toy Story*'s roots in the offices of Pixar's then-home in Richmond, California have worked to frame North America as the standard bearer of computer-animated film production. Yet in 2009, *The New York Times* ran a short feature titled 'Animation Upstarts Are Joining the Fray', which squared the rising volume of computer-animated films (fourteen in 2009 compared with five in 2008) to the multitude of independent production companies now competing for their share of the Hollywood animation market. The influx of certain 'newcomers' was, on the one hand, still fixed to US-based studios Snoot Toons (*Battle for Terra* [Aristomenis Tsirbas, 2007]) and the Exodus Film Group (*Igor* [Tony Leondis, 2008]), while major American studios like DreamWorks were also noted as intending to 'ramp up production' by 'delivering five films every two years' (Barnes 2009). However, the main focus of the article was Ilion Animation Studios, a Madrid-based animation facility founded in 2002 and whose blockbuster computer-animated feature film *Planet 51* (Jorge Blanco, 2009) coincided with 'event' releases by Pixar, Sony, Twentieth Century Fox, and Imagi Studios in Hong Kong.

In the twenty-three years that have elapsed since *Toy Story*, the computer-animated feature film has become a global business, and many studios have extended the computer-animated film industry beyond the geography and industrial filmmaking systems of Hollywood. Computer-animated films continue to be produced and distributed in countries such as Spain, Germany, Argentina, Hungary, Japan, Brazil, Turkey, Holland, India and with the release of the twenty-minute *Buz-e-Chini/The Goat*

(Abbas Ali, 2012), Afghanistan. Since 2008, animation has emerged at the 'forefront' of the New Korean Wave, with 'Korea's own computer-generated cartoons [. . .] met with unprecedented levels of global success' that has reinvigorated the Korean animation industry (Jin 2016: 18). In China, and despite origins as far back as the work of the Wan Brothers in the 1940s, animation has likewise 'come into its own' and 'become a nation-building industry' thanks to CGI (MacDonald 2016: 1–2). The recent Oriental DreamWorks venture by DreamWorks Animation (with China Media Capital, Shanghai Media Group and Shanghai Alliance Investment) in 2012, and whose debut feature *Kung Fu Panda 3* (Jennifer Yuh Nelson and Alessandro Carloni, 2016) became China's highest grossing animated feature (Brzeski 2016), further bears out the lucrative place of computer animation within the Chinese film market.

Richard Neupert similarly considers French computer-animated films such as *Renaissance* (Christian Volckman, 2006) – a black and white, futuristic science fiction feature – as having redefined animation as 'economically important, aesthetically vibrant, and culturally crucial to France's persistently impressive national cinema' (2011: 149). The success of the more recent *A Monster in Paris* (Bibo Bergeron, 2011) once again 'proved that France could produce a world-class digital feature with the sorts of spectacle, musical numbers, and engaging characters that one would find at Aardman, DreamWorks, or Pixar' (Neupert 2015: 350). Indeed, British animation studio Aardman, whose reputation had been founded on stop-motion 'claymation' techniques pioneered in *Chicken Run* (Peter Lord and Nick Park, 2000) and *Wallace & Gromit: The Curse of the Were-Rabbit* (Nick Park and Steve Box, 2005), had themselves entered the computer-animated film market in partnership with DreamWorks for *Flushed Away* (David Bowers and Sam Fell, 2006). Aardman's second feature, *Arthur Christmas* (Sarah Smith, 2011), was produced in collaboration with Sony Pictures Animation, a specialist animated film production company newly formed in May 2002 as a sub-division of Sony Pictures Entertainment.

Many other countries have acclimatised to the possibilities for computer-animated film production. *Khan Kluay* (Kompin Kemgumnird, 2006) is the first Thai animated feature film since the cel-animated film *The Adventure of Sudsakorn* (Payut Ngaokrachang, 1979), with a sequel *Khan Kluay 2* (Taweelap Srivuthivong, 2009) released three years later. *The Emperor's Secret* (Riina Hyytia, 2006), *The Adventures of Alyonushka and Yeryoma* (Georgi Gitis, 2008), *Goat Story* (Jan Tománek, 2008), *Gnomes and Trolls: The Secret Chamber* (Robert Rhodin, 2008), *RPG Metanoia* (Luis C. Suárez, 2010), *Xero Error* (Ashraf Ghori, 2010), *3 Bahadur* (Sharmeen Obaid Chinoy, 2015) and *Bilal: A New Breed of Hero* (Khurram Alavi and Ayman Jamal, 2016) are the very first computer-animated feature films to be produced in Finland, Russia, Czech Republic, Sweden, Philippines, United Arab Emirates, Pakistan and Saudi Arabia respectively. Costing $21 million, *Underdogs* (Juan José Campanella, 2013) is the most expensive Argentine film of all time, and the most expensive Latin American animated feature ever. *Wicked Flying Monkeys* (Alberto Mar, 2015) was described in the US trade press as 'the biggest film production to date from Mexico's Anima Estudios' (Hopewell 2015), while *El Americano: The Movie* (Ricardo Arnaiz and Mike Kunkel, 2016) is first co-production between Mexican and US studios. The Cape Town-based Triggerfish, the studio behind computer-animated films *Zambezia* (Wayne Thornley, 2012) and *Khumba* (Anthony Silverton, 2013), is known as the 'Pixar of South Africa' (Szalai 2013). Within these local productions, Denmark and Belgium have particularly vibrant computer-animated film industries, the latter spearheaded almost entirely by the figure of Ben Stassen. Founded by Stassen in 1994, nWave Pictures have produced six computer-animated films (all directed or co-directed by Stassen), including *Fly Me to the Moon* (2008), *The House of Magic* (2013), *The Wild Life* (2016) and *The Son of Bigfoot* (2017). For *Variety*'s Guy Lodge, the nWave studio represents 'a marker of just how swiftly Euro animation houses are catching up with their Hollywood counterparts' (2014).

Many European computer-animated feature films are obtaining greater visibility among international audiences via the vast distribution networks provided by US partner studios. *Planet 51* was distributed by Sony (although distribution of Ilion's next feature *Mortadelo & Filemon, Mission: Implausible* [Javier Fesser, 2014] was handled by Warner Brothers); *Wicked Flying Monkeys* by Lionsgate; while two Spanish computer-animated features, *Tad: The Lost Explorer* (Enrique Gato, 2012) and *Capture the Flag* (Enrique Gato, 2015), marked the first time a major Hollywood studio (Paramount Pictures) had acquired worldwide distribution right for Spanish films following their strong domestic box office. Between February 2010 and August 2017, nWave also held a long-term production partnership with StudioCanal, which exploited their direct distribution territories (UK, France, and Germany) and provided theatrical distribution for their computer-animated films in the North American market. Several Hollywood studios such as Illumination Entertainment, DreamWorks Animation, Paramount and MGM have recently taken advantage of the increasing eminence of these international animation facilities by outsourcing computer-animated film production, mostly to effects studios in France. In 2014, Ilion Animation was also invited 'to bid against other animation studios to provide animation services on the Paramount Animation movie' (Hopewell 2015), reflecting the attraction of continental Europe and its quality of production services to the larger US conglomerates.

The thematic similarities between pairs of computer-animated films produced by Hollywood – including *Shark Tale* (Vicky Jenson, Bibo Bergeron and Rob Letterman, 2004), *Finding Nemo* and *Shark Bait* (Howard E. Baker and John Fox, 2006); *Madagascar* (Eric Darnell and Tom McGrath, 2005) and *The Wild* (Steve Williams, 2006); *Ratatouille* and *Flushed Away*; and *The Book of Life* (Jorge R. Gutierrez, 2014) and *Coco* (Lee Unkrich, 2017) – has been matched by the rise of the transnational computer-animated 'mockbuster'. Mockbusters are traditionally 'low-budget films that are unapologetic rip-offs of recent big-budget films' (Booker 2011: 49). Examples of this practice include the computer-animated features made by Brazilian company Vídeo Brinquedo, whose straight-to-video *The Little Cars* (Cristiano Valente, 2006), *Ratatoing* (Michelle Gabriel, 2007), *Tiny Robots* (Michelle Gabriel, 2008) and *Little Bee* (Michelle Gabriel, 2009) are mockbusters of *Cars*, *Ratatouille*, *Robots* (Chris Wedge, 2005)/ *Wall-E* (Andrew Stanton, 2008) and *Bee Movie* respectively. The rhetoric of these imitative mockbusters seems to enact a longstanding core/periphery model between North America and other national cinemas. Yet these 'local' responses to the blockbuster computer-animated films of contemporary Hollywood animation continues the range of domestic mockbusters that similarly mine the cultural visibility of more 'official' computer-animated productions. Renegade Animation (US), Allumination Filmworks (US), Simka Entertainment (US), Brightspark Productions (UK) and Phase 4 Films (Canada) have all produced and distributed computer-animated film mockbusters, evidencing how the manufacture of low-budget copycat features has remained a 'largely American practice' (Frelik 2014: 249) just as much as popular Hollywood cinema has historically been reworked and remade within ulterior national contexts. At the same time, the discourse of originality and resemblance that supports the mockbuster trend reflects the international capital of the computer-animated film as a popular global form.

Despite the clear international reach of computer-animated filmmaking, and the numerous low- to mid-budget features produced worldwide (typically financed at around 20% of the cost of Hollywood computer-animated films), many non-US studios are admittedly still playing 'catch up' with the major Hollywood animation studios. Where previously years separated North American computer-animated films, the gap is now a matter of months, especially as the big American studios have the capabilities to release two tent-pole feature films per year supported by high-profile merchandising and marketing campaigns (Pixar with *Inside Out* [Pete Docter, 2015] and *The Good Dinosaur* [Peter Sohn, 2015] in 2015; Disney with *Zootopia* and *Moana* [Ron Clements and John Musker, 2016] the following year). Since *Shark Tale* and *Shrek 2* (Andrew Adamson, Kelly Asbury and Conrad Vernon, 2004) in 2004, DreamWorks have (aside from 2009) released two computer-animated films annually, spiking at three releases in both 2010 and 2014. Computer-animated feature film production evidently remains of growing importance to the North American film industry, and a lucrative and highly profitable business. Yet the particular strengths of American animation as an industrial art form can be squared to its stable studio infrastructure and quality of creative personnel.

The New American Cartoon

Beyond the name recognition of John Lasseter (Disney/Pixar) and Jeffrey Katzenberg (DreamWorks), computer-animated films have proven a magnet for attracting high-profile directors from live-action film into animation for the first time. The involvement of eminent directorial figures with a renowned pedigree in live-action cinema, such as Robert Zemeckis (*The Polar Express* [2004]; *Beowulf* [2007]; *A Christmas Carol* [2009]), George Miller (*Happy Feet* and *Happy Feet Two* [2011]), Zack Snyder (*Legend of the Guardians: The Owls of Ga'Hoole*), Gore Verbinski (*Rango*), and Steven Spielberg and Peter Jackson (*The Adventures of Tintin: The Secret of the Unicorn* [2011]), has afforded a whole new level of artistic credibility to feature-length animation. Andrew Adamson (*Shrek 2*), Andrew Stanton (*Finding Nemo*), Chris Wedge (*Ice Age* [2002]), Brad Bird (*The Incredibles* [2004], *Ratatouille*), Phil Lord and Christopher Miller (*Cloudy with a Chance of Meatballs* [2009]), Gil Kenan (*Monster House* [2006]), and Jimmy Hayward (*Horton Hears a Who!* [2008]) are also all filmmakers that have moved into live-action feature film production following their work directing computer-animated films.

The digital rejuvenation of US animation has further transformed the American cartoon by reprising something of a classic Hollywood sensibility. If Golden Age filmmaking in the studio era had the 'Big Five' and the 'Little Three' as part of its vertically integrated supply chain, then the computer-animated film industry of contemporary Hollywood operates according to an analogous structure, with a 'Big Five' of Pixar, DreamWorks, Disney, Illumination Entertainment and another studio, Blue Sky. Founded in 1987 following the demise of computer technology company Mathematical Applications Group, Inc., Blue Sky Studios began, like Pixar, as a visual effects company, and in 1997, were acquired by Twentieth Century Fox to produce computer-animated feature films. Fox had already sought to break into lucrative feature animation themselves with the founding of Fox Animation Studio in 1994, headed by ex-Disney character animator Don Bluth. However, Fox's unit closed in 2000 having produced only two feature films, *Anastasia* (Don Bluth and Gary Goldman, 1997) and *Titan A.E.* (Don Bluth and Gary Goldman, 2000), and their partnership with Blue Sky (which is now a subsidiary of Twentieth Century Fox) was specifically intended to produce competitive computer-animated feature films.

It is these 'Big Five' that currently account for the majority of mainstream computer-animated film production in Hollywood, and as of late 2017 have contributed a total of seventy-six computer-animated films between them (Pixar nineteen; DreamWorks twenty-nine; Disney nine; Blue Sky twelve; Illumination Entertainment seven). However, these studios' market dominance is not the only analogue to 1940s Hollywood. The loyalty that many employees have to specific animation facilities has provoked further comparisons between contemporary computer-animated film production and studio era filmmaking. The Pixar studio's operations are not far from 'Hollywood of six decades ago' (Feeney 2009), insofar as the authorial signatures of individual expression circulate within stringent industrial parameters. Pixar have outwardly promoted their production culture according to a classical studio template, emphasising close creative and long-term relationships with personnel, lack of migration between studios, and a loyal stable workforce. Many other creative figures are synonymous with computer-animated film production through studio affiliation, such as Chris Wedge and Carlos Saldanha (Blue Sky Studios); Pierre Coffin and Chris Renaud (Illumination Entertainment); and Conrad Vernon and Tom McGrath (DreamWorks Animation) amongst many others. The terms under which Pixar 'blazed a trail for computer-animated films' (Meinel 2016: 8) can be no less understood according to its formation of an industry template rooted in these same discourses of studio exclusivity. The Pixar Brain Trust – a creative consortium that emphasises cohesive in-house filmmaker collaboration – was closely followed by the inception of the Disney Story Trust (also by Lasseter) and then the Warner Brothers Think Tank, which comprises both live-action and animation directors as part of its talent group.

Given the vibrancy of contemporary computer-animated filmmaking, it is perhaps unsurprising that Dietmar Meinel speaks of a current state of 'intensified competition' (ibid.) supporting the North American animation market. Particular rivalries between Pixar and DreamWorks have been widely documented in hagiographic corporate histories, and their creative enmity has invited comparison with the fruitful Golden Age competition between Walt Disney and Warner Brothers. Kathleen McDonnell remembers how the simultaneous release of DreamWorks' *Antz* (Eric Darnell and Tim Johnson, 1998) and Pixar's *A Bug's Life* in the late 1990s 'saw the start of what was termed the Animation Wars' (2005: 71). This 'war' was publicly fought at the 2002 Academy Awards in the category for Best Animated Feature, an honour created to respect the high quality of computer-animated films and to recognise their revitalisation of US animation. Describing the competition between DreamWorks' *Shrek* (Andrew Adamson and Vicky Jenson, 2001) and Pixar's *Monsters, Inc.* (Pete Docter, 2001) for the category's inaugural prize, Paul Karon anticipated that within the Hollywood film industry the future of animation 'is probably healthier than many have predicted' (2002: 36).

It is difficult to comprehensively quantify the good 'health' of contemporary computer-animated films, and to critically explain what is not only a mainstay of contemporary Hollywood cinema but now a mass cultural phenomenon. When a Buzz Lightyear action figure spent fifteen months orbiting the Earth aboard the Discovery Space Shuttle in May 2008, his catchphrase 'to infinity and beyond' became dramatically fulfilled. The elderly protagonist of Pixar's *Up* (Pete Docter, 2009), Carl Fredericksen, is currently an ambassador for the Hear the World Foundation initiative, while the eponymous green ogre Shrek has been the spokesperson for the Department of Health and Human Services' (HHS) obesity campaign across America since 2007. But the reputation and regard of computer-animated films among both critics and audiences demands further exploration, because, as Barry Langford points out, it is 'enormously difficult to compute popularity' (2005: 19). The central argument of this book is ultimately that the feature-length computer-animated film constitutes a unique, but as yet undetermined and unrecognised, genre of contemporary cinema.

There is certainly something regular and uniform, even generic, about computer-animated films. This homogeneity is undoubtedly a function of a Hollywood industry well versed in exploiting the commercial stability and security of sameness afforded by repeating pleasures. Geoff King points out that it is 'not hard to make sense of genre from an industrial perspective' (2002a: 118), and the packaging of computer-animated films according to what this book argues is a successful narrative and characterological formula has strengthened the business and commercial structures of contemporary Hollywood's highly 'animated' film industry.

Criticisms of similarity between computer-animated films have equally supported discourses of volume and oversupply. Writing in the midst of Hollywood's computer-animated film surge of 2006, Laura M. Holson noted that 'while animation continues to be popular with families, audiences complain that it is suffering from too much sameness, with movie plots and characters looking increasingly alike' (2006). Rather than straitjacketing or impeding their close analysis through an emphasis on their many continuities, this book argues that genre provides a critical framework for better understanding the repeating content, style and formal codes of communication of computer-animated films.

The purpose of what follows is therefore to identify the features of the computer-animated film that act as a promise of content: the generic data with which they have been encoded, and the combination and prominence of particular features across multiple computer-animated films that mark them as distinctive. The recognition of a computer-animated film genre should not run counter to the identification of their singularity, or violate their formal specificities. The establishment of a meaningful genre framework groups multiple film examples together, but creates an 'orderly genericity' (Langford 2005: 265) among a collection of popular cinema forms not normally considered in this way. Yet while genre as an interpretive label has been greatly underestimated within their critical lexicon, computer-animated films have attracted a diverse range of attention and theorisation as the field of 'animation studies' has expanded almost parallel to their commercial and critical popularity. This introduction therefore continues by tracing something of this scholarly path, whilst using the story of how the computer-animated film's multitude of pleasures has been told to present several broader concerns of the book along the way.

The Reality Effect

The elasticity of 'digital cinema' as a critical label bears out a degree of variance to a cinema that is (post-) produced, distributed and exhibited digitally. William Brown argues there are 'many digital forms and filmmaking practices', including 'digital animations, such as *Toy Story*', which fall under the auspices of a possible digital cinema (2013: 13). The contribution of digital animation and CGI within a mainstream Hollywood cinema context, however, remains largely understood through the framework of computer-based special or visual effects (North 2008; Prince 2012; Brown 2013; Purse 2013; Whissel 2014; North et al. 2015; Turnock 2015; Keil and Whissel 2016). The imbrication of digital imagery with particular kinds of popular film genres, namely the action, science fiction and fantasy genres, and with a focus on live-action/CG composites, has meant that computer-animated films have been mentioned only briefly as a footnote within visual effects discourse. Numerous other theorists, by comparison, have held a stronger stake in the computer-animated film, getting to know its aesthetics, style, narratives and characters in a multitude of ways.

The most fundamental assumption about computer-animated films is that they perform an aesthetic function, offering finely tuned realistic-looking images of unprecented detail, resolution and surface texture. The popular and critical appreciation of their visual complexity are firmly embroiled in discourses of control (of the film image) and management of its visual (illusionist, simulationist, mimetic) possibilities. By confronting head-on the seduction and spectacle of convincing computer graphics, certain phenomenological accounts citing the computer-animated film counter any critical assumption that the boundaries of film sensorium and embodied spectatorship are policed solely by experimental and avant-garde film practices, or that they operate chiefly outside Hollywood within international art cinemas. Paying particular attention to how *Toy Story*'s slick, pristine computer-generated imagery beckons our fingers, Jennifer M. Barker writes that the film's nostalgic charm is inextricably linked to both its 'tactile allure' and the 'surface of its skins' (2009: 44–5). Vivian Sobchack is no less enamoured by the aesthetic detailing of *Toy Story*'s digital imagery, distinguishing the redolence of its digital surfaces and the toys' manufactured shell that are presented to (and for) enjoyment by the body's senses (2004: 54). Such a turn towards the 'haptic visuality' (Marks 2000) of digital imagery, and the situating of computer-animated films among theories of affect and sensuous experience, belongs to a longer history of academic writing that had responded to computer-animation's impressive capacity for visual realism. As a reaction to Hollywood cinema's shifting aesthetic and stylistic repertoire throughout the 1990s, computer-generated imagery had, from its inception, been exhaustively examined as an emerging technology of persuasive realistic representation (Prince 1996).

Discourses of realism no less inform the animation industry's development of computer graphics. Progressions in texture and shadow mapping, the calculation of colour dispersal and the accuracy of raytracing light paths have brought a hitherto unseen sophistication to digitally animated aesthetics. The result is that, for David Bordwell, computer-animated films are 'overstuffed' in their *mise en scène*, and so detailed in their surface accuracy as to 'display a cinematic sophistication that fits contemporary tastes in live-action movies' (2011: 231). However, in the immediate post-*Toy Story* period, Andrew Darley (1997; 2000) and Julia Moszkowicz

(2002) sought to move the critical discussion of digital realism within the computer-animated film context beyond any narrow focus on the ability of computer graphics to hold up a mirror to organic reality, and the creation of digital images that simply corresponded to the 'light, colour, texture, movement and sound' (Prince 1996: 23–37) of natural phenomena. Terms like 'second-order realism' (Darley 1997) were suggested as useful categories to determine the visual regime of computer-animated films by speaking more explicitly to a perceived hybridisation of image-making technologies. For example, Darley asked of *Toy Story* 'is it cartoon animation, three-dimensional (puppet) animation, live-action or, perhaps, a combination of all three?' (2000: 84). This optical illusion of the analogue would, in time, be subsumed by – and collapsed into – the dominant category of photorealism, particularly as new media theory became increasingly attentive to CGI's capacity for cinematographic verisimilitude. As a similarly 'second-order' visual discourse of photographic realism, photorealism quickly confirmed 'the simulacral nature of digital images' in the way that 'they look not like original reality, or real life, but like copies of that reality' (Brown 2013: 27). Darley and Moszkowicz thus heralded the first wave of computer-animated films for their ability to refashion or 'remediate' (Boulter and Grusin 2000) cinematic realism and photography, expressing their broader affectation for lens-based media as part of their dominant photorealistic agenda. Borrowed by film theorists from the language of new media (to cite Lev Manovich's [2001] work on digital cinema), the audacious 'remediation' of the codes of live-action cinema and the development of photorealistic effects (motion blur, depth of field, simulation of anamorphic lenses) can be understood as a digital (re)production of a cinematographic register.

It is certainly not uncommon for the popular and critical lexicon of computer-animated films to report with renewed enthusiasm on the sophisticated levels of realism achieved in the post-photographic age of heightened simulation. Paul Ward points out how realism remains an 'unavoidable heuristic' (2002: 132) for CGI given the polished glossiness and synthetic sheen of digital aesthetics. However, the limitations of what computer-animated films are able to accomplish and where they can go stylistically are governed by self-imposed regulations for production. William Schaffer (2004) and J. P. Telotte (2010) have each described how Pixar's computer-animated films strike creative bargains with the real, adopting a compromise position that checks the received teleological narrative of realism with the expressive possibilities of the cartoon. When Sobchack similarly asked 'what do we want from animation?' (2006: 172) in an analysis of *Final Fantasy: The Spirits Within* (Hironobu Sakaguchi,

2001) she both declared and unmasked the 'myth' of total animation and the assumed 'authentic' address of digital imagery as a way of responding to a cluster of computer-animated films that had 'shied away [. . .] from character 'realism of any kind but emotional' (ibid.: 173). The scholarly negotiation of the fluctuating (rather than fixed) levels of realist representation has prompted a wealth of neologistic terms such as 'third realism' (Cotta Vaz 1999), 'photosurrealistic' (Apodaca and Gritz 2000), 'spectacular realism' (Lister et al. 2009), and 'irreality' (Sobchack 2006: 179), all committed to defining a computer-animated film aesthetic that operates *in excess* of realism: that is, marking a concession to the not-quite-real within digital representation.

Challenging the view that computer graphics are universally driven by an underlying realist hypothesis, Patrick Power (2008) envisaged a possible future for computer-animated films in which there would lie a greater range of formal expression. This possible future has since been partially realised by a computer-animated film industry that is increasingly turning towards 'painterly' rendering and image processing techniques, either by compositing cel-animation together with cutting-edge CGI, or in the digital replication of hand-drawn styles. Disney's *Bolt* (Byron Howard and Chris Williams, 2008) pioneered Disney's NPR (non-photorealistic) aesthetic, which countered the 'hard clean geometric solutions' characteristic of 'CG algorithms' (Lusinsky et al. 2009). By employing the 'raypainting' technique of editing detailed brushstrokes into larger three-dimensional block colour models, and then buttressing these NPR processes with 'tools from film such as exposure and depth of field' (ibid.), *Bolt* offered a new painterly direction for computer graphics. For Helen Haswell (2014), Pixar and Disney's nostalgic evocation of organic and imperfect hand-drawn animation traditions (pen-and-ink, artistic illustration) in its shorts *Day & Night* (Teddy Newton, 2010), *La Luna* (Enrico Casarosa, 2011) and *Paperman* (John Kahrs, 2012) also provides a corrective to the net visual objective of computer-generated images as that of heightened verisimilitude. However, Power had already found tentative evidence of new 'expressive advances in CG features' (2009: 119) in the soundscapes of Pixar's earlier *Wall-E*, and the Seussian exaggeration of character design in *Horton Hears a Who!*, which each pushed at the boundaries of the digital's presumed telos of naturalism.

The visual achievements of the computer-animated film are certainly a central concern of this book, and in particular the identification of a set of formal devices that exist at the juncture where software meets film style. Informed by wider technological discourses and the status of animation as an industrial art form, this book not only theorises computer-animated films through their unique set of formal features, but connects elements of film style to animation practice and the computer-animated film's unique production contexts. Certain chapters argue that the distinctiveness of computer-animated films can be located not just within the impressive accomplishments of photorealist simulation and the pleasure in the detail, but in the particular coherency of their stylistic range and formal repertoire. Chapter 4, for example, focuses on the exploitation of the virtual screen space through the innovative perspectives of capricious anthropomorphic characters, whose industrious activity creates a visual style (rooted in a non-anthropocentric point of view) that coexists with the systems of classical Hollywood continuity. In Chapter 5, the computer-animated film's re-evalution of everyday objects, including the detailed depiction of junk, waste and discarded rubbish, is used to identify how they regularly play across the poles of microscopic representation and magnification, drawing on the opportunities afforded by scale to creatively re-define cultural detritus through both its abundance and user potential.

Greater scholarly intercessions have recently been made on behalf of computer-animated film narratives that are becoming progressively smarter and more self-reflective about the discourses of realism that inform them. Well-versed in the technological and larger industry pro-cesses involved in computer-animated film production, Telotte (2010), Thomas Elsaesser and Malte Hagener (2010) discussed the ways realism has been co-opted into the 'stuff of narration', which 'catches-up' the spectator in their own 'simulacrum effect' (Telotte 2010: 204). Whereas Darley initially argued that *Toy Story* is 'about realist and illusionary qualities, not character or plot' (2000: 87), it has become increasingly dif-ficult to cleave form from content. The last two chapters of this book, for example, explore how the computer-animated film's pursuit of cinematic realism can be anchored to its strong comic verve. If contemporary visual culture has sounded the death knell for photographic cinema through the impact of digital (forms of) cinema, then Chapter 9 explains how character interaction with elements of film form (logo sequences, closing credits and widescreen matte bars) harnesses the very elements of cinema's formal grammar as a way of extending the boundaries of the 'deconstructive' cartoon tradition. Chapter 10 similarly focuses on how the technical realisation and persuasive simulation of digital images that appear to be photographic are part of the computer-animated films' comic repertoire. It argues that the ability of the virtual camera to simulate the nuances of anamorphic lenses, 'cinematic perspective' (Prince 2012: 95) and focal lengths are actively reworked by the computer-animated film as fresh sites for comedy. With the critical boundaries of identity being continually redrawn to account for the intersection of live-action cinema with digital technology (Manovich 2005; Cholodenko 2008), and at a time when broader definitions of 'animation' remain the subject of intense theoretical debate across film and media studies, computer-animated films work through discourses of digital realism to interrogate the identity of computer animation as a medium of illusion.

Antz meets Adorno

Taking up the mantle from the mushrooming of academic interest in Disney Feature Animation during the mid-1990s, a growing body of ideological criticism directed at the computer-animated film has distinguished how their narratives work ideologically as reflections of shifting social conditions. In this age of *Antz* 'meets Adorno' (Strzelczyk 2008: 208), ideological criticism has certainly afforded computer-animated films increasing theoretical visibility and a greater level of critical focus across multiple disciplines. Computer-animated films are not ideologically innocuous forms of commercial, family entertainment, but are rich in political allegory and serve to encode certain hegemonic values. They have been interpreted as allegorical expressions, or barometers, of an underlying social, political and economic problematic, read as instruments of cultural pedagogy that reiterate normative ideologies and discourses about race, class, gender and sexuality.

The symptomatic interpretation (in Bordwell's terminology [1989]) of computer-animated films has therefore yielded compelling and often contentious readings that have split these digital texts 'apart at the seams', and penetrated into the cracks that 'riddle' their formal coherence (Comolli and Narboni 1977: 7). As a taxonomy of the computer-animated film's political functioning, such readings operate at the juncture where the 'shiny reflective surface of the *Toy Story* movies' (Botting and Wilson 2004: 70) meets the unconscious critical desire to examine the perversely utopian world of the taboo or prohibited. Yet not all ideological analysis is unambiguously critical. Richard Stamp (2004) argues that even 'insidious' ideologies drawn from the computer-animated film coexist with socio-political possibilities of critique, equipping children with tools to manoeuvre around racial, gender and sexual dynamics at a stage in their lives in which they are learning society's most valuable lessons.

Computer-animated films have ultimately provoked the 'same old pedagogies' of gender and sexuality that Elizabeth Marshall and Özlem Sensoy (2009) argue normally come with the territory of animation's ideological underpinnings. The provocative ideological readings of computer-animated films and their narratives' insensitive reiteration of normative Western ideologies commonly identify the role of stardom and the voice (and their relationship to wider concerns of computer-animated film performance, as examined in Chapter 6). Strzelczyk argues that the angst and neuroses of Z in *Antz* are borne out by voice actor Woody Allen and his characteristic Jewishness. For Suzan G. Brydon the 'high-pitched commands' of clownfish Marlin in *Finding Nemo* similarly contribute to the 'mothering' of his character, and he uses phrases 'stereotypically attributed to mothers' policing of children' (2009: 139). In the case of *Shrek 2*, the casting of Eddie Murphy and Antonio Banderas are central determinants in the confirmation of Donkey and Puss as reflecting (and reflective) of contemporary cultural stereotypes (Brabham 2006), in particular the negative portrayal of 'black' and 'Latino' characters. The allying of black actor Murphy's energetic voice and quick-fire delivery with images of a donkey (a 'work animal') makes the computer-animated character 'appear tasteless, offensive, and racist' (Pimental and Velázquez 2009: 13). The gradual critical turn within film studies towards screen acting has pitched up the volume of the voice in cinema (Smith 2008; Neumark et al. 2010). Such analysis of vocal performance includes a greater appreciation of inflections of tone, pitch, rhythm, metre, modulation, timbre, delivery and intonation. The computer-animated film no less resuscitates the voice as a performance element, and Chapter 7 examines how the voice of a screen star speaks with authority by examining vocal performance in relation to elements of character design.

The ideological critique of computer-animated films has tended to focus on the uniformity of ideology and cultural politics within individual texts. By examining the rhetorical devices of *The Incredibles*, for example, David Hastings Dunn makes the argument that the film 'begs to be read as an allegorical tale justifying US foreign policy under George W. Bush' (2006: 559). Close readings of *Monsters, Inc.* also offer the view that the film is a 'clever dramatisation of the problem of declining energy supplies', raising awareness in geographical and environmental research about crafting a 'future of child-friendly cities' in post-industrial societies (Tranter and Sharpe 2008: 299). Yet studio authorship has also been a convenient way of theorising the narratives, themes, characters and ideological operations across a larger corpus. The Pixar studio's synonymy with digital animation and their historical contribution to three-dimensional computer graphics has been the focus of numerous critical accounts that have enforced the studio's business evolution and corporate relationships with Apple/Steve Jobs and Lucasfilm/George Lucas (Paik 2007; Price 2009; Sito 2013). Recent book-length investigations into Pixar's feature and short film canon (Velarde 2010; Wooden and Gillam 2014; Rösing 2016; Meinel 2016; Herhuth 2017) have also served to ground the vexed issue of 'representation' within the throes of a rhetorical naturalisation (and stabilisation) of ideological expression. The identity of Pixar's computer-animated films as 'cultural, political, and social texts' (Meinel 2016: 15) has paved the way for extremely rich enquiries into character construction (gender, sexuality). While much of this book deals with the tribulations of characters (as journeyers; as non-humans; as animators; as actors), Chapter 8 will examine how the physicality, solidity and nuances of personality equipping these digital bodies contribute to the computer-animated film's comic register. Interpersonal relationships are 'the driving forces' (Finklea 2017: 89) behind many computer-animated films, and Chapter 8 discusses how the emotional expressivity within individual characters supports the construction of nuanced models of gender.

Many Pixar-centric studies have permitted the ideological analysis of computer-animated films to move beyond broader labels of the 'children's film' (Booker 2010; Cheu 2013) and 'family film' (King et al. 2010; Brown and Babbington 2015; Brown 2017) to which they are often assigned and explored as a larger animated group. However, a genre 'by definition entails narrative, iconographic, characterological and conceivably ideological conventions' (Langford 2005: 265), and one of this book's lines of enquiry is how computer-animated films transcode or relay particular ideological positions, attitudes, themes, narratives and values as a wider collection of films. For example, the computer-animated film's repeating journey narrative – discussed at length in Chapter 2 – engages the collective mentality that Judith Halberstam (2011) has identified as part of the ideological 'audacity' of recent animated features. These 'Pixarvolt' films are characterised by narratives advocating communitarian revolt and rebellion against corporate domination, resulting in improvised social relationships and collective action. Whereas M. Keith Booker has argued that children's films consistently promote an 'individualist mind-set' (2010: 175) in keeping with an American capitalist system, 'Pixarvolt' films signify an alternate ideological message. For Halberstam, *Robots*, *Finding Nemo*, *Over the Hedge* (Tim Johnson and Karey Kirkpatrick, 2006) and *Bee Movie* address the unruly child through queer embodiment, the dual rejection of the family and coupled romance, and instead enforce collective states of rebellion (therefore challenging any neo-liberal 'be yourself' attitude) (Halberstam 2011: 29).[2]

Beyond their contribution to the journey narrative structure, the visual pleasure and spatial dimension of these rebellious, revolting collectives will be investigated in Chapter 3 according to the computer-animated film's formal strategies of world-building. The swarms, crowds or 'digital multitude', as Kristen Whissel (2014) terms it, which populate computer-animated film worlds have generally been discussed for their ideological implications for de-individualisation of mass society. Florentine Strzelczyk (2008) connects the insect colony in *Antz* to a pre-fascist Weimar Republic; Steven C. Combs (2002) compares *Antz* with *A Bug's Life* according to Daoist (Taoist) thought; and Christopher Falzon (2007) observes the social and political dimension of *Antz* and its reflection of a modern totalitarian existence. But Chapter 3 explores the properties of the digital multitude as a dynamic optical effect that illuminates the scope and expanse of the fictional space. However, the very formation of activist groups bound by communal activity across computer-animated film narratives ultimately mirrors Halberstam's own desire to 'think collectively' about them. By broadening the critical conversation around computer-animated films via 'ideological-generic criticism' (Klinger 1984: 30–44), Halberstam maps their complex formal geography and textual system through the cinema/ideology relation. The grounding of ideology within generic textuality enables the computer-animated film to be studied for their orthodoxies and conventions, viewed relationally rather than in isolation. However, to carry out the ideological critique of a computer-animated film, and their inscription of cultural images, practices, attitudes and discourses, is to analyse the richness and density of meanings contained within its complex textual strategies.

From Technicist to Textualism

Invested in the politics of representation, the wealth of ideological criticism directed at the computer-animated film bears out something of the emergent textualist approach that has come to replace the instrumentalist or 'technicist' approach to digital imaging, which Darley (1990) identified at the very start of the 1990s as the dominant mode of thinking. Towards the end of computer-animation's second decade, Maureen Furniss admitted that the majority of books written on the subject 'focus on techniques, providing instructions on how to use various software packages' (1999). Long-running visual effects journals and popular magazines including *WIRED*, *Cinefex* and *Cinefantastique* continue to prize computer-animated films in these 'technicist' terms, adopting and extending the informative, highly technical tone of industry-based papers routinely presented at annual events in the computer graphics calendar (Street 1998). But as critical literature surrounding computer-animated films gains momentum in volume and scope – and as theorists from multiple disciplines become acquainted with their artistic attributes and visual qualities – the 'technicist' approach has been joined by approaches that are predominantly 'textualist' in focus.

Textualist approaches to film analysis are traditionally formalist, shifting focus onto a film's textual attributes and formal codes: its conventions, systems of organisation, norms and modes, and their effect on the spectator. Such approaches have a different emphasis than ideological criticism. They are less inclined towards the analysis of the socio-political and historical forces shaping the text and, as Garrett Stewart argues, are 'committed to more cinematographic specificity than one finds in the ideological critique of the apparatus per se' (1999: 319). With a greater accent placed on form and convention, textualist approaches have opened the valve on the study of computer-animated films, leading to a new emphasis on their formal vocabulary. Notable among such accounts is a more nuanced consideration of sound design, musical composition and melody (Wells 2009a; Hayward 2010; Whittington 2012; Goldmark 2013), and the deft contribution of unified sound-image relations within animated storytelling (although such accounts have tended to overwhelmingly focus on Pixar's short film format).

Textualist accounts have also advanced the knowledge and appreciation of the self-reflexive narrativisation by computer-animated films of realism (as Telotte, Elsaesser and Hagener all describe), but in some instances has been instrumental in its re-evaluation. Aylish Wood has argued that computer-animated films are not wholly powered by discourses of 'encroaching realism', but by the textual inscription of their technology (2007: 25). No longer attributable to the kinds of reality effects described by Darley and Moszkowicz, computer-animated films such as *Monsters, Inc.* and *The Incredibles* momentarily convey their aesthetic specificity *as computer-animation* through scale, vicarious camerawork and depth of space. Textualist approaches ultimately promote the difference and, most importantly, the differentiation of computer-animated films, guiding an understanding of their specificity within the multifarious field of animation – with its multiple forms and techniques – but also among critical discussions of contemporary digital culture. In reframing computer-animated films as a film genre, such texts begin to acquire relative distance and autonomy from the 'techno-genre' (Manovich 2001: 207) into which they were born, and from which they might otherwise never escape.[3]

With their emphasis on a film's formal properties, purely textualist approaches have been questioned on the grounds that they are markedly ahistorical and unreflective of cinema as a social practice. However, textualist approaches need not be at odds with a parallel consideration of contextualist or historical accounts. Mark Allen Peterson argues that 'Although the formal features of texts – binary oppositions, tropes, intertextualities, and so forth – cannot in themselves validate particular meanings, the close reading of texts is likely to remain significant to the anthropology of media. Texts *do* have formal features' (2005: 119). Chapter 1 plots the textualist trajectory for subsequent chapters by asking similar questions in relation to film genre. Drawing on relevant genre theory, the opening chapter argues for the computer-animated film's formal codes of signification as historically and technologically contingent, informed at every turn by a host of animated and non-animated texts, but also by key developments in digital technology. This book argues that the generic identity of computer-animated films emerges from the analysis of their shared formal features, and of the relationships between such elements. Qualities that seem incidental in a single computer-animated film take on greater meaning when connected to or allied with the consistency and repeating presence of these characteristics in other films. This book explores how over 200 computer-animated films have crafted a specific set of expectations through the deployment of consistent, repeating textual features. To recall Damon Knight's widely repeated definition of the slippery genre of science fiction, computer-animated films 'mean what we point to when we say it' (1967: 1). By employing a genre-based approach to these lively forms of feature-length narrative fiction, this book brings into sharper clarity *what it is we talk about when we talk about computer-animated films*, but also why it matters that they are discussed in such genre-based terms. Genre is a methodology that allows this book to develop new terms of critical evaluation for a popular and rapidly accelerating cinematic form, one whose style, form and function has not yet been addressed with such breadth and scope in existing academic discourse.

Notes

1. As *Screen International* put it, 'Much has been made this year of the seeming over-saturation of studios/computer-generated titles, with critics and analysts pointing to growing movie-goer apathy' (Bordwell and Thompson 2011: 159).
2. By collapsing the live-action/CG film *Babe* (Chris Noonan, 1995) and the claymation *Chicken Run* into the 'Pixarvolt' genre, Halberstam implies that such 'Pixarvolt' films need not necessarily be computer-animated.
3. Techno-genre is a category that Manovich identifies as comprising computer-animation, multimedia and websites, and at the turn of the new millennium was one that was 'just getting started' (2001: 207).

CHAPTER 1

Falling with Style?
The Computer-Animated Film
and Genre

People think of animation only doing things where people are dancing around and
doing a lot of histrionics, but animation is not a genre. And people keep saying, 'The
animation genre.' It's not a genre! A Western is a genre! Animation is an art form,
and it can do any genre. You know, it can do a detective film, a cowboy film, a horror
film, an R-rated film, or a kids' fairytale. [. . .] And next time I hear, 'What's it like
working in the animation genre?' I'm going to punch that person!

(Brad Bird in Weaver 2013: 231)

Within the discipline of film studies, genre theory has yet to identify the
computer-animated film as a significant mainstream genre of contemporary cinema. Despite claims made by Steve Neale at the turn of the new
millennium that connections between genre and contemporary Hollywood
cinema were being revived and very much 'in vogue' (2002: 1), the genre
status of computer-animated films has been far from secured. Such an
omission is particularly puzzling given the resituating of genre back on
film theory's critical agenda after a 'lengthy period of neglect' (ibid.),
and how its return within recent film criticism was intended to address
those emerging cycles and trends now operating within contemporary
Hollywood. Such a statement of scholarly purpose might have been
expected to include computer-animated films, given the shifting industrial context of studio animation, the popular chord struck with critics
and audiences by computer-animated feature films, and the acceleration
of academic interest surrounding the animated medium more generally.
Timothy Corrigan has, for example, summarised the first decade of the
new millennium as one that exhibited an overwhelming 'fascination with
animation' (2012: 14–15), an attraction fuelled by the wedding together of
traditional animated practices with digital technologies in the immediate
post-millenial period.

This chapter identifies the ways in which the shifting, contradictory
relationship between animation and genre has impinged upon the deline-
ation of computer-animated films as a genre in their own right. It also

establishes the value that can be derived from genre analysis, and the meaningfulness of a genre-based approach for the study of computer-animated films. Just as the process of defining a genre as opposed to a mode, cycle, series or formula has been wrought with difficulty and contradiction, there is much contention and conflict over whether genre remains a suitable descriptor for animated films. Such questions hinge upon whether animation itself is qualified as a medium, or whether it is better described as a style or technique. Daniel Goldmark has argued that 'animation is *not* a genre; it is a technological process that creates a particular (highly idiosyncratic) means of visual representation' (2005: 3). However, this is certainly not the view held by every genre theorist seeking to place animation in the throes of generic classification (for example, the 'cartoon' appears among the 'new sites' for genre study offered by Neale [2000: 31]). This book stakes its claim that animation is not a genre, but an expressive medium involving particular kinds of image-making techniques. Yet given how animation comes in multiple styles and forms, and is achieved through diverse techniques and practices, computer-animated films can be considered a specific genre of animation, and of contemporary popular cinema more broadly. However, this chapter begins by unpacking the function of genre in light of the computer-animated film, and examines how the application of generic structures to their narratives has tended to enforce director Brad Bird's view regarding animation's correspondence with, and ability to 'do', recognisable live-action genres.

Genre/Parody/Intertextuality

Submitting computer-animated films to an iconographic treatment of genre – an approach widely used in late 1960s and early 1970s genre criticism (Kitses 1969; Alloway 1971; McArthur 1972) – involves the recognition of broad motifs, themes, archetypes and plot structures as the basis for shared commonalities. The longevity and durability of this structural approach to genres among contemporary analysis has led to the itemisation of computer-animated films according to their most obvious generic allegiance, situating their narratives within familiar generic boundaries. M. Keith Booker, for example, has listed the genres into which computer-animated films most obviously fit, stating that *A Bug's Life* 'draws in important ways on the gangster genre', *Monsters, Inc.* turns to the 'horror/monster movie genre', and that *Up* is 'essentially an entry in the adventure film genre' (2010: 84, 110). While the challenges of post-classical Hollywood cinema have often been squared to its greater permeability and porosity between genre boundaries (leading to postmodern traditions of genre-bending and hybridity), the iconographic analysis of generic affiliation towards the computer-animated film paradoxically restates the stability of these same boundaries for easy recognition.

While the oversimplification of Hollywood's genre past has prompted a revising of the presumed integrity and fixity of film genres, the qualification of computer-animated films via pre-existing genres are not miscalculations made by the genre theorist, or iconographic errors gone unnoticed by the animators. Just as animation has historically demonstrated an overwhelming tendency to take the 'familiar characteristics of a live-action genre and place them with the animated context' (Wells 1998: 171), computer-animated films no less beg, borrow and steal from the narrative structures and thematic concerns that marshal the parameters of generic meaning. *Hotel Transylvania* (Genndy Tartakovsky, 2012) and its 2015 sequel shares with *Monster House* a reliance upon the tropes of the horror film; *The Nut Job* (Peter Lepeniotis, 2014) and *Ozzy: The Great Furscape* (Alberto Rodríguez and Nacho La Casa, 2016) draw their inspiration from the drama of the heist film genre; *Kung Fu Panda*, alongside its two sequels *Kung Fu Panda 2* (Jennifer Yuh Nelson, 2011) and *Kung Fu Panda 3*, push explicitly against the margins of the martial arts film; *Monsters vs. Aliens* (Conrad Vernon and Rob Letterman, 2009) is DreamWorks' homage to 'B' monster movies such as *The Blob* (Irvin Yeaworth, 1958), *The Fly* (Kurt Neumann, 1958) and *Attack of the 50 Foot Woman* (Nathan H. Juran, 1958); and the studio's *Megamind* (Tom McGrath, 2010) and *Captain Underpants: The First Epic Movie* (David Soren, 2017) spoof the resurgence in superhero movies (especially the adaptations of Marvel comic books) currently proliferating across contemporary US cinema.

By treating genres in this way, computer-animated films can be understood as foremost examples of genre parody, whereby pre-existing genres become 'resuscitated' in ways that are 'directly connected to (and constituents of) the genre being spoofed' (Harries 2002: 281). Animation lies in close proximity to film parody through its potential for extreme moments of 'inversion', 'literalization' and 'exaggeration' that traditionally support parodic activity (ibid.: 7). For Jonathan Gray, animation as a medium 'greatly increases scope for exaggeration and literalization' (2006: 67), as parody's language of the implausible, the impossible and the illogical are well-served by animation's ability for subversion, revelation and visualisation. Both parody and animation are thus rhetorically enunciative, insofar as they are equally committed to the weight of 'the idea', performing (and defining) that which is being visualised and made intelligible through the image (animation) or the act (parody).

When considered as footnotes to more established generic systems, computer-animated films can be utilised to explore the longevity of certain film genres, and their enduring place in contemporary cinema. *Cloudy with a Chance of Meatballs* and *Cars 2* (John Lasseter, 2011) revisit two genres – the disaster and spy film – that have waxed and waned in significance throughout Hollywood film history, while *Sing* (Garth Jennings, 2016) capitalises on the recent revival of the jukebox musical format across post-millennial Hollywood, if not the return of the American film musical more broadly. The generic verisimilitude of *Toy Story* similarly provides an important basis for considering how the Western genre 'lives on [. . .] as a permanent part of Hollywood's generic repertoire available for periodic renewal' (Langford 2005: 74–5), far from reflecting any decline of interest in the frontier myths of the American West. For Elliot West too, 'Westerns are in', thanks to the computer-animated films *Toy Story 3* (Lee Unkrich, 2010) and *Rango*, a 'town-taming Western' that features an 'animated chameleon as sheriff and the familiar comic trope of mistaken identity' (2012: 290). Gore Verbinski's first computer-animated film targets a number of classic Western archetypes and individual spaghetti Westerns from *Django* (Sergio Corbucci, 1966) and *The Good, the Bad and the Ugly* (Sergio Leone, 1966) to *High Noon* (Fred Zinnemann, 1952) and *A Fistful of Dollars* (Sergio Leone, 1964), as well as including intertextual references to Robert Altman's neo-noir *Chinatown* (1974) and Francis Ford Coppola's war epic *Apocalypse Now* (1979).

Through their engagement with the familiarity of live-action genres, computer-animated films can be considered one of the most active intertextual fields of contemporary visual culture. As Mikhail Iampolski argues, intertextuality 'superimposes text on text, meaning on meaning' (1998: 28), and whether organically embedded or obtrusively sign-posted, affectionate homage or irreverent parody, computer-animated films routinely underscore the co-presence of residual and implicit film genres through a stockpile of intertextual quotations. When counting the numerous film references, allusions and intertextual citations in *Antz*, for example, Martin Barker admits that 'there are probably more than I spotted' (Barker and Austin 2000: 78). Computer-animated films ask to be *worked out* and *worked through* according to their strong dialogical engagement with recognisable genre components, participating in the invitation, promotion and orientation of the spectator as connoisseur. As both a pluralistic viewing strategy and formal set of principles, then, parody is 'a specific mode of intertextuality that capitalizes on its ironic play between texts' (Harries 2000: 24), and it is this interminable quality of citing and reciting that parallels how computer-animated films are able to dually *use* and *use up* genres for their own gains.

Case Study: *Shark Tale*

DreamWorks' *Shark Tale* is the first computer-animated film to offer a sustained interrogation of the codes and conventions of a recognisable live-action genre, intertextually indebted to the familiar generic mechanisms of the gangster film. Despite visual allusions to both *Jaws* (Steven Spielberg, 1975) and *Titanic* (James Cameron, 1997), it is the gangster film of early 1930s Hollywood as defined largely through the Warner Brothers studio – including *Little Caesar* (Mervyn LeRoy, 1931) and *The Public Enemy* (William A. Wellman, 1931) – that provides *Shark Tale* with its set of stable narrative and character archetypes. The film recasts the image of the mob family as an unlawful unit of sharks, pufferfish and octopi, who live as a subaquatic syndicate (or 'food chain') in a series of lavish coral milieu.

Shark Tale is certainly persistent in exploiting the 'fish-eat-fish world' of underwater organised crime, where kidnapping is 'just business' but where 'coldblooded' refers simply to the shark's biological make-up and 'swimming with the fishes' is literalised by the narrative's sunken ecology. The casting of actors Robert De Niro (as Don Edward Lino), Michael Imperioli (as Frankie Lino) and Vincent Pastore (as Luca) in *Shark Tale* explicitly trades on the ethnic stereotype of Italian-American masculinity central to the thirties' gangster film that shaped Hollywood's mafia and mobster mythology. The Italian-American gangster was, for Peter Bondanella, a 'model for the new urban, Prohibition-era gangster obviously modelled on Al Capone' (2006: 183). The 'link between criminality and Italian heritage' (ibid.: 173) was further canonised in the iconicity of *The Godfather* (1972–90) trilogy, and by Martin Scorsese's multiple mobster films of the 1970s. Not only has De Niro been central to the gangster cinema of post-classical Hollywood, but both Imperioli and Pastore starred in television programme *The Sopranos* (David Chase, 1999–2007), a mob drama about New Jersey-based Italian-American crime family. Scorsese himself also voices the character of loan shark Sykes in the DreamWorks film.

Shark Tale has attracted criticism for its discourse of 'racialized anthropomorphism' as a consequence of its ethnic caricaturing of 'New York Italians', replete with rituals such as a 'Catholic burial, performed in Latin', as a way of defining a particular form of white American masculinity (King et al. 2010: 41). But the film's persistent dialogue with the cinematic history of gangsters bears out the transformative possibilities of

animation within the context of genre parody. *Shark Tale* shows animation to be an oppositional medium, one entirely appropriate to parody's
fundamental attitudes of affectionate admiration and aggressive disregard,
which in turn allows the film to get close to (but remain fully distant from)
its target text. Gray argues that when scenarios, characters and dialogue
as we might know them to be in their primary context are 'turned into a
cartoon' they are suddenly seen through 'fresh eyes' (2006: 66). Animation
is able to afford 'a second level of aesthetic comparison and contrast'
(Dunne 2001: 147) through its distinct visual language, which is inherent
to the medium's inventive re-appropriations. *Shark Tale*'s treatment of
the gangster genre is therefore one of a presence-absence. The film is
entirely creative in revealing its own connections to the Mafia through
its degrees of genre literacy, which allows and invites its narrative to be
understood through its density of allusions.

Case Study: *Hoodwinked*

The visual language and shorthand of familiar genres have certainly
been gifts for the expressive scope given to animators as they rework
and dismantle generic expectation in a multitude of imaginative ways.
The Red Riding Hood adaptation *Hoodwinked* (Cory Edwards, Todd
Edwards and Tony Leech, 2005) produced by the Kanbar Animation
studios re-tells Charles Perrault's fairy tale through a contemporaneous
detective story that utilises an unusually fragmented, divergent narrative
style. *Hoodwinked* not only recollects the shifting chronology of both film
noir and 'hard-boiled' crime cinema (like *Shark Tale*), but borrows the
complex storytelling techniques of 1990s and 2000s Hollywood cinema
that rejects classical lines of causality. In its non-chronological and
repeating organisation of fairy-tale story material, *Hoodwinked* bears the
imprint of what has been variously termed the 'forking path' narrative
(Bordwell 2002), the 'multiple-draft' film (Branigan 2002), the 'database
narrative' (Kinder 2002), 'slipstream fiction' (Hayles and Gessler 2004),
the 'complex' narrative (Staiger 2006), the 'modular narrative' (Cameron
2008) and the hyphenated 'mind-game film' (Elsaesser 2009) as underlying patterns of storytelling in recent cinema.

To varying degrees, these complementary labels and their claims to
address forms of convoluted narration across a multitude of national contexts can be subsumed under the umbrella of the 'puzzle film' (Buckland
2014). For Warren Buckland, the puzzle film involves 'fragmented
spatiotemporal reality; time loops; a blurring of the boundaries of different
levels of reality; unstable characters with split identities or memory loss;

multiple, labyrinthine plots; unreliable narrators; and over coincidences' (ibid.: 5). *Hoodwinked*'s clever organisation and complex shifting chronology, as well as the exclusive lines of action and 'switchpoints' that envisage each possible future of Red Riding Hood 'seriatim' (Bordwell 2002), are used to craft a labyrinthine, multi-version account of Perrault's folk tale. As investigating Detective Nicky Flippers admits, 'We've got four suspects, and that means four stories'. In telling and then re-telling the fairy-tale events in a non-linear fashion, and using a plethora of narrative voices (Red, the Wolf, Granny Puckett, and the Woodsman), *Hoodwinked* expresses a sophisticated narrative complexity and intricate weaving together of plotlines, which manipulates the fairy-tale genre through its convergence with the narrative logic of post-classical (largely Hollywood) cinema and its multiplicity of unreliable narrators (Figure 1.1).

The Limits of Genre

Beyond supporting a critical appreciation of the computer-animated film's parodic activity towards genres, an iconographic synopsis towards a possible generic affiliation certainly proves useful for the consumer contexts in which film genres operate. To help spectators navigate through cinema's dense genre jungle, broadcast schedules, marketing strategies, VHS, DVD and Blu-Ray rental facilities, library catalogues and online shopping outlets are predicated on generic shorthand that clusters together specific films to provide easily identifiable signifiers. It is perhaps, therefore, useful to know that computer-animated films such as *Kaena: The Prophecy* (Chris Delaporte and Pascal Pinon, 2003), *Ark* (Kenny Hwang, 2005), *Battle for Terra*, *Star Wars: The Clone Wars* (Dave Filoni, 2008), *Space Chimps* (Kirk DeMicco, 2008), *Space Dogs* (Inna Evlannikova and Svyatoslav Ushakov, 2010), *Space Chimps 2: Zartog Strikes Back* (John H. Williams, 2010), *Mars Needs Moms* (Simon Wells, 2011), *Escape From Planet Earth* (Cal Brunker, 2013), and *Space Dogs: Adventure to the Moon* (Mike Disa, 2016) all demonstrate a visible alliance to science fiction storytelling. Their replaying of recognisable iconography situates them within a different iconographic realm to that of the wartime-comedy *Valiant* (Gary Chapman, 2005); the Frankensteinian hunchbacked horror of *Igor*; or the sports underdog narrative of Mexican computer-animated film *A Rooster With Many Eggs* (Gabriel Riva Palacio Alatriste and Rodolfo Riva Palacio Alatriste, 2015). But while fixed genre clusters may provide an 'easily sharable and consistently applicable vocabulary' (Altman 1999: 89) to their narratives and character archetypes, computer-animated films have modified the rules of the generic game.

Figure 1.1 Frame grab from *Hoodwinked* (2005) (Kanbar Animation/The Weinstein Company). The film parodies the Little Red Riding Hood fairy-tale narrative through its adoption of contemporary Hollywood storytelling conventions.

Live-action genre labels prove unsatisfactory in practice due to their inability to account for a broad range of computer-animated films. Particular computer-animated films are also more resistant to genre identification than others (resulting in increasingly tenuous links), and are more reflective of the truthfulness of genres as always in flux, that is 'always *in* play rather than simply being *re*played' (Neale 2010: 189). *Rio* (Carlos Saldanha, 2011) is a part-musical, part-love story set in the Brazilian city of Rio de Janeiro; *Wall-E* combines comedy, drama and romance with science fiction; and *The Incredibles* melds a family drama with superheroism. Even *Toy Story 2* (John Lasseter, 1999) shifts the Western parameters of its predecessor, and is a film instead identified by Harries as a science fiction parody (2002: 281) alongside *Galaxy Quest* (Dean Parisot, 1999), which also stars US television star Tim Allen (the voice of Buzz Lightyear).

Within the context of computer-animated films, live-action genres are thus a matter of emphasis and predominance. They are exclusive barometers of occasional, strongly fluctuating, generic identity, rather than inclusive markers that fully secure genre status. Writing in the 1970s, Ed Buscombe suggested that a genre 'is not a mere collection of dead images waiting for a director to animate it, but a tradition with a life of its own' (1970: 45). This statement rings particularly true in light of computer-animated films that have been classed as 'animated' only when linked to external generic structures. This chapter, and those that follow, instead ask what computer-animated films might share with *each other*. Certainly, the close association of a single computer-animated film to a live-action genre will give rise to a certain set of attributes. But as computer-animated films manoeuvre intertextually and intersect with the iconography and motifs of already established genres, they simultaneously surrender their own preliminary features. It is these repeating features that can be used to develop the identity of the computer-animated film as a mainstream genre, one that is constituted by a group of films that are becoming progressively 'familiar and relatively easy to recognize' (King 2002a: 119). To conceptualise a computer-animated film as belonging to a wider computer-animated film genre shifts animation as a medium beyond processes of live-action genrification, and instead asks on what terms animation may have genres of its own, and whether such 'genres' deviate from those found in live-action cinema.

The approach to the identification of a unique genre typology germane to the animated medium offered by Paul Wells is instead to propose seven 'generic deep structures' of animation that reconcile approach and application with the '*essence* of the art' (2002a: 66). Wells does not cleave animated films from live-action genres altogether, but determines the impact of their many intersections and involvements with them. Rather than calling attention to the surface or iconographic manifestations of genre, these 'deep structures' bring into relief the immediacy of an animated film's more profound generic content. This approach enables a variety of texts across multiple animated forms (and created through disparate processes such as cel-animation, stop-motion, glass and sand animation) to be grouped into generic clusters. The iconography of long-standing genres like the Western function as nothing more than a veneer 'hollowed out' by cartoonal form, crafting a conceptual space into which the real generic meanings 'germane to the animated form' are inserted (ibid.: 46). Such a focus on the ingenuity of process, and the particularity of animation's virtues as an artistic practice, opens up the possibility of talking about generic outcomes in the computer-animated film in an altogether different way.

Toy Story can, for example, be examined beyond the economy of expression afforded by its Western icons (saloon, outlaw, cattle yard, heroic cowboy), and instead understood as part of a wider project to catch the spectator up in the film's own effects of illusion. Thomas Elsaesser and Malte Hagener argue that the 'classic movie situation' (2010: 170) of the Western frontier dramatises the shift from traditional chemical photographic process to post-photographic digital animation. The confrontation of Sheriff Woody and a gunslinging villain One-Eyed

Bart (actually a Mr Potato Head doll) neatly plays out the pencil-to-pixel transition inaugurated by *Toy Story*. A 'double reality' is crafted whereby the staging of the Western mini-narrative showcases creative human agency that eventually recedes within computer processing: a new frontier emerging from 'drawing hand to generated pixel' (ibid.). J. P. Telotte similarly suggests that the 'artlessly constructed' cardboard sets denoting the dependable, culturally recognised Western icons actually signals a self-conscious 'surface play' concerning the new illusionary achievements of computer-animated film worlds (2010: 205). *Toy Story*'s familiarity with the Western partakes in a game of illusion or joke of expectation regarding constructed realities, with its narrative knowingly in dialogue with the complex three-dimensional spaces both achievable and available later in the film.

Here in *Toy Story*, the Western iconography is literally 'hollowed out' (by Andy, and by the film), and co-opted into a playful cardboard façade that makes room for the film's broader register of self-reflexivity. It is this narrative treatment of virtual space, and the play of new possibilities in digital depth and dimensionality, which Telotte goes on to trace among *Toy Story*'s (non-Western) 'digital brethren', suggesting that *Monsters, Inc.*, *The Incredibles* and *Cars* are all self-consciously invested in the space of their stories. Computer-animated films can therefore be productively linked according to certain repeating characteristics, demonstrating too that such connections may draw on alternate conditions that operate in excess of familiar genre labels. Computer-animated films may, on the one hand, be powered by the pre-existing iconography of familiar film genres. Yet within this very same process of 'doing' other genres (to recall Bird's terminology), they begin to both create and announce their own specificities. By viewing computer-animated films as connected through their own internal structures and attributes, rather than simply governed by the rule-based familiarity of live-action genres, a host of new properties within their textual systems are brought to the fore. The shifting frames of genre classification (rather than the shifting properties of the films themselves) surface a fresh set of textual attributes. These attributes can help stake a computer-animated film's claim for genericity, and in the process upturn conventional critical accounts that engage with their formal properties. Genre analysis must ultimately make what Langford calls 'meaningful discriminations' about a text, and not simply 'invent absurd refinements of generic denomination' (2005: 7). It is the purpose of this book to activate salient generic criteria, and to outline those features upon which a meaningful computer-animated film genre can be determined and defined.

Genre in Three Dimensions

If to place a film into a genre is to situate it within a discourse of perceived commonalities, types or kinds – thus recalling the original French definition of the term, as well as the Latin *genus* – then the virtual realms and cinematic cyberspaces of computer-animated films immediately offer a conventional stability. Though there is no 'rigid' taxonomy of inclusion and exclusion when erecting generic boundaries, digital technology instantly manages a computer-animated film's entrance into the corpus by embodying one of its most important and irrevocable 'familiar situations' (Grant 2007: 1). Technology has been employed by genre theorists before as both an 'enabling schemata' (Bordwell 1989: 14) and a central determinant in defining animation as a genre (see Moine 2008). These kinds of technically minded approaches persist as a consequence of animation's graphic nature, which blunts 'the usefulness of iconography as a generic arbitrator' (Watson 2003: 157). This leaves technological considerations as a reminder (and remainder) of animation's potential genre status, with Jason Mittell going so far as to identify how a genre category can be defined 'primarily by technology rather than narrative form or content (in the case of animation)' (2014: 121). The ontology of animation certainly interrogates the terms under which genre boundaries have traditionally been erected, and the failure of film genre theory more broadly to accommodate non-photographic forms of image-making. However, there are manifold problems with invoking digital technology as the sole basis of the computer-animated film's genre identity, not least because it is not as stable a negotiator as might be considered (as indicated by the lack of security regarding animation's broader genre status).

The technological characteristics of 'digitality' and 'virtuality' (Lister et al. 2009) that are often assigned to new media are the same conditions used to subsume all computer-based artefacts – including computer-animated films – into the same shared history. Computer-animated films have been made commensurate with a broad 'digital theory' that may address 'anything from the role of CGI special effects in Hollywood blockbusters to new systems of communication (the Net), new genres of entertainment (the computer game) [. . .] or new systems of representation (digital photography or virtual reality)' (Jenkins 2004: 236). Generic classification has come to play a more prominent role in the identification, division and categorisation of new media forms (including the application of film genre theories). But when Andrew Darley declares that computer-animation broadly constitutes 'a form or genre in its own right', the reference to 'computer-animation' is intended to denote all new media types that involve this 'particular way of producing the illusion of movement' (2000: 134) rather than the formal specificity of computer-animated films.

The irrefutable 'digitality' of computer-animated films additionally court concerns about the identification of a corpus, returning to the same kinds of questions that were first asked by 1970s film genre criticism. Andrew Tudor recognised the problem of film genre as that of the 'empiricist dilemma', a loop that first necessitates that films be isolated in accordance to specific criteria (an 'indefinable "X"'), but that such criteria only emerge from the 'empirically established' common characteristics of films (1973: 120–1). Tudor's solution to these issues of categorisation (that 'genre is what we collectively believe it to be') dissolves something of the 'empiricist dilemma' by leaning on a common set of shared beliefs uniting critics and audience. But for Peter Hutchings, this merely 'replaces one problem with another, namely how does one begin to identify the common "cultural consensus" which defines a genre?' (1995: 67). Certain genres are defined according to regulated narrative content, while others by their intense emotional effect on spectators, as work on 'body genres' by Linda Williams (1991) makes clear. Within the context of computer-animated films, this 'consensus' of uniformity and effect is not derived from any shared social consciousness. It is an industry-defined rubric. But the US animation industry and its practitioners *have* shaped computer-animated films to exhibit a further degree of formal specificity, harnessing their 'digitality' in particular ways.

Computer-animated films do tend to convey a uniform three-dimensional visual style, despite the capabilities of digital technology for non-photorealistic rendering. Patrick Power has described the capacity for computer graphics to 'output a naturalistic scene in eclectic styles from cartoon-style to Canaletto' (2009: 121), while cel-shading (also known as 'toon shading') is a cost-effective computer rendering process that substitutes the simplified style of hand-drawn and cut-out animation using digital media. However, the specificity of the visual language of computer-animated films is one that trades in flourishes of depth and dimension. These new screen worlds have a strong spatial imperative, with an impressive volume and heightened agency to their worlds that is hitherto unseen in animated cartoons. This three-dimensional uniformity is unsurprising given that certain software systems have now become industry standard for complex rendering processes. Leading animation and visual effects studios such as Disney DreamWorks, ILM, Animal Logic, Illumination Entertainment, Image Engine and Reel FX, alongside Peter Jackson's WETA Digital and the London-based Framestore/ Computer Film Company (CFC), Ciniste VFX and Double Negative, all use Pixar's proprietary core RenderMan or Maya programs, which have ultimately provided computer-animated films with a shared graphical style. Indeed, in 2006 Thomas Lamarre identified that 'a relatively stable digital look and feel has already emerged' in the kinds of digital animations such as *The Incredibles* 'trouncing' traditional animation at the global box office (2006: 131). The ubiquity of particular software packages has, in many ways, dictated a self-similarity to three-dimensional computer-animated films, and suggests that the visual possibilities for computer graphics have been curtailed by the technology itself. But texts cannot be linked arbitrarily or on their own, but are done so on the basis of cultural practices of production. Generic continuity in the computer-animated film is dually achieved and enacted through the actions of an animation industry that have crafted a heightened three-dimensional aesthetic style as its master image: it helps set the parameters for inclusion by qualifying each film's membership to the genre.

Even considering this increased specificity to the kinds of digital application found in computer-animated films, the spectre of the 'empiricist dilemma' looms large over their potential generic identity. Given what information about computer-animated films is *already known* – namely that they are manufactured digitally and realised through three-dimensional computer graphics – they remain open to accusations that the 'meaning' or 'truthfulness' of the genre will be extrapolated from those films that *already* comprise that genre. In effect, the 'certain kind' of computer-animated film still exists prior to the full network of attributes used to determine exclusion or inclusion. The digital is certainly a fundamental component of the computer-animated film genre, even a strikingly manageable aspect of it. These films' virtual status or 'digitality' is also unlikely to undergo much intense theoretical revision or become subject to radical change. As many genre theorists have pointed out (Browne 1998; Altman 1999), multiple films have undergone a rhetorical process of 're-genrification' over time, implying that films can belong to many genres all at once as the frames of reference are historically repositioned. But these generic gradations are unlikely to befit those feature-length films that are computer-animated, given that their digital identity is not liable to modify beyond all applicability. As a discourse of authentication, the digital is a strong regulating principle and an intrinsic property of these films that confirms something of the genre's visual qualities, suggesting (unlike other film genres developed from literature) its uniqueness to cinema.

While digital technology may help define the genre, it does not exhaust the criteria used to solve the genre riddle completely. If film genres are premised upon formulaic tendencies, as well as necessary degrees of repetition and difference, then the computer-animated film's digitality is simply one 'familiar situation' or relational possibility among many available. The fundamental sharing of a digital aesthetic does not account for the stylistic breadth of computer-animated films. *Beowulf* is a violent fantasy based on the Anglo-Saxon epic poem dated between the eighth and the early eleventh century; *Sunshine Barry & The Disco Worms* (Thomas Borch Nielsen, 2008) is a Danish computer-animated film musical about dancing parasites; *Jonah: A Veggietales Movie* (Phil Vischer and Mike Nawrocki, 2002) conveys a strong Christian morality and is based on the Biblical story of Jonah (albeit relayed with talking vegetables); and *Killer Bean Forever* (Jeff Lew, 2009) tells the story of an anti-hero coffee bean assassin. What is missing, then, is a stable framework with which to interrogate the possible set of relations between what is a remarkably heterogeneous collection of texts.

The (Computer-)Animation of Genre

Genres evolve and mutate in partnership with the theories employed to determine or classify them. A primary feature of the return by film scholars to cinema's many genres during the 1980s and 1990s was a greater sympathy towards the fluid boundaries between genres and the historical (industrial) regimes in which they operate (Neale 1980). Despite the shifting position of genre as both an industrial and cultural process, 'textual codification' remains a much-needed determinant of the genre*ness* of computer-animated films. Discourses of genre do not emerge solely from industrial sources and the circulation of pre-packaged generic labels by the mainstream Hollywood film industry. It is the task of the genre critic to subject the institutionally-defined corpus to further analysis, and to describe its structural agents of generic form.

The critical examination of computer-animated films lacks any real shape or definition at the level of formal structure. The formation of a meaningful computer-animated film genre must pay greater attention to its generic identity as it is located among sharable features and degrees of interconnectedness. It is not simply an industry-defined blueprint that has patterned the production of mainstream animation. It was Rick Altman (1984; 1999) who struck an important balance between diachronic considerations of a genre's historical context with a synchronic, semiotic approach. Mittell (2014: 16) argues that despite being grounded foremost in historicism, the 'centerpiece' of Altman's highly influential textualist model remains the emphasis on genre as a significant attribute of textual structures organised along two linguistic axes, the semantic (*words* or 'building blocks') and the syntactic (*sentence* or 'how spoken'). Within a framework that is both structural *and* iconographic, such formal structures or elements are historically contingent. Film genres are not, as Altman suggests, 'Platonic categories existing outside the flow of time' (1999: 218), but the shifting interrelationship between the semantic (iconographic) and syntactic (narrative and theme) features are a necessary part of a genre's evolving form that invite reflection upon its historical dimension.

In this way, genre emerges as more than just a convenient label to account for computer-animated films in their plurality. Such films are not in a period of dormancy, but are ongoing and present, suggesting their genre status is tied to a particular historical period (emerging in the last twenty years). From this perspective, *Toy Story* cannot be viewed as providing the computer-animated film with its exhaustive generic vocabulary, one that has cumulatively crafted rigid horizons of expectation and governed membership to the genre. Rather, Pixar's debut film inaugurated a loose generic template that subsequent computer-animated films have both added to and subtracted from in equal measure. This is a genre open to negotiation and change. But in determining its possible features, computer-animated films cannot be 'exiled from history' (Altman 1999: 222) or insulated against the impact of technological development. The genre status of computer-animated films is manifest in a particular rhetoric of enunciation, informed by the ritual (industrial) element of the genre as an institutional practice thus comes to bear upon the textual features of the text itself.

The conceptual boundary between the categories of 'animation' and 'film' has remained a site of preoccupation and contention among studies of animation and digital cinema since the 1990s. Alan Cholodenko (1991) has claimed on more than one occasion that all cinema is the progeny of animation, while Alla Gadassik (2010) identifies the blurred lines separating animation from mainstream moving-image production, and the progressive remaking of live-action as simply *another animation*. Yet the conceptualisation of animation in this way risks eroding those specificities holding the medium distinct from other filmmaking practices. Or as the young superhero Dash puts it in Pixar's *The Incredibles*, if 'everyone's special' that means 'no one is'. Just as the desire to find suitable generic structures for animation looks to those germane to the medium – rather than grafting pre-existing genre categories onto animated cartoons – critical emphasis has tended to spotlight how computer-animated films make their presence felt through conventions found throughout their history (though such films are not reducible to them). Wells, for example, has questioned the reading of *Antz* offered by Martin Barker (Barker and Austin 2000), on the grounds that the latter's approach marginalises the film's vocabulary 'intrinsically drawn from the 2D graphic and 3D stop-motion modes of animation', and effaces the traditions of Disney, Warner Brothers and the Fleischer cartoons (2003: 94). Barker focuses, instead, on the fact that in *Antz*, the classic good/evil confrontation of the narrative is combined with star-voice casting (Woody Allen, Sharon Stone, Sylvester Stallone); self-reflexive storytelling; numerous intertextual quotations from live-action cinema; the possible presence of special effects; and the 'contradictory' interplay between the human and non-human characters in the film (2000: 76). Wells' choice of a vocabulary drawn from the history of animation when describing *Antz* (against Barker's downplaying of it), aims to prevent the recession of animation as the computer-animated film's dominant gene, and like Buzz Lightyear, avoid its animated identity irretrievably 'falling with style'.

Claims that animation's formal prerogatives are rooted in the medium's own capabilities, rather than reducible to live-action comparisons, has been central to the formation and subsequent trajectory of animation studies. Michael Barrier, for example, disapprovingly describes Disney's shift towards realism during the Golden Age period as 'parasitic animation, separated from live-action only by the leavening of caricature' (1999: 4). Back in the 1940s, Sergei Eisenstein also recognised that Disney's *Bambi* (David Hand, 1942) replaced the formal expressiveness and visual anarchy of the *Silly Symphonies* with an 'oleographically copied, *emphatically objective* environment' (1986: 99). The digital properties of computer-animated films have subsequently become the basis for plotting new genealogical paths. The formal currency, immersive sensory cues and narrative logic of the computer-animated film have been aligned by new media and animation scholars with a video game phenomenology (on account of the narrow 'ontological gap' [Ward 2002: 133] that exists between computer-animated films and the video game platform). This mutual genealogy nudges the aesthetics and formal style of the computer-animated film towards alternate histories and representational logics, rather than just attributing them, as Jessica Aldred puts it, to 'the adventures of *Bambi*, *Dumbo* and the like' (2006: 163).

The textual legibility of the computer-animated film as a genre is primarily informed by the distinctiveness and creativity of animation as both a medium and a set of formal histories. This book employs the term *computer-animated film* throughout precisely because it is informed by their complex genealogy, rather than strangled by or inoculated against it. It reminds us that an encounter with a computer-animated film is an encounter with traditions of animation, with a digital construct, and with a Hollywood narrative film. In addition, the term computer-*animated* avoids the unwanted connotations of computer-*generated*, a label that semantically privileges mechanised, non-human automation over the flourishes of artisan manual labour. Stephen Prince has suggested that 'computer-generated' remains a poor descriptor, as it implies 'coldly manipulative, soulless, mechanical imaging processes' (2012: 9), while for Aylish Wood 'computer-generated animation' is a term that 'without further elaboration is actually quite vague' (2015: 3). The specificity of *computer-animated film* is therefore intended as a shorthand to connote how the computer of computer-animation replaces the art and not the artist.

Within this book, computer-animated films come close to being what Tzvetan Todorov calls a 'theoretical genre'. Genre-ness is calculated and deduced on the basis of 'abstract' suppositions, prescriptions and properties, and not necessarily on the security of pre-existing genres (which would be, for Todorov, a 'historical genre' [1990: 17]). Though several (but not all) of the features discussed in upcoming chapters *do* have a precedent in earlier animated forms, the medium's own unresolved status as a genre means that computer-animated films cannot be considered a straightforward 'historical genre'. Animation does not predict the generic fate of the computer-animated film, and a more abstract, less historically grounded 'theoretical' reflection is also required to determine the precise terms of its generic identity. The 'theoretical' computer-animated film genre does not exist autonomously outside of the multiple animated texts it accounts for. Rather, the genre's status as 'theoretical' is a product of the rich operations, properties, conditions and conventions that have been shared and revisited across numerous computer-animated films.

CHAPTER 2

Towards a Journey Narrative Syntax

A recurring generic feature of the computer-animated film is the journey narrative, which in its sequentiality of cause and effect enables the genre to follow the tribulations of its many protagonists as they progress through, but also seek to explore, control and master, the expansive and at times chaotic digital terrain. The implementing of a journey narrative structure as its first line of action is as common in computer-animated films as it is distinctive, and can be sub-divided into two interlocking forms, defined in this chapter as the 'flushed away' and 'over the hedge' narratives.

The 'flushed away' journey narrative relies on the spectacle of abrupt geographical disjuncture, which often requires the protagonist to negotiate and quickly adapt to a foreign milieu as a result of their sudden displacement from a customary habitat. The 'flushed away' journey narrative is crucially unplanned and inadvertent: the protagonist is caught unaware by a set of circumstances that substitutes comfort for insecurity. This kind of narrative therefore follows a style reminiscent of the classical Hollywood model with regard to the emphasis that is placed upon the trials of the individual. It also rehearses the disruption or conflict common to such studio era plot patterning, in which the founding stability is compromised by the radical complication and urgency of an encounter with an obstacle. However, unlike the goal-oriented structure of the classical storyline, disruptions in 'flushed away' narratives function as the dramatic catalyst for the subsequent journey. Such disturbances do not, therefore, jeopardise the protagonist's ability to fulfil their intended goal. Rather they intervene in the film's narrative (often towards the beginning) to create an entirely new set of incentives and targets based on their fresh circumstances, and to set in motion the protagonist's acclimatisation and adjustment to them.

Woody and Buzz's accidental fall from Andy's window in *Toy Story*; the kidnapping of Reggie the Turkey in *Free Birds* (Jimmy Hayward, 2013), Blu the macaw in *Rio*, and the army of zoo animals in *The Missing*

Lynx (Raul Garcia and Manuel Sicilia, 2008); the relocation of Kate and Humphrey to Sawtooth National Recreation Area in Idaho in *Alpha and Omega* (Anthony Bell and Ben Gluck, 2010); and the capture of the eponymous snail Turbo by Tito in *Turbo* all follow this narrative pattern. The acquisition of certain skills and knowledges are required by characters to survive this reversal of fortune, despite the opportunities afforded by the journey for unexpected encounters, detours and revelations that occur 'along the way'. *Rango* is a computer-animated film entirely self-conscious about the dramatic possibilities of the journey narrative and its widespread use as motivation for a character's unexpected liberation. *Rango* opens on the eponymous lizard and his overly-dramatic one-man play, complete with his unconvincing accents and a deluded sense of professionalism. But Rango suddenly breaks from his hammy performance, announcing to his fellow cast members 'People, I've had an epiphany! The hero cannot exist in a vacuum! What our story needs is an ironic, unexpected event that will propel the hero into conflict!' The film's broader 'flushed away' journey narrative is subsequently cued to the self-reflexivity of this state-ment, and Rango is unexpectedly flung from the safety of his terrarium across a desert highway and into oncoming traffic. The centre of *Rango*'s 'flushed away' narrative lies in the drama of perilous surprise, something that the manipulation of the spatio-temporal logic in the time-travel narratives of *The Magic Roundabout* (Dave Borthwick, Jean Duval and Frank Passingham, 2005), *A Christmas Carol* and *Mr. Peabody & Sherman* (Rob Minkoff, 2014) also make especially clear. But it is equally about the simple re-situating of the protagonist in a new situation against their will. As the young boy Milo screams in *Mars Needs Moms* as he is unintention-ally rocketed up to the Red Planet from Earth, 'I'm caught in here! Let me go!'

Case Study: *Flushed Away*

The process of becoming displaced – that is, the act of becoming 'flushed away' – is itself frequently coded in computer-animated films as extreme or perilous, involving dramatically staged sequences designed to spotlight the character's physical transition between *known* and *foreign* territories. The 'flushed away' journey narrative is therefore posed not only as a geographical disruption and a rupture of the equilibrium, but is a creative and visually dynamic leap *between* connected virtual spaces. The DreamWorks/Aardman animation co-production *Flushed Away* is the blueprint for this type of journey narrative structure, telling the story of a noble pet rat named Roddy St James who is accidentally 'flushed'

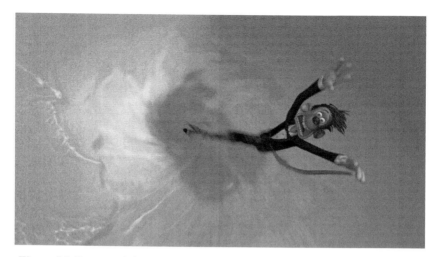

Figure 2.1 Frame grab from *Flushed Away* (2006) (Aardman Animation/DreamWorks Animation). Roddy St James is accidentally 'flushed away' down into the sewers of London.

from his home in Kensington to the secret world of the underground sewers (Figure 2.1). Taken through the sewage pipes and waterworks, Roddy's (literal) downfall is equally the film's opportunity to 'flush' the spectator from one virtual milieu to the other (the separation of Remy from his family in *Ratatouille* unfolds along similar lines, albeit taking place in the underground sewers of Paris rather than those of the British capital). Set to the tune of Australian rock band Jet's 'Are You Gonna Be My Girl?', the physical 'flushing' of Roddy as he is sucked down into the whirlpool of a toilet's current in *Flushed Away* is complemented by the veracity of the camerawork, which augments the spectacle of the rodent's movement through the labyrinthine pipework connecting overground and underground spaces. The presentation of Roddy's journey makes a spectacle out of his spontaneous movement in a bravura sequence that formally illustrates the exhilaration of mobility and the pleasures of travel. As Roddy holds his breath under the cascading water, the camera circles his body from within the pipe, before turning to follow his fall down into the pool below.

The energy of forward momentum in *Flushed Away* is supported by the simulation of water droplets, splashes and turbulent tidal waves. The film's many water-effects sequences, including the climactic tsunami that threatens to engulf Ratropolis, involved the layering of three categories of splashes: 'spherical splashes, crescent shapes, and mist', as well as a fluid simulator that controlled wave patterns (Robertson 2006). However, the behaviour of computer-animated bodies in relation to volumes of water placed the film's journey narrative of movement and motion within technological parameters, requiring the animation of 'splashes created by characters' (ibid.). Scott Cegielski (2006) discusses how the volume of water effects and 'splash emissions' throughout *Flushed Away* required a separate 'Character Splash System', which simulated the deformation of the water surface and splash direction rate as each character waded through the sewer water. Nowhere is the interaction between character and the viscosity of water more present than in the sequence of Roddy's flushing, which provides a striking example of where 'over the course of a shot, the character may travel quite a large distance' (ibid.). The velocity of Roddy as he is taken through the drains of London by the water current is augmented by the film's digital production that, at a distance from the Aardman studio's signature stop-motion Claymation style, permitted an excess of action and surface accuracy within its aquatic set pieces.

Over the Hedge?

The persistence of the 'flushed away' journey narrative within the drama of the computer-animated film is exemplified by its continuing presence in multiple computer-animated features. When canines Duke and Max are inadvertently captured by animal control in *The Secret Life of Pets* (Chris Renaud, 2016), they are rescued by a group of abandoned animals actually known as 'The Flushed Pets'. These 'wild' underground animals reside in the New York sewers, and are vehemently antagonistic towards the more domesticated pets who populate the city. In Walt Disney's recent computer-animated film *Moana*, the eponymous Moana must journey across the ocean to return a small pounamu stone to the mystical island goddess Te Fiti. However, Moana is caught in a typhoon and shipwrecked, prompting her to wash up on an uninhabited island where she meets companion Maui.

However, just as common to the computer-animated film are the journey narratives that can be defined by the label 'over the hedge'. These voyages are signalled as altogether more prepared or expected: a narrative manifestation of an individual character's tenacity, resolve and idealism. Flik's trip to the city to find circus bugs in *A Bug's Life*; Rodney Copperbottom's escape from suburban Rivet Town to Robot City in *Robots*; Valiant's desire to 'fly the nest' and join the Royal Homing Pigeon Service in *Valiant*; Tintin's globe-trotting quest in *The Adventures of Tintin: Secret of the Unicorn*; peregrine falcon Kai's trip to the bird community of *Zambezia*; and Judy Hopps' big move to the urban city of

Zootopia from the rural Bunnyburrow in *Zootopia* are all examples of this narrative form. Characters remain aware of their upcoming excursions, belongings are assembled and a route planned with a clearly-defined goal (the resolution of which may provide the happy ending). If 'flushed away' narratives emphasise the drama of a character helpless in their new circumstances, then these complementary 'over the hedge' narratives illustrate a greater degree of character motivation. Terrain is crossed with a sense of freedom and purpose, rather than fortuity.

The pre-arranged 'over the hedge' narrative can also be borne out of a necessity to restore order from conflict, and thus it often functions as the film's main narratological premise. Shrek must find Arthur 'Artie' Pendragon and announce this young royal heir as King of Far Far Away in *Shrek the Third*; the animals in *Ice Age: The Meltdown* (Carlos Saldanha, 2006) must trek to safety before the glaciers melt away; Yankee Irving must return Babe Ruth's baseball bat to its owner in *Everyone's Hero* (Colin Brady, Daniel St Pierre and Christopher Reeve, 2007) before the next game in the 1932 World Series; and child protagonist Gratuity 'Tip' Tucci must find her lost mother, Lucy, in *Home* (Tim Johnson, 2015). The object of such goal-orientated narratives is therefore staked in a clearly defined external jeopardy, in which character determination is guided by the spectre of an imminent deadline. David Bordwell argues that the trope of the deadline in classical Hollywood storytelling 'asks the viewer to construct forward-aiming, all-or-nothing causal hypotheses: either the protagonist will achieve the goal in time or he will not' (1997: 165). The deadline is central to the 'over the hedge' journey narrative, in which a sense of dramatic urgency, pace and excitement regarding the unfolding action leads to an ongoing crisis of time.

Case Study: *Over the Hedge*

Based on the United Media comic strip by Michael Fry and T. Lewis, DreamWorks' 2006 film *Over the Hedge* is structured by a series of systematic journeys, in which a wealth of unsuspecting forest animals – led by cautious tortoise and group leader Verne – must undertake multiple crossings through dense foliage to collect food. Waking at the height of Spring from their Winter slumber, the animals are confronted with a large hedge, extending in all directions, which has been erected during their hibernation as a consequence of a nearby urban development. Although the animals are initially fearful ('it's obviously some kind of bush'), selfish outsider R. J. the racoon explains that the hedge actually represents the 'gateway to the good life', and he encourages the woodland creatures to

Figure 2.2 Frame grab from *Over the Hedge* (2006) (DreamWorks Animation). The woodland animals prepare to go 'over the hedge'.

go 'over the hedge' to forage food from the gluttonous new suburban community (Figure 2.2). Following their intense preparations, a brief montage depicts the animals' sourcing of goods, and accumulates their sense of mobility and movement. A series of shots shows them hurriedly entering the hedge from left to right, before returning laden with supplies ready for the next winter. Cut to the measure of classical Hollywood storytelling, the 'over the hedge' journey narrative supports the goal-oriented curiosity of the film's protagonists, whose initial scepticism and apprehension at the evolving diegesis gives way to increased knowledge, understanding and comprehension of the world even when (due to the hedge) it is subject to change. However, unknown to Verne, the stakes of these many 'over the hedge' journeys are actually rooted in R. J.'s quest to secretly use the gathered provisions for his own personal gain, as he must replace a wagon of food owned by a threatening grizzly bear. Each industrious journey taken by the animals therefore becomes central to the threat of the deadline for R. J., who has been given only a week (until the next full moon) to replenish the stock.

Just as the journey narrative of *Flushed Away* required developments in the fluid simulation of water in computer graphics (including texture, bubbles, viscosity, energy-in-motion, surface lighting effects, reflectivity), the production of *Over the Hedge* similarly involved fine calculations to approximate the smooth photorealist rendering of natural phenomena. DreamWorks animators worked with a system of 'hedge interactions' as a way of 'realistically deforming and ripping [. . .] the branches and leaves' (Kisacikoglu 2006) as the woodland animals travel regularly through towering flora. Effects animator Gokhan Kisacikoglu explains, 'We placed the characters outside of the hedge and moved them inside gradually during an initialization phase in order to calculate the initial collisions accurately' (ibid.). From the knotted roots to the overlapping leaves, branches in some parts of the hedge were programmed like dominoes to move together when triggered by 'additional forces', and the speed of 'recovery' within these 'branch-to-branch' collisions allowed the hedge to return to its default position (ibid.). As part of their multiple journeys across the film's fictional world, then, repeated character movement through the foliage in *Over the Hedge* demanded the detailing of the precise forces exerted by R. J. and Verne on the vegetation as they embarked upon their frequent foraging expeditions.

Travel and Mobility

Computer-animated films are travel films, and mobility typically defines the character's relationship to the virtual spaces they inhabit. The manoeuvrability and peripatetic behaviour of their primary protagonists, alongside the predominance of the journey or quest style of narrative, perhaps explains why so many computer-animated films connote momentum, motion and directional movement within their titles alone. *In Search of Santa* (William Kowalchuk, 2004), *Thru the Moebius Strip* (Glenn Chaika and Kelvin Lee, 2005), *Mug Travel* (Lim Ah-ron, 2007), *Fly Me to the Moon, The Flight Before Christmas* (Michael Hegner and Kari Juusonen, 2008), *Journey to Saturn* (Thorbjørn Christoffersen and Craig Frank, 2008), *Up, Quantum Quest: A Cassini Space Odyssey* (Harry Kloor and Daniel St Pierre, 2010), *Escape From Planet Earth, Turbo* and *Air Bound* (Tomohiro Kawamura and Yoshihiro Komori, 2015), all gesture to the active engagement that a computer-animated film character has with the three-dimensional fictional world of the film. In *Wreck-It Ralph* (Rich Moore, 2012), the label 'going turbo' is even used to define the serendipitous wanderings and rootless incognito drifting of video game characters as they regularly undertake journeys between video games (known as 'game-jumping').

The stakes of reusing the journey narrative, and its regularity within so many computer-animated films, are certainly rooted in the wider prevalence of this narrative form across numerous historical, cultural and multimedia contexts, including cinema as a 'technology of vision' (Eleftheriotis 2010: 11). For Jane Suzanne Carroll, the 'journey-based narrative' is the 'master story of western civilization' (2011: 11), with many stories and folk tales including pilgrimages and quests. Janis P. Stout (1983) has further traced the enduring image and basic shapes of the journeyer or quester within the American literary tradition that frequently deals with motion and migration. Stout argues the conspicuous presence of travels and voyages is reflective of American national history, in which 'spatial movement has been the characteristic expression of our sense of life' (ibid.: 4). Computer-animated films certainly continue these literary, historical and cultural traditions of journey-centeredness, (re) locational movement and expedition, prioritising the journey narrative as their primary thematic and narrative concern. The journey framework not only enforces a chronology of events, but also crafts the 'chrono-logic' that Seymour Chatman (1980) suggests is part of the double temporal logic of narratives more broadly. The virtues of the journey narrative – as the organisation of a story according to conceptions of travel – lie in its ability to stabilise the 'external' movement through time ('the duration of the presentation' of the film text), but also govern the 'internal' logic too ('the duration of the film's sequence of events') (ibid.: 44). The logical consistency of the 'over the hedge' journey narratives are intended to conclude with the satisfaction of the end (Rodney *does* reach Robot City and the animals *do* reach safety in *Ice Age: The Meltdown*). In the 'over the hedge' journey narrative that also structures the Dr Seuss adaptation *Horton Hears a Who!*, Horton successfully preserves the miniature community of Whoville – who reside in a tiny speck of dust sitting upon a flower – by transporting it to a safe and stable home away from the film's antagonist, the Sour Kangaroo.

Due to its disruptive properties, the 'flushed away' journey narrative more obviously concludes with the symbol of a place as the 'end' that is located anywhere, and may exist in any form. *Flushed Away* chooses to keep Roddy in the underground sewers rather than return him to his domestic bliss overground; *Ratatouille*'s Remy stays to cook in Paris; and Lightning McQueen remains in the dusty and forgotten town of Radiator Springs in *Cars* following his unexpected pit-stop. But such narratives justify these relocations by framing the new locale as an improvement, and the event of being 'flushed away' comes to function as an important act of necessary re-discovery. Roddy finds the sense of community and belonging he is shown to crave, while Lightning McQueen learns a greater appreciation for small town values through his interaction with the local Radiator Springs community. In *Ratatouille*, Remy finally opens a restaurant, 'La Ratatouille', in the heart of Paris, dissolving the prejudice between human and non-human characters to show their peaceful co-existence in the French capital. Staying true to the classical narrative model in which the initial equilibrium is restored in an ulterior form, it is the linear, sequential style of the journey narrative that permits the end of the journey to be renewed as a new destination.

The iconography of *Cars* and its sequel *Cars 2* invites comparison to the particular cinematic traditions of the road movie, mapping their respective 'over the hedge' journey narratives against the drama of the Piston Cup stock car racing season. Pamela Robertson claims that while the road movie might be about 'the journey more than about any particular destination' (1997: 271), computer-animated films maintain their obsession with notions of the 'home'. This fascination exists because, as Corey Creekmur adds, either 'you can't go home again', or 'there's no place like home' (1997: 91). *Flushed Away*, *Cars* and *Ratatouille* all posit the former as a lack of willing to return mitigated by the lure of a developing romance, matching geographical relocation with a new romantic opportunity. Roddy suggestively asks fellow rodent Rita if she 'wouldn't happen to need a first mate', while Lightning decides to 'stop and stay a while' in Radiator Springs, much to the delight of love interest Sally. However, the 'flushed away' journey narrative most commonly equates the 'end' with a return to a Kansas-like (and no place like) 'home'. The forward-directed closure of the computer-animated journey becomes cyclical as the geographic, as well as narrative, resolution takes place in which the 'end' is ultimately expressed as a desire to return to the familiarity and *already known* of the 'beginning'. 'Let's go home', utters Woody at the end of *Toy Story 2*, a weary statement articulating the pull-string toy's wish to return to the sanctuary of Andy's Room. The equilibrium is *restored*, rather than *renewed*, inasmuch as Woody is free from the constraints of living idle as a museum piece, and returns to life as the subject of Andy's affections.

The journey narratives of numerous other computer-animated films have been resolved through the pleasurable satisfaction of a homecoming. *The Polar Express* and *Mars Needs Moms* have their 'flushed away' narratives framed by the protagonists' aspirations to return home (often personalised through the symbol of the family member, or in Woody's case his owner). The homecoming in *Wall-E* is precisely that. The inquisitive robot is a civilising force, returning the human race to Earth following their voyage aboard the AXIOM to (re)make the desolate planet hospitable and homely once again. In *Monsters, Inc.*, protagonists Mike Wazowski and James P. 'Sulley' Sullivan must themselves return human child Boo to her bedroom, following her intrusion into the monster world they inhabit, just as Tulip and Junior must deliver the right babies to expectant families during the climax of *Storks* (Nicholas Stoller and Doug

Sweetland, 2016). In the suggestively titled *Home*, the film's narrative premise concerns the friendly colonisation of Earth by the Boov alien race to examine the politics of settlement and entitlement, and in doing so interrogates what it means to actively establish a homespace. The journey narrative is also large enough to accommodate both the 'flushed away' and 'over the hedge' scenarios. *Up* is a particularly productive example in this respect, not least because it plays with the home as an ideological space of comfort, protection and sanctuary, and incorporates the computer-animated film's two journey narratives by attaching them to its two primary characters. Whereas the balloon voyage of Carl Fredericksen occupies the 'over the hedge' element of *Up*'s broader narrative structure ('so long boys!'), it is the young Boy Scout Russell who embodies the 'flushed away' element of the film. Russell accidentally boards Carl's flying house upon its take-off when in pursuit of the fictitious 'snipe' animal, and in doing so the 'over the hedge' and 'flushed away' strands of the film suddenly merge.

The desire to return, find, locate or discover home is naturally expressed in the more goal-orientated conditions of the 'over the hedge' narrative, albeit motivated by the displacement and alienation of another character becoming 'flushed away'. Bolt the dog, for example, pursues a journey back to owner Penny in *Bolt*. Ryan the lion cub is accidentally imprisoned away from his father, Samson, in *The Wild*, and Marlin must find his young son Nemo in the fish-out-of-water narrative of *Finding Nemo*. In *Strange Magic* (Gary Rydstrom, 2015), the capture of lovestruck fairy Dawn prompts her sibling Marianne to cross the perilous border between the fairy/light and bog creatures/dark lands marked by primrose flowers. Defying her father's commands to stay, Marianne undertakes a journey to restore both her family and her fractious relationship with her sister. All these (often father) figures resolve to locate their separated offspring in ways that position the re-establishment of the family unit as central to the journey narrative's resolution. Or as Manny puts it upon his parting from daughter Peaches in *Ice Age: Continental Drift* (Steve Martino and Michael Thurmeier, 2012) as the tectonic plates shift beneath their feet, 'I will find you'.

It is the logical sense of progression, but also the demand for resolution, destiny and fate offered by the journey narrative that makes it an ideal device around which to shape the action of a computer-animated film. But the value of the journey narrative also permits the development of character attributes and qualities; the evolution and resolution of a narrative that is as much physical (the activity of travel) as it is psychological. In this way, the journey narratives in computer-animated films conform to Rick Altman's model of a 'single-focus narrative', storylines that commonly take the form of 'a journey (whether the literal wanderings of voyagers, the spiritual path of a Dante, or the psychological vagaries of the Bildungsroman)' (2008: 157). Within the computer-animated film's journey narrative, particular characters can resolve inner conflict or feelings of guilt (Marlin eventually finds his son in *Finding Nemo*, Manny returns to his rebellious daughter in *Ice Age: Continental Drift*); learn humility (Scrooge in *A Christmas Carol*); or achieve a sense of self-worth (as with Rapunzel's ascent to womanhood in *Tangled* [Nathan Greno and Byron Howard, 2010]).

Case Study: *The Good Dinosaur*

Set in an alternate universe in which humans and dinosaurs are able to coexist, Pixar's *The Good Dinosaur* demonstrates the continual narrative and visual possibilities of the journey narrative framework. The film's boy-meets-dinosaur premise is initiated by dinosaur Arlo's separation from his family – mother Ida and siblings Libby and Buck – as he is knocked unconscious and swept downstream following his pursuit of a feral caveboy, Spot. Twenty minutes into the film, Arlo's vengeful pursuit of Spot (whom he blames for luring his father, Poppa Henry, to his death) leads to the pair being thrown head first over the gorge's edge into the fast-moving river. The film cuts between close-ups of Arlo's stricken face as he calls out to his mother, to wider landscape panoramas that show in full the apatosaurus being swept away. One particularly violent wave throws Arlo into a rock face, where he falls unconscious and drifts downstream before resting in the twinkling waters of a shallow pool. The 'flushing' of apatosaurus Arlo from his home by the flowing water current is given extra emotional impetus as Poppa Henry was similarly swept away along the ravine (and subsequently killed) during a flash flood earlier in the film. The iconography of water so central to the 'flushed away' narrative (as in *Flushed Away*, *Ratatouille*, *Moana*) is continued in *The Good Dinosaur*, with a spectacular sequence that rapidly switches between over and above the water level as it follows Arlo's parting from his mother and siblings.

As a counterpoint to the stylised design of the dinosaurs (including tyrannosaurus, pterodactyls, styracosaurus, velociraptors) and its occasional human characters, *The Good Dinosaur* employs an intricately photoreal policy for its vast underwater ecology. The many rivers and streams that vein the impressive virtual topography – designed using data from the US geological survey – were rendered using the Houdini FLIP water solver software (also used in the production of *Tangled* and *Cars 2*). The Houdini FLIP program has since supported the rendering of 'lapping waves' and 'thin-surface runoff ripples' in Pixar's short film *Piper* (Alan Barillaro, 2016), which depicts a sandpiper's first encounter with the sea, including the addition of surface foam and simulated whitewater spray details (Serritella et al.: 2016). That *The Good Dinosaur* borrows so heavily from the frontier landscapes of epic Hollywood Westerns, including the work of John Ford and Howard Hawks, enhances the film's investment in the mechanisms of the journey. However, while Arlo's homecoming through the vegetation and rocky landscapes in the shadow of the neighbouring Claw Tooth mountains forms the main emotional thrust of the film, the 'flushed away' journey narrative is exploited to set in motion Arlo's maturation. Previously denied the chance to 'make his mark', given his inability to harvest crops and rear animals on his family's farm, Arlo's moment of 'flushed away' disjuncture cues a change in the timid apatosaurus' behaviour. As both obstacle and guide, the flowing river prompts Arlo to survive out in the wild, and it is only after his journey through nature that he returns home with a fuller sense of purpose.

Collective Action

Journey narratives in the computer-animated film typically begin as singular excursions. Spatial movement and directional values are normally embodied through an individual character suddenly separated from their social group, or who desires to break out from its restrictive confines. Computer-animated films therefore readily adhere to the narrative economy and linearity of the *monomyth* or hero's journey pattern as proposed by Joseph Campbell (1998), in which a single figure is called to adventure as a rites of passage for personal growth and the acquisition of knowledge. Both Roddy and R. J. are coded in the respective fictional worlds of *Flushed Away* and *Over the Hedge* as loners. R. J. announces that he is nothing but 'a family of one', while Roddy's isolated circumstances are expressed through sound and image during an opening sequence that shows him undertaking group activities on his own (set tellingly to the sound of the Billy Idol song 'Dancing with Myself'). A similar ethos of isolation drives Reggie the turkey in *Free Birds*, who proudly but unconvincingly declares 'I'm a flock of one. A lone wolf'. But it is through their respective journey narratives that R. J., Roddy and Reggie are introduced to a particular kind of collective community, one that reflects the computer-animated film's wider re-negotiation of traditional family values.

Computer-animated films show minimal investment in the normative social unit of the nuclear family. Marlin (*Finding Nemo*), Django (*Ratatouille*), Stoick the Vast (*How to Train Your Dragon* [Chris Sanders and Dean DeBlois, 2010]), Lord Redbrick (*Gnomeo & Juliet* [Kelly Asbury, 2011]), Dr Bill Tenma (*Astro Boy* [David Bowers, 2009]), Tim Lockwood (*Cloudy with a Chance of Meatballs*), Buck Cluck (*Chicken Little*), the Fairy King (*Strange Magic*) and King Peppy (*Trolls*) are all single (male) parents. *Hotel Transylvania* and *Epic* (Chris Wedge, 2013) also begin with their respective father figures Count Dracula and Professor Bomba recently widowed. Each film's narrative exploits the lingering loss of the mother to create tensions between these fathers and their sole female offspring. In this way, computer-animated films follow the durable template of Disney animated features, which have regularly turned to the fragmentation of the family unit to trade in single parenthood as part of their representational orthodoxy. As Janet Wasko (2001) and others have identified, the ideological commitment towards 'family friendly' entertainment across Disney animation is at odds with the classical Disney formula that is predicated upon the absence of complete family structures.

Many computer-animated films are therefore strongly invested in the theme of surrogacy, presenting characters whose own journey narrative is implicated in the acquisition of children, and their subsequent adaption (often comically) to the demands of parental responsibility. Villainous Gru in *Despicable Me* relinquishes his role as antagonist and pauses his childhood desire to be 'the greatest villain of all time' to become a surrogate single father to three adopted children, Margo, Edith and Agnes. The third film in the trilogy, *Despicable Me 3* (Pierre Coffin and Kyle Balda, 2017), achieves a similar effect in its treatment of surrogacy and adoptive parenthood by following Gru's new wife Lucy Wilde as she struggles with the challenges of being stepmother to the three girls ('I'm still figuring out this mom thing'). In the opening sequence of another computer-animated film, *Penguins of Madagascar* (Eric Darnell and Simon J. Smith, 2014), three penguin brothers, Skipper, Kowalski and Rico, similarly assume the role of surrogate parents to an orphaned penguin, which they affectionately name Private. In DreamWorks' *Mr. Peabody & Sherman*, the theme of adoption is channelled through Mr Peabody, an anthropomorphic canine who adopts seven-year-old human orphan Sherman as his son, while *Storks* begins with the avian cast adopting a parentless child, 'Orphan Tulip' (as they name her), who is left behind by the Stork Mountain baby delivery service.

As *Storks* and many others exemplify, a great proportion of child characters in computer-animated films are orphans or abandoned children, affording considerable narrative opportunity to nuance the formation of familial constructs. Megamind and Metro Man (*Megamind*), Fernando (*Rio*), Pisces (*Shark Bait*), Lewis and Michael 'Goob' Yagoobian (*Meet the Robinsons* [Steve Anderson, 2007]), Flynn Rider (*Tangled*), Po (*Kung Fu Panda*) and Félicie (*Leap!* [Éric Summer and Éric Warin, 2017]) are all figures devoid of their real biological parents. The musical number 'Darkness, No Parents' sung by Batman in *The LEGO Movie* (and repeated during the film's closing credits) is explicit in drawing attention to the character's visible lack of a stable parental unit. The spin-off sequel, *The LEGO Batman Movie* (Chris McKay, 2017) further checks Batman's narcissism and arrogance by detailing his orphan origin story. Not only does Batman visit an orphanage to deliver Batman-themed merchandise ('Hey orphans, look who's here!'), but the superhero himself becomes a foster father to Dick Grayson.

That is not to say that computer-animated films have been entirely immune to more traditional depictions of the family. *The Incredibles* and *Shrek 2* source much of their comedy from familial dysfunction (including similar sequences set around a dinner table), while *Brave* (Mark Andrews and Brenda Chapman, 2012) is emotionally invested in the tribulations of a fractious mother/daughter relationship (though these three films less readily conform to a 'journey' narrative pattern). *Mars Needs Moms* is a particularly exceptional case. The film reaffirms the family unit as necessary by stressing the 'correct' social structures in which children should be raised, articulating the necessity of a mother and father unified through marriage. While the aliens harvest maternal figures from Earth to rear their own young, they renounce this insidious practice at the film's climax and admit that children are 'meant to be raised by parents'.

However, the journey narratives of the computer-animated film are typically employed to impress upon the protagonist an unconventional social group. They are subsumed by a collective mentality that functions as a welcome surrogate for the traditional family structure. Dennis Tyler argues that across the majority of Pixar's computer-animated films, the family 'is not simply the biological entity of the nuclear family, but rather a grouping of individuals who care for each other whether technically related or not' (2013: 269). Tyler draws primarily upon the competing 'broken home environments' of Carl and Russell in *Up* to illustrate the contemporary cultural landscape and changing nature of the family. He points out that Carl's raw grief at the death of his wife Ellie, alongside Russell's ambivalent and incomplete homelife (it is hinted that his parents have separated), carves a space for the realisation of a new kind of family unit. These new models of responsibility are a pattern of the 'family' repeated at length across numerous computer-animated films. *Kung Fu Panda* mobilises the archetypes of the *wuxia* or 'martial hero' genre of Chinese narrative fiction to frame the personal journey of panda protagonist Po. The film utilises the martial arts team of the Furious Five to provide Po with a more supportive social network, replacing his otherwise unfulfilling domestic life and naive (adoptive) father figure (by the third film, Po has both a foster and biological father, but no mother).

These complex, shifting familial relationships bear out Judith Halberstam's argument that many contemporary animated narratives mobilise a particular kind of address towards the 'disorderly child'. The attraction of the 'flushed away' journey narrative in particular connects to Halberstam's suggestion that children 'live according to schedules not of their own making' (2011: 47). However, computer-animated films more generally challenge the frozen logic of the family and its normative structures, rejecting the two-parent model for the intrigue and excitement of rebellious collective action. Nuclear families are deferred in favour of a menagerie of unusual toys, ants, bees, pigeons, robots, fish, snails, cars and rats, which band together to replace parental figures and allow computer-animated film narratives to instead trade in values of 'group bonding'. The 'flushed away' journey narratives of *The Ant Bully* (John A. Davis, 2006) and *Epic*, for example, emotionally rehabilitate their respective protagonists by teaching them the value of kindness and hard labour through unexpected communal activity. Shrunk down to miniature size, both Lucas Nickle and Mary Katherine 'M. K.' Bomba learn about the world by having to live so close (and even underneath) its surface. In *Monsters vs. Aliens*, bride-to-be Susan Murphy tellingly rejects marriage to obnoxious weatherman Derek to spend her life with an oddball army of monstrous characters.

The impact of the collective, and of cross-species alliance and co-operation, has been pursued further in Pixar's *Monsters University* (Dan Scanlon, 2013). The film situates the young and vulnerable Mike Wazowski within the Oozma Kappa fraternity, a group of 'misfit' monsters of differing species and diverse ages. The film circumvents individual-oriented success and delights in the unexpected friendships formed among this failing, rejected collective. The orphan narrative of *Penguins of Madagascar* also allows the film to reflect on the stakes of a family structure that is formed through chance ('You've got us, we've got each other. And if that ain't a family, I don't know what is'), while *The LEGO Batman Movie* climaxes with the musical number 'Friends are Family'. In its emphasis on what it means to be close (and with lyrics including 'We're not related but here's good news, friends are the family you can choose'), this song verbalises the value of non-normative adoptive relationships, and the place of friendship as a worthy substitute for blood relatives. As these computer-animated films make clear, viable family units need not be made up of heteronormative nuclear families. Rather, they can emerge from any other affiliation or grouping that provides the emotional nourishment previously provided only by a more conventional familial structure.

Beyond its contribution to the computer-animated film's internal coherence, both 'flushed away' and 'over the hedge' journey narratives also provide spectators with a virtual tour of their film's expansive digital terrain. Giuliana Bruno has suggested that such 'touristic' journeys in cinema are those of a 'devouring gaze [that] is hungry for pleasure and spectacle consumption' (2002: 82). Although Bruno is making an analogy between film (and more specifically cinema-going) with tourism as a leisure activity, the scope and breadth of the computer-animated film world also appeals to such spectatorial cravings. The journey narratives map out the virtual space as a backdrop for the characters' movement through both entirely fictional spaces and real-world locations (further discussed in the next chapter), which are signposted through historically formed iconography and encode the fictional world with particular socio-cultural and geographical data. However, these round-the-world voyage narratives do not reduce the computer-animated film to nothing more than a series of destinations, or cast its narratives as episodic and punctuated by the accumulation of 'foreign' spaces. The process of spatial exploration casts the spotlight on travelled space and experience, providing a series of geographical encounters indulging in the pleasures of revelation and discovery. Spectators are invited to identify with the protagonists and their goals, and to simultaneously appreciate the artistry, scope and design of these virtual panoramas. When Remy first glimpses the sumptuous Paris skyline in *Ratatouille*, his incredulity matches the spectators' own sense of wonder ('Paris? All this time I've been underneath Paris? Wow!'). Their 'touristic' gaze is satisfied by Remy's movement across the fictional world that reframes the action, quenching the spectators' thirst for spectacle through the sequence's careful co-ordination as a dramatic reveal.

The strong geographical brevity developed in the computer-animated film provides a striking example of what Sue Beeton (2005) identifies as the underdeveloped area of 'film-induced tourism', in which animated landscapes are used as publicity material by tourism organisations. Set predominantly around the area of Sydney Harbour in Australia, computer-animated footage from *Finding Nemo* was used by the Australian Tourism Commission (ATC) with the intention of enticing American travellers back to the country following the uncertainty of the US economy, and knock-on effects of the Iraq war (Mitchell 2003). The Malagasy tourism industry similarly hoped that the release of *Madagascar* would swell the country's turbulent economy and boost its flagging tourist trade, while *Kung Fu Panda 2* was even awarded a marketing prize by China's National Tourism Administration in November 2011 for promoting the city of Chengdu (following an earthquake that devastated the city in 2008).

'Movies are always better . . . especially sequels'

Computer-animated films draw upon and perpetuate the mythology of the spaces and geographical icons they visit, using the mechanisms of the journey narrative to support their unique language of visual description. Yet journey narratives are also stories that are designed to enhance and organise the computer-animated film's particular features, providing spectators with a guided tour of (the 'building blocks' of) its generic world. In this way, they hold a specific relationship to industrial processes of film franchising and sequelisation. Indeed, just as Andrew Tudor has identified the incessant process of 'sequelling' that has become a feature of horror films since the 1980s, sequels are an especially notable and highly striking convention of the computer-animated film (2002: 106–7). In recent work on the film sequel (Jess-Cooke 2009; Jess-Cooke and Verevis 2010; Henderson 2014; Klein and Palmer 2016), computer-animated films feature as examples of popular cinema that have fully exploited the possibilities for repeating pleasures. Stuart Henderson goes as far as to argue that when taken together, Pixar's *Toy Story* films serve as an 'exemplar of the sequel form's potential' (2014: 167). Or, as Boingo the Bunny puts it in the *Hoodwinked* follow-up *Hoodwinked Too! Hood vs. Evil* (Mike Disa, 2011), 'Movies are always better . . . especially sequels'.

Computer-animated films are certainly emblematic of the intensification of what Thomas Schatz calls the 'franchise mentality' (2009: 30) in the conglomerate era of Millennial Hollywood. These are films firmly implicated within discourses of cross-media promotion, pertaining to their exploitability as 'tentpole' projects and popular forms of 'merchantainment' (Hardy 2010: 31). Robert Sickels (2011: 95) argues that computer-animated films are a particularly 'desirable' investment for contemporary movie studios because they lend themselves well to concomitant ancillary revenue. Promoted across an array of interlinked entertainment and media products, computer-animated film narratives flow across several media platforms, which in turn suggests that the film's narrative and its characters are so large that they 'cannot be contained within a single medium' (Jenkins 2006: 95). But while the 'robust afterlife' (Bordwell 2006: 3) of computer-animated films is remarkably plentiful, their post-cinema existence does not unfold entirely within the synergistic home video entertainment marketplace, or the terrain of subsidiary merchandise and spin-off consumer products. It now increasingly takes place within the confines of the cinema auditorium, with computer-animated films having ushered in a shift towards the *multi-part* rather than strictly *multimedia* franchise.

A computer-animated film rarely exists in isolation. Most have theatrically released sequels and prequels (and in some instances multi-episode television spin-offs), which expand upon the precedent of an original to pattern the network of supplementary texts that trail in its wake. Such follow-up texts are commonly announced in their multitude, batched together in production slates and pipelines with the promise of more, and more than one, to come. Schatz points out that Pixar's computer-animated films are one of the 'dozen or so single-film franchises' operating today. Jason Sperb argues that 'Pixar long resisted the lure of sequelization' (2016: 105), yet three out of the five examples that Schatz lists have subsequently acquired feature-length sequels, with *Monsters, Inc.*, *Finding Nemo* and *Cars* spawning *Monsters University*, *Finding Dory* (Andrew Stanton, 2016), *Cars 2* and *Cars 3* (Brian Fee, 2017), respectively, in addition to the studio's enormously successful *Toy Story* trilogy and their upcoming sequel to *The Incredibles*. There are eight feature-length entries in Crest Animation's *Alpha and Omega* series (2010–17), and DreamWorks Animation currently has four computer-animated films with (multiple) sequels – *Shrek*, *Madagascar*, *Kung Fu Panda* and *How to Train Your Dragon* – with a sequel to *Trolls* and *The Boss Baby* (Tom McGrath, 2017) already in production. Disney's next two animated features, the upcoming *Ralph Breaks the Internet: Wreck-It Ralph 2* (2018) and *Frozen 2* (Rich Moore and Phil Johnston, 2019) are also sequels to existing computer-animated films, while Illumination Entertainment has already announced planned sequels to *Minions* (Pierre Coffin and Kyle Balda, 2015), *Sing* and *The Secret Life of Pets*. Films produced by other US studios, such as *Ice Age*, *Open Season* (Jim Culton and Roger Allers, 2006), *Happy Feet*, *Happily N'Ever After* (Paul J. Bolger, 2007), *Space Chimps*, *Cloudy with a Chance of Meatballs*, *Rio* and *The LEGO Movie* also all have follow-up films that reflect the industrial identity of a contemporary Hollywood cinema that is, perhaps more so than ever in its long history of sequelisation, turning to franchise filmmaking and the transfer of story material into a follow-up. However, multiple computer-animated films produced outside Hollywood, such as *Appleseed* (Shinji Aramaki, 2004) and *Resident Evil: Degeneration* (Makoto Kamiya, 2009) in Japan; *Impy's Island* (Reinhard Klooss and Holger Tappe, 2006) in Germany; *Winx Club: The Secret of the Lost Kingdom* (Iginio Straffi, 2007) in Italy; *Daddy, I'm a Zombie* (Ricardo Ramón and Joan Espinach, 2011) in Spain; *Kikoriki: Team Invincible* (Denis Chernov, 2011) and *The Snow Queen* (Vladlen Barbe and Maxim Sveshnikov, 2012) in Russia, and *Yugo & Lala* (Wang Yunfei, 2012) and *Dragon's Nest: Warriors' Dawn* (Song Yuefung, 2014) in China, also all have sequels that permit spectators the pleasure of 're-digesting their favourite storyline or star in a part-two blockbuster' (Jess-Cooke 2009: 8).

The inclusion of short form animation within the Hollywood film industry's increasing computer-animated output has awakened the traditions of the Golden Age seven-minute cartoon (see Klein 1993). Standard Pixar practice has been to accompany the theatrical exhibition of its feature-length productions with a short unaffiliated with the narrative of the main feature. Sustaining the studio's own short form origins and its heritage in television commercial production, these shorts endure as testing grounds for animators and directors to hone their craft prior to feature-length duties. Perhaps less well-known is the terrain inhabited by another set of Pixar films released under the banner of the Home Entertainment Shorts. These are a secondary cycle of 'spin-off' films packaged on DVD releases, whose mini-narrative arcs dovetail with the Pixar studio's feature-length films. These latter shorts have become a standard part of computer-animated film franchising, typically pursuing the tribulations of supporting characters (the 2006 *Cars* short *Mater and the Ghostlight* directed by John Lasseter and Dan Scanlon), or showing events unfolding parallel to the main narrative, as in the spin-off to *Wall-E* titled *Burn-E* (Angus MacLane, 2008), or *The Legend of Mor'du* (Brian Larsen, 2012), which connects to *Brave*. With contemporary Hollywood cinema 'infused with recycling and repetition' (Jess-Cooke 2009: 1), many North American animation studios have registered their commercial interests in spin-off shorts as much as feature-length sequels, which in their narrative organisation and character development are underscored with discourses of continuity and repetition, deviation and departure.

Between 2010 and 2016, for example, Illumination produced ten supplementary Minions shorts as part of their *Despicable Me* franchise, which operate tangentially to the narrative arc established across the feature films. Both the DVD releases of *The Lorax* (Chris Renaud, 2012) and *Sing* were packaged alongside three shorter 'mini movies'; *Dawn of the Dragon Racers* (John Sanford and Elaine Bogan, 2014) is a computer-animated short that featured on the DVD/Blu-Ray/digital release of *How to Train Your Dragon 2* (Dean DeBlois, 2014), and is one of four spin-off short films within the franchise, while *Norman Television* (Habib Louati and Boris Jacq, 2016) is a four-minute computer-animated film included on the DVD of *The Secret Life of Pets*. In the case of *Almost Home*, a prequel to *Home*, the film premiered before the theatrical exhibition of *Mr. Peabody & Sherman* and another computer-animated film sequel, *Rio 2* (Carlos Saldanha, 2014). The computer-animated short film *Puppy!* (Genndy Tartakovsky, 2017), which accompanied the recent theatrical release of *The Emoji Movie* (Tony Leondis, 2017), serves as a narrative bridge between *Hotel Transylvania 2* and *Hotel Transylvania 3* (Genndy Tartakovsky, 2018). Yet it is not uncommon for such shorts to function as precursors to (or commonly in lieu of) a feature-length sequel. Examples include *Club Oscar* (Vicky Jenson, Bibo Bergeron and Rob Letterman, 2005), *Hammy's Boomerang Adventure* (Will Finn, 2006), *Super Rhino* (Nathan Greno, 2009), *Megamind: The Button of Doom* (Simon J. Smith, 2011), *Tangled Ever After* (Nathan Greno and Byron Howard, 2012), *Frozen Fever* (Chris Buck and Jennifer Lee, 2015) and *Riley's First Date?* (Josh Cooley, 2015), which function as abridged sequels to *Shark Tale*, *Over the Hedge*, *Bolt*, *Megamind*, *Tangled*, *Frozen* and *Inside Out* respectively.

There are fundamental expectations that the wave of 'sequelling' accompanying each computer-animated film must meet. Pat Brereton (2012: 156) argues that *Toy Story*, for example, cannot end tragically. Resolving the Woody/Buzz conflict, Pixar's film incorporates an open-ended story structure in such a way as to both accommodate, and even anticipate, the possibility for more sequels, albeit with minimal disruption to the 'chrono-logic' of the original story. The *Toy Story* franchise has certainly continued to exploit the lack of fixedness to its narratives. The recent Toy Story Toons series of three theatrically exhibited shorts – *Hawaiian Vacation* (Gary Rydstrom, 2011), *Small Fry* (Angus MacLane, 2011) and *Partysaurus Rex* (Mark Walsh, 2012) – has sustained and expanded the *Toy Story* mythology long after the events of *Toy Story 3*, satisfying the audience's desire (and paving the way) for more of the same. Yet the multi-film form of computer-animated films is particularly conducive to supporting the shape of the journey narrative structure. This is because the journey itself can be staged as a broader meta-narrative stretched across the franchise, made to continue seamlessly from one computer-animated instalment to the next.

The journey narrative established in DreamWorks' *Madagascar* has been notably resistant to closure, and has become well-supported by the structure of the franchise's (to date) three feature-films. The first in the trilogy establishes the moment of 'flushed away' disjuncture, as anthropomorphic animals Alex, Marty, Melman and Gloria are mistakenly shipped from the comfort of a New York zoo to become marooned on distant Madagascar. The 2008 sequel (subtitled 'Escape to Africa' and advertised with the tagline 'Still Together. Still Lost') takes place as the animals attempt to flee the island, only to crash land in the African plains. *Merry Madagascar* (David Soren, 2009), a twenty-two minute Christmas-themed television special broadcast on NBC, transports spectators to sometime between the first and second films (thus becoming a 'interquel', 'intraquel' or 'midquel') (Wolf 2012a: 207). The plot of *Merry Madagascar* is the resumption of the quartet's futile attempts to flee Madagascar, this time in a homemade hot air balloon ('It may not be pretty, but we're headed to the city!'). The third feature-length instalment, *Madagascar 3: Europe's Most Wanted* (Eric Darnell, Tom McGrath and Conrad Vernon, 2012), continues the original chronology and follows the animals' ongoing attempts to return to Central Park Zoo from Africa, trailing them from Monte Carlo to Rome and finally London. Enabling the spectator's 'touristic' exploration of the virtual space, the final *Madagascar* film climaxes with the lost animals rejecting the sanctuary of captivity, and permanently joining a travelling circus. Now perpetual voyagers, Alex, Marty, Melman and Gloria ensure that the journey narrative, which first began in the original film (and that was subsequently extended and expanded across the franchise) will always remain in motion.

Franchises are signs of the potent and pervasive economic pressures exerted on contemporary cinema. If the film 'ain't broke, don't fix it'. Just repeat it. Geoff King argues that Hollywood today commonly 'eschews genre logic' and places greater stress upon a franchise mentality and the lure of 'series, cycles, remakes and sequels' (2002a: 144). Computer-animated films lend themselves to franchising and enable individual studios to emphasise their own 'legally restricted brand-name or franchise products' (ibid.). But the repackaging of the journey narrative across franchises, cycles and series allows for a clear expansion and nuancing of the genre's broader diegesis, with each new computer-animated film affording the opportunity for another journey to occur within a more extensive fictional universe. Each additive segment of travel and motion implies a fictional space that has organised itself into a series of stories, which are then told anew by the next instalment of the franchise. As the museum tour guide (later revealed to be La Muerte, ruler of the Land of the

Remembered) puts it in *The Book of Life*, 'All the world is made of stories'. The next chapter therefore shifts the spotlight onto world-building and the specific kinds of fictional spaces in which the genre's many journeys take place, identifying how computer-animated film worlds are unique virtual environments that assume a place within a continuum of dynamic and diverse animated screen worlds.

CHAPTER 3

Notes on a Luxo World

Between its first screen appearance in Pixar Animation Studio's computer-animated short *Luxo Jr.* and its subsequent adoption by the company as its corporate logo, the Anglepoise 'Luxo' lamp featured in four educational shorts: *Light and Heavy* (John Lasseter, 1991), *Surprise* (John Lasseter, 1991), *Front and Back* (John Lasseter, 1991) and *Up and Down* (John Lasseter, 1991), all created for the long-running US children's television programme *Sesame Street* (Joan Ganz Cooney and Lloyd Morrissett, 1969–). Each of the thirty-second vignettes framed the curious lamp character within loose narratives of worldly exploration. Learning concepts such as the behaviour of objects under duress, gravity, depth, dimensionality and perspective were all realised through the playful actions of the sentient spotlight. While other test animations made by Pixar during the studio's formative period – such as *Beach Chair* (Eben Ostby, 1986) and *Flags and Waves* (Bill Reeves and Alain Fournier, 1986) – were colour visualisations primarily designed to test the proficiency of their proprietary RenderMan software, the investigative actions of the Luxo character across these early shorts actively inducted spectators into the specific circumstances and conditions of these new computer-animated film worlds. Through the impressionable Luxo's inquisitive behaviour, animators were able to facilitate spectators' entry into such screen spaces, priming them for what to expect of digital animation's new fictional worldhood by playing out the logic of its own spaces.

Given how its curious actions were qualified through lifelike movements and unfolded within a narrative space charged with a recognisable reality, the Luxo character seemingly moved according to a familiar 'hyperrealist' set of conditions, a representational schema standardised by Walt Disney and central to the orthodoxy of his animated formula (Wells 1998: 25–6). John Lasseter had, of course, already applied the principles of traditional animation – including the 'illusion of life' techniques of Disney's 'Nine Old Men' animators – to three-dimensional digital animation during the production of *Luxo Jr.*, presenting his approach at the SIGGRAPH industry conference on computer graphics in July 1987 (Lasseter 1987: 35–44). Yet, just as the cel-animated feature *Snow White and the Seven Dwarfs* (David Hand, 1937) conventionalised the hyperrealist framework for the hand-drawn animated style, the arrival of the feature-length computer-animated film cemented hyperrealism as the dominant aesthetic impetus governing these emerging digital worlds. Hyperrealism continues to regulate the events and action(s) across feature-length computer-animated fictions, and within an animated context explains something of their worldly constitution. Indeed, without the verisimilitude of a hyperrealist sensibility, Buzz Lightyear really would be able to fly (rather than simply 'fall with style') in *Toy Story* and Carl Fredericksen would have little need for helium balloons to raise his house from its foundations in *Up*. The elderly widower could, instead, call upon animation's effortless ability to bring into disrepute gravitational laws, as epitomised by the hapless Wile E. Coyote, who was often suspended in a state of comic inertia during his failed pursuits of the Road Runner in Warner Brothers' *Looney Tunes* cartoons.

Highly evocative and elusive, despite being rigidly rule-bound and fictionally incomplete, the worlds of feature-length computer-animated films certainly present scholarship with a unique theoretical challenge. Thomas Lamarre points out that 'digital media promised to produce amazing new worlds, things never before seen' (2006: 131). At the same time, however, the worlds of the computer-animated film can be theorised according to many of the relationships to world-building by which all animated worlds have been categorised. Such relationships overwhelmingly coalesce around issues of realism whilst embracing their constructedness as ontologically finite, occluded screen spaces. Paul Wells has summarised the world-making capabilities of animation, arguing that animators are responsible for 'every aspect of what is a highly detailed process of *creating* a world rather than merely *inhabiting* one' (2002a: 26, original emphasis). The description of animated worlds offered by Alexander Sesonske back in the 1970s that cartoon worlds are not '*the* world' plays out a familiar preoccupation with attributing fictionality to animation's foundational *un*reality (in Cavell 1979: 167–8). These kinds of commonplace assertions have, perhaps, underscored too heavily the boundary between reality and illusion in the critical conception of animated worlds, spotlighting animation as a product (and project) of heightened illusionism in ways that have wrapped fictionality solely around its status as non-realistic media. Each of those elements cited to incriminate animation, whether concerns of its fictional construction, its borders and boundaries and wider incompleteness, is a matter of course for all of cinema's fictions. The charges of fictionality brought against animated worlds by scholars such as Sesonske can ultimately be levelled at live-action filmmaking too, and find an unexpected corollary in a live-action cinema no less constructed, shaped and sculpted. V. F. Perkins, for example, identifies an often-overlooked 'compromise position' occupied by the photographic narrative film, in which a 'fictional "reality" is created in order to be recorded' (1993: 61). In a more recent essay detailing cinema's capability for creating visually arresting worlds, Perkins adds that it should be a necessary recourse for all fictional analyses to 'illuminate artifice, not deny it' (2005: 34). Worldhood, he suggests, is 'not primarily an issue of realism' (ibid.). Animation is undoubtedly a special case when situated alongside such discourses of fictional world-making, affording an alternative logic to understandings of film fictionality. But the default manner in which animation has been critically evaluated does little to lay the groundwork for examining the identity or scope of computer-animated films, or the complexity of their fictional worlds.

The identification of the digital as renewing cinema's fictional worlds and their regeneration and rejuvenation at the hands of technological developments are demands that can only be satisfied by a fresh approach to world creation in the computer-animated film context. While such digital spaces convey degrees of continuity with prior animated worlds, they also demonstrate multiple points of rupture. To distinguish the transformations and salient points of contact that computer-animated films make with cinema's other types of fictional worlds, this chapter returns to the early years of computer animation by introducing 'Luxo' as a valuable descriptor that brings into focus the unexplored area of computer-animated film worlds. Luxo is a term that is not only historically bound to the development of computer-animated filmmaking within America during the 1980s and 1990s but, as this chapter contends, also works to afford a degree of specificity to a particular type of screen world within contemporary digital culture.

Leakage, Labour and Luxo

The value of Luxo to definitions and classifications of computer-animated film worlds is no less significant today, over thirty years after the lamp's first screen appearance. The impact of digital technologies upon contemporary filmmaking practice, and the increasingly hybrid, composite illusionism of mainstream Hollywood in particular, has given rise to a range of fictional film worlds to which the broad label *computer-animated* might be legitimately applied. Within cinema's ever-broadening spectrum of digitally enhanced environments, it is perhaps useful to both discriminate and qualify where 'computer-animated films' fit within such a sliding scale of digital processing and manufacture. In *Waking Life* (Richard Linklater, 2001) and *A Scanner Darkly* (Richard Linklater, 2006), for example, animation overlays pre-existing live-action footage via the process of interpolated Rotoscoping, applied using the digital tool Rotoshop (created for *Waking Life* by American computer programmer Bob Sabiston). These hybrid films thus re-conjure a particular kind of computer-animated world (albeit replicating a flattened, hand-drawn style) by superimposing a computer-animated fiction on top of a pre-existing, live-action one.

Contemporary filmmaking also mixes highly persuasive digital imagery with sophisticated matte paintings, detailed miniatures and models in the construction of putatively live-action worlds. *Sky Captain and the World of Tomorrow* (Kerry Conran, 2004), *Sin City* (Robert Rodriguez and Frank Miller, 2005), *300* (Zack Snyder, 2007), *Speed Racer* (The Wachowskis, 2008), *The Spirit* (Frank Miller, 2008), *Alice in Wonderland* (Tim Burton, 2010) and *Hugo* (Martin Scorsese, 2011), alongside the recent *Star Wars* (George Lucas, 1999–2005), *Lord of the Rings* (Peter Jackson, 2001–3) and *The Hobbit* (Peter Jackson, 2012–14) film series, typify how the increased practicality of all-digital environments has expanded the range of computer-animated worlds. The mechanics of these films' production present a digital update to the rear-projection processes of the classical studio era. Their often sophisticated application of digital technology negotiates the 'clumsy sublime' of these earlier projections by erasing the visual incongruity between character and place, while simultaneously maintaining the 'artificiality and glaring implausibility' of earlier, pre-digital forms of diegetic world construction (Mulvey 2007: 3). Within these digital environments, actors are required to (inter)act in front of vast green and blue screens (known as a virtual backlot), or in minimal sets with animatronics, props and prosthetics, while computer graphics, in the words of Jay Boulter, seamlessly 'fill the world' (2005: 24).

With *computer-animated* worlds now defined by their striking multiplicity, the term Luxo will be expanded in this chapter to connote those fictional worlds specific to the computer-animated film. It does not account for digitally traced Rotoscoped worlds, or three-dimensional virtual scenery achieved via digital projection common to live-action/computer-generated composites. Luxo worlds are of an alternative mode of production and different visual order. They are simulated virtual environments not captured in the real world, but rather are modelled, shaped, sculpted and recorded from within a computer. As Burr Snider wrote back in December 1995, '*Toy Story* was shot entirely on location – in cyberspace' (1995). Put simply, a Luxo world can be thought of as a computer-animated fiction achieved through a fluid act of production, and not as a fictional world crafted separately in *post*-production.

Just as 'generic verisimilitude' (Neale 2000: 28) as a dimension of genre codifies generic expectations into an implied set of laws and pre-structured agreements circulating between industry, text and spectator, Luxo ultimately functions as a shorthand that makes discriminations about how spectators are to grasp fictional meaning within this particular cartoon context. A Luxo world can *only* be a computer-animated film world. It is a fictional space that both *preserves* and is the *preservation of* the computer-animated films as a particular kind of contemporary cinema. Charged with disclosing the many particularities of these digitally animated worlds, we might therefore unfold Luxo as a synonym for - or a term closely allied with - the 'animatedness' of the computer-animated film. Drawn from Sianne Ngai's work on animatedness as a quality rooted in unbridled hyperactivity and exaggerated energy (2005), here it is a catch-all term used to verify the computer-animated film's many qualities and specificities as the dominant mode of contemporary animated fiction.

It has certainly been a prerequisite of animation scholarship to unfold along the fault lines of animated difference. The accelerating academic interest in animation as an inherently spatial art, and the recent spate of critical writing that has matured around the subject of animated worlds, has affiliated the virtues of animated filmmaking with its particular world-making capabilities (Wood 2006; Telotte 2010; Buchan 2011; Crafton 2013). Suzanne Buchan has defined animated worlds as those 'realms of cinematic experience that are accessible to the spectator only though the techniques available in animation film-making' (2006: vii). The textual implications of what Buchan has labelled animation's 'special powers' has been maintained across many formal appreciations of animation's range of performance spaces. Animated worlds are certainly gifted, accomplished enough to progress, transition, adjust, reform, flatten and become spatially discontinuous at will. Computer-animated films are no less prone than other types of animation to creatively accent their achievements when presenting their worlds. Describing the climactic door chase sequence from Pixar's fourth feature film *Monsters, Inc.*, Aylish Wood outlines a sudden 'leakage' of computer animation onto the screen interface that pushes the technology beyond merely reproducing 'a series of pre-existing conventions' (2007: 25). This 'leakage' occurs when the digital becomes notably inscribed into the text, making spectators witness to an event that surfaces both the artistic expertise of the filmmakers and the innovative presence of 'elements that could only be effectively achieved through digital animation' (ibid.). The standout visibility of the technology momentarily engenders an exhibitionist mode of address pushing at the accepted boundaries of live-action possibility. A Luxo world must therefore be critically evaluated as a representational and fictional space revealed to the spectator, *and* the world of its origins on a computer screen. The two strands are interrelated and inseparable, part of an essential cause and effect relationship between the unseen process of activating or giving life and the new kind of arresting screen activity witnessed by the spectator. The animatedness of Luxo worlds thus arises as a shorthand not just for the strengthening of animated artifice (rather than its rejection) but also as an attestation to a certain visibility or 'leakage' of labour.

Revelations of animated work represent a highly apposite intervention into the appreciation of computer-animated screen spaces. Vivian Sobchack has argued that the themes of automatic precision, regulation and oppression in *Wall-E* – despite the film's many 'formal achievements and narrative complexity' – efface the effortful qualities of its digital production (2009: 390). For Jennifer M. Barker, digital technologies omit the effortful authenticity and labour of cel-animation, with a frictionless fluidity that excludes the discontinuous, 'jerky, slightly imperfect illusion' of frame-by-frame cel-layering (2009: 137). Beyond the frailty and fallibility of hand-drawn techniques, computer-animated films such as *Wall-E* equally elide the 'laborious struggles' and stuttering, sporadic movements characteristic of stop-motion. For phenomenologists such as Sobchack and Barker, these qualities of non-digital animation enable it to play across the poles of animate and inanimate, and act as a reminder of 'how difficult it is to be animate, to be alive, to struggle against entropy and inertia' (Sobchack 2009: 390). Exploring the features of a Luxo world helps identify how spectators remain privileged observers to a digital thumbprint in a computer-animated film world: that is, the collective trace or impression of its animatedness left behind by the animators. It is the formal dynamism, virtuosity and staggering complexity of these new worlds that manifest the residual labour of their collaborative and sophisticated digital production. The digital thumbprint within a Luxo world is less a clumsy, revealing remnant of its fictionality and more the visible mark of its arresting worldhood. By addressing various aspects of their worldliness, including their growth and cultivation inside a computer program and the unique kinds of digital characters who populate such screen spaces, this chapter argues that computer-animated films are those that visibly *labour* while not *labouring*. These worlds do not settle, but are charged with an enlivening, 'animate' quality that invites spectators to keep up with the action. It is here, then, spread widely across the geography of its fictional Luxo world, that computer-animated films most forcefully harness elements of their particular animated identity. As the insect Colonel Cutter puts it when surveying the achievements of the underground colony in *Antz*, 'Look at what these workers have done'.

The Question of Fiction

All fictional worlds within the cinema are founded upon interstitial qualities, pulled between elements of reality and their own fictional constituents. Perkins writes that a fictional film world, though 'not ours', may share our own real-life histories, as well as 'our economy, our technologies, our architecture, and the legal systems and social forms' (2005: 19). Relevance and recognisability for a computer-animated film similarly exists as variant gradations on a spectrum of fictionality, rather than according to a simple binary opposition between the real and the unreal. Multiple levels of recognition are built into a Luxo world, whether presenting an unspecified milieu, or invoking more familiar iconography that establishes a real-life location with both great economy and little scope for contradiction. Computer-animated films also mix their stylistic register, marrying entirely fictional environments alongside worlds that often invade realist topography. *The Adventures of Tintin: Secret of the Unicorn*, for example, introduces a fictitious Moroccan fishing port and semi-independent state named Bagghar. This fictionally real location situates a Luxo world as simultaneously *in* and *beyond* our real-life world. Tintin's Morocco is recognisable as *our* Morocco. It is marked by Arabic and Berber dialects, flowing *djellaba* clothing, bustling *souks* and street vendors, and the ornamental cornices and crenellated arches of Moorish *riad* architecture. But despite its audiovisual proximity to the real world, Bagghar belongs entirely to, and is an invention of, the formal achievements of the fiction.

The animatedness of computer-animated films permits Luxo worlds to stake a very different territory than other fictional environments, providing another separating principle between those states of reality and illusion that extend beyond broader conceptions of 'location'. Just as photographic cinema inhabits the 'compromise position' between fictional construction and realism, a Luxo world adopts another kind of compromise aesthetic that settles depictions of reality with its own perceptible animatedness. Many scholars have set out to map the computer-animated film's 'compromise' visuality to better understand the nature of its worlds. Martin Lister, for example, has defined Pixar's aesthetic style as a visual combination of 'spectacular realism', which involves 'sophisticated rendering of depth, lighting, texture, and so on' with more 'cartoon-derived codes' pertaining to character design, action, comedy and movement (Lister et al. 2009: 151–5). The term 'third realism' has been originated within the pages of *Cinefex* by Mark Cotta Vaz to similarly describe the conjunction of dimensional photorealism with the flourishes and freedoms of illustration (1999: 41–50).

It is also not uncommon for scholars to lean on more familiar vocabularies to describe the particular visual skewing of real-world conditions in its representations. In his recent book on the historical transformation(s) of animated space, J. P. Telotte places the design policies of Pixar within a long chronology of animated worlds, which always seem 'to point in the direction of both a real space and a fantastic space' (2010: 15). It comes as little surprise that a vocabulary drawn from the genre of fantasy has appeared so widely in discussions of computer-animated film worlds. The recent resurgence of academic interest in the workings of fantasy itself correlates with the upturn in the number of 'pure fantasy films' in the immediate post-9/11 period (Cornea 2007: 266). But the recourse to fantasy equally stems from the fact that animation has also regularly been considered a 'fantastic' visual medium. Donald Crafton is not alone in arguing that the 'settings, landscapes and stages' that cartoon stars occupy are 'fictional worlds that we like to believe in, all the while knowing them to be fantastic' (2013: 16). Fantasy, here, is implicated in animation's ontological disassociation from photographic cinema, once again subsuming discussions regarding the fictionality of animated worlds within ontologically specific concerns of the medium's inherent non-indexical quality.

The 'in-between' state of a Luxo world is manifest not just in an aesthetic style in which a creative bargain between fictionality and animatedness is struck, but bleeds into the kinds of actions and events that might be permitted to occur within these computer-animated spaces. Katherine Sarafian, producer of *Brave*, reveals the myriad of possible terms for computer-animated worlds:

> Pixar's digital universe is not a hyperreal world, nor is it a surreal world, nor a real world that mimics life. It is an *other*world, neither more nor less real than the actual, physical world outside. It is wholly different at the same time that it is familiar. (Sarafian 2003: 216)

Despite Sarafian's suggestion that Pixar are involved in the creation of 'other' worlds, their fictional worlds (as with the majority of computer-animated films) cannot be considered 'Other' in the manner that James Walters (2008) has recently theorised. In fact, Luxo worlds do not pose themselves as alternative, imagined or other, and are rarely supernatural. Computer-animated films are also not built to the same blueprint of fantasy and magic that has held such strong ideological currency across the Walt Disney Corporation's various business and multimedia enterprises, and especially packaged in their feature-length animated output. The strange visual reality and viewing pleasures of the computer-animated film are, perhaps, closer to an associated or overlapping category of fantasy, known as Low Fantasy (sometimes called magical realism). Magical realism is a mode of fantasy with very few cinematic examples, and despite efforts by Frederic Jameson (1986) in the 1980s to conjoin it with cinema, it remains primarily the reserve of particular kinds of literature. It has, however, been a term deployed to identify the ontology of animation: that is, describing all animation as a type of cinema that can 'create their own worlds' (Berleant 1991: 183).

Computer-animated Luxo worlds can be understood as an emerging cinematic mode of magical realism. These films exist *outside* any broad definition of science fiction: a mode of speculative fiction that, unlike magical realism, 'does not have a realistic setting that is recognisable in relation to any past or present reality' (Bowers 2004: 28). Luxo worlds do, however, deviate from magical realism in one significant way. Arnold Berleant points out that magical realism conventionally evaporates 'the significance of the distinction between the real and the unreal', thus providing a continuous slippage between the magic of fantasy and reality (1991: 183). However, computer-animated films preserve such a distinction within its worlds, not permitting their animatedness to slip continuously into real world so that their specificities might become lost. Their narratives operate at the border, by retaining animatedness and playing with their degrees of difference from live-action film. Computer-animated films do not want spectators to mistake them for live-action worlds, however. Making use of a stylised, caricatured aesthetic, despite the heightened level of mimesis afforded by technological advancement, is just one of the processes by which these films creatively, imaginatively and playfully remind spectators of their animatedness. The design policies in operation in a Luxo world bring computer-animated films up to the edge of live-action reality, only to recoil from the opportunity for realistic representation.

Luxo begins to emerge as a particularly valuable descriptor for computer-animated films for three reasons. First, terms like hyperrealism, spectacular realism and third realism tend to prioritise the dominance of the real by suggesting that the new, interstitial aesthetic of computer-animated films is a modification *to* a dominant realist register *by* animation (a heightened or exaggerated version of reality). Luxo, by comparison, authenticates the computer-animated film's formal achievements as a creative product *of* animated technique (emphasising animatedness). Second, Luxo conceptualises animatedness by avoiding reference to heavily loaded terms such as fantasy and science fiction, and certain affiliate descriptors such as dream-like, enchanted, surreal, paranormal, magical and supernatural. Not only have such concepts remained subject to ongoing theoretical revision across several disciplines, they are not satisfactory as explanations for the types of world produced in computer-animated films. Third, Luxo constitutes an umbrella term under which the hybrid visual style of computer-animated films coexists with the kinds of events, activities and relationships that are bound together through a certain visibility of the processes by which they are made. Crafton has suggested that 'live-action environments are selected, constructed, and manipulated as much as cartoon environments, but the techniques for doing so are disguised, creating a natural believability, a cinematic trompe l'œil that passes for reality' (2013: 146). But the invasion of realistic representation by animation highlights the stress placed upon the retention of animatedness. Computer-animated worlds make few attempts to 'pass for reality'; rather, they regularly deliver spaces that are visibly powered, and not paralysed, by the animated labour involved in their production as their status as (computer) animation is announced in a number of ways.

Harnessing the Digital

A Luxo world's virtual production contributes to several of its achievements. Luxo worlds exist inside a computer independently of the film that takes place there, and independently of the spectators' act of watching. These spaces are persistent worlds: mapped, built and surviving three-dimensionally. Individual sets, reminiscent of those in stop-motion, are physically modelled to scale using a host of pliable materials, before being remodelled and rendered inside a computer. Even those computer-animated films achieved through motion-capture processes, including *The Polar Express*, *Beowulf* and *The Adventures of Tintin: The Secret of the Unicorn*, have their fictional worlds crafted inside a computer, into which the captured performances are immediately inserted. Performers climb wire-frame sets and handle rough props that correlate to digital equivalents. No green/bluescreen processes are involved (and thus no virtual environment enveloping the actors). When these performances are viewed 'live' on a computer monitor, the pre-existing three-dimensional world is instantly composited into the film frame, giving the illusion that each actor is performing directly within the virtual Luxo world with minimal pause or lag.

The virtual creation of Luxo worlds in this manner holds a strong practical value. Frederick Betz argues that, stored digitally, computer-animated worlds are simply 'easy to alter' (2001: 210). Or, as Stuart Mealing puts it, 'one advantage of computer generated sets, as opposed to hand-built models, is that they can be destroyed as often as you like and then restored at the touch of a button' (1998: 40). Luxo worlds are equally more forgiving when it comes to the practicalities of computer-animated filmmaking. Computer-animated films are, as with much animated and non-animated cinema, highly collaborative efforts. As the opening credits of *Cloudy with a Chance of Meatballs* playfully announce, this is 'A Film by A Lot of People' (the 2013 sequel modifies this disclaimer to declare 'Another Film by A Lot of People'). The virtual geography of a Luxo world enables the multiple production staff including animators, visual development artists, production designers, directors of photography, set supervisors, set dressers and art directors to work simultaneously and seamlessly within the space of the same location. Available from any computer terminal, a Luxo world is more accessible than the material sets of stop-motion animated worlds (which are often duplicated to improve workflow). The persistent nature of Luxo worlds is also especially conducive to the production of computer-animated film prequels, sequels and spin-offs as discussed in the previous chapter. David A. Price notes that *Toy Story 2* 'reused digital elements from *Toy Story*, the making of which had left behind a kind of digital backlot' (2009: 182). Any number of environments can therefore be summoned from the copious digital archives, revisited and remade as new performance spaces in the latest cinematic instalment as part of a cost-effective economy of production.

The mathematical codes known as 'fractals', which underlie the creation of Luxo worlds, are equally significant for determining how the animatedness of computer-animated film worlds marks their unique topology. Coined by mathematician Benoît Mandelbrot in 1975, the dominant features of fractals are their self-similarity, scaling invariance and strict rules of repetition, insofar as they connote patterns that repeat at various levels of magnification (1983: 34). As an individual tree branch grows and then divides, it produces a miniature 'version' whose microcosmic shape emulates that of a fully grown tree. Similar relationships exist in the branching of rivers and of smaller streams, and between enormous mountain ranges and more diminutive rock formations. Computer-animator Loren Carpenter adapted fractal patterning when making computer-animated shorts during the early 1980s, drawn to Mandelbrot's writing on fractals in his pursuit of developing landscapes structured to the apparently random patterns found across the natural world. Presented at the SIGGRAPH computer graphics conference in 1980, Carpenter's two-minute film *Vol Libre* (1980) was the first to employ fractal-generating algorithms to accurately simulate the fractal geometry found within natural geography. With a visual effect evoking time-lapse footage, virtual mountain ranges and rock formations in *Vol Libre* suddenly emerge from simple polygon shapes during the course of the film's duration as calculated by Carpenter's natural algorithm. The strong fractal dimension of the building of Luxo worlds more accurately matches the mathematical code (at an atomic level) that governs the geological shapes, curves and contours of the real world. Thus, while both hyperrealism and fractals work as critical terms to define animation's formal relationship with realism, the latter is related to the specificity of computer-animated film worlds that are virtually grown within a computer program. Fractals suggest the unique algorithmic code base of computer-animated films (rather than the cel base or clay base of other animated forms). By understanding a Luxo world as a fractal fiction, the digital identity or animatedness of the computer-animated film can be cast on the side of fictional world creation, rather than entangled with longstanding discourses of realism.

The grow-divide structural order central to fractal geology has remained the fundamental building block of feature-length computer-animated films, used as an underlying mathematical code that generates the most intricate of virtual landscapes. Malcolm Cook has recently argued that 'fractals serve as a way for nature to self-inscribe through the technology of computers, refiguring, but not resolving, the nature/culture dichotomy in new ways' (2015: 58). Although the ridges and plateaus of the fictional Paradise Falls in *Up* were sculpted to resemble the vast Tepui mountains of Venezuela, the self-regulation patterning of fractals enabled an accurate replication of jagged rocks and dense surrounding jungle. Growth algorithms were similarly used to cultivate the lush foliage central to *Over the Hedge*, while in *Flushed Away* fractal geometry created the smaller detail of foam lather floating almost imperceptibly on top of the film's underground river system (Robertson 2006).

There are two principal ways that computer-animated films may choose to invite spectators to marvel at the accuracy, detail and visual complexity of their fictional worlds generated through the fractal algorithm. Stephen Prince has identified how a computer-animated environment can effortlessly 'nudge out the physics of actual light behaviour' (2012: 69). The food in *Ratatouille*, as Prince explains, was primed and shaded using subsurface scattering systems of light and additional 'bounce lights' to create a warm, glowing candescence that cheated physical lighting systems used in live-action film. The objective was to enhance the sophisticated texture and fine detailing of its array of edible objects, correlating the enhanced visibility with a heightened level of appeal. Light is an attribute of *Ratatouille*'s animatedness: an animated addition that makes Luxo an even more resonant term for describing computer-animated film worlds. Cast from the light of Luxo, these new worlds are particularly enlightened and illuminated, their desirability continually spotlighted with each and every frame. However, a Luxo world is equally illuminated through the specific capabilities of the virtual camera that marvels at the accuracy and expanse of fractal growth.

The fractal graphics of *Vol Libre* 'tricked the eye in numerous ways, seemingly depicting a fully detailed world that scaled, titled and panned accurately' (von Borries et al. 2007: 128–9). It was, of course, not the world that tilted or panned but the multi-directional camera placed within the fiction itself. Notwithstanding developments in the multi-plane camera at the Walt Disney studio during the 1930s, the camera in cel-animation typically maintains its place in one position. It is the individual film cels (comprising the fictional world) that are incrementally moved frame by frame. In the creation of a Luxo computer-animated world, the inverse relationship between the camera apparatus and the world is true. Computer-animated worlds remain spatially fixed. It is the mobile, vicarious camera that moves through the space, particular viewpoints chosen and pre-determined within the fictional world to the denial of others. Spectacular shots such as those accompanying Bob Parr's (Mr Incredible) arrival on Nomanisan Island, an uncharted volcanic landmass in *The Incredibles*, as well as the entire opening sequence through the dust clouds in *Wall-E*, formally reprise the vicarious camerawork so impressive in Carpenter's *Vol Libre*.

The elaborate flamboyance of the long take is also a particularly common element of the (presentation of those) Luxo worlds found in computer-animated films produced through motion-capture technology. This is a formal feature that can be attributed to the camera's lack of spatial constraints as it builds a world separate from the motion-captured performances. Computer-animated films raise intriguing questions about the function of editing within the digitally assisted long take. The potential flexibility of unbroken screen time is compelling within a medium that historically takes editing as a relatively 'invisible' process, one that effaces its frame-by-frame or stop-motion construction for a more continuous understanding of movement. Nonetheless, certain sequences are designed to draw attention to the camera's unrestrained and unrestricted animated

Figure 3.1 Frame grab from *The Adventures of Tintin: The Secret of the Unicorn* (2011) (Amblin Entertainment/Paramount Pictures). The bravura virtuosity and extended mobility of the virtual camera.

capabilities, including the virtuosic excess of the 'Ticket on the Loose' sequence from *The Polar Express*, which follows the serendipitous and fortuitous behaviour of a golden ticket fluttering in the wind, the opening shot of *A Christmas Carol* that swoops through a digital Dickensian London, and the Moroccan chase scene in *The Adventures of Tintin: The Secret of the Unicorn* (Figure 3.1). These continuous shots fit under what Deborah Tudor has defined as 'array aesthetics' in non-animated cinema driven by its digital content. Rethinking the shot as the 'basic cinematic unit', these computer-animated films provide spectators with moments in which they are able to 'access information within one shot that would not be available from one point of view' (2008: 99–100). Through the spectacle of the long take, these films additionally provide a stylistic correlative or counterpoint to their many journey narratives, while visually conquering the virtual space through the logic of extended mobility.

Case Study: *Frozen*

In the case of Disney's commercially successful computer-animated film *Frozen*, the mathematically predictable patterns of self-similarity central to the fractal geometry of fictional world creation are reflexively acknowledged within the context of an extended musical display. Disney technical director Lewis N. Siegel (2014) explains that consideration was given throughout the film to details of frost and snow shading, the refraction of light through transparent ice blocks, and controlling variations of snow strength (soft, crunchy, viscous, powdery). Yet, *Frozen* is highly explicit in folding its own digital construction back onto itself, as through its anthemic musical number 'Let it Go' the film rousingly performs the spectacle of fractal growth.

Banished from the kingdom of Arendelle and separated from her sibling Anna, Queen Elsa marches alone through the snow, having left behind an eternal winter. During the song's latter stages, Elsa both tentatively and then defiantly describes her hidden capabilities of cryokinesis that are now free to burst from her body in the spectacle of creative flurry. Gesturing first with her foot, and then again with hands previously encased in protective gloves, she chants, 'My power flurries through the air into the ground, my soul is spiralling in frozen fractals all around', a line that is delivered as Elsa conjures and levitates an ornate ice structure from the snow-covered mountain below. While continuing *Frozen*'s preoccupation with frost and ice – from its opening shot of a spiralling snowflake to its earlier numbers 'Frozen Heart' and 'Do You Want to Build a Snowman?' – the virtuosity of 'Let it Go' as predicated on the instantaneous control of ice is inevitably embroiled with discourses of world-building. If fractal mathematics both reveal the underlying order of nature's chaotic construction *and* permit animators to sophisticatedly simulate snow as a natural phenomenon, then the allusion made by Elsa (as superanimator) to fractal geometry crystallises the very structures of a computer-animated film world. Elsa's active multiplication of snowflakes in all directions ultimately personalises the randomised creation of digital structures in *Vol Libre*, while the symmetry of irregularity that underlies fractal systems in the natural world suitably expresses the character's own ambivalent sense of order and chaos.

Masses and Multitudes

The computer-animated film evidently makes demands on its spectators for a more active reading of its animated spaces. But the play with the ontological infinity of the virtual horizons works in conjunction with the affinity between spectators and the digital population residing within the fiction. The animatedness of computer-animated films invites spectators to consider the relationship between the fictional Luxo world and its characters as particular residents of the fiction. Characters are, of course, a key element of all of cinema's world-building activities. Uri Margolin argues that 'narrative must be about a world populated by individuated existents' (2010: 406). Luxo worlds are bound by certain cultural and historical parameters, but are not entirely impervious to fictional disruption in the form of fictionally anonymous characters. *Ratatouille*, unfolding in the modern-day French capital, uses the character of Chef

Auguste Gusteau to provide an entirely fictitious history of Fine French Cuisine. The fictional Gusteau crafts Paris an alternative history. He does not transform the city into an alternative or other-wordly place. This is because Gusteau constitutes part of the 'unifying consistency' of fictional worlds, and one of the primary ways worldness has been defined by scholars. A fictional world, Tanya Krzywinska argues, must 'have a history', and 'past events that constitute the current state of affairs' (2006: 386). In *Ratatouille*'s fictional world, Gusteau is a primary component of *this* history of Paris, one in which the idolised chef did own a prize-winning restaurant booked five months in advance.

Perkins has also considered the role played by fictional characters, who since they are in a world 'their knowledge of it must be partial, and their perception of it may be, in almost any respect, distorted or deluded' (2005: 26). With his initially unwavering belief that he is a real Space Ranger, Buzz Lightyear is the benchmark here, though the eponymous canine in *Bolt* similarly believes he holds impossible superpowers in the real world (unaware of his carefully managed involvement in a fictional television programme). Both *Toy Story* and *Bolt* dramatise the partiality of characters' knowledges, defining them in relation to sustained delusion and misinterpretation. But what distinguishes Luxo worlds is the degree to which they are enabled by the technology to be populated in altogether different ways.

Computer-animated films are traditionally ensemble films with strikingly large casts, aside, of course, from those occasions where the narrative calls for the fictional world to be stripped of its population. A pivotal flashback sequence in *Cars* reveals how the thriving town of Radiator Springs off Route 66 became a sparsely populated, forgotten community with the arrival of the highway interstate. The ruined and tarnished Luxo worlds of *Wall-E* and *9* (Shane Acker, 2009) also bear the harsh scars of their fictional histories, with indelible traces of apocalyptic events that have altered each screen world from its original, populated state. But Luxo worlds are conventionally densely inhabited. Crowd simulation software refined during the late 1990s, including Attila and Dynasty, has been a core component of computer-animated film production. When rendering the flowing river of rodents in *Ratatouille*, an updated crowd system was mandatory to accommodate the rats as a featured foreground element. Pixar animators David Ryu and Paul Kanyuk (2007) explain how the secondary rodent crowds required the same level of 'nuanced articulation' as primary animated characters (known as 'Hero' animation), who are typically more detailed and given more expressive movements in their individual skeletal and joint structures. The result was a believable rat colony that ebbed and flowed, and whose coordinated behaviour and fluid momentum was a symptom of the complex animation pipeline implemented.

Beyond their heightened visual detailing and physiognomic believ-ability, characters in the computer-animated film can therefore be defined through the allure and attraction of their volume and quantity. To recall Kristen Whissel's term, the 'digital multitude' has become a signature feature of a Luxo world and its particular kind of population (2014: 59–90). MASSIVE (Multiple Agent Simulation System in Virtual Environment), the commercial crowd system used for *The Ant Bully*, *Happy Feet*, *Up*, *Wall-E* and *Brave*, as well as the DENIZEN program developed to populate the vibrant city of San Fransokyo in *Big Hero 6* (Don Hall and Chris Williams, 2014), draw attention in their name to the impressive scale and visual complexity with which such systems operate. Vast crowds, hoards, armies and swarms are used as a dynamic optical effect, which exploits and consolidates the vastness of the fictional space. Frenetic onscreen anarchy provides delectable diegetic presence, as the multitude moves from background to foreground and along horizon lines, their movements through the space showing and showcasing its expanse.

The fleeing townsfolk raised into panic that the 'sky is falling' in *Chicken Little;* the waddle of penguins dancing in the Antarctic's polar landscape in *Happy Feet* (Figure 3.2); the roaring Scottish natives in *Brave*; the cheering college monsters gathered for the annual scare games competi-tion in *Monsters University*; and the animal talent queueing around the block for a chance at fame in *Sing* are all large-scale multitudes collected within the film frame predicated on their visual abundance and profusion. The *mise en scène* of these films is often designed to augment the sense of organised chaos, emphasising the vibrant activity of a crowd participating

Figure 3.2 Frame grab from *Happy Feet* (2006) (Animal Logic/Warner Bros. Pictures). The elaborate excess of the digital multitude fills the computer-animated film frame.

in complex interactions with the impression of organic movement. The hive in *Bee Movie*, for example, is mapped through spaghetti junctions and a monorail system, while in *Antz* the vast underground colony is similarly organised by a network of interconnecting tunnels and routes dug deep into the soil. The arteries of this underground metropolis (parallels to Fritz Lang's early silent film are clear) are pulsing with insect workers, each action enhancing the heightened levels of background activity.

Spectacular *moments of multitude* arbitrate the spectators' exposure to a Luxo world. The multitude inhabits the fictional world three-dimensionally, providing a dynamic play of foreground and background spaces that is unachievable to the same degree in cel-animated cartoons. A visual polyphony, computer-animated characters flow effortlessly into the recesses, alcoves, corners and cavities of the fictional Luxo world. Such spatial connections between populace and virtual space are best demonstrated by *Wall-E*. During the film's climax, the large (and, due to their oversized and obese stature, enlarged) human characters are suddenly thrown from their hover chairs as the AXIOM spaceship violently tilts. Freed from their regulated pathways, they helplessly cascade, tumble and pour through the space(ship), disrupting the rows of recliners while bumping, knocking and striking one another, before eventually coming to rest in a large mound collected in one of the AXIOM's many corners. The 'digital multitude' can thus be evaluated for its contribution to world-building, and in particular as a site of animatedness distinguishing a fictional Luxo world. The population in a computer-animated film is inseparable from the world in which it resides, and there is a placement of characters that *opens up* the world by simultaneously *filling in* its spaces. These associations between the populated and the population are an attribute of a Luxo world's production. Whereas in cel-animation characters are literally layered on top of the world (the background cels) and photographed frame by frame, in computer-animated films characters are built three-dimensionally, usually out of clay, before these sculptures or 'maquettes' are scanned into a computer and then inserted into the world (a process known as blocking), dressing the set with their residency. Characters require a performance space in which to manoeuvre and an environment that houses their behaviour, and the various computer-animated spaces are refined to accommodate their many virtual bodies.

Another vital element of the multitude relates to the fluctuating levels of autonomy, automaticity and artificial intelligence given to its various constituent parts. The multitude is regulated by complex animation cycles that furnish loops of activity and behavioural impulses. Run primarily using technological scripts, which provide an automated system of agency, characters function, as computer scientist Ann Marion argues, like 'puppets that pull their own strings' (in Brand 1989: 95). Just as virtual geology pushes up the fractal landscapes in an automatic, programmed fashion, certain characters within the multitude may be choreographed to remain idle, while others turn and shuffle randomly without awkwardness. The sophistication of the crowd simulation software allows each member of a multitude to be governed by a set of unique directives and instructions. Isaac Kerlow notes that in *A Bug's Life* 'there were over 430 crowd shots with about 600 distinct crowd characters' (2004: 362). Sarafian adds that rather than build one ant and 'copy and paste' it into batches, the technology enabled specific attributes and behaviours (such as curiosity, anger, incredulity, happiness and nervousness) to govern over a thousand ants in one shot (2003: 217). This degree of independence permits individuals to be identified within a group, a living organism such as a colony or a hive broken down into its constituent parts. The narratives of nonconformity in *Antz*, *A Bug's Life*, *Bee Movie* and *Ratatouille* reflect such fragmentation of the multitude through a protagonist who rejects that which is pre-programmed, whether rebuffing a regimented dance routine (*Antz*) or declining their allocated labour roles (*Bee Movie*).

Luxo worlds are busy worlds. The heightened levels of activity and vibrancy, and the multiple planes of action, which draw in our viewing eye, are one of its most defining features. In this way, Luxo worlds can be viewed as central to a culture of exchange between cinema and video games, a platform whose worlds are similarly acts of style and products of rhetoric. To borrow a term popularised within the video game sphere during the 1990s, Luxo worlds can be considered a particular kind of 'open world'. Indeed, the release of *Toy Story* in 1995 is historically continuous with the proliferation of such three-dimensional open world platforms released during the 1990s, including *Doom* (1993), *Quarantine* (1994), *Descent* (1995), *Stonekeep* (1995), *Super Mario 64* (1996), *GoldenEye* (1997) and *Grand Theft Auto* (1997). Jettisoning the conventional 'level' format in which gameplay sediment accumulates as the gamer progresses, an open world video game provides a vast, expansive and highly detailed virtual landscape that 'gives the player a world that seems limitless' (Lukas 2013: 57). Many open world games, for example, include a map either as a backdrop to the seemingly unscripted, nomadic in-game experience, or as a printed accompaniment. For the production of *Monsters, Inc.*, *Cars* and *Monsters University* detailed maps were produced of the Monstropolis, Radiator Springs and university campus locations respectively, awarding each environment a geographical coherence and revealing the state of affairs within the virtual territory. With spectators sutured into a logical, appealing and ambitious space, Luxo worlds are rich and richly developed environments that feel spatially, and indeed formally, open. Fractal geometry builds the vast digital world, one whose impressive brevity is spotlighted first through candescent lighting, and then again by vicarious camerawork that carves through the geography. High-density flocking crowds then enter and exit the frame: a particular kind of ambient virtual population comprising (often hundreds of) self-directing characters purposefully negotiating the three-dimensional terrain.

Drawing the Line

If a Luxo world is opened up by its internal richness, then what might be at stake in the broader openness with which it is experienced? Stanley Cavell suggests that 'a painting *is* a world; a photograph is of a world' (1979: 23–4). He argues that 'you can always ask, of an area photographed, what lies adjacent to that area, beyond the frame. This generally makes no sense asked of a painting' (ibid.). A Luxo world certainly does not, and cannot, exceed the portion glimpsed, and thus it 'makes sense' that computer-animated films encounter their edge at the film's frame. But we might say that computer-animated films playfully engage with the loss of their centripetal frame, and gesture towards the centrifugal spatial qualities of photographic cinema. The sheer scope of a Luxo world and its levels of spatial freedom involve computer-animated films in a playful illusion that narrative is a single, unfolding plotline progressing through a broader fictional space in which many other possible narratives remain unrealised. By constructing its Luxo worlds as spatially open, computer-animated films ultimately provide a striking example of Jean Mitry's observation that 'a film is a world which organises itself in terms of a story' (in Andrew 1984: 76). All animated worlds *are* the film organised for the purposes of a story, and their creation from scratch is an unavoidable act of narratology. But a Luxo world presents its events as if they were unfolding *of* a world. This is because the film frame threatens to burst at the seams with its visual information (and indeed the practices of intertextuality across multiple computer-animated films achieves this fictional 'leakage'). But this only plays with the existence of a frame at all. The spectator glimpses a snapshot of a densely populated and rich world that is slipping, or, in the case of the climactic AXIOM sequence in *Wall-E*, literally falling off the edges.

By mapping something of its lively cinematic geography, the Luxo world can be further linked to two areas of interest across recent animation scholarship: the views advanced by cultural theorist Paul Virilio concerning the blur and 'lost dimension' of modern life, and the business and motive actions of the animated line. As we have seen, computer-animated films have been examined by Sobchack for effacing their labour. According to this reasoning, our stuttering lived experience does not take solace in digital imagery, and instead finds a greater corollary in the lapses, imperfections and spatial disjuncture of cel-animation and stop-motion. But by invoking the fluidity and fluency of a Luxo world, and its particular sites of animatedness, a claim can be staked that computer-animated worlds *do* replicate something of our modern experiences. Virilio has argued for the elusiveness of reality within a modern crisis of the physical dimension as homogeneous and continuous. Time has overtaken space, with speed now the 'primal dimension that defies all temporal and physical measurements' (Virilio 1991: 18). Computer-animated films are a staple of moving image culture, but they are also a culture of animated images that move. Their worlds embody the 'speed spaces' outlined by Virilio. The open-ness of their worlds, but also the busy activities of those who reside there, places emphasis upon the world as action and the proficiency of the pictorial space. As Virilio has added in a recent interview, 'whoever controls the territory possesses it. Possession of territory is not primarily about laws and contracts, but first and foremost a matter of movement and circulation' (in Armitage 2000). In its scale, behavioural complexity and variance, the multitude certainly dominates the Luxo world, ebbing and flowing through the space to draw attention to the haste with which it moves. In short, such groupings come with (and belong to) the territory. But the behaviour of the multitude only stands as emblematic of the surrounding fictional world. Luxo worlds are not homogeneous spaces, but are loaded with fluctuating urgencies of movement and uneven and heterogeneous speeds.

The visible energy of a Luxo world finds another analogue in the recursive and repeating animated line, a fundamental feature of animation enforcing its animatedness. Computer-animated films are built from multiple conceptions of the line: basic information lines of binary codes, as well as detailed wire-frame matrixes used to create the details and decor, including characters. The computer-animated space might even be explicitly partitioned by lines of continuous marks made upon its textual surface. These include the hurrying procession of ants that adorn the colonies in *Antz* and *A Bug's Life*, the luggage conveyor belts in the climactic airport sequence of *Toy Story 2*, the impressive library of doors in *Monsters, Inc.* suspended on rails, the Honex Corporation's twisting monorail system in *Bee Movie*, and the AXIOM's automated pathways in *Wall-E*. But just as the expressive freedoms and transformative activity of the animated line (as graphical inscription) belong to animation to distinguish it from live-action, computer-animated films create fictional worlds that appear to draw and then redraw themselves. A Luxo world continually lays bare the vibrancy of its own existence, foregrounding its distinctive ontology and its animatedness though the spectacle of its multi-directional characters, and the open world of which they are a vital part. Émile Cohl made it impossible (though not frustratingly so) for the spectator to predict the fate of his ever-changing and highly improvisational animated line in *Fantasmagorie* (1908). A Luxo world is similarly arresting and gratifying because its spaces are filled with an impulsive energy. As a fictional realm, it is ultimately one of agency: highly industrious and perpetually on assignment. Computer-animated films offer up (and open up) their many screen worlds for our appreciation and enjoyment, and in doing so draw and redraw the cartography of the animated map. It is the vibrancy of a Luxo world, and the proficiency of its pictorial space, which will be taken up in the subsequent chapter.

CHAPTER 4

Computer-Animated Films and Anthropomorphic Subjectivity

The prevailing orthodoxy concerning the construction and engagement with fictional animated characters is their organisation around behavioural patterns that are anchored to recognisably 'human' psychology, intentionality and proportion. At the root of this representational regime lies the creative model of anthropomorphism, a term whose etymology can be traced back to sixth-century Greece, combining ἄνθρωπος (ánthrōpos) defined as human and μορφή (morphē) meaning shape or form. Invested primarily in the perception, presence and impression of consciousness, anthropomorphic representation holds particular currency within the histories and traditions of the animated cartoon. Patrick Power argues that persuasive 'anthropomorphic personification' is ultimately a defining register of animated aesthetics, so 'pervasive in cartoon and 3D feature animation that it is virtually synonymous stylistically with these genres' (2008: 37). Animation's evolution from hand-drawn to digital systems, from painted cel to single-point pixel, has done very little to moderate or destabilise the frequency of anthropomorphic representation across the medium's visual grammar. The earliest cycle of computer-animated shorts produced under the creative guidance of John Lasseter at the Pixar Animation Studios during the 1980s followed the Golden Age blueprint of Walt Disney and Warner Brothers by assuming a strong anthropomorphic approach. *Luxo Jr.*, *Red's Dream* (John Lasseter, 1987), *Tin Toy* (John Lasseter, 1988) and *Knick Knack* (John Lasseter, 1989) centred upon the activity and agency of an anglepoise lamp, abandoned unicycle, child's musical toy and snow globe, objects whose sudden sentience ran counter to the human involvement typically required to fulfil each item's function. Pixar's commercial projects and television advertisements made during this late-1980s/early-1990s period (for Listerine, Gummi Savers and Tropicana, amongst others) similarly provided a space in which filmmakers such as Lasseter, Andrew Stanton, Pete Docter, Jan Pinkava, Jeff Pidgeon and Galyn Susman honed their craft by pushing at the boundaries of anthropomorphic characterisation, at the same time as they tested the visual possibilities of emergent computer graphics.

With the release of *Toy Story* and the arrival of the feature-length computer-animated film format, 'persuasive' anthropomorphosis had reached, in the words of Andrew Darley, an 'extraordinary' level (2000: 91). Indeed, the relatively short history of computer-animated filmmaking remains strongly interwoven with anthropomorphic characters and images. While biologically recognisable humans (and, in some instances, 'super' humans) do jostle for prominence as protagonists, 'humanised' animals and non-humans more regularly function as narrative agents populating these three-dimensional digital worlds, occupying and inhabiting virtual spaces through their residency and contributing to their plentiful '"fullness" of people' (Heath 1981: 179). Supporting both single stories and entire series, anthropomorphism remains the computer-animated film's default register, no less embedded within its screen narratives than it is implicated in those wider marketing and promotional enterprises that inform contemporary consumer brand culture (Lanier et al. 2014).

Within the history and representational field of animated anthropomorphism, however, little distinction has been made between the pre-war era of Gertie the Dinosaur, Felix the Cat and Mickey Mouse, the anarchy of Looney Tunes' talking ducks and 'wabbits', and the spate of contemporary digital anthropomorphs that are assigned complex personalities in advance of (or in conflict with) culturally 'assumed' personae that stem from an animal's 'unwitting' semblance and mimicry of human conduct (Gould 1987: 504). Mainstream computer-animated films have ultimately been subsumed into a broader creative anthropomorphosis, which represents a 'curious mix of "fantasy" and "reality" in which the spectator can recognise human traits in [. . .] animal figures' (Wells 2002b: 161). By contrast, the newly digital constitution of anthropomorphism has fundamentally altered the way in which anthropomorphic representation and animated animality can function within an animated context. The guiding principle of this chapter, then, is to approach and elucidate anthropomorphism by forging a more fluid connection between the digital constructs of anthropomorph and diegetic world. To do so will involve some semantic reconfiguration, thinking more conceptually about the form or morphē component of the anthropomorph that is increasingly being raised into prominence at the expense of any prevailing humanness (ánthrōpos). By interrogating more directly the in-between and fractured identity of the anthropomorph as a hybrid figuration between poles of animacy and inanimacy, this chapter argues how computer-animated films have exploited the non-human morphē element of its characters – over any prevailing interest in their fluctuating degrees of human connotation – to control virtual space through anthropomorphic subjectivity. With digital environments now glimpsed through the eyes of others, the virtual space has become increasingly articulated through a multiplicity of limited, broadened and unstable perspectives, with the increased manoeuvrability and peripatetic behaviour of the anthropomorph yielding new spatial orientations and possibilities for disparate fields of vision. Supported by developments in computer-animation and a virtual camera unencumbered with positional constraints, embodied anthropomorphic point of view in the computer-animated film is anchored to the nomadic sauntering of sentient non-human characters who are prized for their subjective abilities as ulterior forms or morphēs, rather than valued for their strict paralleling of human behaviour. Such a switch of emphasis both licenses the mastery of geographic exploration by computer-animated anthropomorphs across the virtual terrain, but also reconfigures the received narrative surrounding the function of these most enduring of character archetypes.

A Special Relationship:
Anthropomorphism's 'Animated' History

Despite the widespread integration of animal and human intelligence across art, culture and religion, from Egyptian gods and deities, spiritual pre-Paleolithic shamanist culture, children's literature and folk tales (Beatrix Potter, George Orwell), mythology's divine beings and scientific examinations of animal behaviour, many writers have reflected upon why animated films have been consistently gripped by anthropomorphosis, their worlds often anthropomorphous in invention and design. Recent scholarship has not only tackled the topic of animated anthropomorphs in their multiplicity and variance, but also tied the very history of animation as an early twentieth-century medium to 'the spectacle of anthropomorphism' and the visual pleasure of 'seeing something move *as though* it were human' (Riffel 2012: 5). As agents of narrative and supported by discourses of visual and behavioural familiarity, animated anthropomorphs certainly permit the aesthetic exploration, dilution, exaggeration and satirising of the machinations of the human condition (psychology, intent, behaviour, socio-cultural hierarchies) through devices of allegory and analogy, symbolism and signification. Such meaningful anthropomorphic characters therefore function as 'pragmatic' solutions, part of an 'anthropocentric' explanatory concept insofar as they evidence how humans are able to 'make sense' of 'the deeply enigmatic and often hostile world in which they inhabit' (Lanier et al. 2014: 37) through the ascription of human connotation.

Allied to the ability of animated anthropomorphs (as visual phenomena or simulacra) to carry a host of implicit meanings, the attribution of human-like qualities to non-human (often animal) characters as they intentionally act, and move seamlessly within, an animated space, has been theorised as a fundamental requirement of character design. Anthropomorphism is a representational strategy of accessibility, continually revived by animators to pique spectator recognition, interest, empathy and compassion in the animated figure being observed. Cognitivist Torben Grodal (1997: 89), for example, argues that:

> When watching a visual representation of phenomena without any centring anthro-pomorphic actants, we often 'lose interest' owing to lack of emotional motivation or the cognitive analysis of the perceived, a fact which many makers of experimental films have discovered when presenting their films to a mass audience.

Lasseter had certainly highlighted the value of anthropomorphism when giving his well-received and influential industry paper at the SIGGRAPH conference in July 1987, in which he discussed the necessity for appeal and personality across computer-animated characters. Speaking at length about the digitally animated short films *The Adventures of André and Wally B* (Alvy Ray Smith, 1984) and *Luxo Jr.*, Lasseter observed how the desire for anatomical magnetism and perceptible 'charm' was rooted in the display of numerous human archetypes that compensated for the fact 'the live-action actor has charisma' (1987: 35–4). For the early pioneers of computer-animated technology, this allure (and the success of the character to be read as 'true' by the intended child audience) was communicated through an anthropomorphic schema: humanlike body dimensions matched with the hypothetical behaviour of objects under a range of disparate emotional states. Lasseter's particular 'concentration' on his characters' eyes was a key principle of the filmmaker's approach to anthropomorphism, one predicated on spectators' ability to coherently register the 'direction and purpose' of computer-animated figures through a sensitivity to their ocular cues (including their 'stark black pupils' and 'erratic blinking') (Neupert 2016: 40–1).

The ubiquity with which the cartoon form has been driven by an anthropomorphic impulse stems from the synonymy between animation and anthropomorphism as artistic models. Both are rhetorical strategies in service of characterisation: invested in degrees of personification, the impression (and impassion) of consciousness, and the presumption of subjectivity. Tim Tyler's description of anthropomorphism as 'The practice of attributing intentionality, purpose, or volition to some creature or abstraction that (allegedly) does not have these things' (2003: 269) could reasonably be offered as an explanation of animated technique and its predilection for movement, illusory action and the vigour of expressive agency. Yet animation simultaneously *obliges* any anthropomorphic imperative as an autonomous, *visualisation* and *elaboration* of conscious thinking. It is a medium that can dilute or attenuate a variety of representational positions within anthropomorphism as a social phenomenon, animating the kinds of civilising approaches to the non-human which, as Cliff Hamilton suggests, is something us humans have been undertaking for 'as long as there has been a developed form of communication' (1983: 166). Psychologists have examined at length this widespread phenomenon of *pareidolia* and the hard-wired, intuitive presumption of human consciousness that sees faces within places (separate from *apophenia*, or the visibility of meaningful patterns and connections in irregular data clusters). Within a clinical environment, the systematic misidentification of a particular stimulus according to degrees of personhood and human physiognomy has been a staple of the psychological Rorschach inkblot test, and has contributed to examinations of children's brain skills of perception, recognition and comprehension.

Pixar's *Monsters, Inc.* is highly explicit in drawing attention to the dramatic possibilities enabled by such 'false' information processing, and the role of animation in supplementing the unconscious projection of personality at the centre of anthropomorphic thinking. *Monsters, Inc.* opens at bedtime on a restless, agitated young boy, who, during one of his nervous glances towards his cupboard door, briefly glimpses a slithering tentacle draped ominously over his bedroom chair. Shutting his eyes and summoning the courage to look again, the young boy is soon relieved to discover that the cause of his discomfort was merely the sleeve of a protruding jumper. Yet in *Monsters, Inc.*, the boy's unconscious attribution of humanlike form through *pareidolia* as a process of 'magical thinking' (Zusne and Jones 2014: 77) is made concrete by the monstrous reality of the scenario. In an inverse disclosure, the initial impression of monstrosity and its 'realistic' demystification is itself a false reveal. The child (as anthropomorphiser) was correct in his original assumption, and the jumper is indeed a monster's extended appendage, albeit belonging to a creature who proves physically inept and, as a result, fails to pass what is nothing more than a scare simulation. Through its anthropomorphic agenda, then, *Monsters, Inc.* discloses how animation is capable of extending the terms of anthropomorphism as a psychological process by actualising the cognitive phenomenon of witnessing humanlike configurations. The 'intentional stance' (Kennedy 1992: 93) fundamentally embroiled within anthropomorphism – that supposes non-human desire, mental propulsion and predictive behaviour – is here made complicit in a deception. The anthropocentric perception of monsters by the child in *Monsters, Inc.* is offered, in turn, as a visual *possibility*, an *inaccuracy* and then a *certainty*.

The overriding discourse of 'humanisation' entwined with the anthropomorph is, as many animation scholars (Sandler 1997; Wells 2009b) have made clear, part of the history of (how spectators have engaged with) animation, and thus expectedly finds a place within theories germane to an understanding of the medium. Anthropomorphism lies at the cornerstone of Sergei Eisenstein's writing on 'plasmaticness', reflecting the allure that the Russian filmmaker and formalist felt towards Disney cartoons, and how scientific 'categories of zoology' were unsettled through their seductive (and empathetic) anthropomorphic fantasy (1986: 4). An Eisensteinian ecstasy towards the anthropomorph has continued to underscore the figure's sustained visual curiosity and increasing prevalence within the contemporary era of computer-animated cinema. Power argues that 'the idea of a rat in a restaurant would normally evoke disgust, but Remy the rodent/chef anthromorph in *Ratatouille* is more likely instead to engage and intrigue aesthetically' (2008: 26). Such admiration for the captivating anthropomorphic form within Pixar's culinary comedy supersedes the spectators' distaste towards the rodent's skilled preparation of gourmet cuisine. For Power, the magnetism of the anthropomorph is squared to its liminal, in-between identity, with the anthropomorph 'on the edge of chaos, both at once' (ibid.: 23), insofar as it is caught within a transitional cycle of change between ánthrōpos (humanity) and morphē (form). The animated anthropomorph ultimately shimmers as an intrinsically ambiguous and fragmented agent, a mix of competing (and reciprocating) personalities and scenarios, and split by the rhetorical separating body the boundary or 'slash' that divides 'rodent/chef' in Power's description. The 'slash' is a semantic synecdoche confirming the anthropomorph's chaotic identity as a combination of multiple forms, a schizophrenic tension inhabited by the constituents of ánthrōpos and morphē that has prompted Paul Wells to coin the '*Madagascar* problem'. Referring to the DreamWorks computer-animated film franchise that includes an assured African lion, hypochondriac giraffe, energetic zebra and sassy New York hippopotamus as its main cast, Wells describes the often tricky negotiation of animal (natural) and human (cultural) discourses within the politics of anthropomorphic identity. He points to a mutual dependency between human socialisation and the preservation of 'true animal actions, behaviour and primal motivation', a relationship that supports the 'inner logic' (Wells 2009b: 22) of anthropomorphosis as animation's common representational strategy.

Despite the ongoing participation of computer-animated films with an anthropomorphic register, this chapter argues that their many humanised animal narratives have ultimately engaged the confrontation of animism and humanism with a greater degree of fluidity between those components either side of the 'slash'. Animators have looked to rigorously take advantage of the etymology of the anthropomorph by confronting its fractured and hybrid state. The presence of the paradigmatic 'slash' in Power's description (separating Remy as 'rodent/chef') certainly raises important questions about which of the two identities in the anthropomorph should be ranked most 'animate'. However, this chapter does not reinforce the slash as fixed or immovable, nor does it eliminate it entirely, as each move would only muddy the waters even further. To begin to examine how computer-animated films typically meld together human and non-human registers, this chapter conceptualises the division between ánthrōpos and morphē as an altogether more porous channel through which ánthrōpos and morphē are permitted to interface and collide. The consequence of this representational shift towards form (morphē) at the expense of humanity (ánthrōpos) is that computer-animated film narratives have increasingly mined the non-human element of the splintered anthropomorph for its expressive, creative potential.

Ánthrōpos/Morphē

The new legibility of the non-human, morphē characteristics in computer-animated film anthropomorphs is openly registered through a style of performance that frequently withdraws from ánthrōpos (attribution of human characteristics), and instead more readily inscribes elements of form as an opposition or complement to familiar humanlike qualities. In his discussion of puppet/puppeteer interaction, John Bell usefully speaks of 'the weird concept of letting the object determine the action', a process that is underpinned by 'figuring out' how 'structure determines movement' (2008: 7). The assumption that human activity is the overwhelming blueprint for a non-human's presumed emotions is destabilised in computer-animated films by the persistence of the morphē as an essential form of the anthropomorph that never alters. It is the anthroporph's morphē (rather than its human connotation) that is ultimately permitted to take centre stage, interceding into the 'action' to both signal and dictate a mode of acting no longer committed to human-centred appeal. This gives licence for computer-animated films to navigate beyond traditional performance styles, and instead inaugurate a new form of 'method acting' that hinges upon – and exhibits the spectacle of – the magnetism of the morphē.

Drawing its design policy from Tex Avery's animated short *One Cab's Family* (1952) and *Susie the Little Blue Coupe* (Clyde Geronomi, 1952) made at the Disney studio – and with character names indebted to Isaac Asimov's short story *Sally* (1953) – Pixar's *Cars* franchise immediately throw into relief the performance potential of the morphē. Within each film's creative process of automobile customisation, emotion in these sentient 'smart' cars is expressed through a familiar anthropomorphic design: eyes across the windshield, with mouths positioned over the front grille above the bumper. Yet each vehicle's anatomical coherency (key to the projection of 'emotion', 'personality' and 'charm') and the application of human descriptors are often placed subservient to – or at least in dialogue with – a new level of engagement with the language of the object. These cars do not 'age', they rust, while a burst tyre constitutes nothing more than minor injury (though an oil spill is an embarrassing sign of incontinence). Cars of a particular vintage additionally cough and splutter, and their imperfect, 'aged' bodywork is often matched with old-fashioned, outdated views. This is most obvious in the characters of Mater, a redneck tow truck, but also ageing hippie Fillmore, who as a VW Type 2 camper van with psychedelic paintwork plainly gestures to 1960s American counterculture. Bell acknowledges that in the case of the automobile's perceived cultural value, 'cars have their own personalities, marked by make, color, size, style, and power' (2008: 172), something that each *Cars* film dramatises through multi-faceted characters that successfully support our emotional investment over the course of a feature-length movie (the first two *Cars* films are the longest in the Pixar oeuvre). However, despite each film's capabilities for convincing human-like automobiles acting and *re*acting for our spectatorial pleasure, the discursive power of the performances in the *Cars* series hinges upon the exposure of communicative cues fundamental to their status as cars (typically, mechanical deficiency). The sporadic lapses into morphē momentarily alleviate the anthropomorph's degree of humanity, and reminds spectators of the authentic (if fallible) 'bodies' of cars by equating, in the case of *Cars 2* villain Miles Axelrod, a leaking engine with public humiliation.

The computer-animated film's attraction towards the authentic form of the non-human can, however, be further disclosed through narratives in which anthropomorphs are obliged to shed any acquired humanlike characteristics or identity (ánthrōpos), and instead fully encouraged to embrace their true morphē. In *Shark Tale*, compassionate great white shark Lenny is rejected by his criminal shark family for his unforgiveable vegetarian preferences. Just as Bruce the Shark in *Finding Nemo* attends underwater self-help classes to rehabilitate his natural carnivorous tendencies, Lenny's latent vegetarianism is perceived as a 'flaw' within his true sharkhood, one that has been widely understood among ideological criticism as a symbol of Lenny's 'odd' sexuality and performance of gay masculinity (King et al. 2010: 45). In *Bolt*, the eponymous canine must actually *learn* true animal actions following a pampered career spent in front of television cameras: a profession that has systematically rid him of typical dog skills. A protracted musical montage expresses the dog's attempt at burying bones and fetching sticks ('it's really a dog thing'), and the acquisition of 'dogness' is invoked by the film to develop the cross-species romance between Bolt and feline companion Mittens against the backdrop of the former's procurement of true animalism.[1]

Case Study: *Zootopia*

In the first teaser trailer for Walt Disney's computer-animated film *Zootopia*, which premiered on 11 June 2015, the word 'anthropomorphism' appears onscreen to give shape and definition to the film's modern civilised world and its humanised animal citizens. Dismissed by the voiceover narration as simply 'a big fancy word' that describes how animals 'walk around on two feet, they do not go to work nude [. . .] and they use technology', *Zootopia* self-reflexively folds animation's representational history back onto itself by acknowledging the principles of anthropomorphism embedded within the medium's many animal stories. *Zootopia*'s hyper-consciousness towards traditions of 'the animal' as a common point of access and spectatorial engagement in animated storytelling continues throughout its main narrative trajectory. The film follows the journey of idealist Judy Hopps, a police academy valedictorian who moves to the city of Zootopia with the intention of smoothing over latent animal/animal tensions, but is immediately assigned desk duty rather than allowed on the city streets. Disney's film uses its diverse animal cast to trade in themes of institutional corruption, bias, racism, bigotry, sexism and xenophobia, with rabbit Judy (and her companion Nick Wilde, a fox) often subjected to vehement opposition on account of their species.

Divided by hysteria, fear and political protests, *Zootopia* also constructs its characters as splintered and divided, having to accommodate ánthrōpos and morphē as a set of competing identities in flux. Within the histories of the cartoon, *Zootopia*'s anthropomorphic agenda fully realises what Wells calls the 'bestial ambivalence' and the 'animal/human divide' (2009b: 26) that conventionally underscores animation's animal problem. The values of ánthrōpos and morphē that coalesce within the anthropomorph are thrown into relief during Judy's first case, which involves the psychotropic effects of toxic flowers that cause the animals to 'go savage', and rescind their reserved humanity by switching to their feral animal state. There are multiple verbal references to the implications of non-human behaviour no longer subordinated by its assimilation into a dominant humanity ('That killer instinct is still in my DNA'; 'It's in their biology'). *Zootopia*'s unruly animals are thus an act of rebellion against the strategies of humanity imposed upon them. The film's engagement with its characters' baser instincts and 'uncontrollable, biological urge to maim and maul' (as Judy puts it) situates the film amid a complex set of dichotomies: cultured/unrefined, civilised/wild, prey/predator, hospitable/destructive, instinct/inference, tolerant/prejudiced. Positioned as the film's main narrative premise, anthropomorphism and anthropomorphic difference subsequently provide *Zootopia* with the stakes of its drama, whilst reflecting the pleasure (if not the centrality) of how talking animals can be made visible to the spectator within a cartoon context.

Animal Behaviour

A network of relationships is clearly erected in computer-animated films between ánthrōpos and morphē as factors of identity held in delicate, even interchangeable, compromise. Yet by awarding space for the anthropomorph's primal instinct, base behaviour or the recuperation of an underlying morphē, these are films that actively interrogate what it means for a particular kind of animal or object to become subject to consciousness. Furthermore, if humanlike 'actants' drive the spectators' relationship of complicity with the anthropomorph, then qualities and meanings drawn from the non-human morphē element permit ulterior connections with objects and animals of the world, and emphatic distinctions to be made regarding non-human ways of being. Sidestepping dominant criticisms levelled at anthropomorphic thinking by scientific studies that 'guard against unwarranted attribution of human characteristics to other species' (Keeton 1967: 452), computer-animated film anthropomorphs are thus no longer burdened with the anthropocentric teleology of humanity, but are instead free to indulge gestures and rhythms that are rooted in their non-humanity. Indeed, the sporadic exclamation of 'squirrel' made mid-sentence by anthropomorphic canine Dug in *Up* not only verbalises the involuntary resurfacing of the character's suppressed morphē (otherwise disguised in his technologically assisted proclivity for human speech), but literally speaks to the ongoing recovery by computer-animated films of a more non-human oriented vocabulary.

Given the emphasis placed by computer-animated films on the morphē as it able to suddenly cut across, interrupt, invert and guide the behaviour of anthropomorphs, a fruitful antidote to this new mode of digital anthropomorphism is the affiliated concept of therianthropy. One of many hybridised figurations of mythology that collate human and animal points of reference, the human/non-human ratio that structures therianthropy bears out precisely how computer-animated films have plotted new paths for traditions of animated anthropomorphism that are more readily anchored to a presiding non-humanity. Therianthropic images, according to Simon Baker, combine 'the form of a beast with that of Man', but do so in a manner that relates to the metamorphosis *from* original human form *into* animality (2001: 108). Combining ánthrōpos with θηρίον (theríon), meaning beast or wild animal, therianthropes exist as human figures with animal features, traits or tendencies, and are characters especially common to mythology and the fantasy genre. However, the manner in which Eisenstein describes the poetisation of 'man in an image – in the form of an animal' articulates a strong therianthropic rather than anthropomorphic mode of thinking in early animated storytelling (1986: 48). In this way, therianthropy (and affiliated concepts such as zoomorphism) emerges as a potentially useful animal/human rubric for identifying several representational norms of traditional, rather than digital, animation.

Prior to the advent of digital technology, animated characters were typically therianthropic avatars for the animators who created them: cel-animated constructs that privileged human connotation over an engagement with their non-human morphē. Walt Disney's twenty-sixth animated feature, *The Great Mouse Detective* (Ron Clements, Burny Mattinson, Dave Michener and John Musker, 1986), offers an obvious analogue to contemporary computer-animated anthropomorphism. The 'mouse detective' character in the Disney film's title prefigures the rodent/chef dualism of *Ratatouille*'s Remy, and thus corroborates (rather than invalidates) the splintered identity that underpins the animated anthropomorph as a crossbreed figure. Closely following a therianthropic representational style, the grafting of human schemata, mannerisms and intellect upon Basil the eponymous mouse/detective forfeits several nuances of rodent behaviour. He communicates little about mousehood and the tribulations of being a rodent living in nineteenth-century London. Functioning as essentially a human clothed in beast (in this case rodent) form, Basil has more in common with the biological reality and lifestyles of humankind. He smokes a pipe, plays the violin and his mouse hole residence on Baker Street (*our* Baker Street, of human proportions) is decorated with antiques and a roaring log fire. There is minimal engagement with his rodent identity (his morphē) and the film, like many of its cel-animated predecessors, opts instead to paint its worlds as strikingly therianthropic.

Animation scholars may query this assumption that pre-digital animation (and particularly Disney) failed to fully confront the anthropomorph's morphē component. What about the celebratory musical number 'Everybody Wants to be a Cat' from *The Aristocats* (Wolfgang Reitherman, 1970)? Or Lumière's 'Be Our Guest' song-and-dance routine in *Beauty and the Beast* (Gary Trousdale and Kirk Wise, 1991), in which he claims to 'do tricks' with his 'fellow candlesticks', or the hyperactive Genie in *Aladdin* (Ron Clements and John Musker, 1992), who constantly restates his mythological status as a supernatural force, explaining through song that Aladdin has 'never had a friend like him'. However, 'Everybody Wants to be a Cat' is rendered a paradox by the cats that perform it. The felines have little trouble playing instruments, singing and dancing in a way that recognisably approximates to human form (just as King Louie's desire in *The Jungle Book* [Wolfgang Reitherman, 1967] to 'be like' Mowgli, or Louis the alligator's wish to be a 'human being' in *The Princess and the Frog* [Ron Clements and John Musker, 2009] seems equally redundant given their proclivity at song, dance and in the case of Louis, playing the trumpet). Secondly, Lumière and his companions Cogsworth and Mrs Potts in *Beauty and the Beast* are *literal* therianthropes, cursed to live as a candelabra, clock and teapot respectively. Yet all are switched back into their original *human* bodies to resume their prior roles as maître d', major-domo and housekeeper. *Beauty and the Beast* thus anticipates Disney's later therianthropic characters Emperor Kuzco (*The Emperor's New Groove* [Mark Dindal, 2000]) and Tiana and Naveen (*The Princess and the Frog*), whose switch from their magically induced morphē of mammal (llama) and amphibian (frog) are similarly reversed once the characters have redeemed prior moral indiscretions. Finally, the supernatural Genie, whilst not strictly a therianthrope, is nonetheless morphed into a loose human appearance during the film's emotive 'happily ever after' climax. His *Pinocchio*-like quest to be 'set free' is satisfied through his visual transformation into human shape, thereby reversing villainous Jafar's own transition from human to genie (suitably, the sorcerer then returns to humanity in the sequel). These metamorphoses back to human form contrast with Princess Fiona in DreamWorks' irreverent computer-animated film *Shrek* who, in an emphatic rejection of ánthrōpos, openly shuns her human identity to remain what Lord Farquaad dismisses as a 'disgusting' ogre. The sequel *Shrek 2* does include sequences in which Shrek and Fiona each lapse into human semblance, but now it is their ánthrōpos selves that are framed as abnormal, and so both are restored to their 'authentic' ogre (morphē) identities in a shared pact of true love. A similar fate befalls therianthrope Dr Cockroach in the studio's more recent *Monsters vs. Aliens*, whose extradiegetic transformation into an insect from his original human is one that the film chooses never to rectify.

Case Study: *Ratatouille*

The computer-animated film's progressive investment in the morphē of its characters reaches a climax in *Ratatouille*, Pixar's aforementioned culinary comedy telling the story of rat-turned-chef Remy. Brad Bird's film takes its place alongside Disney's *The Great Mouse Detective* in a popular 2D animated rodent tradition, which began with Mickey Mouse's *Plane Crazy* (Walt Disney and Ub Iwerks, 1928), but which also contains *The Rescuers* (Wolfgang Reitherman, John Lounsbery and Art Stevens, 1977), *The Devil and Daniel Mouse* (Clive A. Smith, 1978), *The Secret of NIMH* (Don Bluth, 1982), *Heidi's Song* (Robert Taylor, 1982), *An American Tail* (Don Bluth, 1986), *The Rescuers Down Under* (Hendel Butoy and Mike Gabriel, 1990), *An American Tail: Fievel Goes West* (Phil Nibbelink and Simon Wells, 1991) and television series *Tom and Jerry* (Hanna-Barbera, 1940–), *Danger Mouse* (Brian Cosgrove and Mark Hall, 1981–2; 2015), *Tube Mice* (Sara Bor and Simon Bor, 1988) and *Biker Mice From Mars* (Rick Ungar, 1993).

What distinguishes *Ratatouille* from this rat pack is a consistent admission of protagonist Remy's own rathood at the expense of anthropomorphic impersonations of human beings. The film begins with his voiceover narration, which laments the basic 'problem' that he is a rat. 'This is me', he concedes, in a gesture that self-consciously verbalises the inherent tensions and schizophrenia of a human/non-human character. Remy's admission also directly reverses the crisis of identity experienced by villainous Ratigan in *The Great Mouse Detective* who claims that he is, in fact, 'not a rat' but a 'big mouse'. Though Ratigan's riposte is designed to address 'humanity' as the act of being humane and benevolent, his words also reflect how the film preserves a fundamental humanity (ánthrōpos) to its characters over that of their 'rathood' or morphē. Indeed, as an animated revision of Professor James Moriarty in this Sherlock Holmes retelling, the strongly humanised Ratigan is dressed in a bespoke tailored grey suit, top hat, white gloves and an embossed gold cane, despite his sporadic lapses into a more feral physicality.

Within the context of other computer-animated films, however, Remy's narration in *Ratatouille* also serves another purpose. Evoking Woody's angry retort to Buzz Lightyear in *Toy Story* that he is 'just an action figure', Weaver's 'you da ant' praise to fellow insect Z in *Antz*, Samson's motivational dictum in *The Wild* that 'you're a lion, *be* a lion' and Socrates the lion's admission to chimpanzee Toto in *Animals United* (Reinhard Klooss and Holger Tappe, 2010) that 'playing Monkey must be fun', *Ratatouille*'s narration instantly establishes the self-reflexive treatment of one of animation's defining characteristics, that of using animals as characters. Later in the film, Remy accompanies his father Django to an exterminator shop, whose window is adorned with a macabre display of dead rats, poisons and rat-traps. Reviewer Andrew Osmond notes that this sequence reminds Remy how 'rats and humans are natural foes' (2007: 66), yet it simultaneously brings into relief their incompatibility as species *through* a visceral confrontation with the rats' own mortality and existence as vermin.

The graphic shop window display therefore resolves a conundrum posed earlier in the film, in which Remy is heard briefly squeaking in his native rat tongue, rather than the American accent of stand-up comedian Patton Oswalt who otherwise provides his speaking voice. The abrupt switch from human vernacular to high-pitched squeaks makes audible the inherent tensions of identity embedded within the anthropomorph. This moment also suggests that any shift away from ánthrōpos to morphē is neither finite, nor is it irreversible, but a fluid 'dialogue' between the two possibilities.[2] Anticipating Dug's highly comic 'squirrel!' proclamation in *Up*, the 'slash' dividing Remy's character is therefore carefully constructed to allow the digital character frequent, but perceptible, slips into non-human identity. *Ratatouille* therefore encourages the audience to rethink the potential (im)balance of human representation and animality across animated anthropomorphism, offering a glimpse into how computer-animated films might begin to restructure its human/beast binary.

Focalisation and Fictions

By erecting a more permeable and fluid boundary between ánthrōpos and morphē, the anthropomorph of the computer-animated film has itself 'morphed' into more than simply a figuration of human resemblance. Rather than hold an anthropomorphic mirror up to human form and mimic its distinguishing characteristics or traits, these films have begun to unravel the tensions and connections between ánthrōpos and morphē, the animate and inanimate, subjects and objects. In the computer-animated feature-film, there is a greater investment in the volatility between the two poles, a deeper interest in objects *as objects* rather than objects *as humans*:

rats-as-*rats*, rather than rats-as-*chefs*. This reversal in agency from human ánthrōpos to non-human morphē is, however, most commonly articulated in computer-animated films through dynamic point of view subjectivity, a degree of perspectival intrigue and a continuous innovation of spectator viewpoint. The computer-animated film's engagement with the morphē has, this chapter suggests, produced multifarious axes of action. The varying of angles and the reorganisation of the spatial coordinates within these fictional worlds is the product of an anthropomorphic eye (the eye of the anthropomorph) that is in constant positional flux. Transmitting the story in this manner creates a style of anthropomorphic narration couched in more vivid and visually dynamic terms, with a new saliency and forcefulness that has its roots in an anthropomorph who has rejected its human essence in favour of exploring the dynamic potentials of its morphē.

In tune with this new animated treatment of anthropomorphosis, the anthropomorph itself has shifted into new territory and begun to assume alternate textual properties. Characters such as Remy have evolved into more prescriptive and functional agents: part of the computer-animated film's textual system, which controls, expands, modifies, limits and alters spectators' access to that which unfolds in its fictional worlds. Through an engagement with their subjectivity, the spectator is optically guided by the anthropomorph through various diegetic *matter*, transforming it into *meaning*. The visual methods by which the spectator discovers and explores the fiction's spatial constituents and dimensions are not detachable from the anthropomorphic perspectives from which they have been shown. As the hub of such diegetic information, the anthropomorph thus becomes, in Gérard Genette's terms, a narrative 'focalizer' of the constructed fiction (1988: 72). Focalisation describes the angle of vision 'from which the life or the action is looked at' (in Stam, Burgoyne and Flitterman-Lewis 2005: 82). It is a term that can become a verb ('focalising' or 'to focalise') or adjective ('focalisor'), in a way that point of view and perspective cannot (Bal 1985: 143), and so it provides an expedient way of examining the computer-animated anthropomorph's dynamic interaction with its digital world ('the focalised'). These films regularly (re)construct their fictional worlds by using the spatial proximity of the anthropomorph (as a dominant focalisor), and the array of unexpected angles of vision that can emanate from it. One additional point to consider when examining how plot action or events are filtered through anthropomorphic perception is Seymour Chatman's work on 'diegetic consciousness'. This term pertains to the intellectual, emotional and perceptual parameters of a character in relation to its place in the fiction (Chatman 1990: 146). All that we *need to know* of the computer-animated world is, in fact, often all that we *can possibly know* from the anthropomorph's mediating perspective and primary consciousness (a primacy or immediacy to diegetic events). Personalising the space in this manner creates the world as aesthetically and stylistically anecdotal, a virtual reality that is visually channelled through the anthropomorph's individual activities, movements and viewpoints within, through and across it. Anthropomorphism in the computer-animated era can, therefore, be recast on the side of diegesis, and involved in a wider discourse of fictional world creation, transmission and representation. Computer-animated worlds are not solely 'lived' through an anthropomorphic humanity or recognisable 'actants', but through an engagement with the anthropomorph's 'diegetic consciousness' that is heavily inflected by its *other* identity as a non-human.

Let us return to *Ratatouille* alongside another computer-animated film, *Bee Movie*. Both have their worlds continuously narrated through disorientating, dynamic perspectives and an innovation of viewpoint that owes a debt to the computer-animated film's increased engagement with morphē. Ten minutes into *Ratatouille*, Remy and his brother Emile are confronted with a shotgun-wielding Grandma trying to rid her house of a rodent infestation. The action traverses both horizontal and vertical planes, and it is the manoeuvrability of Remy and Emile as they scatter that takes the sequence through a variety of spatial levels: from floors, to tables, kitchen tops, along gas pipes and structural beams, to an explosive climax upon a swinging chandelier (which, in a comic epilogue, crashes to the floor to return the sequence back to a human level). A similar exploration of space occurs in DreamWorks' *Bee Movie*. The film tells the story of oppressed worker bee Barry B. Benson, whose nonconformist attitude leads him to reject the labour of the Honex Industry workforce, and instead assume a more active role away from the production line. During his first flight outside the safety of the hive with the Pollen Jock Flying Corps, insect Barry becomes attached to the fur of a tennis ball. This unfortunate act prompts a kinetic sequence in which the spectator follows the ball's unstable trajectory as it is served and traverses the net back and forth between the players. The ball then inadvertently leaves the court, propelling Barry into a maze of New York traffic, from which he is then sucked into the labyrinthine engine of an oncoming motorcar, the camera following his negotiation of the vehicle's pumps and pistons (Figure 4.1).

The viewing positions tendered during these sequences are unconcerned with satisfying a live-action promise, instead foregrounding the numerous capabilities and potentials of anthropomorphic representation. The space is consistently reconstructed and reframed through a sustained volley of conceptual and innovative viewpoints, the source of which being

Figure 4.1 Frame grab from *Bee Movie* (2007) (DreamWorks Animation). Barry's point of view restructures the geography of the virtual space.

Remy, Emile and Barry, whose anthropomorphic eye is privileged over that of the other human characters who partake in the scenes. The visual experience of each sequence thus emerges from the immediacy through which each event is diegetically narrated, and the function of the anthropomorph as a focalisor of the action in soliciting such narrational modes. But within each film's broader allegiance towards the anthropomorph's subjectivity, it is ultimately the morphē identity, or 'morphē eye', which is rendered most dominant, and central to how the scene (and its narrative drama) is transmitted. The camera did not need to occupy such intrusive, exploratory and dynamic positions; the animators could certainly have located it elsewhere, telling the story from more conventional, 'grounded' places within the fictional world. But it is the energy of the non-human morphē eye and its aptitude for spatial discovery that is used to inscribe the spectator into the world, and skew their perception of the events that unfold there. Remy and Barry's 'take' on the scene – their own specific focalised angle of vision as rat and bee protagonists – is animated to be the spectator's own viewing position (Figure 4.2). The sequences *as they are shown*, and the viewpoints disclosed, engage with the anthropomorph at the new level of morphē. The spectator is not confused by the text's subjective strategies, nor do the films yield to a disorder that edges the spectator closer towards absolute incoherence and abstraction. Rather, *Bee Movie* and *Ratatouille* absorb and invite the audience (through the figure of the anthropomorph) to participate in a spectatorial game that sharpens their awareness of the virtual realm and its spatial dimensions.

Figure 4.2 Frame grab from *Ratatouille* (2007) (Pixar Animation Studios). The
pleasures and perils of anthropomorphic subjectivity.

The action that takes place in computer-animated films is mediated and
mobilised by the mobility of the anthropomorph, and by the filmmaker's
increased investment in the diverse potentials of the morphē. Yet such is
the aptitude of the virtual camera (a revolutionary technical development
operational beyond wholly animated cinema) that it is licensed to *ignore*
the anthropomorph and manoeuvre *anywhere* it chooses. This is something Mike Jones is keen to stress when describing the spatial composition
and vanishing points of the virtual camera in *Monsters, Inc.*, one that
moves 'in a way that defies time and space, ethereally beyond it' (2007:
236). Conceiving the unrestricted virtual camera as a 'phenomenon of
intangible and abstracted presence', Jones actually turns to the humanis-
ing effect of anthropomorphosis, suggesting there is an 'anthropomorphic
embodiment' to the digitised space that creates the illusion that it has
its own point of view: an 'eye' because it is an 'I' (ibid.: 237). However,
this attribution of an omnipotent perspective downplays the concrete
textuality, tangibility and presence of the anthropomorph as a particular
resident or inhabitant of the fiction. In fact, it is the virtuosity of a virtual
camera no longer restricted by human positioning, or by its status as
physical apparatus, which can permit the relocation of subjectivity *into*
the anthropomorph's 'eye' in the first instance, a figure that through
anthropomorphism itself already exists in the text as an animate 'I'.

Deleuze and Gaseous Perception

This new tactile treatment of an anthropomorphic eye/I in computer-
animated films subsequently 'anthropomorphises' the spectator as an
embodied navigator of the virtual space. Such a process permits what

Giuliana Bruno calls embodied tours of the 'cine-city', a term especially resonant with the vigorous *Ratatouille* and *Bee Movie* sequences, in which the spectator shifts from a 'static contemplator' into a mobilised anthropomorphic state undertaking journeys in virtual space (Bruno 2002: 56). With perception freed from the physics of human perspective and allied to the non-human (Remy, Barry), computer-animated films can be illuminated by the systems of subjective variation and fragmentation formulated around what Gilles Deleuze has called 'gaseous perception'. This is an abstract, free-floating mode of expression that Laura U. Marks describes as akin to drug-induced delirium (2000: 161). Breaking with the normal conditions of human subjective experience allows the audience to achieve an open flow of 'hallucinogenic' perception that can be said to be experienced by objects, which are situated in their position of uncontaminated objectivity. As Deleuze puts it, this is 'the pure vision of a non-human eye, of an eye which would be in things' (1986: 81). Not only do these observations accord with computer-animated films' repeated reliance on non-human protagonists to tell its stories – from garden gnomes (*Gnomeo & Juliet*) to penguins (*Penguins of Madagascar*) – but the purity of a subjectivity 'in things' describes a spectatorial disengagement from human compositional logic. Gaseous perception therefore fits within the broader shift occurring in the anthropomorphic representations of computer-animated films *away* from ánthrōpos (human subjectivity), and *towards* the possibilities of the morphē (the object or 'thing'). Although unrelated to his brief comments on animation made in *Cinema 1* and instead theorised in relation to mid-twentieth century American experimental cinema (Stan Brakhage, Michael Snow, Jordan Belson, Ken Jacobs), Deleuze's 'gaseous' conceptualisation of decentred point of view perception free from anchor points nonetheless seems to fit with the heterogeneous virtual spaces tended by – and through – the anthropomorph. There is certainly something compelling and 'hallucinogenic' about a computer-animated 'cine-eye' (itself an anthropomorphic means to describe cinema) that behaves like the randomised movement of a molecule or, for that matter, a rat or bee. Even the etymological roots of hallucination in Latin – meaning *to wander mentally* – are reflected in the capabilities of Remy and Barry for sporadic and erratic behaviour as they negotiate the geography of their own 'cine-city'.

By not separating its viewpoints from the purposeful focalised subjectivity of non-human agents, computer-animated films naturally tender a different kind of 'free-floating' subjectivity not as fully amorphous as the 'gaseous' mode of perception engendered for Deleuze in 1960s experimental film (which resisted the creation of a centralised subject).

This is despite the increased flexibility of digitally assisted film production and computer-animation that enables a more intuitive virtual camera, one whose own continuous 'free-flowing movement' described by Jones (2007: 237) more readily aligns with the altered, hallucinogenic state and audiovisual sensorium central to Deleuze's notion of a 'gaseous' cinema. However, even with perspective conducted through the anthropomorph as an agent of irregular perception, computer-animated films are no less 'at the service of variation and interaction' (Deleuze 1986: 80). The rhythmic pacing and action of the enlivened non-human (that is, crucially, exploited for its virtues as such) foreground the flux of randomness in movement; those spaces and dimensions that are visible but become momentarily occluded; and the reflexive play on digital technology's capabilities for transgressive spatial orientation. Both *Ratatouille* and *Bee Movie* can ultimately be considered 'gaseous' insofar as they involve multiple sequences whose spectacle derives from a boundlessly shifting composition and the connections *between* multiple diegetic points. William Brown argues that 'for Deleuze, cinema becomes gaseous when it escapes human perception and abandons its otherwise all-pervasive anthropocentricism' (2012: 268). The non-anthropocentric (perhaps, newly morphē-centric) cinema accessible in computer-animated films (re)makes the virtual space and its perspectives not as solid, but as a highly gaseous set of spectatorial experiences. The *mise en scène* of *Ratatouille* and *Bee Movie* frequently emphasises the momentum of subjectivity as both de-centring force and chaotic impact, rooted in the very intensity (and uncertainty) of proximity yielded by the anthropomorph's agitated, airy non-human body.

The dislocation from physical constraints and spatial experimentation, following the disorientation stimulated by hallucinogens, is therefore not a delusion or mirage, for it has its roots in the concrete textuality and diegetic presence of the anthropomorph. *This* is the method, the 'drug', which can induce in spectators such animated hallucinations and the gaseous state. Deleuze's claim that the gaseous 'cine-eye' (Dziga Vertov's non-human eye) is 'not the eye of a fly or of an eagle, the eye of another animal', obtains additional significance in computer-animated films because their 'cine-eye' is often precisely that (1986: 83–4). Their many 'animalised' embodiments even coexist with abstracted perspectives made available by the subjectivity of objects not conventionally anthropomorphised as humanlike subjects in scientific or social cognition (due to their lack of obvious physiognomic markers), such as a baseball and bat (*Everyone's Hero*) or garden vegetables (*Cloudy with a Chance of Meatballs 2* [Cody Cameron and Kris Pearn, 2013]). Shifting away from the stable point of view of human subjects to the decentred and 'gaseous' anthropomorph takes us into another, perhaps more obvious, area of Deleuzian philosophy. Through an embodied 'cine-eye' – whether a fly (*A Bug's Life*), an eagle (*Valiant*) or a penguin (*Happy Feet*) – computer-animated films enact Deleuze and Felix Guattari's concept of 'becoming-animal' which, despite being not strictly an anthropomorphic impression of humanity, remains concerned with the partition between human and animal (1987: 265). Here, 'becoming' is attained through an 'unnatural participation' predicated on penetration and spectatorial embodiment. Creative and fictional 'becoming' is intrinsically related to animated anthropomorphism as an artistic process. It recalls both Winsor McCay (how *would* a mosquito operate) as well as Lasseter, who declared at SIGGRAPH that anthropomorphic characters are embodied according to a fictionalised and hypothetical thought process.

The point of view (POV) shot becomes an intriguing tactic of 'becoming' in this respect, especially as it involves the unnatural merging of human with anthropomorphic eyes. A subset of the eyeline match, the POV shot features in a wide range of computer-animated films as a technical flourish and emphatic display of subjective alignment (if not allegiance). Towards the beginning of *Toy Story*, for example, the embodied agency of Woody signifies the broader narrative shift away from human (Andy) to non-human (toy) perspective. As Woody glides down the bannister towards the arms of his owner, the disorienting angle of vision cues an adjustment in the film's address to the spectator, one that is allied to the degree of consciousness and newly suggested animate life behind the cowboy doll's painted eyes. In *Toy Story 3*, the point of view shot becomes a similar device of drama. During a sequence at Sunnyside Daycare, the behaviour of the riotous, rampant children towards the plastic playthings is registered through Buzz Lightyear's point of view, as the space ranger confronts (with his comically fixed, moulded grin) the looming mouth of a toddler that presses down upon Buzz's plastic visor. Structured around what Edward Branigan calls the 'point/glance' shot and the 'point/object' shot (1984: 1), the repetition of point of view in computer-animated films spotlights its status as a key component of their visual language, as well as confirming its role in labelling anthropomorphic characters as emphatic focalisors. But it is also a stylistic device deployed by computer-animated films to involve their audience in a rhetoric of Deleuzian 'becoming', whether this is 'becomings-rat [*Ratatouille*], becomings-insect [*Antz*], [or] becomings-wolf [*Hoodwinked*]' (Deleuze and Guattari 1987: 265).

It would be something of a misnomer to discount how computer-animated films, as examples of mainstream narrative cinema, are not structured by an overarching 'classical' model of narration, one that traditionally privileges an illusionist, transparent textual system rooted in diegetic coherency and legibility. Many computer-animated films adhere to the logic of classical storytelling (establishing shot, continuity editing, 180-degree rule, shot/reverse shot) at the same time as they fully confront the dizzying possibilities of anthropomorphic subjectivity, thereby revealing a push-pull relationship in their formal style between the visual bravura of animated intervention and a more restrained 1940s/1950s Hollywood classicism. *Toy Story*, as Rupert Neupert argues, adheres 'comfortably within many conventions of classical Hollywood storytelling', just as *A Bug's Life* 'follows fairly classical shot composition with a very functional pacing and some intensified continuity editing' (2016: 92, 134). Charles Tesson in *Cahiers du Cinéma* similarly argues that with *Toy Story 2* 'the classical style of the *mise en scène* guarantees the character's humanity' (in ibid.). While computer-animated films make use of classical 'human-centred' perspectives (and human characters) in their configuration of diegetic space, this is nuanced by a more erratic, variegated articulation of the digital environment attributable to the activity of the anthropomorph. With human characters and their perspective featuring as merely a component of the image, the attraction of computer-animated film anthropomorphism, then, involves the spectators' ability to momentarily reject their own ánthrōpos, cross species and take an embodied (rat's-eye or bee's-eye) tour of the virtual world in the skin of another kind. The heightened flexibility of the anthropomorph as a non-human morphē permits it to surmount the limitations of a human (ánthrōpos) eye that is an otherwise fallible and immobile receptive organ. Through the animator's exploitation of non-human morphē over that of the figure's human connotation or ánthrōpos, the anthropomorph of computer-animated films ultimately becomes the pinnacle of putting 'perception into things', into 'matter', the pure vision of a non-human eye (Deleuze 1986: 83). During each of these 'becomings', the spectator (as perceiver) relinquishes power over the fiction to the anthropomorph, and must accept its subjectivity and its morphē as the mediating interface.

A Plasmatic Fiction?

Networked across a variety of computer-animated films, the anthropomorph has given the filmmaker license to experiment with the spatial horizons of the digital world through conceptual perspectives and orientations, without impediment. The anthropomorph's sporadic behaviour and dynamism of movement (anchored to the morphē of its existence) continuously makes available a range of proximities and observation points, deployed to involve the spectator in a rhetoric of *seeing things differently* through the inhabiting and embodiment of place and space. Computer-animated anthropomorphs provide a fluid interchange of observation points and axes of action, constantly reframing or 'deforming' the action to allow the spectator to perceive the events taking place in the fictional worlds through a highly inventive cinematic eye. Within this intensification of anthropomorphic subjectivity and its raising to a higher pitch of emphasis, the anthropomorph itself enlivens all corners of the virtual world in which it resides. Just as the library of mobile doors in *Monsters, Inc.* descend, dip, spiral and rove through the fictional space during the film's climax, the anthropomorph similarly crafts for the spectator innovative and inventive entry points into the virtual geography. The fictional world is transformed into an open (and open*ed*), multidimensional state of omnidirectionality in which no one angle is privileged, but whose spatial coordinates are made variant through the continual exchange of the horizontal and vertical axes of action. The arrangement of pixellated space and binary code in the computer-animated film frame becomes activated in its entirety by the kinaesthesia and virtual virtuosity of the anthropomorph, whose gaseous, molecular contact with the virtual cartography is able to 'animate' each pixel of this digital domain into agency.

Such connections between character and fictional world return computer-animated films to one of the defining virtues of anthropomorphic representation within animation, that of Eisenstein's notion of 'plasmaticness'. There are certainly distant echoes of Eisenstein's voice in Tobey Crockett's use of 'protean' to describe his own fluid conception of a digital diegesis, particularly the discourses of power and powerlessness that he argues underscore 'the emergence of a new subjectivity which comes with the territory' (2009: 118–19). Yet computer-animated films return to, and revaluate, 'plasmaticness' through the interactions between the anthropomorph and the fictional world that contains it. The 'slash' that splinters human and non-human identities can be reconceptualised as a new plasmatic channel, through which ánthrōpos and morphē frequently intersect and collide to form new power relations and anthropomorphic constructs. While animators may be heirs to anthropomorphic representations from hand-drawn techniques *past*, they have implemented digital technologies of the *present* to instil in the boundary a new protoplasmic instability that allows a more flexible engagement with the morphē. The 'plasmatic' energy of the 'slash' is subsequently transferred to the surrounding virtual world through the anthropomorph's subjectivity, which reorients spectator viewpoint in a process that renders the dynamic digital space highly changeable. The 'plasmatic' experience of a film's fictional world retains the same powers of seduction for the spectator as the animated line did for Eisenstein in the 1930s; its spontaneity, its freedoms and its omnipotence. The fictional milieus of the computer-animated film have ultimately begun to adopt many of the values associated with the anthropomorph, through their mutation into intensely *subjectivied* locales: a toy's story, a bug's life, a shark's tale and a bee's movie (the recent release of *A Fox's Tale* [György Gát and János Uzsák, 2009], *A Turtle's Tale* [Ben Stassen, 2010], *A Mouse's Tale* [David Bisbano, 2015] and *A Stork's Journey* [Toby Genkel and Reza Memari, 2017] speaks to this continual anthropomorphic 'possession' of the narrative material). But the often discontinuous, disorienting exploration of 'plasmatic' place and space within a world, and the ability of the spectator to 'dynamically assume any form' (Eisenstein 1986: 21) or, for that matter, any morphē, fail to compromise the validity of the fictional world as a world. The focalising of computer-animated film fictions by the mediating force of the anthropomorph, and its capabilities for reorganising their world's spatial coordinates, is part of a deliberately frenetic, aesthetic experience in which the spectator is constantly *shown* the geography of the virtual environment, rather than simply left to *see* it.

Notes

1. The recent release of Blue Sky's *Ferdinand* (Carlos Saldanha, 2017), in which a non-violent bull (voiced by American professional wrestler John Cena) must learn to fight, suggests that the computer-animated film retains a vested interest in the push-pull relationship between ánthrōpos and morphē within the construction of its characters.
2. Alex the lion (*Madagascar*), grizzly bear Boog (*Open Season*), chimpanzee Comet (*Space Chimps*), Nat the preteen fly (*Fly Me to the Moon*), Bolt the dog (*Bolt*), Reggie the turkey (*Free Birds*), Duke the mongrel dog (*The Secret Life of Pets*) and Bo the Donkey (*The Star* [Timothy Reckart, 2017]) are some of the other computer-animated film characters who have been heard in their true morphē or animal parlance, rather than the linguistic proficiency of their (often 'star') voice actors.

CHAPTER 5

Object Transformation and the Spectacle of Scrap

The Luxo worlds of the computer-animated films are highly resourceful and marked by heightened levels of vibrancy, inasmuch as they are organised by a specific register of non-human agency, which grants any object the opportunity for a life of its own. But these films' resourcefulness can be equally attributed to their inventive treatment of those objects that remain fully inarticulate entities, inauspicious items consigned to linger as inanimate, lifeless matter. With respect to such artefacts, computer-animated films are liable to reject more traditional codes of anthropomorphism by refusing to bestow upon them any intention or volition. This hierarchy of importance arbitrates the transformative potential of the commodity within a Luxo world, explaining why some objects are able to cross the threshold into anthropomorphic identity while others simply endure as inanimate 'stuff'. Maurizia Boscagli argues that 'what defines stuff is its amorphousness as accumulation, assemblage, jumble of objects; a blur between borders and defined categories, what's left in the aftermath of (now waning) cultures of abundance' (2014: 11). As a consequence of a hyper-consumerist culture, the 'disactivated' object not only finds anchorage between the heavily politicised poles of production and consumption, but such 'stuff-objects' are enlivened through 'the human as participating in matter' (ibid.: 2).

Computer-animated films have broken new ground for the transformative possibilities of such objects through an altogether more functional series of renovations. Given the pliant and polymorphous vigour of animation's worlds (from the heavily surrealist qualities of Émile Cohl to Disney's 'plasmatic' form), as well as the digital's capability for instantaneous protean metamorphosis, it might be expected that computer-animated films would more readily pursue a transformative agenda predicated on the exhibitionist visual spectacle of quick change and the vacillating, wavering physical integrity of objects. However, animators engage (or not) with unstable objects, whose durability, fragility, volatility and fluctuating value offers a series of opportunities for activation and animation. Yet devoid of personification or any sentient semblance of life, these objects (as 'stuff') become expressively 'animated' in alternate ways that confirm the spectator's presence inside a computer-animated film world. As this chapter makes clear, these are films that frequently modify a range of objects by giving them new and often highly industrious functions, a shift from the articulation of a point of view *in* things to an engagement with the potential (after)life *of* things.

In computer-animated films, beauty in the form is realised through the creative flexibility of the function, suggesting how *things can matter* without altering *the matter of things*. Robert Wisnovsky's distinction between the categories of 'existent' and 'thingness' within the ontology of objects is useful here, not least on account of its resemblance to the competing poles of ánthrōpos and morphē that collide within anthropomorphic representation. Wisnovsky explains that to refer to an object as an 'existent' addresses not *what* the object is or what makes it one thing rather than another, but to enforce '*that* the object is – i.e. an existent'. This description recalls the terms of ánthrōpos as signifying a human *being*, or an object viewed in light (or, perhaps, in *life*) of its existence, actualisation and appearance. By comparison, Wisnovsky notes that 'the "thingness" of a cat – its catness – is what sets it apart from a horse, whose thingness, of course, is horseness' (2005: 1008). In centring on the differentiating qualities that set that one object apart from another, 'thingness' (an object's 'whatness') can be equated in animation to its morphē or form that gives definition to its shape and structure.

The concessions made within anthropomorphic representation to the 'thing'/morphē of characters as discussed in the previous chapter are therefore equally upheld by computer-animated films in their failure to turn away from the truth of material substance. Computer-animated films are, in other words, invested in the potentials of things (and their 'thingness'). Objects are prized according to their utilitarian value – that is, their constructive worth or usefulness – whilst animators seek to preserve physical relationships and properties (specific to the morphē), rather than collapsing an object's material honesty within the spectacle of metamorphosis. Any kind of object residing in a Luxo world has the potential to be unlocked and re-animated in this manner, to be suddenly freed from the obligation of fixed identity. However, the fascination of computer-animated films frequently lies in the simplest of objects and ornaments. Dan North explains that just as early cinema audiences 'may have been fascinated by rustling leaves, water and other simple natural views, now there is a trend for celebrating the CG rendering of simple things' (2008: 151). Such mastery over the 'simple things' is most commonly realised through the computer-animated film's preoccupation with discarded waste, trash, junk and detritus: acted upon in equally 'simple' ways in order to reconfigure their perceived worth.

Garbage, as Boscagli makes clear, is both dangerous and disruptive, unruly and unstable. It is 'stuff in its most extreme form', a realm of disposed objects that occupy a peripheral space 'beyond official taxonomies of value' (2014: 228). But this marginal residence on the cusp of meaning is what makes formless garbage, junk and rubbish so seductive and summons the potential possibilities of its disuse. Computer-animated films creatively engage with the life cycles and degrees of obsolescence through which the most common of objects conventionally live. Choosing not to follow Remy's disdain for barely edible leftovers in *Ratatouille* ('what we're stealing is, let's face it, garbage!'), these are films consistently drawn to the treasures of the unspectacular, accumulating and recycling superfluous bits of detritus, litter and scraps.

Consider the piles of junk cascading ominously towards an incinerator in *Toy Story 3*; the chase sequence through the municipal depot and car junkyard in *Underdogs* and *Barnyard* (Steve Oedekerk, 2006); the post-human landscapes laden entirely with trash in *Wall-E*, *Mars Needs Moms* and *Yak: The Giant King* (Prapas Cholsaranont, 2015); the floating ruins of dead cities suspended in the sky in *Dragon Hunters* (Guillaume Ivernel and Arthur Qwak, 2008); and the avalanche of discarded food forming Mount Leftovers in *Cloudy with a Chance of Meatballs*. It is within such disorganised clutter and unwanted remnants that computer-animated films seek out their treasures, prizing the spectacle of those things whose values can be made foreign through imported mechanisms that disengage the waste object from its initial purpose. Re-energised and re-valued in this way, even the garbage so derided by Remy in *Ratatouille* is awarded a new life as it is cast by computer-animated films in new roles. As one of the inquisitive ragdolls puts it when surveying the discarded wastelands portrayed in *9*, 'these ruins are full of riches'.

Case Study: *Antz*

Through its engagement with the fascination of everyday mess, DreamWorks' *Antz* immediately outlines the computer-animated film's investment in cast-offs, unwanted commodities and the politics of trash culture that render their screen spaces the liveliest of scrapheaps. Its narrative seizes upon a multitude of discarded objects appropriate to its fictional world, in this case New York, and reassigns them new innovative

Figure 5.1 Frame grab from *Antz* (1998) (DreamWorks Animation).
The desired detritus of Insectopia.

identities. Lying undiscovered and known only through fabled accounts, the idyllic wonderland of Insectopia in *Antz* is revealed upon its discovery by protagonists Z and Princess Bala to be an accumulation of decaying and decomposing food collected at the foot of an overflowing litter bin (Figure 5.1). If the spectator becomes quickly acquainted with the irony of Insectopia's worthlessness, the diminutive ants remain oblivious to the paradox of their 'paradise'. Astounded by the towering monumental space that holds their gaze, Z and Bala instead revel in the luxury and opulence of their new surroundings ('Have you ever seen anything more beautiful in your life?'), and through their adoration of the enveloping waste the ants (re)value the clutter found in this land of abundance and perishable plenty.

The scattered rubbish, discarded refuse and debris is here salvaged from irrelevance and triviality, its prior rejection and shelf life relinquished in favour of a new afterlife predicated on frivolity and childlike amusement. While Z excitedly plays in the fresh surface fungus of an infected dough-nut to form the shape of an angel (thereby recalling a popular childhood game), Bala enthusiastically 'rides' a worm as it snakes like a rollercoaster through the bore holes of a damaged, mouldy apple. Away from the rigid, ordered economy of the ant colony, the cascading waste at Insectopia pre-sents freedom and instant reward without the monotonous labour, and as such its utopian qualities provides the ideal backdrop for the two noncon-formist characters' growing affections. The cross-class alliance between worker ant Z and Princess Bala is forgotten in the excitement of romance. Their shared engagement in rubbish cultivates a unity that bypasses their social categories normally held distinct, and fuelled by their autonomy they return to incite the whole colony's collective uprising against its authoritarian military generals at the film's climax. A haven of appeal and invitation, Insectopia holds an exuberant new life as the longed-for place of perfection for its anthropomorphic ants, whilst offering a key moment in *Antz*'s broader Marxist credentials (Falzon 2005). But for the spectator, the narrative significance of Insectopia serves to multiply and revive those renounced things that are piled up to comprise it, literally offering spectators *food for thought* as (though the actions of Z and Bala) *Antz* recycles biodegradable waste products as an imaginary paradise.

Glamorous Garbage and Junk Cities

Antz is far from the only instance of cultural detritus retrieved and redeemed in such explicit and sustained acts of worship. *Over the Hedge* valorises cans of garbage thrown out by a neighbouring residential human community as an attractive alternative to traditional foraging ('welcome to paradise!'). R. J. the racoon takes pleasure in revealing the ritualistic eating habits of suburban America (food *as identity* and *status*), before tipping over the 'gleaming silver cans' filled with unwanted scraps to the excitement of the woodland creatures (food *as survival* and *pleasure*), who proceed to rummage through its relative treasures. Rubbish is also served in the cafeteria of *Monsters University*, tipped directly from the litter bins onto food platters as the monstrous students eagerly tuck into the edible leftovers. *Bolt* includes a similar sequence in which discarded scraps are celebrated as a plentiful bounty by its hungry anthropomorphic cast.

Robots also concentrates its values – and the incentives of its protagonist Rodney Copperbottom – on regaining and reclaiming the tarnished and corroded. The film stresses the preservation of outmoded robots (known as 'Rusties') with little exchange value, and the salvaging of second generation parts over new expensive upgrades, subscribing throughout to Rodney's philosophy that 'you can shine no matter what you're made of' as it fully embraces the lingering presence of the forgotten within the aesthetics of trash. A similar ethos of recovery drives the character of Hamegg in *Astro Boy*. A robot repairer and owner of an underground robot fighting ring, Hamegg exclaims 'I love robots! Especially the discarded ones. The more banged up they are, the more abused . . . the more I like getting them back on their feet.' Just as *Toy Story* champions Sid's toys cobbled together from broken remnants by making a spectacle out of their troubling identity as waste products, *Robots* and *Astro Boy* similarly focus on the capacity, rather than negativity, of what to *do* with what is broken and wrecked in its celebration of fragmented 'things' free from an encoded social value or context. As Hamegg decries in disbelief, 'Can you believe someone threw this away?'

The scrap hoarded within the computer-animated film's many worlds positions the genre within a vibrant lineage of 'thinkers, artists, and film-makers who are formulating a cultural politics out of trash's disruptive power' (Boscagli 2014: 228). From Duchamp's readymades and *objets trouvés* to Dadaism, cubism and modernists such as Richard Stankiewicz, Joseph Cornell, Robert Rauschenberg and Ed Keinholtz, twentieth-century art has been alive with investments in the formal possibilities of junk as raw material for unprecedented creativity. Whether collapsed into postcolonial and postmodernist discourse, or viewed as a commentary on globalised obsolescence and resourcefulness, interest in an aesthetics of trash (that is, assembled from fragments not planned as material for art) has not solely been the preserve of art and cultural historians. Barthes, Baudelaire, Bergson, Benjamin, Foucault and Heidegger all theorised the production of 'things', while the consolidation of 'thing theory' has placed emphasis on the emergence of an object's 'thingness' as a consequence of fault ('when they stop working for us') (Brown 2001: 4). The politicisation of rubbish within computer-animated films, and the manner in which common refuse so often functions as the trigger for inspired and innovative interpretation, certainly invokes the long and diverse history of modern art made from rubbish. Lawrence Alloway argues that the activities of junk art were made possible by the 'throw-away material of cities, as it collects in drawers, cupboards, attics, dustbins, gutters, waste lots and city dumps'. He writes that 'junk culture is city art. Its source is obsolescence' (Alloway 2006: 79). However, the panoply of junk collected throughout computer-animated films is both *from* the city and can now *constitute* the city.

A particular trope in this regard is the recycling of rubbish and waste as the backdrop for entire communities. Random objects are frequently put to practical use within highly 'animated' landscapes that are built from the ground up, lively junkspaces predicated on discourses of regeneration and renewal. Not simply scrap cast off by the forward momentum of urban progress, junk in the computer-animated film often functions as the basic elements of the Luxo world's architecture, coding these screen spaces as 'trashy' sites of innovation and places of (re)construction. The worlds of *Valiant*, *The Ugly Duckling and Me!* (Michael Hegner and Karsten Kiilerich, 2006), *Fly Me to the Moon*, *Air Bound* and *The Tale of*

Despereaux (Sam Fell and Robert Stevenhagen, 2008) are all crafted from discarded waste, while the Wild West town of Dirt located in California's Mojave desert in *Rango* incorporates empty, rusting gasoline canisters among its makeshift saloons and shop fronts.

The spectacle of scrap, both organic and electronic, as it assumes new forms provides a Luxo world with heightened levels of visual detail, and offers spectators the ordinary pleasure in the recuperation of trash (as art) through its practical inscription as a fully-functioning 'cine-city'. Roddy's accidental discovery of an underground sewer version of 'London' ten minutes into *Flushed Away* reveals a micro-city composed entirely of reclaimed items. Everything from the architecture to the modes of transport in this subterranean metropolis is compositional. This is a seductive, vibrant micro-city whose culture and technology are based on scavenged junk leftover by the culture residing above. Chipped porcelain mugs, traffic cones, odd buttons, discarded food, a jukebox and an old boot are all sculpted together into a stylised version of London's familiar skyline. A clock hung inside a gilded gold frame and mounted on a salvaged washing machine evokes Big Ben, which overlooks LED advertisements that reprise the entertainment junction of Piccadilly Circus. Yet *Flushed Away*'s recreation of tourist London is not limited to land. Recalling the passenger steamboats moored on the River Thames during the early nineteenth century, rodent tourists board a sewing machine (doubling as a river bus), whose route along the waterways runs adjacent to a phone box and toilet cubicle arranged in the architecture of Tower Bridge. These rat-made channels that vein the city are themselves home to a plenitude of makeshift vessels kept afloat by the buoyancy of tin cans. The most famous boat is the Jammy Dodger owned by scavenger Rita, which is built from tennis balls, license plates, a bike chain, rusty screws and other objects well-worn through multiple uses.

The pre-formed consumer products laying waste 'up top' in *Flushed Away* are remembered 'down below' by this habitat that creatively intervenes into and arrests the object's flow from the factory to the scrapyard. By 'clogging [. . .] the sleek flows along the approved routes of capital' (Boscagli 2014: 229) – an image particularly prescient given Roddy's journey *as waste* through London's waterpipes – *Flushed Away*'s alternative vision of the capital reveals the appeal of anachronistic artefacts no longer dependent on the culture from which they have been expelled. The underground 'London' to which the cultured Roddy arrives is not simply a repository for the forgotten and the discarded. It is an inventive realm that as with many computer-animated films draws in the spectator (and Roddy) through acts of creation, range and variation, and the spectacular re-making of that which is already made. But in suggesting a more moderate existence that underscores their proclivity for recycling and reuse, *Flushed Away* reveals how the switch in functionality (that identifies the city as a culture predicated on its sustainability) is primarily achieved through the manipulation of scale.

Diminutive Pleasures

Fluctuations in the size, weight and dimension of characters and objects have a long history in animation, openly embroiled within its culture of quick change as part of what Scott Bukatman calls the medium's 'sustained elaboration of metamorphic possibility and reflexive play' (2012: 16). From the Disney short *Giantland* (Burt Gillett, 1933) and the grotesque growth of Ursula in *The Little Mermaid* (Ron Clements and John Musker, 1989) to the absurd physical humour of the MGM cartoon *King-Size Canary* (Tex Avery, 1947), animation has fully exploited the potential of dimensional disjuncture, whilst taking a cue from wider traditions of fantasy fiction, fairy and folk tales (Lewis Carroll, Jonathan Swift, Mary Norton) that employ magical devices of physical reduction and amplification.

It is certainly not uncommon for computer-animated films to draw upon a similar language of scale and dimension to resize the pleasures of looking. *Jimmy Neutron: Boy Genius* (John A. Davis, 2001), *The Ant Bully*, *Thru the Moebius Strip*, *Igor*, *A Christmas Carol*, *Despicable Me*, *Space Chimps 2: Zartog Strikes Back* and *A Monster in Paris* all incorporate sequences of dynamic miniaturisation through the (often comedic) shrinking of individual characters into minuscule proportion, a device that shifts the spatial coordinates of the world that contains them. By comparison, *Shrek 2*, *Monsters vs. Aliens*, *Hoodwinked Too! Hood vs. Evil* and *Minions* all mine the spectacle of excessive growth to enlarge its protagonists. For critic David Denby (1998), *Antz* operates as a 'terrific joke about scale', one that is initially told in a visual gag contained within its very first image. When a silhouetted New York skyline (marked by the Empire State Building, Chrysler Building and World Trade Center) is bathed in radiant sunlight, the enlightened image reveals not a panoramic cityscape of Manhattan, but angled blades of grass merely resembling skyscrapers built to various heights, shapes and designs. The perceptual implication of *Antz*'s 'lawnscape' constitutes a playful moment of misdirection, and invites the spectator to immediately reconceptualise and reformulate their response to (the values attributed to) the most unspectacular of milieu.

Beyond its contribution to animation's metamorphic aptitudes, the manipulation of proportional rules in computer-animated films can be utilised as a visual shorthand to quickly dispense with any object's established function. Object transformation occurs when the spectator is dropped into a miniature space, inaugurating a state of induced smallness that through its investment in size, stature and scale inversion recalls the position of children in relation to adulthood, looking *up* (rather than down) at a world often built for those who are much bigger. Released by the Canadian comic book publisher Arcana Studios as its debut computer-animated feature, *Pixies* (Sean Patrick O'Reilly, 2015) tells the story of a tiny army of fairies who follow a human, Joe Beck, into his 'human-sized' world to retaliate against his dumping of rubbish into their underground village. The fairies' sudden traversing of suburban America allows *Pixies* to manipulate proportion and perspective as, led by the Pixie King, they navigate the dangers of their new environment. Crossing the threshold of proportional absurdity to momentarily be made miniature, the spectators of many other computer-animated films are similarly invited to take up residence in new monumental spaces composed of the waste products of urban life, and to see(k) the bigness now made available in that which is small. The possibilities of miniaturisation and magnification are firmly implicated in the regimes of anthropomorphic subjectivity, as shifts in size permit new perspectival contact with the 'stuff' of the diegetic world (including creating new opportunities and hazards within familiar terrain).

With new access to the house 'that can be set on a pea', or that which could be 'hidden under a tuft of grass', spectators thus enjoy and experience something close to what philosopher Gaston Bachelard calls the 'interior beauty' of the miniature, given access to one of the last 'refuges of greatness' in these micro-communities (1994: 148). When young boy Lucas Nickle is shrunk from human size to ant proportions in *The Ant Bully*, for example, his transgression into the miniature world 'hidden under a tuft of grass' presents a new kind of monumental space emerging from his resizing, including the threat of enlarged raindrops and oversized jellybeans. In *Epic*, seventeen-year-old Mary Katherine 'M. K'. Bomba is similarly confronted with the newly enormous perils of the natural world when she is accidentally shrivelled to the size of the tiny humanoid 'Leafmen' soldiers. Coupled with the visual drama of size, both *The Ant Bully* and *Epic* additionally use miniaturisation as a device to emotionally rehabilitate their stubborn protagonists, teaching them the value of kindness and hard labour through unexpected communal activity that comes from their sudden 'drop' into a smaller group.

As Susan Stewart argues when discussing the appeal of the miniature, the 'world of things can open itself to reveal a secret life', exposing not just a set of actions but a narrative and history 'outside of the given field of perception' (2003: 54). Computer-animated films are likewise drawn to the values of miniature thinking. Through the reciprocal configuration of miniaturisation and enlargement, spectators are invited to look closer and reflect upon the actual size of the cultural detritus, junk and everyday objects being reassembled in unconventional ways, suddenly privy to the terms of its 'secret life'. It is ultimately a specific type of fictional world in which a broken pencil is used as a wooden leg (*Flushed Away*), a single plant leaf is able to function as a parachute (*Ice Age: Dawn of the Dinosaurs* [Carlos Saldanha and Mike Thurmeier, 2009]), wristwatches can be worn as belts (*Rio*), a solitary matchstick can become a streetlamp (*The Tale of Despereaux*) and a rusty tin can provides buoyancy as a life raft (*Minuscule: Valley of the Lost Ants* [Hélène Giraud and Thomas Szabo, 2014]). Colliding with a newly available dimensional quality that is rooted in the spectators' induced smallness, the retention of an object's material properties both anchors the success and arbitrates the suitability of its very transformation. The social and political significance accrued by an object thus operates secondary to an investment in its materiality. The computer-animated film and its industrious acts of functional transformation awards new degrees of strength and security to objects rooted in their resizing. As a correlative to the dominant twentieth-century scientific and cultural narrative of compact, portable technology, the increased smallness of its junkspaces makes full use of the crevices and corners of a Luxo world, whilst the view tendered from inside these minuscule realms ascribes new monumentality to an environment suddenly partial and far-reaching in its enveloping enormity.

Case Study: *A Bug's Life*

The computer-animated film's culture of reclamation engenders a kind of objectified 'role-play', one that celebrates the enduring, haunting presence of waste matter and material by efficiently working on (and with) the often broken and discarded fragments of the spectator's own civilisation. In Pixar's *A Bug's Life*, the 'big city' visited by Flik as part of the character's desire to prove his worth outside Ant Island is, in fact, a collection of discarded cans and takeaway boxes, arranged to recall the familiar geography of Times Square. As a parody of New York City, the downtown architecture of so-called 'Bug City' has boxes for frozen bagels and jumbo pretzels doubling as skyscrapers; fairy lights re-purposed as elaborate neon lighting displays (recalling the arrival of neon signage in Times Square during the 1920s); and an empty soup can now home to a dive bar, complete with a penknife countertop and an array of disreputable clientele.

Figure 5.2 Frame grab from *A Bug's Life* (1998) (Pixar Animation Studios). The 'big city' recycles junk as insect architecture.

If the thrilling abandonment of Z and Bala obfuscates their ability to detect Insectopia as a structure of rubbish in *Antz*, then Flik's amazement at his surroundings ('wow, the city!') is humorously offset against the truth of the architecture (Figure 5.2). Stained and scruffy at the corners, the rejected packaging has been re-energised as a bustling modern metropolis, one that, as the local transport system announces, offers locals (and visiting tourists like Flik) trips to all destinations including 'the septic tank' and the 'empty bean can'. This kind of playful urban regeneration in *A Bug's Life* both acknowledges and twists twentieth-century projects of large-scale renewal. With junk as the building blocks of its rapidly growing settlements, the film visualises the social reform of disused landscapes into areas of increased prosperity (despite fleeting evidence of a homeless bug playing music for money) and the creation of a communal, cosmopolitan location where insects go to be seen, play cards and drown their sorrows.

In *A Bug's Life*, the oversize (but, seemingly, now small) spectator encounters from the 'inside out' the film's Luxo world of rubbish pregnant with opportunities for new experiences. The film offers a captivating inversion of perspective that enlarges the everyday, and permits spectators to both find and appreciate the large in what is small. Values of magnification and miniaturisation in the computer-animated film therefore unlock objects from the constraints of just one function. Stripped of several of the descriptive characteristics used to conventionally individuate them, these objects are regenerated from eyesores to environments, from waste to worlds. Within such strategies of sustainability, spectators intervene only on the object's latest identity, witnessing the results of its creative restoration and capacity to endure. In *A Bug's Life*, labels and logos may serve as printed reminders of the object's original use (a drink can, a container for food), but this is an identity it has now shed. The original function is rarely made available, and so like the inhabitants of these worlds whose engagement with, and understanding of, the 'empty bean can' will forever remain incorrect, spectators are invited to appreciate the intrigue of an object's potential afterlife.

Pretend Play

Values radiate from everyday objects. These values are formed through their perception by the beholder. Keith Moxey has argued that 'the ways in which objects call to us, their animation, their apparent autonomy, stem only from their association with us' (2008: 142). He concludes that these objects and artefacts 'may haunt us but their autonomy is relative. They cannot exist without the power with which we invest them' (ibid.). Where there is junk in the computer-animated film there is often a visible system of appropriation. The seemingly spontaneous, improvisatory dwellings in *Flushed Away* and *A Bug's Life* are ultimately the outcome of a creative process of interpretation that has situated discarded everyday objects in a variety of new collaborations. As several computer-animated films make clear, central to this assembly are the achievements of characters (functioning as diligent artisans) who purposefully scavenge and engineer the debris of mass culture as a way of furnishing their own environments.

Filmmaker Shane Acker has spoken of world creation and its relation to discarded matter within the post-apocalyptic narrative of his computer-animated film *9*. Describing the industrious actions of the nine homunculi ragdolls who populate the film's barren wasteland in search of survival, Acker suggests 'they are using old, now redundant objects, as new tools, but infuse them with an incredible creative spirit' (in Wells 2011: 100). The manipulation of waste products, junk and discarded objects by the diminutive dolls in *9*, who source their basic necessities from outside (often past) civilisations, are all creative acts of animation. The reordering of the rejected in a Luxo world is determined by its connections to an agent, because devoid of anthropomorphic sentience or personification, this junk cannot free itself from its perceived lack of worth on its own. So while Ralph Bakshi's irreverent cel-animation *Hey Good Lookin'* (1982) opens with a heated verbal exchange between a pile of waste and an anthropomorphic trash can ('you know all this rubble, just passing the time bullshittin'?'), the abandoned Luxo world in *9* remains inarticulate and requires external 'animation'.

Within this rhetoric of creativity, trash is created by sifting, sorting and judicious selection. The imaginative and resourceful attitude of Wall-E (as the last of the Waste Allocation Load Lifter – Earth Class robots) towards his own abandoned surroundings certainly operates in this vein. Methodically picking and poking his way through the rubbish heaps, the robot compacts the unwanted cultural detritus left behind on an evacuated Planet Earth into neat cuboids, which are then are stacked into soaring junk structures as part of his extensive clean-up operation. Glimpsed through the suffocating fog within this stifling post-human world, Wall-E is the sole architect of his own personalised high-rise junk yard, a world-builder and junk artist whose 'trashy' recreations give definition and life to a dead city that has long since atrophied. But it is not only the compression of outmoded material and cultural objects into the stackable building blocks that reforms and reshapes these broken, forgotten remnants of mass culture. A post-mortem into the decaying city reveals how it is Wall-E's creative interaction with discarded artefacts that ushers each object towards a new and innovative functionality.

A surrogate animator whose labour revives identity in the inanimate, Wall-E's proclivity for collecting suggests subject/animator and object/animated are not entirely separable. The film picks out its protagonist from the other (non-functioning) versions of similar design, which now lay defunct by the roadside. Similarly, with humans having long departed aboard the AXIOM spaceship, the last surviving model of his kind must systematically reattribute worth to the homogenised rubbish. Any object recovered from compaction is primed to be recycled and repurposed, designated a spot in Wall-E's organised archive of antiques relating to a long-lost civilisation. Wall-E's personalised cabinet of curiosities, and his philosophy that *everything matters* (and that everything, given the oppor-tunity, *can matter*), crystallises the values that computer-animated films attribute to rubbish. Any object has the opportunity to graduate from matter to matter*ing*. There are no patterns to his selection process during his repetitive labour, only a curious electronic noise emitted by the robot that confirms the object's intrigue. Such excessive behaviour towards possession enables the first switch in the objects to take place; ownership prompting an immediate transformation from a status of *nothing*ness to *thing*ness.

Toy Story 3 is firmly in the shadow of *Wall-E* as it likewise makes a distinction between toys (worth) and junk (worth*less*) founded upon issues of possession. Whereas rubbish is devoid of ownership ready to be reclaimed, the identity *of the toys*, and indeed their status *as toys*, is predi-cated upon a sense of belonging. To be owned is ultimately to be salvaged from abandonment. With shades of the animated musical *The Brave Little Toaster* (Jerry Rees, 1987), which also culminates at a junkyard, Woody,

Buzz and the remainder of Andy's toys must continually fight against their phobia of being downgraded to the rank of trash, and it is this perpetual fear that engulfs them. Despite the villainous Lots-O'-Huggin' Bear's proclamation to his fellow toys that 'we're all just trash waiting to be thrown away', *Toy Story 3* permits its toys salvation from such a future as junk by giving them a present as toys.

The valuations of worth made in *Wall-E*, and the numerous salvage operations described throughout this chapter, can be understood according to ideas of 'symbolic' or 'pretend play' that typically marks early child behaviour. I have argued elsewhere with regards to the regimes of object transformation in the computer-animated film *Up* that the imaginative spirit underscoring pretend play 'involves a child's relations with objects, and in particular a central act of *object substitution*' (Holliday 2016: 28). The manipulation of one object for another (and the variant possibilities engendered by these substitutional activities) replace a mode of play that relies on an obedience towards what Elena Bugrimenko and Elena Smirnova have termed the 'situation' (1994: 294–5). The emergence of symbolic, metaphorical and conceptual representation is central to the child's cognitive and social development, a behavioural stage that runs alongside the maturation of social play (participatory involvement between children rather than solitary actions), but also incorporates the drama of perspective, imitation and imagination. The playful activities of Wall-E as he coerces mounds of discarded waste into new functional identities, appeals to the creative spirit with which children infuse their objects and the false representations bestowed upon them. These transformations are investigational acts rooted in substitutional behaviour: the repurposing of junk and waste to 'stand in' for another more functional entity.

Computer-animated films are littered with substitutional gestures of this kind, staking their interest in the kinds of creative substitutions that have been credited with nourishing and strengthening a child's cognitive development. An oven glove acts as a rodent's bed in *Ratatouille*, while a matchbox becomes a rucksack in both *The Ugly Duckling and Me!* and *The Nut Job*. In *A Bug's Life*, would-be inventor Flik combines 'just an ordinary blade of grass and bead of dew' to manufacture a crude, but fully-functioning, telescope (though the device is immediately ridiculed). It is not uncommon for the industrious behaviour of computer-animated films to be reflected in the actions of aspiring inventors. Dr Cockroach in *Monsters vs. Aliens* is an inventor obsessed with the properties (and even taste) of garbage, improbably turning 'a pizza box, two cans of hairspray ... and a paperclip' into a fully-working super computer. Jimmy Neutron (*Jimmy Neutron: Boy Genius*), Rodney Copperbottom

(*Robots*), Lewis Robinson (*Meet the Robinsons*), Flint Lockwood (*Cloudy with a Chance of Meatballs*), Gru (*Despicable Me*), Mr Peabody (*Mr. Peabody & Sherman*) and, of course, Wall-E are additionally all inventors or creators who plunder their respective Luxo worlds and scavenge for its hidden treasures.

Case Study: *Wall-E*

Activities of object substitution take on greater meaning in *Wall-E*. During one sequence of 'pretend play' ten minutes into the film, the curious android encounters a discarded brassiere among the abandoned cultural detritus. Drawn to the allure of its curved shape, he tentatively positions the lingerie over his binocular eyes believing it to be spectacles. Later, Wall-E imitates a song-and-dance routine copied from his VHS of *Hello, Dolly!* (Gene Kelly, 1969), replicating the movements onscreen by gesturing with a dirty and disused hubcap. Tilting his treasure to mimic a top hat, Wall-E performs not just the musical number for love-interest EVE, but simultaneously forces a switch in functionality. Norman Klein identifies in the transformations of early cel-animation, and particularly the work of the Fleischer brothers, there lies an impression of an image's 'atomic structure' seemingly coming 'unglued' (1993: 64). But adhering to the preservation of the morphē, *Wall-E* stabilises its transformations by avoiding the transmutation of one object into another. Like Chaplin, a figure to whom Wall-E has so often been likened, the robot sanctions multiple roles to engulf even the most unspectacular and broken of objects through the dextrous skill with which he handles them, rather than recourse to the pleasures of 'atomic' instability.

If Insectopia permits the ants to express what Wisnowsky might call their 'antness', then the vast playground of scattered junk allows Wall-E's own 'robotness' (his own morphē) to sporadically manifest. Indeed, for all his numerous capabilities as a fully-functioning android, and there are many, Wall-E's ever-expanding repository of salvaged treasures both amuses and confuses him, and his inability to operate everyday objects carves out a space for their range of possible functions to be performed. By comparison, the sleek and sophisticated EVE is a character through which the film channels an object's 'correct' use, showcased by her skilled handling of the Zippo cigarette lighter, light bulb and Rubik's cube. A new inhabitant to the film's desolate wasteland, EVE comes from a world 'alive with consumption and dead with thought' (Shaw 2010: 395) and it is this that restrains her object substitutions. She is ultimately an extension of the AXIOM's dutiful autopilot that governs the craft's trajectory. EVE's 'robotness' surfaces only when she is entirely autonomous from Wall-E and his objects: when piloted by the regulated trails on board the AXIOM, or in her directive to automatically scour Earth's rubbish for signs of life. But the discarded waste bequeathed to Wall-E once all humanity is evacuated from Earth has developed his eccentric personality and transformed his regulated, automatic existence.

Despite his inquisitive approach and attempts to coach EVE in his own style of 'pretend play', the only object that Wall-E is able to correctly operate is himself. He remains alert to his faults, aware of when he requires upgrade, repair or maintenance. His playful actions with the lingerie and hubcap invite spectators to revel in the android's behavioural (rather than mechanical) deficiencies. As Wall-E's inquisitive activity re-values the cultural meanings of artefacts long since buried, spectators become progressively acquainted with the robot's own morphē and status *as an object*. The android's own 'thingness' is therefore illuminated by his engagement and 'pretend play' with the 'thingness' of others, and so as the inanimate objects lie dormant on Earth ready to be reclaimed, their discovery not only brings each one to life (and *into* a new life), but reanimates the animator himself.

Waste Management

In the grand scheme of things, the average piece of junk is probably more meaningful than our criticism designating it so.
(Anton Ego, *Ratatouille*)

Computer-animated films build their narratives around what it is like to live among (and with) trash. They question the processes and meanings involved in an object's shift to a new function that prolongs its use value, and dually exploit and corrupt the planned obsolescence of a 'thing' by tendering the potential pluralism of its functionality. As complex sites of discourse, the rubbish and waste generated by the material culture of fictional Luxo worlds ultimately gives characters their means of existence. Urban foraging puts on display the recovery of unwanted surplus and catches up its characters in broader networks of obligation and application.

Waste, litter and detritus gesture back to the wasteful economy and irresponsible set of cultural circumstances that fashioned it. The many eco-critical readings of *Wall-E*'s environmentalist impetus (Murray and Heumann 2011; Whitley 2012; Meinel 2014), for example, bear out how its narrative of apocalyptic warning is embroiled in issues of commodity possession, accumulation and (re)distribution as a dramatic backdrop for its systems of functional object modification. Gillian Whiteley argues that 'waste is, of course, an adjunct of luxury. Junk, trash, garbage, rubbish, refuse – whatever we call it – is dependent on economic wealth and excess production' (2011: 4). The many images of sustainability in the computer-animated film are often rooted in cultural inefficiency and excessive materialism. In the case of *A Bug's Life*, the diminutive insects fully exploit the pleasures of excess packaging and contemporary takeaway culture, as the (over) abundance of products enables the expedient engineering of 'green' recycling in the form of a Luxo world's cities and settlements. Though dismissed by his sceptical woodland audience, R. J'.s tirade in *Over the Hedge* against American consumerism and humanity's religious attachment to food is similarly provocative in its political framework, insofar as it verbalises the erosion of interpersonal communication at the hands of food-induced lethargy and unproductivity. Despite his confident hyper-awareness, R. J. himself is not immune to the allure of suburban affluence. The character's sinful gluttony (ultimately redeemed by the narrative's climax) is initially presented in the film's opening prologue, as the duplicitous racoon struggles in vain to grasp a vending machine's last remaining piece of confectionery, showing the character's strenuous desire for packaged junk food that is frustratingly just out of reach.

Computer-animated films can both celebrate and be altogether more phobic about populating their Luxo worlds with abundant images of the torn and the tatty. The wilting vegetation and plant life in *Bee Movie*; the barren landscapes that are 'depleted by the central resources' in *Delgo* (Marc F. Adler and Jason Maurer, 2008); the desolate wasteland partitioned off from the colourful city of Thneedville in *The Lorax* (whose inhabitants sing 'We don't want to know, where the smog and trash and chemicals go'); and the rundown, rusting town of Radiator Springs in *Cars* all pose waste products as the consequence of ecological devastation, anthropological neglect or a simple desire to reduce traffic congestion. Many other computer-animated films convey narratives with strong ecological or environmental themes, such as *The Living Forest* (Ángel de la Cruz and Manolo Gómez, 2001) and its sequel *Spirit of the Forest* (David Rubin, 2008), and *Bunyan and Babe* (Louis Ross, 2017), although perhaps the most explicit of these is *Animals United*, which unfolds against the backdrop of an international climate change conference. Whether celebrations of junk's creative potential or moralising tales on the harsh consumption practices born out of global capitalism, in their very ambivalence computer-animated films disclose the flexibility of its waste matter by implicating such rubbish into new circuits of meaning. These films notice waste in order to be inspired by its messy, unruly visibility. Allied to this, it is the 'meaningfulness' instilled into the 'average piece of junk' that can be identified as one of their most prolific pleasures. When Wall-E ignores the monetary value of a discarded diamond ring and instead becomes fascinated with the hinged mechanism of the trinket's box; when Oh believes Van Gogh's oil painting *The Starry Night* (1889) to be nothing more than dinner in *Home*; or when *The LEGO Movie* treats discarded objects as museum pieces (curated in 'The Relic Room'), such actions are appropriate to a body of computer-animated films in which the conception of junk is entirely relative and relational.

Through their elegiac and empathetic relationship to waste products, computer-animated films enliven objects residing in their Luxo worlds with multiple values and operations, unfastening a range of junk, trash, waste and detritus from what poet Anne Carson calls the 'latches of being' (1998: 4). By introducing a foreign constituent to pilot a single object's identity during their substitutional acts of pretension, Luxo worlds manifest as spaces that are highly *interchangeable* rather than fluidly changeable. But there are multiple limitations in operation, and the transformative vibrancy of these fictional realms resides at the juncture where creativity meets constraint (arbitrated by the regulating principles of the morphē) in ways that establish the parameters of expectation within, and stability of, a Luxo world. Yet by inviting spectators to formulate a new response to a recognisable object, and to become acquainted with the widening of its functional possibility, computer-animated films revel in choreographing the simplest of objects a more creatively innovative routine. It is this compelling and vibrant compatibility between restrained bravura, a resourceful energy and heightened levels of industriousness that makes a Luxo world one of the most exciting and dynamic screen spaces of contemporary cinema.

CHAPTER 6

Pixar, Performance and Puppets

Computer-animated Luxo worlds are worlds of irrepressible energy and vigour. Optically compelling, with arresting activity staged in depth so that it recedes far into the virtual horizon, elaborate compositions stress a Luxo world's monumentality and multitude, and its extremes of life and luminosity. The net effect of virtual environments exhibited in this way is certainly one of spectacle. Such worlds solicit a mode of spectatorial address that is marked by the repeated disclosure of their own heightened intricacy, agency and animatedness. But visual spectacle within a Luxo world is no less a function of the unique kinds of performances made available in, and sanctioned by, these computer-animated screen spaces. Paul McDonald has recently argued that 'all film acting is spectacle' (2012: 171), and while this certainly rings true for the accomplishments of many performers across cinema history, it is the computer-animated film genre that routinely makes a spectacle (out) of animated acting.

Recent writing that has staked a claim for animation as a 'performance art' has brought into relief the intrinsic place of performance within the creative capacities of animation to excite and entertain, and for animated films to be viewed as a 'cultural enterprise based on performativity' (Crafton 2013: xv). Computer-animated films have proven no less a magnet for discussions of acting in animation, and Donald Crafton has recently endorsed Pixar as a studio producing highly 'performative' films. The separate, and yet entirely inseparable, relationship between the computer-animated film and acting, and the clear valuation of performance as an indispensible element, hinges upon the fundamental role played by the animator in the construction of performance. Whether it is the label 'animator/actor' settled upon by Paul Wells (1998: 110), or Stephen Prince's terming of the 'animator-as-actor' (2012: 110), a particularly durable line of critical inquiry has identified performance as resting upon the animator's discipline, expertise and application of their own acting credentials. For Heather Holian, animators are 'the most sophisticated, versatile and total – that is entirely masked and anonymous – professional masqueraders working in the entertainment business today' (2015: 231). The animator's prominent place as the locus for such 'masked' performances has been further sustained across the wealth of practitioner manuals and guidebooks (Kundert-Gibbs and Kundert-Gibbs 2009; Beiman 2010; Hooks 2011; Hayes and Webster 2013), which coach animators in the successful creation of persuasive, autonomous and self-governing characters. Acting also forms a necessary component of the curriculum at the Pixar University, a professional development and education programme established in 2003, and based 'in-house' at the company's Emeryville studio in California. Among the multitude of guest seminars, event lectures and workshops available each day, animators can also take acting lessons and courses in improvisation alongside other typical 'fine art' subjects like painting, drawing and sculpture classes for four hours per working week.

Any appreciation of 'acting' within the feature-length computer-animated film context is, however, complicated by the particular conditions governing the creation of a screen performance. Animated acting is an expansive, fluid construction borne out of a unique combination of animated gestures and mimes, all choreographed to a dubbed vocal track. An *exploded* view of the genre's performance divulges the multiple artistic presences that mediate the spectacle of computer-animated film acting. Performance in the computer-animated film is co-authored, not belonging to the individual but a product of the collective. The 'performance *of* animation' (Crafton's term for the unseen work undertaken by animators) is rarely singular, but a highly complex enterprise involving a plurality of creative personnel, including directors, animators and voice artists operating within separately defined spheres of labour. Performance is a through-line traceable from the initial pencil sketch artists through to the modellers who manufacture clay sculptures and resin castings known as maquettes, before the final stage: a 3D digital, wire-frame scale model. Each phase refines and develops that which precedes it, continually recombining and transforming the character's performance.

Animators working on computer-animated films conventionally work on shots or sequences too, rather than individual characters. The assigning of shots or sets of shots (rather than specific characters) to animators means that they 'ultimately complete between 90 seconds to less than ten minutes of final footage, which is usually scattered throughout the film' (Holian 2015: 232). The industry-level division of performance among multiple 'actors' working together more obviously codes computer-animated film acting as fundamentally collaborative. During the standard production of a Pixar feature film, 'twenty to thirty animators frequently contribute incrementally to the same character throughout the course of a production' (ibid.). Yet the achievements of the animators and artists mean the conditions of production are not reflected in those of reception. The spectator never ceases to believe in the ontological consistency or unity of the performance, even as they are simultaneously made aware (often extra-textually through 'bonus' features attached to DVD releases) that each performance is the product of an accumulation of labour. It is nonetheless increasingly challenging to discuss performance in the computer-animated film in the same terms as those advanced by the recent spate of writing on acting in the cinema, which has typically sought to reaffirm the elusive skills that reclaim the cinema for human performers. If Andrew Klevan reminds us ('because we are prone to forget') that a 'living human embodies a film character' (2005: 7), then the conditions of computer-animated film acting complicates how such performances can be authored and attributed.

A more expansive and inclusive concept of performance is required to accommodate a computer-animated film genre not wholly explainable in traditional terms of 'acting'. Computer-animated films, as Prince argues, offer 'some of the most affecting performances in modern cinema' (2012: 102). But they call for fresh ways of understanding the terms of these screen performances that acknowledge how its range of actors do not 'perform' in the same way. Computer-animated films are not replete with the same kinds of 'mindful' bodies (Clayton 2010) inhabiting live-action cinema who are conscious of the recording apparatus. It is certainly a prerequisite that computer-animated films involve a cast of entirely virtual characters rather than flesh-and-blood actors (*Happy Feet*, *Wall-E*, *The LEGO Movie* and *Sausage Party* [Conrad Vernon and Greg Tiernan, 2016] are the only computer-animated films have any form of live-acton footage, amounting to a few minutes). But this shortage of human actors onscreen spotlights the unique spectrum of bodies that the genre is populated with, and those conditions under which such bodies are able to perform.

This chapter identifies the multiple points of contact and divergence between the computer-animated film and the centuries-long tradition of 'performing objects'. Implicated in Western discourses of puppet theatre and typically held distinct from cinema, performing objects have been defined by Frank Proschan (1981; 1983) as material images of humans, animals, or spirits that are created, displayed, or manipulated in narrative or dramatic performance. John Bell has since expanded Proschan's original definition of performing objects to include artefacts such as scroll paintings, peepshows, masks and narrative sculptures, alongside the various 'stuff, junk, puppets, masks, detritus, machines, bones that people use to tell stories or represent ideas' (2008: 2). These objects function as a dual site of significance and signification, inserted between the human performer and spectator who are simultaneously trained upon the object engaged in performance. Puppetry has been described as both the oldest and most developed mode of the performing object tradition. Puppet theatre is the dominant form in which agency is transferred to an inanimate, material object, coerced into a deliberate surrogate for otherwise human-centred routine.

Traditions of puppetry support a critical investigation into computer-animated film performance because they ultimately preserve, rather than undermine, the genre as a particular type of animation. Puppetry sharpens our awareness of the particular onscreen/offscreen separation that occurs in the computer-animated film between occluded performer/animator and performing object/character, exposing how the moving force and apparent agency of computer-animated bodies are determined extrinsically. This chapter argues that computer-animated film characters can be conceptualised within traditions of string puppetry and marionette performances in ways that traditional cel-animated characters and stop-motion figures cannot. Within many critical discussions of *avatars*, *synthespians* and *vactors* (a neologism of virtual and actors), the digital is often viewed as an accessory that hides or invalidates performance (Wojcik 2006). It is regarded to be a prosthesis displacing the actor as the bearer of signs, and thus remodels performance as a concern of post-production. As Sean Aita has recently claimed, 'it is this extremity of mediation – the uncoupling of physical appearance from the requirements of the casting process – that has made it difficult for commentators and critics to determine the level of actor contribution' (2012: 256–70). Such concerns have certainly precluded any great understanding of the manifold ways in which the computer-animated film expands a discussion of contemporary screen performance. But the genre accepts the puppet as a replacement for the live, lively and living human body and celebrates, rather than disguises, its virtual sites of signification within the onstage/offstage partition fundamental to its stagecraft. By extending the vocabulary of the computer-animated film to appreciate its status as a form of modern puppet entertainment, this chapter examines how the many characters populating a Luxo world are able to *act*, but that this is a function of them being *acted upon* in many compelling ways.

Computer-Animated Films as Performing Objects

From the intricate shadow puppet prologue and epilogue of *Kung Fu Panda 2* – inspired by Chinese artwork and striking for their visual complexity and sophistication – to the 'little puppet shows' within the musical number 'I've Got a Dream' from *Tangled*, computer-animated films have regularly demonstrated a vested interest in the spectacle of puppet performances. Inspired by the art of puppetry, computer-animated film narratives commonly grant spectators the intrigue of a puppet/puppeteer relationship. The 'constant pulsation' that Henryk Jurkowski (1983: 31) describes between the object in performance and the human performer has been a gift for the expressive scope given to animators as they explore the qualities of puppet/puppeteer contact. Best remembered in this spirit is *Ratatouille*, a film premised upon a playfully implausible conception of performer/puppeteer interaction. 'I'm not your puppet, and you're not my puppet-controlling guy!' exclaims human chef Linguini, as he is involuntarily orchestrated into agency by rodent Remy, who pulls on the strands of his hair just as a marionette is moved through the manipulation of its strings.

Computer-animated films regularly establish certain discrepancies between the talented and the surrogate, animator and animated, and afford the spectator opportunity to linger over the creative 'pulsation' of puppet and puppeteer in increasingly innovative ways. To protect the ant colony from a horde of villainous grasshoppers in *A Bug's Life*, the ants (under the orders of Flik) build a persuasive puppet replica that can be manoeuvred by the insects through a system of pulleys. In *How to Train Your Dragon*, protagonist Hiccup fashions a wooden and leather tail for a wounded Night Fury dragon (whom the young Viking christens Toothless). Orchestrated with his foot inside a harness, Hiccup's invention permits him to perform with the creature by using his crude contraption and, in a real-time act of puppetry, direct the dragon's movements. Puppet spectacle plays no less a significant role in the recent prehistoric Pliocene narrative of *The Croods* (Kirk DeMicco and Chris Sanders, 2013). Makeshift puppet shows are twice enacted by humans to entice the affections of the film's army of fantastical creatures. Characters perform with rod-operated creations that loosely approximate the physical look and gesticulations of those prehistoric animals the puppets are designed to beguile and entice ('I don't think our puppet looks scared enough!') (Figure 6.1). Thrusting the 'acting sticks' into the hands of primeval cavegirl Eep during one such show, caveman Guy quizzes his fellow Neanderthal over her acting credentials, asking her 'How's your acting?'.

Figure 6.1 Frame grab from *The Croods* (2013) (DreamWorks Animation Studios).
Primitive rod puppets operated by hand.

Case Study: *Toy Story 3*

Visions of the puppet in performance are especially pronounced across
the *Toy Story* films. Scenes of puppet–puppeteer interaction begin the
first *Toy Story* film and mark the climax of the third in the trilogy. Such
bracketing of the series stresses the puppet as a 'theatrical figure moved
under human control' (McPharlin in Tillis 1992: 21). During the first few
seconds of *Toy Story*, a Mr Potato Head Doll is thrust into the film frame
as the spectator becomes instantly folded into the fantasy space of childhood play. But it is the corresponding puppet scenes of *Toy Story 3* that
imbue puppet/puppeteer engagement with a greater narrative purchase.
Now leaving for college, toy owner Andy delivers his cherished childhood
playthings to an infant named Bonnie, whose shyness around adults is
replaced with an unbridled energy and animated demeanour when playing
with toys. Handing over each of his toys to their grateful new owner,
Andy cannot help but initiate an impromptu performance with objects,
and the duo soon delight in making Woody the Cowboy, Buzz Lightyear
and Mr Potato Head the centre of their own repertory theatre ('Oh no,
Dr Porkchop is attacking the haunted bakery!' 'The ghosts are getting
away!').

During the fun and frivolity, it is now Bonnie rather than Andy who
begins to orchestrate the toys' movements and perform with their bodies.
As Woody's new owner, Bonnie guides the doll's agency. This verifies
both her new relationship with the wooden toy, but also authenticates
the handover from Andy to confirm Bonnie as Woody's new puppeteer.
Most poignantly, it is Bonnie who raises Woody's arm to wave goodbye
to Andy. These passages at the climax of *Toy Story 3* are intended to

rhyme with the scenes of Andy's playtime that open the first *Toy Story* film. Not only does Andy reprise many of his signature playtime gestures, clasping Woody on his neck and bouncing him up and down, but Bonnie also repeats several of the playful actions that have visually defined Andy's puppet playtime.

At its finale, then, *Toy Story 3* climaxes the trilogy's use of a puppet–puppeteer contact to spotlight the adequacy of ownership. Bonnie's active imagination and puppet performances enforces her separation from the villainy of Sid in *Toy Story*, but also the motives of toy collector Albert 'Al' McWhiggin in *Toy Story 2*, who decides to preserve Woody in a glass cabinet, refusing to perform with the doll as a puppet. But Bonnie's lively puppet performance convinces Andy of her suitability by approving ownership through her willingness to assume the role of puppeteer. As Andy himself reveals to Bonnie as he entrusts her with his beloved Woody doll, 'somebody told me you were good with toys'. It is therefore through scenes of unbridled puppet/puppeteer interaction that *Toy Story 3* is able to mark the resolution of Andy's toy story that has been the locus for each of the three films. By extension, the implication is that Bonnie's own authored toy story is only just beginning.

The Labour of Puppetry

GRU: What are these?
AGNES: Puppets! You use them when you tell the story.
(*Despicable Me*)

Computer-animated films have continued to mount an increasingly apparent vision of performing objects. From the shadow puppetry that decorates the closing credits of *Legend of the Guardians: The Owls of Ga'Hoole* and the well-worn Ebeneezer Scrooge string puppet in *The Polar Express*, to the Mexican baroque-style carved wooden puppets that become characters in *The Book of Life*, their investment in the visual pleasures of puppet performance is one that creatively 'doubles' the kinds of interaction between animators and their digital objects. Puppetry has progressively entered into the lexicon of computer-animated film production as industry shorthand to describe the creative interrelationship between the *performer* (animator) and *performed* (character). The impression of continuity between computer-animated films and puppetry is typically founded upon the assumption that they share many of the same basic approaches. Since the earliest Pixar shorts, computer-animated films have been positioned as a successor to stop-motion animation as its 'closest living relative' (Lee 1989: 77). But the genre actually cross-pollinates stop-frame techniques with those associated with marionette theatre, and evokes the wealth of string marionettes (as well as rod or hand puppets) moved within a live performance setting. Sianne Ngai has argued that:

> The difference between characters animated in the form of marionettes pulled on strings [. . .] and characters animated by stop-motion photography seems to be a difference in their capacity to create an illusion of independence or autonomy. At a purely visual level, stop-motion characters seem less manipulated than puppets. (2005: 374)

The unique features inscribed onto virtual characters illustrates how computer-animated films rework the conditions of marionette performance. In the early phases of production, virtual human and non-human bodies are reduced to their most basic workable geometry, comprising a series of faces (known as polygons). Rotations give definition to the figure's expressional range, from shaping the mouths to widening the eyes, in tandem with the complex musculature supplemented with connective tissue, elasticity of tendons and the flexing of skin. Animators inscribe onto non-human and human figurations skeletal structures complete with a degree of anatomical coherency, and delineate appropriate head and body areas. The jointed segmentation and individual limbs of computer-animated bodies are then affixed to a series of *avars* (animation variables) through a process known as rigging. These *avars* provide particular articulation points for the animator as they remotely operate the character's armature and steer its (human or non-human) complex endoskeleton. Shrek the ogre has 180 *avars* in his face alone, while *Toy Story*'s Woody has 212 (and 712 in total across his string puppet body) (Tillis 1992: 186), including points on his eyebrow that can furrow, raise, arch, sneer and act surprised at the click of a mouse.

The *avars* on computer-animated film bodies afford greater freedom and fluency, increasing their scope of expression and smoothness of motion. The potentials of gesture, sound and choreography of rhythm – actions that qualify the character's performance – are more controllable in computer-animated films than in physically-based puppets (though more *avars* come with greater expense). The first toys and insects puppets of *Toy Story*, *Antz* and *A Bug's Life* represent something of a progression from the stiffness of early stop-motion puppet animations. This includes Vitagraph's *The Humpty Dumpty Circus* (1898), *The 'Teddy' Bears* (1907) – a re-telling of Robert Southey's *The Story of the Three Bears* made by Edwin S. Porter using stuffed toy animals – and Ladislas Starewicz's *The Cameraman's Revenge* (1912) that featured preserved grasshoppers and beetles enacting a tale of 'infidelity and retribution in the insect world' (Telotte 2010: 38). However, the DreamWorks/Aardman co-production *Flushed Away* deliberately adopts a compromise position that re-situates digital performance within the expressive freedoms of stop-motion. A team of animators at DreamWorks set out to reproduce the stop-motion plasticine aesthetic of its British-based partner studio Aardman, with a stop-motion rig transposing their 'unique performance style' (Costello 2006) onto a computer-animated world. The intention was to emulate the limited facial expressions of their moulded clay counterparts, including the monobrow, frown lines, replacement mouths and the look of pre-modelled plasticine heads as if 'sculpted with traditional modeling tools' (Costello 2006:). In *Flushed Away*, certain formal restrictions governed the expressivity of its characters to faithfully integrate clay stop-motion ('claymation') puppets efficiently with the computer-animated feature film for the first time.

The multiple *avars* controlling the movement of computer-animated characters, alongside the hinged movements and volumetrics that power the skin, muscle and flesh underneath computer-animated bodies, not only authenticate their bond to puppetry, they also hold the computer-animated films distinct from performances achieved through other animation techniques. In stop-motion animation, there are no such 'strings' governing the incremental movement of three-dimensional objects. As Richard Weihe suggests, such strings 'are invisible, indeed, non-existent. Their function is replaced by the technique of frame-by-frame animation' (in Buchan 2011: 104). By comparison, computer-animated films incorporate precisely those string *avars* traditionally absent from stop-motion processes in its methods of movement. The puppetlike distinctiveness of computer-animated films also extends to their difference from those performances achieved through traditional hand-drawn methods. Steve Tillis makes clear that the two-dimensionality of cel-animation as a 'painterly art', as well as the distinct articulation points and control mechanisms involved in the creation of movement, dislocate hand-drawn techniques from traditional puppet praxis. So whereas Tillis claimed in an earlier account of performing objects that 'animation, as such, is not really at issue with the puppet' (1992: 23), puppetry has become a more significant concern of the computer-animated film.

Practitioners have certainly been invited to reflect upon the labour of their animated work as approximating a form of computer-animated string puppetry. Pixar's proprietary 'Marionette' animation program casts computer-animators in the role of puppeteer, while the studio's earlier 'Menv' (Modelling Environment) software used to articulate character movements was renamed 'Puppets' to further inscribe the animator as puppet-master. Brian Stokes has even suggested to puppeteers sceptical of computer-animated films that now 'you'll know they are made up of virtual objects arranged in a hierarchy much like your marionette' (2003: 22–3). The perspective that computer-animated films are a puppet progeny of marionette theatre has often been alluded to within the films themselves. In fact, computer-animated films often support their narrative investments into the creative interrelationship between puppet and puppeteer with passages informed by the disclosure of the workings of their computer-animated puppets.

In *Robots*, the chaotic gesticulations of Bigweld Industries' gatekeeper Tim evoke a Punch and Judy hand puppet show. Another character, antagonist Phineas T. Ratchet's father Bob, is suspended by looping chains from the ceiling of Madame Ratchet's Chop Shop, visually aligning his performance with traditions of string-marionette theatre. But *Robots* also unveils the nuts and bolts of puppet production during its opening sequence, by focusing on the arrival of newborn android Rodney Copperbottom. Rodney is boxed and delivered in his constituent parts, and then assembled with ratchets, rivets and screws in this unique (re) vision of childbirth. Despite the exhausting twelve-hour 'labour', Mrs Copperbottom exclaims with emphatic glee that 'Making the baby is the fun part'. Reversing the Pinocchio narrative, *Astro Boy* (loosely based on Osamu Tezuka's *manga* and *anime* series) also makes a spectacle out of artificial automatons and their creation (another computer-animated film *Pinocchio 3000* [Daniel Robichaud, 2004] is a similar futuristic retelling of Carlo Collodi's novel *The Adventures of Pinocchio* [1883]). In *Astro Boy*, shots linger over the complex circuitry that comprises the skeletal framework of Toby, an uncanny robot facsimile produced by grieving robotocist Dr Bill Tenna to replace his deceased son ('it looks just like him, doesn't it? A perfect replica').

Computer-animated film puppets typically offer a greater economy of production and faster workflow than in stop-motion, with build pipelines that allow 'CG puppets to be quickly put together' (Costello 2006). But the intrigue of puppet labour and the manufacturing of its 'workable geometry' continues to loom large over the genre, especially in scenes that function as a surrogate for the kinds of interaction between animators and their performing objects. The renovation of Woody at the hands of toy restorer Geri in *Toy Story 2* and the opening sequence of *9* both call upon the attentive craftsmanship and dexterity of the 'hand of the artist' (Crafton 1979) to spotlight the artistry of puppet manufacture. If the restoration of Woody hinges upon the frailty of the cowboy doll's jointed segmentation and the weakness of his articulation points, then *9* champions its cast of 'puppet people' (to use *9* animator Matthew Teevan's term [2011: 86]) as altogether more durable. The untimely death of their human animator, following his completion of the final knitted doll in *9*, charges each creation with a greater resilience that belies their fragile armature and delicate multipart skeletons. Each of these sequences, then, nuances the perspective of the computer-animated film as an elaborate puppet show that entrances its audiences through similar presentational modes. This is a genre that achieves its performances through a multitude of expressive and impressive puppets, each one submitted to the human hands of the animator in dramatic performance to, in the words of *Despicable Me*'s Agnes, 'tell the story'.

The unique qualities of computer-animated film production further align with features of puppet theatre. Karen Prell, an ex-puppet animator with sixteen years' experience at the Jim Henson Company, was recruited by Pixar founder Ed Catmull during the late 1990s at a time 'when computer animation started replacing film and television puppetry' (Prell 2012). Catmull was 'intrigued by her [Prell's] puppet acting experience', and the performance skills she had honed in real-time puppetry on *Sesame Street*, the final season of *The Muppet Show* (1976–81) and *Fraggle Rock* (1983–7). The migration of Prell to computer-animated filmmaking suggests a potential correlation between the virtual manipulations of three-dimensional digital puppets moved 'live', and the rod (and hand) operation of Jim Henson's celebrated 'muppet' creations (see Shershow 1995). Describing the fourteen shots she animated on *Geri's Game* (Jan Pinkava, 1997), Prell reveals that 'It was so much fun getting into Geri. [. . .] If you think of him as a 3D puppet, he's so amazingly expressive' (in Robertson 1998: 28). The orchestration of computer-animated puppets and their limbs in this way re-inscribes a computer-animated film world as an alternate kind of live performance setting in which figures are 'worked' within a three-dimensional (rather than scenic) screen space.

Each puppet action is also instantly recorded at the precise moment that it is cued. DreamWorks animator Marek Kochout explains that 'Instead of taking an actual image on a camera, the computer is recording it, so then you can play it back at speed and it moves' (in Johnston 2011). Keyframe animation systems interpolate intervening frames between those set manually by the animator. Generated by the software, these interim or intermediate movements supplement the parameters already inputted to produce continuous bodily movement (deformation, positioning, orientation), and complete any given action. The continuously recording, but also creating, computer involved in the production of computer-animated films permits a fluent integration of character movement, rather than the incremental separation of postures and poses in stop-motion frame-by-frame (and the individual drawings of cel-animation). The technology replaces the linearity of these processes by allowing animators to return to tweak individual frames, responding to the action in real time in a continuous feedback loop with the animator to create a particular 'liveness' to the performance. In computer-animated films, the technology is therefore able to record movement. With stop-motion, it merely creates its illusion.

Case Study: *Toy Story 2*

More than any computer-animated film, *Toy Story 2* draws attention to the specificity of the computer-animated film's puppet performances, bringing into relief their status as a form of modern puppet entertainment. Learning his buried history as a popular culture icon, Woody the Cowboy stares captivated at his own string-puppet performance in 'Woody's Roundup', a Western adventure series enacted with 'wooden' marionettes in the style of *Howdy Doody* (1947–60) and Gerry Anderson's thirty-nine-episode Supermarionation series *Four Feather Falls* (1960). Each episode of 'Woody's Roundup' (until its unforeseen cancellation) is an allusion to an outmoded media form marked by visual cues that connote a sense of the 'vintage'. But the fictional puppet history of Woody in 'Woody's Roundup' gestures towards the character's reality as a computer-animated film performer, and the conditions under which his puppet performance is recorded for spectators' pleasure. Rather than an elaborate self-portrait, 'Woody's Roundup' functions as an intrusive X-ray, exposing the cowboy doll's unique puppet origins (just as the toy advertisement in *Toy Story* precipitates Buzz Lightyear's existential crisis of identity). The black-and-white tint of the television – on which the grainy VHS is displayed – even evokes the X-ray's radiographic and radiological power, irradiating the shots of Woody and 'diagnosing' the truthfulness of his puppet biology (Figure 6.2).

'Woody's Roundup' makes visible the marionette strings that govern Woody's rickety, saccadic movements and the jerky agitations that contrast to the fluidity with which he otherwise moves. It also spotlights the pivoted movement and sectioned body of the cowboy doll, including his every notch and worn imperfection, as he dances through the flimsy, two-dimensional painted backdrops. Jerome Christensen has queried the connection between the film's multiple Woodys, dismissing the television edition by refusing to acknowledge it as an 'earlier version of a self that had evolved, metamorphosed, or somehow acquired a personality' (2012: 336).

Figure 6.2 Frame grab from *Toy Story 2* (1999) (Pixar Animation Studios).
'Woody's Roundup' discloses the truthfulness of the cowboy doll's puppet biology.

This distinction holds because of the separation that Christensen enforces between 'Woody the puppet and Woody the toy' (ibid.: 332). Animated by Prell's husband and ex-'muppeteer' Mike Quinn, 'Woody's Roundup' is not a false memory but a revelatory video representation of the puppet spectacle of computer-animated films, including the duality of obstruction and exposure that governs the agency of its puppet characters. Both 'Woody's Roundup' and *Toy Story 2* recuperate Woody into a recorded marionette theatre. The cowboy doll gazing transfixed is no less a 'filmed' puppet-in-performance than the one he glimpses on the television screen. When the watching Woody then starts to re-enact the movements and gestures from his 'Woody's Roundup' performance, the two sets of marionette strings become irrevocably, yet fascinatingly, tangled.

Motion Capture and Marionettes

Reviewing puppet history and praxis offers an insight into the computer-animated film as a new kind of puppet performance space, whilst enabling a more flexible and expansive (re)definition of what has traditionally been understood as digital puppetry. Recent critical investigations situating computer-generated imagery as an annexe to the performing objects tradition have tended to afford generality to motion-capture as the dominant mode of 'cyber' or 'virtual' puppetry. As a technique that conventionally transcribes human activity and movement (bodily, facial) through motion sensors (physical *avars*) that are relayed via computer software, motion-capture maintains the human body as the primary control mechanism. In fact, as Barry King asserts, it 'grips it like an ever-tightening glove' (2012: 278). The technology manifests the labour of animated performance through a real-time correspondence between contribution and animation, without any pause or lag. Within the context of the computer-animated film, motion-capture has been used sparingly rather than exhaustively. *The Polar Express, Monster House, Happy Feet, Beowulf, A Christmas Carol, Mars Needs Moms, The Adventures of Tintin: The Secret of the Unicorn, Happy Feet Two* and the German action-adventure *Tarzan* (Reinhard Klooss, 2013) are the only computer-animated films (to date) to have embraced the performance possibilities of the technology. The disclaimer contained within the credits to *Ratatouille* (declaring motion-capture to be a 'performance shortcut') reflects unease about the way the technology has been aligned with traditions of animated acting (see Furniss 2000; Freedman 2012). Pixar's announcement that *Ratatouille* is '100% Genuine Animation' indicates how motion-capture has been uncoupled from its possible animation lineage despite its contiguities with the Rotoscope process.

Motion-capture is likewise a technique that is not indigenous to the computer-animated film. It has a sustained screen life in live-action/computer-generated composites, conventionally aligned with the high production values and visual spectacle of Blockbuster fantasy and action cinema. Popular discourse and industry publicity have also contributed to motion-capture's *myth of authorship* in which there is a perfect accord between actor and animated performance. Describing the motion-capture performance of Anthony Hopkins in *Beowulf*, Animation Supervisor Kenn McDonald recognises how a single motion-capture actor can help 'drive the performance, [and] the twitches he [Hopkins] used to create his character will be consistent throughout' (in Wolff 2007). In truth, however, there is little requirement for the performer and resultant performance to align exactly, and many computer-animated films using motion-capture have eschewed the consistency afforded by a single actor. For *Mars Needs Moms*, actor Seth Green provided the motion-capture movements and voice for nine-year-old protagonist Milo, only for his vocal performance to be replaced by child actor Seth Dusky during the film's post-production. Actor Gary Oldman (motion-capture) and child actor Ryan Ochoa (voice) also contributed to the composited performance of Tiny Tim in *A Christmas Carol*. Practices such as these align motion-capture with other types of animated acting in which multiple actors combine to create one animated performance. The technology can also be placed in conversation with cinema's wider tradition of dummies, doubles and stand-ins that have meant different bodies, rather than just one actor, can be used for the same character. The performing objects of computer-animated films therefore expands a discussion of puppetry beyond those (exceptional) films that use motion-capture technology. Puppetry becomes an altogether more inclusive category that identifies the particular methods by which their many performances can be both achieved and appreciated.

Puppetry is also a primary site of animated specificity or animatedness, further implicated within the dynamic cinematic geography of computer-animated films and the heightened vigour and vitality of their worlds. This is because animatedness has been understood as an excess or surplus of animation, one that typically manifests in an 'exaggerated performative character', and a certain quality that 'separates the automaton from the autonomous, the regulated from the resistant' (Bukatman 2012: 21). These same features of uncontainable energy have been conceptualised according to their degrees of association with the movements of a puppet. For Ngai, animatedness is not just rampant vitality or positive wilfulness, but an 'exaggerated responsiveness to the language of others that turns the subject into a spasmodic puppet' (2005: 21). To be animated is, therefore, to submit to a defenceless state as if controlled by an invisible other: erratic and unbridled activity seemingly the product of a hidden puppet master whose manipulations enforce the subject's separation from the inanimate.

The 'puppetlike' connotations of animatedness envisaged by Ngai – relating to an oversupply of energy and the visible manifestation of 'high spiritedness' or unrestrained force – certainly evoke the etymological origins of 'motion' as the sixteenth-century English word for 'puppet show' (used to occasionally denote the term puppet) (Gross 2011: 66). Animatedness also indicates how the specificity of performance in the computer-animated film contributes to the agency and arresting activity of its Luxo worlds. Their puppet performances enmesh one idea of animatedness (those specificities or qualities holding computer-animated films distinct) together with animatedness as heightened expressiveness and excess vigour. The puppet is therefore not just part of what individuates the performative illusion of computer-animated films (the juxtaposition of the puppet and the hidden activity of an operator), it also suggests something about why such lively and 'animated' acting is so appealing in the computer-animated film. These puppet performances create a fluctuating urgency that enlivens the virtual space by making it seem receptive to invisible control. Part of the attraction and desirability of computer-animated films lies in their democratic treatment of performance. Their visual field always appears available and hospitable to the arrival of new enlivened puppets. Spectators are routinely made witness to a range of (soon-to-be anthropomorphic) objects on the cusp of unexpected 'spasmodic' activity.

To call upon Aura Satz and Jon Wood's term for the endowment of 'a curious, [and] at times uncategorisable collection of things with the capacity for voice, speech or expression', a computer-animated film is replete with any number of 'articulate objects' (2009: 15). But there presides an instability to performance, even a rejection of acting, which contributes to the computer-animated film's allure. As the previous chapter argued, not every object is necessarily primed for agency. The inanimate plastic dolls in *Flushed Away*, for example, deprive rodent protagonist Roddy of his desired companionship. Reversing the *Toy Story* narrative, the dolls' moulded and immobile expressions are a counterpoint to Roddy's range of facial features and heightened expressiveness that confirms his computer-animated ancestry. Just as Wall-E trawls the earth's surface for keepsakes (discarding some, keeping others), animators source the terrain of a Luxo world to find and decide upon its 'articulate objects', and coerce them into a screen performance. The computer-animated film thus has many points of 'articulation' readymade as potentially 'spasmodic'. Reflecting the puppetlike disposition of its inhabitants, the computer-animated film and its worlds fascinate through its many moving parts.

Puppetry's peculiar fascination is further rooted in the spectators' simultaneous processing of the illusion and mechanics of that illusion, the outward sign and its inner workings. Negative reactions towards the puppet typically call upon a vocabulary drawn from the uncanny and grotesque, which describes its 'fundamental strangeness' (Gross 2011: 4–5). As Tillis identifies, the puppet occupies a place 'within the margin of doubt' (1992: 65), and he has described the effect of the puppet's 'double vision', arguing that 'the puppet invariably exposes the presence of the operator behind it, even if it occludes that presence by taking focus as the site of the operator's performance' (1996: 115). This chapter argues that it is the perceptual challenges posed by the performed puppet, and the recognition of its paradoxical modality as both manipulated object and autonomous character, which are a principle pleasure of computer-animated film performance. Multi-faceted characters are enacted through a specific set of utterances, impulses and gestures that support emotional investment and elicit sympathy. The spectator thus remains conscious that any acting by digital puppets involves the work of an animator. In this way, the puppet cannot help but implicate the puppeteer. Without them, puppets are dead matter. For the puppet to act it must *enact* the animators' contribution and make visible the traces of their effort and exertion. As a popular form of digitally mediated acting, then, performance in the computer-animated film is not undermined by the visible absence of the film actor, but rather enlivened by the particular terms of their occlusion.

CHAPTER 7

Monsters, Synch:
A Taxonomy of the Star Voice

The ascription of speech as a dynamic sound form to the computer-animated film's performers foremost constitutes these puppets as articulate and enlivened subjects. Performance across computer-animated films is certainly more than the vocal element, and many have been praised for their abilities to rehearse and recall the virtues of silent film acting (Hooks 2012). Several characters act in a measured fashion, personified by a screen performance keyed through mute responsiveness. But others are defined entirely through their proclivity for verbal communication, falling victim to speech as a signifier of their character. The presence and expressive power of the voice typically gives computer-animated films one of its most distinct performative stamps, and their linguistic richness is supported by a range of characters that protest, splutter, complain and argue as they become impassioned and animated agents granted sudden verbal excess. Framed by recent critical writing on the eloquence and impact of the voice in cinema, this chapter argues that computer-animated films provide the ideal place to (re)discover and examine the voice as an expressive technique within the armoury of animation's performance rhetoric.

The voice is a necessarily concentrated instrument of performance within the practicalities of computer-animated film production. It is typically the actor's only contribution and the sole evidence of their participation (though this is less true in the case of motion-capture technology). While recording sessions are commonly taped and played back for the animators' visual reference, the vocal performance 'has to work independent of body language and facial expression' (Paik 2007: 174). Karen Paik describes the numerous demands placed on an actor who 'must be "on" for hours, doing take after take without the benefits of sets, costumes, or even other actors' (ibid.). The computer-animated film voice is also a stream of recorded speech purified inside an aurally deadened studio, delivered and archived with a degree of sonic sterility. These are voices 'unencumbered by the extraneous and uncontrollable noise ("dirt") of live-action film production' (Macallan and Plain 2010: 245). The computer-animated voice is a clean voice, distilled from audible contamination and conducive to audio-mixing techniques such as 'panning' that spreads the sound signal into a multi-channel sound field. Helen Macallan and Andrew Plain suggest that the fundamental gluing of voice to body in computer-animated voice acting may mean that 'voice panning will be increasingly identified as a defining characteristic of animation' (ibid.).

Certain developments in sound recording technologies and equipment have also proven especially valuable for the practicalities of animated voice-work, including portable recording devices and sound samplers. Compression on digital sound files and their complex layering has also alleviated logistical issues of negotiating complementary schedules between vocal performers, which necessitate that separate streams of vocal audio are seamlessly edited together. It is this clarity of sound recording, quality of mixing technologies and increased storage capabilities in the production of star sound that has enabled American actor Paul Newman to appear retrospectively in *Cars 3*. Newman's vocal performance as Doc Hudson – achieved via unused audio recordings of the actor during the production of *Cars* – provides a sonic equivalent to what Lisa Bode has termed 'posthumous performance', which conventionally relies on digital recombination and technological mediation to resurrect a screen performance 'after the originators are long dead' (2010: 66).

Since the emergence of the computer-animated film, Claude Brodesser and Ben Fritz have proposed a three-tier system that structures the majority of its voice work. They argue contemporary animation studios are bound by the desire to '1) get superstars; 2) get recognisable names; 3) get an unknown' (2005: 1, 68). This chapter is concerned with the dominant categories of 'superstars' and 'recognisable names', and the ways in which the star voice functions as an integral performance element within the construction of acting in the computer-animated film. Their narratives are unable to draw on aspects of stardom generally located in the photogenic organisation of familiar human physiognomy, and so instead rely upon the phonogenic aspects of an identifiable star voice. For Philip Drake, the immediate familiarity that a spectator has with a star's iconic voice identifies such performers as ideal candidates for animated voiceover. He argues that 'the voice of the star is a potent sign in the idiolect in that it is often read, like the body, as the site of "presence"' (2004: 75). The expressive materiality of the star voice and its audio 'visibility' are certainly conducive to the looseness and fundamental separation between sound and image in computer-animated film voicework. Stars are mediated figures, and their voices operate disjunctively 'as something detachable from the star's personality' (Bordwell et al. 1988: 73). Held independent from the body, the star voice is a potent performance sign with the ability to embody the appeal and attraction of a star, manifesting their stardom in vocal form.

Within film production in Hollywood, the star's voice is central part of their capital. The recognisable properties of a star voice are therefore ideally suited to computer-animated films in which the voice itself, as William Whittington suggests, functions as a 'kind of special effect [. . .] much like the image-sound relations found in puppetry' (2012: 383). The star throws their voice through the technologically-mediated act of ventriloquism into these computer-animated puppets, who momentarily borrow it on loan. Such is the potency of star speech that it works against the concealment of the dubbing process that is fundamental to the vocal performances across the genre, and is accepted by spectators rather than rejected (unlike spectators' responses to the poor synchronisation of sound in live-action cinema). But the potency of the star voice is problematised by the manifold post-production dubbing practices involved in the construction of computer-animated film speech.

Polyglot Performance and Accented Animation

Computer-animated films can be understood as multiple language versions, with their many characters polyglots for the countless languages they can (be made to) speak. Many computer-animated films produced by animation studios in the US and UK have been successfully re-dubbed for re-release abroad, either to replace or coexist with an English-language or subtitled edition. Particular institutional infrastructures support these global dubbing practices, unsurprising given that 'dubbing is the primary mode of audiovisual translation' within the internationalising of animation (Montgomery 2017: 85). For example, Disney Character Voices International is a subsidiary of the Disney Corporation specifically responsible for the international translation and dubbing of its animated feature films. *Frozen* was dubbed into forty-one different languages, while *Moana* was the very first Disney feature film to be dubbed by the division into Tahitian.

The desire to attract more localised audiences through voice acting has additionally led to 'tailored' versions of computer-animated films, which emphasise national specificity and highlight the lucrative role played by the wider industry of dubbing. The character of receptionist Loretta Geargrinder in *Robots* was re-cast as actress Natasha Lyonne (US), television presenter Cat Deeley (UK) and radio host Jackie O (Australia) in line with the specifc country of release (television writer Lowell Ganz's performance as Mr Gasket was also re-dubbed by radio broadcaster Terry Wogan for the UK theatrical run). In *Cars 2*, the role of retired racing car Jeff Gorvette was also re-dubbed, with different regional drivers cast for the film's international exhibition (Jeff Gordon in the US and UK; Fernando Alonso in Spain; Sebastian Vettel in Germany; Jan Nilsson in Sweden; Vitaly Petrov in Russia). The character of Harv, Lightning McQueen's agent in the original *Cars* film, was likewise switched from American actor Jeremy Piven to UK television personality Jeremy Clarkson for the British version. UK television stars Fiona Phillips (*Shark Tale*) and Jamie Oliver (*Ratatouille*) were similarly replacement casting for UK re-dubs of American features, while international footballers Manuel Neuer and Antoine Griezman performed in the German and French-language versions of *Monsters University* (as 'Frightening' Frank McCay) and *The LEGO Batman Movie* (as Superman, replacing Hollywood actor Channing Tatum) respectively.

In 2013, *The Hollywood Reporter* noted that 'A typical animated tent-pole is dubbed for 39 to 40 territories' compared with 'a more typical live-action movie [that] usually is dubbed into 12 to 15 languages' (Siegel et al. 2013). As animation that speaks in tongues, many computer-animated films produced outside North America have, in the reverse process, been re-dubbed with high-profile Hollywood stars to replace the original voice cast who may otherwise be unknown outside of their country of origin. *Dragons: Destiny of Fire* (Eduardo Schuldt, 1997), originally in Japanese Peru; *Kaena: The Prophecy*, *Dragon Hunters* and *Asterix: The Mansions of the Gods* (Alexandre Astier and Louis Clichy, 2014) in France; *Boo, Zino & the Snurks* (Lenard Fritz Krawinkel and Holger Tappe, 2004) and *Animals United* in Germany; *Midsummer Dream* (Ángel de la Cruz and Manolo Gómez 2005), *Tad: The Lost Explorer* and *Spirit of the Forest* in Spain; *Free Jimmy* (Christopher Nielsen, 2006) in Norway; *A Fox's Tale* in Hungary; *Dino Time* (Yoon-suk Choi and John Kafka, 2012) and *Red Shoes and The 7 Dwarfs* (Sung Ho Hong, 2017) in South Korea; *Plumíferos* (Daniel De Felippo and Gustavo Giannini, 2014) in Argentina; and *Delhi Safari* (Nikhil Advani, 2012) in India are just some of the computer-animated films that have all obtained an English dub as part of their North American release. In the unprecedented case of *Kung Fu Panda 3*, the film was actually produced in two languages simultaneously, with 'characters' mouths and body language [. . .] animated twice to match the nuances of both [English and Mandarin]' (Brzeski 2016). Within this international distribution of contemporary Hollywood animation, computer-animated films provide strong multilingual narratives that fully embrace linguistic difference. The linguistic analogy of 'accented cinema' invoked by Hamid

Naficy to explain transnational migratory, exilic and diasporic cinema (including the 'deterritorialized conditions of the filmmakers' [2001: 4]) seems particularly appropriate to an 'accented' computer-animated film genre that is sonically formed across the interstices of diverse cinematic practices and national borders.

The dubbing process is certainly more feasible and accepted in animation as a medium than it is in live-action cinema. Within the specificities of animation as a particular kind of sound cinema, the animated voice is itself a dubbed voice and lip-synching becomes 'as much of an issue in the original as it is in the translated version' (Ferrari 2010: 45). But the intricate network of re-voicing practices can bring into disrepute the star's vocal input. Jeff Ulin contests that 'when Tom Hanks does not play the part [of Woody in *Toy Story*] in the German version, nor Eddie Murphy [as the Donkey in *Shrek*] then those actors do truly do not ever appear in the film' (2010: 157). Local industrial practices have, however, managed to maintain star consistency. Hollywood stars have their voices replaced by specialised dubbing artists who, over time, become the specific 'foreign voice' of that star. Anne Karpf suggests that this process strives to 'preserve a sense of "authenticity" in the voice', while in some transnational cases the dubbed star voice can become 'more authentic than the actor's own' (2006: 251).

Beyond compromising the potency of star voicework, a second issue raised by star voice dubbing in the computer-animated film is the value of impersonation and imitation. During the automated dialogue replacement (ADR) and looping processes that are used to obtain a more intelligible and stable sound, an accepted element of the star's working responsibility is that they 'will do some dubbing or post-synchronisation of the voice during sound re-recording' (McDonald 2000: 9). Yet certain bilingual stars can also utilise their vocal talents to essentially re-dub their own star voice for a film's release abroad. Spanish actor Antonio Banderas re-voiced his eponymous role in *Puss in Boots* (Chris Miller, 2011) in five separate languages (English, Italian, Latin American Spanish, Castilian Spanish and Catalan) (Siegel et al. 2013). For *The Book of Life*, Mexican actor Diego Luna voiced protagonist Manolo Sanchez for the North American release of the film, just as he had done in the Spanish re-dub. In *Zootopia*, popstar Shakira dubbed Gazelle in both the English-language and Spanish releases.

Yet the specific phonological features and recognisable enunciation of the star voice mean that it can be accurately impersonated by sound doubles when the original star is unavailable. Vocal mimicry of this kind has proven a particular feature of the computer-animated film's transmedia flow, in which star sound is multiplied across a range of consumer products. Star voice impersonations remain particularly rife in video game spin-offs, though they become more of a necessary requirement where the original star voice actor passes away between computer-animated film sequels. Examples include Blake Clark replacing Jim Varney as Slinky Dog in *Toy Story 3* and Lloyd Sherr replacing George Carlin as Fillmore for *Cars 2* and *Cars 3*. The vocal bifurcation of the star voice through sound doubles is a (frequently necessary) practice that reflects a desire by studios to preserve the vocal continuity of a computer-animated character who spectators expect to speak in a certain 'star' way.

It is, however, more commonplace for stars to reprise vocal roles for feature-length computer-animated film sequels, and the attraction of the multi-part computer-animated film franchise is often the return of the primary ensemble star cast in the latest instalment. There are a few exceptions, including the replacement casts for low-quality, direct-to-video sequels (*Open Season 2* [Matthew O'Callaghan and Todd Wilderman, 2008], *Happily N'Ever After 2: Snow White Another Bite @ the Apple* [Steven E. Gordon and Boyd Kirkland, 2009] and *Surf's Up 2: Wavemania* [Henry Yu, 2017]). But computer-animated film sequels traditionally use the star voice as the repeating constant within the sequel's own agenda of repetition, reiteration, return and renewal. The voice of a star is a connective between films that manifests both the star actor's popularity, but also evidences their capital as a useable and re-usable Hollywood commodity. Stars are more likely to be replaced for subsequent television series adaptations due to the lower budgets afforded to small-screen programming, though it is not unprecedented for the original voice actors to perform in both (in the case of 'themed' television specials such as *Scared Shrekless* [Gary Trousdale and Raman Hui, 2010], *Toy Story of Terror!* [Angus MacLane, 2013], *Toy Story That Time Forgot* [Steve Purcell, 2014] and *Olaf's Frozen Adventure* [Kevin Deters and Stevie Wermers, 2017]). Produced by Disney Television Animation, the recent *Big Hero 6: The Series* (2017–) also marks the return of the original feature film's main voice cast.

The many screen bodies assigned to the star voice across computer-animated films is often (but not always) a non-human and always (though not often) one whose performance can be distinguished in relation to the persona or iconography of the star. The aim of this chapter is to unpack the fluctuating levels of correspondence between the star voice and the animated image to illustrate the voice within the creative puppeteer/ puppet relationship. Proschan asserts that 'puppets, of course, cannot speak for themselves' (1981: 528), and the coexistent presence of the vocal performer alongside the animator completes the screen performance. But it is not just the vocal performer who must 'actualise' character qualities through vocal inflection. Involved in the transference of the true star origin of words into new animated bodies, animators and a multitude of creative personnel 'actualise' the star voice into variable pitches of emphasis, dialling up the star's involvement to a range of disparate volumes through schemes of performance. In the computer-animated film, there are ultimately many processes of ventriloquism in operation. The animators, in collaboration with the star performer, speak in compelling unison. The porosity of the audio and visual allows star speech to be textually cued in ways that contribute to the liveliness of the performance. The impact of the star voice in the computer-animated film is, as this chapter argues, dramatically achieved through (and derived from) the creative ventriloquism of its delivery.

The Problem of Star Sound

The abundance of star sound across computer-animated films has been attributed to two particular milestones within animation's very recent history: Robin Williams's energetic delivery and heavily improvised vocal performance as the Genie in *Aladdin*, and the 'revolving door' (Gray 2006: 84) of celebrity guest voice actors in *The Simpsons* (Matt Groening, 1989–) But the 'starry-eyed' (Bevilacqua 1999) leaning towards star voices that defined the US animation industry in the 1990s was rapidly intensified by the advent of the computer-animated film. Starr A. Marcello contends that animation of the 1960s and 1970s was 'much less interested in the use of major movie stars than it is today' (2006: 63). Computer-animated films continually attract a host of Hollywood stars and high-profile performers, making (the presence of) a star voice into a particular requirement for contemporary animated cinema.

Among the top eight most commercially successful stars of North American cinema during the 1990s – Tom Hanks, Jim Carrey, Tom Cruise, Mel Gibson, Harrison Ford, Mike Myers, Will Smith and Bruce Willis – five have performed in computer-animated film voiceover, often doing so more than once (including multiple roles in a single film) (McDonald 2000: 103-4).[1] Among the following decade's most successful box office performers, almost half the top ten had provided the voices for computer-animated characters: Samuel L. Jackson (*The Incredibles*), Hugo Weaving (*Legend of the Guardians: The Owls of Ga'Hoole*), Owen Wilson (*Cars*) and Ian McKellen (*The Magic Roundabout*). As of 2016, eight out of the top twenty highest grossing film stars of the year at the US domestic box office had voiced computer-animated film characters – Kevin Hart (*The Secret Life of Pets* and *Captain Underpants: The First Epic Movie*), Matt Damon (*Happy Feet Two*), Chris Evans (*TMNT* [Kevin Munroe, 2007] and *Battle for Terra*), Chris Pratt (*The LEGO Movie*), Dwayne Johnson (*Planet 51* and *Moana*), Benedict Cumberbatch (*Penguins of Madagascar*), Emily Blunt (*Gnomeo & Juliet*) and Channing Tatum (*The LEGO Movie*, *The Book of Life* and *The LEGO Batman Movie*) – thereby highlighting the significance of computer-animated voiceover within a star's body of work.

Many of the current discourses surrounding star voice acting outline the detrimental impact of 'celebrity voice actors' (ibid.: 63) and the profitable business of animated voice work. When combined with the revenue generated by excessive merchandise, tie-ins and the requisite multi-film franchise, voice acting can offer a cost-effective return for a vocal performer who may be 'on set' only occasionally (albeit in recording sessions that can extend over a period of several years). Depp's voice work on *Rango*, for example, was completed in a tight twenty-day window, while Woody Allen recorded all his dialogue for *Antz* in only five. The abridged schedule suggests voice acting is an ancillary, extra-textual endeavour undertaken by stars between more demanding live-action roles.[2]

The perceived authority of the star within computer-animated film voicework is also made culpable for clouding the merits of the trained voiceover artist, and taking work 'away from the core group of voice actors' (Bevilacqua 1999). Despite such widespread resistance towards star voices radiating from the specialised voice-acting community in America, the involvement of stars in computer-animated films has ultimately dissolved much of the stigma typically attached to animation voice-work. Experienced voiceover artist Billy West admits 'years ago, celebrities wouldn't bother with cartoons; they'd look down their nose at them. But since they crashed the party here, nobody looks down their nose at it' (in Godfrey 2011). There is also increasing evidence that the star voice in computer-animated films is challenging the Hollywood film industry's history of overlooking voice-acting as a creative discipline, which has been generally perceived as 'somehow a lesser form of acting' (Wojcik 2006: 71). In particular, Depp's performance in *Rango* renewed the debate as to whether the Academy of Motion Picture Arts and Sciences should introduce its own award for animated voiceover. In April 2011, the *Voice Over Times* started an online petition for the Oscars to originate a Best Voiceover Performance category, the objective of which was to 'achieve a measure of recognition for voice actors that is on-par to on-camera actors' (Parkin 2011).

The computer-animated film's commitment to the star's vocal presence, alongside their ability to attract established performers willing to enter the voiceover business, typically remains the reserve of popular discourse. Only recently have scholars such as Rayna Denison (2008; 2017), Rebecca Asherie (2012) and Colleen Montgomery (2016; 2017) begun to unpack the 'dense network of meanings' that surrounds star voice acting, as well as other types of voice and vocal performance that appear within computer-animated features (Holliday 2012). Vocal performances by stars can be sealed off from its other sounds, and more closely intertwined with aspects of computer-animated film performance. To identify how the star voice is made to creatively coalesce with the animated image, this chapter turns to the work of sound film theorist Michel Chion.

Chion has discussed the auditory and visual aspects of film in terms of an illusory 'audiovisual contract' operating between sight and sound. This 'contract' is crafted around what he terms 'added value', in which screen images can assume certain 'phrasings' according to how they are enriched and contextualised by a film's carefully chosen soundscape (1994: 5). Such 'added value' is especially operational in the area of synchresis. A neologism produced out of the combination of 'synchronism' and 'synthesis', synchresis is defined by Chion as 'the spontaneous and irresistible weld produced between a particular auditory phenomenon and visual phenomenon when they occur at the same time' (1994: 63). From the 'monstrous yet inevitable' agglomerations which emerge from discontinuous image/sounds in experimental film, to the rousing non-diegetic orchestral music of Hollywood blockbusters, synchresis refers to the spectators' mental fusion (and acceptance) of sound and image as compatible when they accompany each other onscreen.

Chion's work on synchresis is particularly valuable to the study of the star voice in the computer-animated film, given that the concept of 'added value' is a fundamental act of ventriloquism. The 'phrasing' of an image by sound is a ventriloquial act that structures vision by 'rigorously framing it' (ibid: 7). It suggests possession of a puppet by ventriloquist's speech so that it may seem to speak for itself. But synchresis is by definition a phenomenon of cinema that occurs in reception. It is a 'reflex psychological phenomenon that depends on our nervous and muscular connections' (Chion 2000: 205). Computer-animated films fully exploit the spontaneous coupling of sound and visual events, and the attribution of concomitance that spectators do as a psychological matter of course. Chion argues that synchresis is 'not totally automatic' but also 'a function of meaning'. In the computer-animated film, synchresis is a product of the finely tuned textual organisation of sound and image, the specific 'phrasing' of which emerges from the particularities of their mutual reinforcement.

This chapter argues that the three categories of *anthropomorphic*, *autobiographic* and *acousmatic* synchresis frame the computer-animated film's dominant 'synchretic' unions, and reflect the manifestation of the audible momentarily colliding with the visible through nuances of performance. Each category implicates the use of the star voice in what Roland Barthes has called 'fascinated listening'. While 'hearing' is simply a physiological phenomenon, Barthes suggests that 'listening' involves a more alert (and psychological) activity and the attentive 'deciphering' of that who is speaking (1985: 245). Such categories relate to the degrees of attachment that the star vocal track has with the performance (and design) of the puppet speaker. The terms anthropomorphic, autobiographic and acousmatic synchresis thus revise the tensions between star image and screen performance that Richard Dyer (1979) outlined as 'selective use', 'perfect fit' and 'problematic fit'. The computer-animated film genre exploits those elements comprising the 'structured polysemy of the star image' (ibid.: 3) for the expressive and performative possibilities of the computer-animated image. This chapter contends that the star voice is a much more active ingredient in the construction of performance than has hitherto been identified, and that a greater interrogation of the voice critically engages with the charges brought against star voice casting in the computer-animated film.

Anthropomorphic Synchresis

The dramatic impact of anthropomorphic synchresis derives from the star voice's synchrony with a mutated (and non-human) visage or bodily form. The spectator's blindness to the vocal source is tempered by the maintenance of the star's primary physical features, skilled vocation, or elements of their persona, albeit playfully channelled through the genre's anthropomorphic register. Anthropomorphic synchresis balances the morphē with an ánthrōpos or humanity that is closely tied to the star's extra-filmic identity. It is a category of representation that rewards the spectators' disentanglement of the specific qualities of the star image from the anthropomorphic character that performs in a fictional computer-animated film world.

The performance of Puss in Boots, Z in *Antz* and Finn McMissile in *Cars 2* all revisit the prior screen roles of each character's voice performer (Antonio Banderas, Woody Allen, and Michael Caine respectively). The eponymous character of Puss in Boots is deliberately evocative of Banderas's role in the live-action *The Mask of Zorro* (Martin Campbell, 1998) and its sequel *The Legend of Zorro* (Martin Campbell, 2005); *Antz* mines the neurosis of protagonist Alvy Singer, played by Allen, in *Annie Hall* (Woody Allen, 1977); and Finn McMissile owes a debt to Caine's connections with 1960s British spy cinema. More recently, Hong Kong martial artist Jackie Chan's recurring role as Master Monkey in the *Kung Fu Panda* series lends a degree of credibility through the actor's historical affililation with the *wuxia pian* and kung fu traditions. Marcello has identified how such 'persona typecasting' in the computer-animated film has been defined as an increasingly awkward correspondence between a star's real-life personality and computer-animated character, rather than the suitability of an actor for a role. In these terms, the star is conceived as having obscured the path that the character would have taken had a specialist vocal performer (and non-star) been cast in the role. But it is the creative methods by which the genre stages the meeting of the audio and the visual that reinforces and secures this particular synchresis effect.

Shark Tale's approach to anthropomorphic synchresis is to remind spectators of its ensemble cast through the details of character design. Actress Angelina Jolie's full lips, high cheekbones and pale skin were transposed onto her aquatic character (a sultry and seductive lionfish named Lola) (Figure 7.1). These anthropomorphised features foster a continuity of appearance between Lola and Jolie's other notable screen roles during the 2000s – *Lara Croft: Tomb Raider* (Simon West, 2001), *Original Sin* (Michael Cristofer, 2001) and *Mr. & Mrs. Smith* (Doug Liman, 2005) – by selecting and re-animating her 'dark hair, equally dark

Figure 7.1 Frame grab from *Shark Tale* (2004) (DreamWorks Animation). Seductive lionfish Lola (voiced by Angelina Jolie) and anthropomorphic synchresis.

large eyes, [and] the high arch of her sculpted eyebrows' (McDonald 2012: 179). But the film also gives primacy to Jolie's assertive and assured star persona that, as Paul McDonald argues, is additionally constructed around her 'bankable' sex appeal and 'trademark dark, pouting sensuality' (ibid.). Within the ventriloquised puppet performance of Lola, *Shark Tale* places Jolie's star voice into a specific audiovisual configuration that differs from her vocal roles in the *Kung Fu Panda* films (in which she voices a South China tiger), and *Beowulf* (Jolie plays a supernatural, metamorphosing reptilian, albeit one that is no less rooted in her habitual sensuality).

Anthropomorphic synchresis also accounts for those instances where stars perform as skewed, anthropomorphic 'versions' of themselves. *Surf's Up* (Ash Brannon and Chris Buck, 2007) transforms professional surfers Kelly Slater and Rob Machedo into penguins, while musicians Dolly Parton and Elton John become garden gnomes in *Gnomeo & Juliet*. A short sequence from *Bee Movie* acknowledges this tendency to bring sound and image together via the process of anthropomorphic synchresis. Appearing in a parody of Larry King's CNN programme *Larry King Live* (1985–2010) entitled 'Bee Larry King', protagonist Barry B. Benson draws attention to the fact that King's physical features and behavioural facets have been re-appropriated within an anthropomorphic context, joking that 'they have a Larry King in the human world too'. Bee Larry King has Larry King's signature suspenders and 'old guy glasses'. He also 'always leans forward', has 'pointy shoulders' and 'squinty eyes'.

The coupling of King's distinctive gravelly, baritone voice and New York accent with a character design that acknowledges aspects of his media identity, crafts a particular kind of synchretic collusion between the audio qualities of King's star voice and the performance of the character. *Bee Movie* creatively scores King's voice to the actions and activities of Bee Larry King in ways that diverge from his other vocal performance in *Shrek 2* and *Shrek the Third* (in which he voices the androgynous Doris the Ugly Stepsister). The attractiveness of anthropomorphic synchresis therefore lies in the porosity of the non-human animated figure, which absorbs numerous aspects of the star. It is the captivating 'hit' between the star's speech and aspects of the character's performance that enables a jolt of recognition in the spectator, and the 'mental fusion' of the synchresis is stimulated.

Case Study: *Cars / Cars 2*

Best remembered in the spirit of anthropomorphic synchresis are the many automobile characters that populate Pixar's *Cars* franchise. Many of the films' voice actors are affiliated with the world of racing, including former NASCAR Champion driver and commentator Carrell Waltrip ('Darrell Cartrip'); British racing driver David Hobbs ('David Hobbscap'), ESPN/ABC sportscaster Brent Musburger ('Brent Mustangburger') and sports announcer Bob Costas ('Bob Cutlass'). Current British Formula One driver Lewis Hamilton appears in *Cars 2*, whilst an automotive version of Michael Schumacher visits Radiator Springs in the 2006 original, where he greets tyre shop owners Guido and Luigi ('There is a real Michael Schumacher Ferrari in my store!'). However, the vocal performance of US talk show host Jay Leno ('Jay Limo') in *Cars* is another example of how anthropomorphic synchresis is rooted in the creative act of 'theming'. A silver and white Luxomobile Limousine, Jay Limo fronts 'The Jay Limo Show', and in his design recalls the distinctive grey hair and facial features of Leno himself. Even John Lasseter is revised as 'John Lassetire' in *Cars 2* as appropriate to the film's automobile theme, and is voiced by the Pixar co-founder.

Complementary to its use of anthropomorphic synchresis within specific character designs, the original *Cars* is also highly self-conscious in narrativising the very role of the voice as a performance element within computer-animated film acting. The recurring presence of US comic actor and voice artist John Ratzenberger – who spectators now expect will appear in a minor voice role in each of Pixar's features – is one of the key ways in which 'each Pixar film works in allusions to earlier films' (Booker 2010: 92). Ratzenberger's privileged place within the Pixar films is made a particular feature of *Cars*. During the film's closing credits, a drive-in movie theatre is showing motorvehicle 'versions' of previous Pixar features, here titled 'Toy Car Story' and 'Monster Trucks, Inc.' (by the release of *Cars 2*, the same theatre has now updated its listings by showing 'The Incredimobiles'). This cartoon coda 'doubles' anthropomorphic synchresis, as here *Cars* re-animates characters from other Pixar films as sleek automobiles, thereby collapsing other computer-animated films into its visual register of car modification. In *Cars*, this recalling of the studio's own computer-animated films is mediated by the vocal presence of Ratzenberger, whose character Mack the Truck watches with increasing unease those scenes that include the actor's previous appearances (as Hamm in *Toy Story*, and the Abominable Snowman in *Monsters, Inc.*, as well as P. T. Flea in *A Bug's Life*). As Mack retorts upon hearing his vocal likeness through Pixar's cartoon canon, 'They're just using the same actor over and over. What kind of cut-rate production is this?'

Autobiographic Synchresis

The vocal performances of British musician Sting and American actor Ray Liotta in *Bee Movie*; Joan Rivers and British media entrepreneur Simon Cowell in *Shrek 2*; US rock star Steven Tyler in *The Polar Express* and Frank Thomas and Ollie Johnston (two of Disney's legendary 'Nine Old Men' animators) during *The Incredibles* can be understood according to the narrower category of autobiographic synchresis. This is a performance type that maintains the recognisable qualities carried in the voice again without aural corruption, but replicates the star's physiognomy with similar fidelity (thus jettisoning the expressive possibilities of anthropomorphism). In autobiographic synchresis, the emphasis is on the presence of stars as themselves in ways that are reliant upon the weight of extratextual connotation behind their appearance. In *Fly Me to the Moon*, which tells the story of three insect stowaways smuggled aboard the Apollo 11 spaceflight in July 1969, American astronaut Buzz Aldrin voices his younger 1960s computer-animated self (a 'real' voice that contrasts with the young version of baseball star Babe Ruth in *Everyone's Hero*, who is voiced by actor Brian Dennehy). Aldrin's vocal performance in *Fly Me to the Moon* is reflective of a particularly emerging area of digitally-mediated performance. Computer graphics have provided new opportunities to complicate the corporeality of film acting, deteriorating the star's body through digital ageing, or recreating their youthful appearance using techniques of virtual age regression (Pallant 2012).

However, Aldrin's heavily 'youthed' performance in *Fly Me to the Moon* is significant because it distinguishes a potential split within autobiographic synchresis, and identifies instances across the computer-animated film where there is a desire to accurately replicate the familiarity of a star's face to match their voice. Examples of this practice include the digital presence of Korean pop singer Psy who features in the closing credits to *The Nut Job*; comic-book writer Stan Lee's short appearance in *Big Hero 6*; and Johnny Depp as American journalist and author Hunter S. Thompson in *Rango* (a role he had previously played in *Fear and Loathing in Las Vegas* [Terry Gilliam, 1998]). It is also common for those computer-animated films utilising motion-capture to faithfully and convincingly recreate the facial characteristics of their ensemble star voice cast. Stephen Prince argues the designs of Anthony Hopkins and Jolie in *Beowulf* are 'intended to look as photorealistic as the digital animators can make them' (2012: 117). The visual and aural recognisability of these kinds of performances are to a degree 'autobiographic' insofar as they maintain a photorealistic accuracy to their 'star' physiognomy as a way of complementing the truthfulness of the voice. However, the roles being played are always fictional, thus collapsing their effect into that of the offscreen/onscreen and actor/character binary in live-action cinema. Within the particular pleasures of autobiographic synchresis, voice actors play themselves (rather than performing in 'roles' as characters), thus confirming a Luxo world as a realm in which entirely fictional personalities can and do coexist with real-life celebrities.

Typically brief in screen-time and often self-reflexive in tone, both autobiographic and anthropomorphic synchresis can be united together under the umbrella of the film cameo, as roles of 'short but memorable duration', often by an actor 'who is usually a major film star or entertainment figure' (Goble 2010: 90). A cameo has narratological and formal implications, as it is 'often an odd moment, hanging in time, pausing the progress of the story and inviting the viewer to ponder some tangential implications of the story's consequences' (Mathijs 2013: 146). Yet the fleeting presence of a star in the computer-animated film foregrounds the line of critical inquiry that has discriminated against the star voice as nothing more than 'celebrity testimonial' (Pringle 2004: 131). The marquee name of a star can certainly prove to be a valuable asset, and used to sell the film on the basis of the star's high-profile involvement. During the opening credits to *Antz*, for example, a magnifying glass meanders over the bright white screen, picking out the name of its extensive cast (including Woody Allen and Gene Hackman) to literally enlarge and expand their presence. A similar technique of emphasis is used to spotlight the US voice cast of *Free Jimmy*, with the star names (Woody Harrelson, Samantha Morton) emblazoned on posters, billboards and advertisements during the film's opening sequence. *Fly Me to the Moon* even climaxes with the real-life appearance of Aldrin, whose sudden arrival within the diegesis halts the film's closing credits ('Stop the credits!') as he unexpectedly walks into the shot to pause the film's forward momentum, thus leaving the narrative 'hanging in time'. Aldrin explains that contrary to the film's events, 'there were no contaminants, no flies, on the Apollo 11', in a short sequence that momentarily combines the youthful computer-animated portrayal of the astronaut with his real-life equivalent. Finally, Aldrin's autograph appears etched in the bottom left of the screen. If the voice, as Barthes has suggested, operates as an 'intimate signature of the actor' (in Pavis 1998: 435), then Aldrin's verbal statement coupled with his physical presence and 'autographing' of the film's final sequence, authenticates *Fly Me to the Moon* through the credibility of his endorsement (Figure 7.2).

However, it is the art-historical origins of 'cameo' that reposition the star voice beyond the perspective that it is simply a marketing tool

Colonel Buzz Aldrin
Lunar Module pilot, Apollo 11

Figure 7.2 Frame grab from *Fly Me to the Moon* (2008) (nWave Pictures/Summit Entertainment). The real Buzz Aldrin halts the closing credits to validate the film's lunar narrative.

employed as leverage to attract audiences. Cameo is an artistic practice that involves the carving of a human figuration (originally of imperial types or dignitaries) brought into relief through colour contrast, and by raising it above a background plane. Initially carved from gemstones (sardonyx, agate, amethyst and chalcedony), but also shell and glass during the early Roman era, cameos are typically found on jewellery, such as brooches, amulets, medallions or pendants. The cameo's disjuncture between raised decoration, and that which remains on a lower plane, evokes the ways in which animators can illuminate the presence of a star and creatively profile their involvement. The star voice 'cameo' of anthropomorphic and autobiographic synchresis is then accented through elements of character design and performance. Through such animated acting, a star's vocal performance can be shaped into varying degrees of visual prominence, carefully sculpted to enhance its boldness against the film's surface.

Acousmatic Synchresis

The third category of acousmatic synchresis relates to an audiovisual arrangement in the computer-animated film that manipulates the multitude of associations that can be tied to the recognisable star voice. 'Acousmatic' is a term adapted by Chion from French novelist Jerome Peignot to describe sound one hears without seeing its source. A director is able to obscure the origin of the voice for the purposes of mystery and intrigue, before 'de-acousmatizing' it and divulging its cause later through what Chion calls 'visualized' sound (1994: 72). It is a prerequisite of the computer-animated film that the true source of the sound will always remain acousmatic, insofar as a mediating digital surrogate speaks in place of the star. Such disembodiment is foundational to the genre's synchretic logic. Spectators accept speech from that which cannot speak, and perceive the voice as a function of a character devoid of larynx, oesophagus and other biological markers. But the currency of acousmatic synchresis is one of disguise more than reveal, playing upon the intrinsic separateness of the visible and the audible that synchresis, as Chion argues, would otherwise help the spectator to overcome.

Acousmatic synchresis is primarily directed at the star voice and its possessor, engaging with the voice as assignable to the star. It formally postpones the textual meeting between sound and image, prolonging the spectators' process of synchresis until the animated image 'catches up' with the voice. Acousmatic synchresis is, therefore, a device often used to orchestrate the mechanics of the star entrance, employed at the moment at which vocal omnipresence (the unseen star speaker) suddenly emerges as computer-animated presence. The opening sequence of *Cars* functions as emblematic of acousmatic synchresis with its introduction of American film star Owen Wilson. The actor's South Texan drawl and elongated intonations are heard, seemingly in voiceover narration, against a black screen, soliciting the spectator to 'audio-view' the scene and its scarcity of image (the sequel *Cars 3* replays this sequence verbatim). Listening to the star speak without any trace of their image transforms the star voice into an *acousmêtre*. This is what Chion calls a kind of hidden, mysterious 'acting shadow' (1999: 21). When Wilson's automobile character Lightning McQueen finally appears – literally out of the darkness of his container – to assume ownership of the star voice, the not-yet-seen enters the field of vision, luxuriant light bathing the sleek contours of the motor vehicle. Formally shaping *Cars* as a star 'vehicle' for Wilson, acousmatic synchresis can also be staged to trouble the star voice's attribution and aggravate how it comes to be anchored within the fictional world. The entrance of Billy Crystal as green, one-eyed monster Mike Wazowski in *Monsters, Inc.* involves a particularly light-hearted act of audio misdirection. As Sulley's alarm clock ticks over to '6:05' and the radio sounds, the spectator believes that Crystal's recognisable voice is that of a smooth-talking disc jockey. However, a camera pan reveals that Mike is actually standing over the sleeping Sulley as the true source of the star speech, delivering his news bulletin and forecast that it 'looks like it's going to be a perfect day'.

Many computer-animated films extend the vocal attributes of its characters and the power of the star voice by opening with voiceover narration.

For Sarah Kozloff, the power of verbal narration lies in its ability to 'taint' information 'with subjectivity', as the visual immediately succumbs to 'narratorial mediation' (1989: 13). *Puss in Boots, Megamind, The Wild, Happily N'Ever After, Chicken Little, Igor, The Croods, Tangled, How to Train Your Dragon, Escape from Planet Earth, Epic, Wreck-It Ralph, Rise of the Guardians, Mr. Peabody & Sherman* and *Norm of the North* (Trevor Wall, 2016) all open with this device to (sonically) introduce key characters in a highly personal fashion. In the computer-animated film, these opening voiceovers confirm the primacy of the star voice, intensifying and privileging its familiar materiality. But such voiceovers additionally craft a temporal delay in disclosing the screen speaker, reproducing a kind of Barthesian 'fascinated listening' that delights in the spectators' anticipation of the 'de-acousmatic' reveal. In the first scenes of *Antz*, for example, spectators hear Woody Allen's identifiable voice and fast-delivered delivery, but are refused a screen source in which to place his speech. There is a notable delay before the vocals are 'de-acousmatized', and the prolonged reveal of insect Z as he speaks in Allen's recognisable New York accent amplifies the moment the star voice becomes inserted into its new non-human source.

Case Study: *Happy Feet*

Although the narrative of *Happy Feet* is seemingly predicated on the energy, vigour and skill of movement as a form of expression and site of performance, the film also spotlights the importance of the voice, and is much about the aural power of 'song' as it is about the visual spectacle of 'dance'. *Happy Feet* takes its cue from protagonist Mumble, the film's solitary non-singing emperor penguin, and his acquisition of a heartsong so that he can find a mate. However, to the disdain of his father, Mumble is unable to find his voice and instead displays a proclivity for tap dancing that marginalises him from the rest of the penguin herd. Philip Hayward describes *Happy Feet* and its register of 'concentrated vocality' with regards to the re-inscription of penguins' vocal communication 'as human vocal singing' (2010: 91). However, through its register of acousmatic synchresis, *Happy Feet* demonstrates a heightened awareness of how the voice can be grafted onto the animated body to construct performance. This awareness is figured through the vocal performance of Robin Williams, an actor and comedian well-known to American audiences since the 1970s, and central to the emergence of star sound within an animated context.

In *Happy Feet*, Williams voices three characters, a rockhopper penguin named Lovelace, Cletus the seal, and a male Adélie penguin named

Ramón. Among these roles, Lovelace is both *Happy Feet*'s omniscient narrator and a character whose mythology within the film's fictional world is predicated upon his vocal, rather than visual, qualities. Indeed, Lovelace's concealment is carefully orchestrated to maximise the temporal delay that supports the process of 'de-acousmatizing'. Prior to his (visual) reveal forty minutes into the film, Lovelace addresses the audience with a knowing gesture to his occluded onscreen presence, teasing that 'You've heard the voice. Now you're about to meet the one-and-only Lovelace in the flesh, right here, right on, right now!' This comment discloses the attraction of acousmatic synchresis as a technique of performance, and how in computer-animated films it playfully frustrates any simultaneous experience by the spectator of sound and image together. It perhaps also acknowledges Williams's contribution to star voice acting in animation by more readily making a feature of his vocal delivery.

For Chion, acousmatic sound 'intensifies causal listening in taking away the aid of sight' (1994: 32), and *Happy Feet*'s positioning of the spectator as initially blind to the visual elements of Lovelace's character strengthens his first appearance. *Happy Feet* also presents its own vision of ventriloquy once again rooted in the manipulation of sound and its source. Later in the film, as Mumble's attempts at a heartsong for love interest Gloria prove futile, it is Ramón who hides out of sight as the young emperor penguin simply mimes along pretending to sing his version of Frank Sinatra's 'My Way'. When taken together with Lovelace's protracted reveal, this sequence presents another instance of how *Happy Feet* emphasises the potential for listening conditions based on the invisibility of the sound source. Ramón's act of ventriloquism falsifies the authenticity of the musical number, but like Kathy Selden's dubbing of Lina Lamont in *Singin' in the Rain* (Stanley Donen, 1952), it is the convincing synchronisation of auditory and visual elements that secures the illusion of a complete performance. *Happy Feet* therefore strengthens the impact of the voice by consistently situating the allocation of sound within a series of sleight of hand sequences that, in the case of Mumble's fabricated heartsong, fully showcases the performative possibilities enabled by dubbing.

The Pleasure of the (Star) Voice

By hinging upon the recognisability of a star voice, and the fact that many computer-animated film characters are first introduced through their oral qualities, acousmatic synchresis is more directly implicated in the criticisms levelled at star voice-casting. While the non-celebrity, career voice actor is praised for their vocal manipulation, range and versatility, the star voice has to merely turn up and 'sound like him-or-herself to guarantee audience recognition' (Marcello 2006: 64). Computer-animated films certainly adhere to an implicit audiovisual contract that extols the virtues of the star's vocal signature by maintaining its sonic purity. The recognisable traits of the star's voice are rarely disrupted by any kind of aural corruption. Stars in the computer-animated film typically speak as themselves, rather than adopting speech impediments, national inflections or dialects, unidentifiable twangs and regional accents.

There is occasional evidence of this practice: Mike Myers' Scottish brogue in the *Shrek* films; Ian Holm and Frances McDormand's French accents in *Ratatouille* and *Madagascar 3: Europe's Most Wanted* respectively; Steve Carell's Eastern European inflection in *Despicable Me*; Williams's flamboyant Hispanic lilt as Ramón in the *Happy Feet* films; and Alec Baldwin's Russian accent as Nicholas St. North in *Rise of the Guardians*. Chion has argued that 'for a single body and a single face on the screen, thanks to synchresis, there are dozens of allowable voices' (Chion 1994: 63). But stars are expected to sound a certain way, and computer-animated films traditionally maintain the acoustic potency and purity of the star's idiosyncratic voice as part of its audio repertoire. Such preservation of the star voice is not just a concern of character authenticity, but maintains the authenticity of the star and the impact of their vocal purity. Just as ventriloquism is itself a form of illusory deception, the computer-animated film exploits, rather than resists, the fundamentally ventriloquistic identity of its audiovisual construction by delighting in the recognisable star voice's animated reassignment. Acousmatic synchresis maintains its allure through the (delayed) creation of new synch points of sound and image, marking the union of visual and aural events in unexpected and never-before-seen creative synchrony. Unlike the reveal of the Wizard in *The Wizard of Oz* (Victor Fleming, 1939), the aura of the voice does not crumble due to its demystification and 'de-acousmatizing' disclosure. Rather, acousmatic synchresis hinges upon the fascinating moment in a computer-animated film at which spectators, to borrow Walter Murch's phrasing, witness 'old friends dressed up in new clothes' (in Chion 1994: xviii).

Acousmatic synchresis therefore underlies what is fundamentally enjoyable, engaging and 'irresistible' about star voice casting in computer-animated films. By prolonging the disclosure of the reconstituted star speaking in a computer-animated film for the first time, their narratives exploit the star voice within 'the opportunities provided by thinking with our ears' (Bull and Back 2003: 2), whilst fully exploiting the audiovisual deceit involved when the star voice is relocated. The creative scoring of the star voice to puppet performer in the computer-animated film, and the multiple 'fits' between star persona and screen performance that can be achieved, solicits spectators' curiosity about the cinematic bodies that speak in a voice they (may) know. Computer-animated films stoke the spectatorial game of speculation and deciphering undertaken by viewers who decode a vocal performance as the product of a star (*that sounds like*, *that could be*) and try to award the voice a real-life origin. The manner in which the star voice is 'actualized', and the multiple gradations that govern how it is given textual definition, situate the star voice as a significant part of the anatomy of the computer-animated film's puppets. Star speech is placed in certain audiovisual configurations that reflect the intersection of animation (visible) with (audible) as they creatively 'hit' one another.

Notes

1. Tom Hanks in the *Toy Story* franchise and *The Polar Express*; Jim Carrey in *Horton Hears a Who!* and *A Christmas Carol*; Mike Myers in DreamWorks' *Shrek* movies; Will Smith in *Shark Tale*; and Bruce Willis in *Over the Hedge*. Hanks voiced a total of six characters in *The Polar Express*, while eight characters were voiced by Carrey in *A Christmas Carol*.
2. McDonald's (2000: 104) analysis of Tom Hanks' stardom during the 1990s, for example, omits the actor's voiceover work in *Toy Story* and *Toy Story 2*. Hanks' vocal performance as Woody features only as an addendum alongside his uncredited appearances during the decade, with the focus instead on his successful live-action roles.

CHAPTER 8

From Wile E. to Wall-E:
Computer-Animated Film Comedy

Select any two animals, grind together, and stir into a pot. Add prat falls, head and body blows, and slide whistle effects to taste. Garnish with Brooklyn accents. Slice into 600-foot lengths and release.
(John Hubley and Zachary Schwartz, 'Animation Learns a New Language', 1946)

The recipe for computer-animated film comedy draws upon an alternate set of ingredients than those involved in the creation of other types of animated humour. The guidelines proposed in 1946 by ex-Disney layout artist John Hubley, and the founder of United Productions of America (UPA) Zachary Schwartz, offer a readymade formula for a particular kind of American cel-animated cartoon produced during the classical studio era. However, while computer-animated films do cast their comic net wide, they do not support the wild and extreme expressions of wit founded upon disruptions of spatio-temporal unity and unorthodox patterns of behaviour. They jettison the effortless violation of expected and accepted logic, which has traditionally manifest an array of extreme sight, spot and blackout gags, physical buffoonery and the unprecedented ability of the cartoon to literalise 'puns, proverbs and metaphors' (Thompson 2005: 148). Humour drawn from the rejection of physical and spatial laws, metamorphosis and transposition of form, and manipulations with colour have been displaced from the centre of the computer-animated film's investigations. Exaggerated degrees of physical distortion and degradation of the animated body operate outside the accepted hyperrealist agenda of a Luxo world, while the 'head and body blows' at the centre of animation's history of violence have been replaced with a less ferocious treatment of its characters.

Computer-animated films without a strong comic verve are rare, and while there are examples of films that are less family-oriented – *Final Fantasy: The Spirits Within*, Kevin Munroe's latest instalment of the Teenage Mutant Ninja Turtles story *TMNT*, and *Beowulf* – the synonymy between comedy and the computer-animated film foregrounds several significant issues. Thomas M. Leitch suggests that a genre's comic intent, that is, its target as one 'which seeks to make viewers laugh', would normally be sufficient to qualify it as comedy (2002: 9). 'Unless', Leitch contends, 'it is animated, in which case it will be classified as a cartoon' (ibid.). This chapter argues that comedy does not fully subordinate or subsume the computer-animated film within (or under) the genre heading of comedy, designating 'computer-animated' as merely a type, division or sub-genre of comedy, as is the case with the associative labels *black*, *romantic* or *musical* comedy. Following the modal rather than generic approach to film comedy, and given there is 'no single adequate theory of comedy' (King 2002b: 5) more generally, this chapter argues that comedy is worked into the stable, solid genre of the computer-animated film in particular ways, leading to a range of comedic orthodoxies that both define, and are defined by, the specificities of their worlds. Comedy is one of the final refuges of the genre's animatedness, and it is these qualities of animated difference that secure the computer-animated film's generic structures. The language of contemporary computer-animated film comedy therefore obeys traditions of cartoon humour insofar as comedy functions as its own statement of variance and otherness. But as this chapter will argue, computer-animated films have closed off many of the established avenues through which animation's 'comic craziness' (ibid.: 21) has traditionally been pursued.

The story of animation's exceptional comic arsenal and the medium's prolonged relationship to comedy is one that remains mostly untold. Paul Wells points out that despite the fact that comedy 'is assumed to be at the core of most animated films', it remains an 'intrinsic, but largely uninterrogated vocabulary' (1998: 127). The conclusions offered in the next three chapters are therefore intended to complement the recent typologies of animated humour (Thompson 2005; Goldmark and Keil 2011; Buchan 2013; Wells 2013). This particular chapter, however, argues that the computer-animated film's jocular system and methods of its merry making pose something of a challenge to Kirsten Thompson's assumption that 'despite all this exciting new technology, much of animation still uses the old sight gags, pratfalls and verbal humour that have been around for over seventy years' (2005: 151). Far from regurgitating these dominant comic paradigms, computer-animated films convey their own sense of humour that reworks and expands upon pre-existing theories of animation comedy. However, just as there is no universal theory for comedy in the cinema, no single approach to studying comedy in computer-animated films can satisfactorily encompass their unique brand of comedy, and the shifting terms of its precise 'gagology' (Durgnat 1969: 185). Computer-animated films are not all built to the same comedic template, neither is there a standalone film that outlines the genre's full range of comic effects. There are, however, certain comic orthodoxies and recurring gags to which computer-animated films regularly turn to generate its laughs, and it is this chapter that identifies the range of comic material that can be found across their narratives.

A Happy Feat?

Computer-animated films contain the multiple 'points of access' (King 2002b: 153) that characterises mass-marketed comedies, and in particular animation, currently produced across contemporary Hollywood. As part of their sustained attraction to a demographic of both adults and children, computer-animated films build upon an established 'hallmark' of animated comedy, that of parody (as examined in Chapter 1), which alongside social critique and satiric commentary flourished within the propagandist ideology of wartime animation (Shull and Wilt 2004). The dismantling of particular genres, alongside subversive caricature, parodic swipes at celebrity culture and heightened self-reflexivity, situate computer-animated films as continuous with many staples of animated comedy that have marked the irreverence of the medium since the Golden Age of the American cartoon, by appeasing adult audiences through their volley of self-conscious gag structures. In satisfying the interests and tastes of younger viewers, computer-animated films have also jettisoned overtly salacious, risqué or racist humour as a source of comedy, relegating any divisive content to occasional quips and oblique but innocuous metaphors. Noel Brown suggests that the multi-layered appeal of computer-animated films made by Pixar and DreamWorks enabled them to fill the vacuum in Hollywood left empty during the 1990s by the decline in 'adult-driven domestic comedy' (2012: 184), with feature-length animation quickly reasserting its position among the family market.

Overt sexual and racist humour is less evident in the computer-animated film too than in the controversial terrain of 'forbidden' animation, an area of adult animation that Karl F. Cohen (1997) describes as inviting censorship through a sustained emphasis on alcohol, drugs, sexual content, profanity and off-colour vulgarity. Yet, operating beyond the mass-marketed conservatism of Hollywood, contemporary computer-animated films from outside the US are more in line with these controversial traditions in ways that have broadened the representational scope of CGI. Digital techniques have replaced cel-animation in sexually explicit Japanese *hentai* pornography, while Shinji Aramaki's computer-animated film trilogy *Appleseed* (2004–14) taps into the coverage of adult themes refined since the 1980s within the theatrical and homevideo histories of Japanese anime. However, there are a number of computer-animated feature films aimed largely at adult audiences increasingly produced across Europe. Norway's first computer-animated film, *Free Jimmy*, incorporates sex scenes alongside moments of drug-taking, violence and swearing; *Ronal the Barbarian* (Kresten Vestbjerg Andersen, Thorbjørn Christoffersen and Philip Einstein Lipski, 2011) is an adult Danish computer-animated film that parodies the sword and sorcery sub-genre of fantasy; and the recent Turkish computer-animated film *Bad Cat* (Mehmet Kurtuluş and Ayşe Ünal, 2016) is firmly in the mould of Ralph Bakshi's *Fritz the Cat* (1972), and is a film that outgrossed both *Zootopia* and *Kung Fu Panda 3* at the Turkish box office. By comparison, and despite their many allegorical and political readings, computer-animated films produced and distributed within the Hollywood system have been generally marked by child-friendly, family-oriented comedies supported by normative socio-political meanings that continue the 'conservative ideology of cartoons' (Thompson 1980: 119). In this way, the recent release of *Sausage Party* marks something of a turning point for computer-animated film comedy.

Case Study: *Sausage Party*

Sausage Party is the first computer-animated film to be rated R by the Motion Picture Association of America. Produced in Vancouver by Nitrogen Studios and directed by Conrad Vernon, it is a computer-animated sex comedy telling the story of anthropomorphic hot dog sausage Frank who, alongside love interest Brenda (a hot dog bun), is separated from the rest of his pack during a supermarket aisle spill. The subsequent narrative cuts between Frank and Brenda's journey to find their respective cliques, and the other foods' growing realisation that their ultimate future in the supposedly utopic 'Great Beyond' of the kitchen is one in which they are actually cooked (tortured) and eaten (killed).

Within the currents of contemporary Hollywood film comedy, *Sausage Party* stakes out its particular territory according to the tropes of the 'lad flick' trend that 'came to prominence in the late 1990s against the backdrop of anxieties about a "crisis in masculinity"' (Hansen-Miller and Gill 2011: 36). The film embraces the homosocial trajectory of these bromance narratives in which 'homophobic humour serves to consistently disavow and deflect the homoerotic potential among the characters or between male audiences and those onscreen' (ibid.: 44). The frequent vulgar exchanges between male sausages Carl, Troy and Barry are particularly reliant on the comedy of mocking same-sex intimacy, turning on Barry's misshapenness ('you deformed nerd') and alluding to his effeminacy ('I guess you're weird and a pussy!') to attack his lack of confidence and weak physicality. For David Greven the heroes of bromance cinema similarly defy 'leading man standards' and are, like Barry in *Sausage Party*, 'physically unconventional looking, out of shape, out of work' (2016: 105). The casting of Seth Rogen, Jonah Hill, James Franco, Paul Rudd, Danny McBride and Craig Robinson in *Sausage Party* further contributes to the identity of the film as a particular form of post-millennial male comedy. When taken together, this repeating cycle of actors are central to the recent Hollywood tradition of early-2000s 'beta male' comedies (typified by the work of writer, director and producer Judd Apatow), in which the focus on (often hapless) men of a 'post-college age or older' is exploited to showcase the 'regressive state of American masculinity' (ibid.: 108–9). Their presence in *Sausage Party* works to not only affirm and contextualise the crude gestures to male/male affection (including its explicit consumation in the film's final 'orgy' scenes), but underscores the discourses of failure, defensiveness, misogyny and racism that typically define the bromance narrative's articulation of disaffected, cynical twenty-first century manhood.

Yet *Sausage Party* is not just a 'beta male' reinvigoration of animation's anthropomorphic tradition through its combining of a 'food–come–alive' narrative premise with the archetypal bromance humour of 'penises and semen' (ibid.: 109). It also functions as a commentary on Vernon's own history within computer-animated filmmaking as director of *Shrek 2*, *Monsters vs. Aliens* and *Madagascar 3: Europe's Most Wanted* (he has also worked creatively on thirteen other computer-animated films for DreamWorks since *Antz* in 1998). The film's producer and voice star Rogen described *Sausage Party* as an 'R-rated Pixar movie' (in Tapley 2016), and the film deliberately subverts the rigidity of the template crafted by Pixar and DreamWorks for computer-animated films. The film alludes to both *Monsters, Inc.* and *Brave*, and parodies Remy's puppeteering of Linguini in *Ratatouille* (by having a human controlled via his scrotum). The film's climax – during which the characters are exposed as 'something called cartoons' and voiced by celebrity actors 'in another dimension' – also reflexively acknowledges how performance and acting in computer-animated films are typically constructed. *Sausage Party* therefore obtains its comic impact from its identity as a new kind of genre parody, perhaps marking the first moment where the computer-animated film as a set of recurring narratives and characters became fully recognisable and available for parodic treatment.

Thrills of the Chase

If computer-animated films *can* be connected to prior forms of comedy in animation, then the journey narrative (as examined in Chapter 2) is significant in re-imagining the economy of the chase cartoon, a constrained mini-narrative of tightly-plotted action that structured cartoon comedy as early as the 1920s, though it eventually diluted and 'died' with the onset of the Vietnam war-era and wider cultural 'backlash against violence' (Lehman 2007: 180). As a storytelling structure, the chase traded in a particular state of anarchy, underpinned by its velocity, acceleration, nonsense, frenetic activity, but also its unpredictability (despite its formulaic nature). Whether anchored to the relentless pursuit of the Road Runner by Wile E. Coyote, or Tom's obsession with capturing Jerry that repeated in increasingly elaborate Sisyphean cycles, the chase strikes as funny because of the dynamic between chaser and chased. The journey narrative thus shares with the chase the likelihood of hazards, of rhythm and movement, dealing in the comedy of survival alongside the intrusion, intersection and comedic conflict of incongruous worlds that are suddenly made to collide. But the computer-animated film has notably extended the streamlined economy, suspense and reasoned system of the cartoon chase narrative.

No longer 'sliced into 600-foot lengths', computer-animated films come in feature-length duration, demonstrating their obedience to greater classical virtues of narrative coherence and causal logic. Computer-animated films have been allied to what Stanley Cavell has theorised as the 'comedy of remarriage', as well as a variety of other 'romcom' structures (Davis 2009), while *Shrek* has also been credited as 'a virtual remake of the main plot line of the classic screwball comedy *It Happened One Night* (1934)' (Booker 2010: 153). *Antz, Shark Tale, Flushed Away, Cars, Alpha and Omega, Cloudy with a Chance of Meatballs, Rio, The Book of Life, Strange Magic* and *Trolls* are no less explicit in the debt they pay to the structuring principles of the romantic comedy, and largely conform to the 'boy-meets-girl' narrative category outlined by Gerald Mast (1976: 8–9) as one of eight plotlines that typically arrange the comedy film. Wall-E's romantic courtship of EVE in *Wall-E* openly reworks many 'romcom' conventions, albeit through the comic conjunction of mime, charade and intertextuality. *Wall-E* is ostensibly a robot reboot of the Michael Crawford/Marianne McAndrew courtship that plays (and is repeated) on Wall-E's well-worn VHS copy of *Hello, Dolly!*

The appropriation of familiar Hollywood 'romcom' narratives testifies to the ability of computer-animated films to resituate the mutual loathing/

loving, passion and sentiment of potential male/female couples within its own representational heritage of anthropomorphism. Anthropomorphism remains a particularly powerful catalyst for computer-animated film comedy, just as it resides within the genre's capacity to (re)construct the geography of its virtual spaces. Israel Knox explains how the 'spectacle of animals carrying on like human beings, especially by their resort to language' remains 'highly amusing' (1957: 801–12). Philosopher Henri Bergson's theory of laughter similarly gestures towards the comic potential of human/animal assimilation. Bergson argues that 'You may laugh at an animal but only because you have detected in it some human attitude or expression' (2005: 2). The physical and behavioural equivalence of 'humanlike' computer-animated bodies remains a central component of the genre's comic register. Indeed, the farmyard animals in *Barnyard* rescind their animal actions for humorously refined human behaviour when out of human sight, while in *Norm of the North* the eponymous polar bear is coded as exceptional as a result of his ability to act in ways that approximate human form.

As examined in Chapter 4, however, computer-animated films have extended the comic language of anthropomorphism by staging the meeting of human (ánthrōpos) and non-human (morphē) registers as more of an eventful comedic collision, often alleviating the anthropomorph's aspirations for human expression to surface the instinctual element of the morphē. The suave and valiant performance of Puss in Boots from the *Shrek* films is routinely interrupted by his irrepressible and typically reflex feline actions that comically disturb his bravado. His confident entrance in *Shrek 2* is instantly checked by a hairball lodged in his throat (prompting the character to retreat from bipedal to quadruped poses). In the spin-off *Puss in Boots*, the character becomes transfixed by a spot of light that jags across the cobbled stone floors of San Ricardo. The feline abandons his pursuit of the villainous Humpty Dumpty, and instinctively jumps to follow the light's erratic path with catlike exuberance. A similar joke appears in *The Secret Life of Pets*, in which the anthropomorphic cast cannot help but excitedly follow the red light cast from a series of laser pens. Computer-animated films therefore not only inscribe or perform culturally sanctioned ways of defining gendered male and female oppositions (as in the 'romcom'), but simultaneously manoeuvre beyond normative body categories. Typical gender distinctions are rendered a matter of proportion, placed within (and harnessed through) the intrinsic properties of character, contributing to what Sianne Ngai calls the '"thinging" of the body in order to construct it [. . .] as impassioned' (2005: 99). The 'thinging' of performance in the computer-animated film rooted in the comic possibilities of morphē permits the interrogatation and (re)construction of widely held bodily boundaries, and to disclose new performance pleasures arising in the possibilities of inanimate objects 'acting funny'.

The wedding together of anthropomorphism with familiar narrative structures across computer-animated films also recalibrates the dominant 'battle of the sexes' motif of the 'romcom' (Mortimer 2010: 10) as something that more readily resembles the 'battle of the species'. Certain incompatibilities that 'may arise from social status, wealth, conflicting lifestyles and attitudes' (ibid.) certainly remain salient within the organisation of computer-animated film romance. *Gnomeo & Juliet*, in particular, poses the romantic union as transgressive of a class divide, albeit as a playful snobbery between blue/Montague and red/Capulet garden gnomes in its retelling of Shakespeare's star-crossed lovers' story. However, Wells points out that when 'romcom' structures are mobilised within the anthropomorphic context of animation, the tribulations of the 'boy-meets-girl' narrative can be abandoned to explore instead the implications of 'cross-species coupling' (2002a: 62). Anthropomorphism therefore becomes a political device that can radically interrogate non-normative identities, exploring taboo, cross-dressing, gender-bending and alternative sexualities. The unconvincing cross-dressing disguises of Bugs Bunny during his wealth of 'transvestite cartoons' (Sandler 1998: 162) are evoked by male ladybird Francis (*A Bug's Life*) and highly masculine Madame Gasket (*Robots*); Gru, who crossdresses in *Despicable Me 2* as part of a gendered performance at Agnes's birthday party ('It is I, Gru … zinkerbell'); and, most memorably, Buzz Lightyear's trespassing of gender roles as housewife 'Mrs Nesbitt' in *Toy Story*.

The computer-animated film also provides the stage for another orthodox duo of comedy film, adapting the masculine spaces and familiar comic structures of the 'buddy movie'. The 'buddy movie' structure of the computer-animated film is most commonly formed through involuntary and serendipitous events: a mismatched duo thrown into incongruous and highly comedic conflict as appropriate to the unintentional schemes of the 'flushed away' journey narrative. One character is typically reluctant to form a pairing, although any hostility among the duo is progressively dissolved over the course of their union, resulting in a developing friendship. That is not to say that these impromptu duos cannot establish an immediate bond whose strength is tested throughout the narrative (such as fish Oscar and great white shark Lenny in *Shark Tale*). But it is commonplace for the computer-animated film to make use of the 'verbal banter, mutual rescues, [and] a movement from antagonism to affection and support' that Yvonne Tasker (1998: 85) describes as central to the hostile workings of the buddy movie. The pairings of Shrek and the Donkey in *Shrek* ('why are you following me?'), Boog and Elliot in *Open Season* ('What are you doing here?') and Carl and Russell in *Up* ('What are you doing out here, kid?') are all emblematic of the initial disdain that precedes the final origination of new buddies. Boog's retort to Elliot in *Open Season* that 'We are not "We"! It's just "Me"!' not only verbalises the theme of reluctance that typically supports the genesis of a buddy movie structure, but also discloses the contribution of duelling pairs to the formation of non-nuclear 'family' units across computer-animated films.

As a 'fascinating challenge for animation' (Hooks in Barrier 2007), interspecies coupling within the context of computer-animated films can be compared to the strand of 'biracial' buddy films that were part of a sub-genre popularised during the 1970s and 1980s that reflected 'the advancement of African Americans in the decade following the civil rights movement' (Carroll 2003: 73–4). The computer-animated film is certainly able to reconfigure the white male/black male tensions of racial difference central to the biracial buddy movie through the humour of a cross-species clash. Through its pervasive anthropomorphic register, the genre re-negotiates the volatility of black/white experience central to late-1980s Hollywood cinema such as *48 Hours* (Walter Hill, 1982) and *Lethal Weapon* (Richard Donner, 1987), and instead engineers comedy from a (dis)harmony 'of sorts'. In *Ice Age*, for example, Diego admits that Manny the Mammoth and Sid the Sloth are 'a bit of an odd couple', though he might equally be referring to any of the cross-species pairings that populate the genre. Yet the biracial history of the buddy movie phenomenon can itself be sustained through specific choices in voice casting, which reaffirm the presence of a racial boundary even within the alliance of different species. The white/black actor pairings of Mike Myers/ Eddie Murphy in the *Shrek* films; Jack Black/Will Smith in *Shark Tale*; Ben Stiller/Chris Rock in the *Madagascar* franchise; Ashton Kutcher/ Martin Lawrence in *Open Season*; and Jim Parsons/Rihanna in *Home* all enact racial divides at the same time as the characters' own clash of size, shape, stature, design and species visually connotes their conflict within the framing journey narrative.

Stand-Up and Comedian Comedy

The feature-length duration of computer-animated films has placed additional emphasis upon the value of verbal comedy. The widely-held assumption is that the jokes of animated comedy unfold according to that which is *visual*, rather than aspects of sound or dialogue. In answer to the question 'How is animation comedy different?' Jean Ann Wright replies that 'It's above all visual with plenty of sight gags' (2005: 182). However, the recent critical investigations into animated sound and music (Goldmark and Taylor 2002; Goldmark 2005; Wells 2009a; Coyle 2010) have placed greater emphasis on the contributions of soundscapes to the formation of cartoon comedy. Steven Allen in particular has specifically objected to arguments that omit the sonic capabilities of animation, arguing for cartoons (and especially those produced by Tex Avery) to be conceived as 'integrated audio–visual vehicles' (2009: 7–22). Feature-length computer-animated films can equally be viewed in this audiovisual manner, evidenced by the inclusion of *A Bug's Life* under the heading of 'verbal comedy' in Thompson's (2005) summary of the most dominant comedic tropes in animation.

Language and speech are often employed for comedic purposes in the computer-animated film, their narratives synonymous with extensive comic dialogue and carefully constructed verbal witticisms. The recent casting of American television actor Jim Parsons as Oh in *Home*, for example, capitalises on his proclivity for delivering complex dialogue that has become a feature of his role as theoretical physicist Sheldon Cooper in the CBS television series *The Big Bang Theory* (Chuck Lorre, 2007–). The talkative but naive Oh frequently mistakes words and tenses ('I do not fit in. I fit out'), and he regularly mispronounces words and phrases (Will Ferrell's vocal performances in *Megamind* and *The LEGO Movie* are marked by a similar verbal garbling). Computer-animated films certainly sustain the 'joke-oriented' dialogue familiar from the Looney Tunes and Merrie Melodies cartoons, though they are less inclined towards recognisable catchphrases ('What's up, Doc?') or outlandish speech impediments such as Tweetie Pie's 'I Tawt I Taw a Puddy Tat', or Elmer Fudd's exaggerated rhotacism when instructing audiences to 'Be vewwy qwuiet' (Wells 1998: 39). However, despite their strong franchise mentality and sequelisation, computer-animated films do not have the same opportunities to develop character catchphrases in the same manner as the seven minute Hollywood cartoon, or long-running animated serials. There are also limitations to the catchphrase as a device of comedy. A 1994 episode of *The Simpsons* titled 'Bart Gets Famous' parodies the cultural purchase of the catchphrase that, as Chris Turner suggests, 'can easily become a comic crutch, drained of any real humour through overuse' (2004: 61).

A particularly distinguishing feature of computer-animated film's vocal orientation has been the deployment of stand-up comedians in vocal roles. Tim Lawson and Alissa Persons point out that while many voiceover artists of the Golden Age era honed their talents on radio, today 'many are also former nightclub and stand-up comedy performers' (2004: xxvi). Computer-animated films certainly provide evidence of this practice. The casting of former Comedy Store member Tim Allen in *Toy Story*, alongside fellow stand-up comedians Don Rickles (Mr Potato Head), Jim Varney (Slinky Dog) and Wallace Shawn (Rex the Dinosaur), established a blueprint for casting actors with a background in stand-up comedy from which computer-animated films have seldom deviated. Denis Leary (*A Bug's Life*), Ray Romano (*Ice Age*), Billy Crystal (*Monsters, Inc.*), Wanda Sykes (*Over the Hedge, Barnyard, Rio, Ice Age: Continental Drift, Ice Age: Collision Course* [Mike Thurmeier, 2016]), Norm MacDonald (*The Flight Before Christmas*), George Carlin (*Cars, Happily N'Ever After*), Adam Sandler (*Hotel Transylvania, Hotel Transylvania 2*), Jerry Seinfeld (*Bee Movie*) and Patton Oswalt (*Ratatouille*) all amplify the potency of verbal comedy through a confident and sophisticated comic delivery. The long-running NBC sketch comedy show *Saturday Night Live* (1975–) has been a particularly rich field from which computer-animated films have sourced their voice actors. These include: Amy Poehler (*Shrek the Third, Horton Hears a Who!, Monsters vs. Aliens, Hoodwinked Too! Hood vs. Evil, Free Birds, Inside Out*), Jason Sudeikis (*Epic, The Angry Birds Movie* [Clay Kaytis and Feargal Reilly, 2016]), Bobby Moynihan (*Monsters University, Underdogs, The Nut Job 2: Nutty by Nature* [Cal Brunker, 2017]), Maya Rudolph (*Turbo, The Nut Job, Big Hero 6, Strange Magic*), Bill Hader (*Cloudy With a Chance of Meatballs, Inside Out*), Kristen Wiig (*Ice Age: Dawn of the Dinosaurs, Despicable Me 2, How to Train Your Dragon 2, Sausage Party, Despicable Me 3*), Andy Samberg (*Space Chimps, Hotel Transylvania, Cloudy with a Chance of Meatballs 2, Hotel Transylvania 2, Storks*), Kenan Thompson (*Rock Dog* [Ash Brannon, 2016]) and Frank Armisen (*The LEGO Ninjago Movie* [Charlie Bean, 2017]).

The predominance of stand-up comedians with careers outside cinema, or at least actors with connections to the American stand-up comedy circuit, across multiple computer-animated films is often targeted through specific characterisations. For example, the cheery, spirited, forgetful and often rambling personality of Pacific regal blue tang fish Dory in both *Finding Nemo* and *Finding Dory* is well-served by the intuitive impulses and improvisations of comedienne Ellen DeGeneres, who began her stand-up career in New Orleans during the 1980s. DeGeneres' riffing, real-time responsiveness, imbued with a feeling of the unprepared and illogical, offers an excess of verbal material that fully realises the spontaneity and absent-mindedness of Dory's aquatic character. Computer-animated films have ultimately extended the cohesive generic forms and techniques of 'comedian comedy'. This was a comedian-centred form of the studio era offering primacy to the spectacle of the comedy star's film performance, manifested, as Steve Seidman argues, through the 'comedian's awareness of the spectator's presence and the assertion of his own presence [that] both work toward described enunciation' (1981: 5). The same structures of address privileging the comedian's presence are endemic to the computer-animated film. Claire Mortimer's description of Woody Allen in the first sequence of *Annie Hall* fits closely with the introduction of Allen's character in *Antz*. As Alvy Singer, Allen 'strings together a series of gags, in the style of a comedian's stand-up routine' and with 'poignant glimpses of his despair and low self-esteem' (2010: 85). The juxtaposition in *Annie Hall* of the 'deeply personal' with the 'ridiculous' is no less manifested in *Antz* by the meandering monologue of Z as he talks to his therapist (and to the spectator) about his failure to subscribe to 'this whole gung-ho super-organism thing'. Self-deprecating, isolated and showing his anxious 'fear of enclosed spaces', *Antz* utilises the organising force of the virtuoso stand-up performer within the diegetic activities of its Luxo world.

The strong verbal patter of computer-animated films has ultimately crafted new possibilities for the comic union of sound and comedy in animation. Rebecca Coyle suggests that 'an issue that has particularly intrigued animation-sound scholars is that of 'funny music', that is, the ways that music and sound are used for humour' (2010: 13). Within the construction of its comedy routines, however, the hyperrealist approach to sound in the computer-animated film relies upon a more naturalistic application of an appropriate audio track. The abandonment of formal musical numbers has situated the computer-animated film outside an animated comedy rooted in the arrangement of sound. Computer-animated films conventionally jettison the 'patter song' or 'comedy song' (Ghez 2010: 505), the stock-in-trade of the Broadway-style musical-comedy format popularised throughout Walt Disney's Second Golden Age. However, the computer-animated film's recent return to the recognisable movie-musical template, with *Frozen, Moana, Strange Magic, Trolls* and, most notably, *Sing* has significantly reopened the comedic possibilities of the musical number within the genre's comic repertoire.

In their audiovisual composition, computer-animated films therefore eschew the explosive aural dynamics of Warner Brothers, and instead fortify the organic connection between sound and image. Within their *symphonic*, rather than *cacophonic*, sound register (Brophy 2003: 137), eminent film composers of the contemporary Hollywood era such as Randy Newman (*Toy Story* films, *Monsters University*), Thomas Newman

(*Finding Nemo*), Danny Elfman (*Meet the Robinsons, 9, Epic*), John Powell (*Bolt*), John Williams (*The Adventures of Tintin: The Secret of the Unicorn*), Michael Giacchino (*Up, Cars 2*), Hans Zimmer (*Kung Fu Panda 2, The Boss Baby*) and Alan Silvestri (*The Wild, Beowulf, The Croods*) have designed elaborate instrumental scores that fully support the nuanced trajectory and tonal shifts of the computer-animated film's narrative structure. Unlike more conventional forms of screen comedy such as slapstick, or even the episodic patterns of repetition within cartoon plotlines, computer-animated films offer greater scope for narrative peaks and troughs of comedy and pathos, laughter and poignancy. The distinction that Scott Curtis (1992: 202–3) makes between another set of audio categories germane to animation sound – *isomorphic* fidelity and *iconic* analogy – is also applicable to the soundscapes of computer-animated films. Their audio track is rhythmically and *isomorphically* shaped around the images (a technique known pejoratively as 'mickey-mousing'). These synchronised musicological rhythms are not, however, used to create conspicuous effects that achieve their impact through heightened analogy and a degree of jarring incongruity. Rather, the genre's *isomorphism* is rooted in a hyperrealist approach that eschews the comic possibilities of incongruous and inappropriate sounds, and aims instead for an emotive, rousing musical score that is closer to the effect of live-action cinema.

Case Study: *Monsters, Inc.*

Monsters, Inc. explicitly inscribes the stand-up credentials of improvisational comedian Billy Crystal into its narrative events, whilst disclosing the role of sound within the character's comedic armoury. The film's final scenes depict Crystal's character Mike Wazowski performing an acerbic and observational comedy routine to a young boy in their bedroom, reminiscent of a late-night stand-up act in a comedy club ('It's great to be here in your room!'). The fast-paced delivery of Crystal is staged for the awakened child onscreen as an entertaining comic spectacle, as Mike extemporises about his childhood and sports prowess, and tries to engage the drowsy audience in his personal monologue (Figure 8.1). Steve Neale and Frank Krutnik have suggested 'much short comedy is of the comedian comedy kind' (1990: 109), citing animated figures like Bugs Bunny, Daffy Duck and Tweetie Pie who all gesture to camera to signal their deviant behaviour and supposedly onscreen/offscreen split-personality. In the case of *Monsters, Inc.* this short performance is shaped around showcasing Crystal's own history as a comedian (he performed during the 1970s at The Improv and Catch a Rising Star comedy clubs in Los Angeles and

Figure 8.1 Frame grab from *Monsters, Inc.* (2001) (Pixar Animation Studios).
Mike Wazowski's stand-up routine.

New York respectively). Sat perched on a bar stool, Mike's delivery of his well-honed routine reflects how *Monsters, Inc.* literally spotlights the intimacy of 'live' stand-up comedy, couching Mike's act in a wider narrative that is invested in the authority of the voice as an energy supply that powers the city of Monstropolis.

However, with Mike's verbal jokes and wordplay failing to elicit any laughter from the unresponsive child, the one-eyed monster abandons his chatter, and resorts to a clearly-rehearsed physical routine in which he swallows his microphone before regurgitating it back up in a feat of comic flatulence. Only now does the child laugh hysterically, clapping and screaming wildly upon seeing this perfectly executed stunt. Mike is here presented as an anomaly. He is a specific type of stand-up comedian, contrary to the other monsters that work for the 'Monsters, Incorporated' company who resort to all manner of props to stimulate their young audience's laughter, including wind-up false teeth, funny glasses and spinning plates. As Mike himself states, 'Only someone with perfect comedic timing could produce this much energy'. The climax of *Monsters, Inc.* is therefore explicit in adding verbal comedy to the computer-animated film's comic arsenal through Mike's oral skills. Within the newfound desire of the company to 'Think Funny' – the motto that now adorns its Laughter Floor – Pixar's film suggests the necessary coexistence of the comedy of language with physical absurdity.

A History of Violence

In his examination of the sixteen Droopy cartoons directed by Tex Avery during a twelve-year period between *Dumb-Hounded* (1943) and *Deputy Droopy* (1955), Curtis asks, 'why do cartoon characters always have funny voices? Certainly, it is because they have funny bodies' (1992: 202). For Curtis, 'funny' is a synonym for 'distorted' and 'elastic', reflective of the (often literal) eye-popping, nonsensical proportion, infinite flexible body parts, deflating limbs and stretchy heads that manifest the visual language of animation's physical absurdity and the reaching of its threshold of distortion. As one hillbilly tells the audience in Tex Avery's early animated film *A Feud There Was* (1938), 'in one of these here now cartoon pictures, a body can get away with anything', including the impossible recovery of their bodily shapes.

Unless bodily reshaping and exaggerated physical curvature function as a moniker of unprecedented superhumanity (Elastigirl in *The Incredibles*), is an intrinsic feature of an object's design (*Toy Story*'s Slinky Dog), or is a feature of a gelatinous chemical mass (Benzoate Ostylezene BiCarbonate, or B.O.B., in *Monsters vs. Aliens*), an alternate set of rules preside over the *un*distorted and *un*elastic movement and behaviour of computer-animated film bodies. Only a handful of computer-animated films trade in such exceptionalism, and very few present images of metamorphosis. *The Legend of Secret Pass* (Steve Trenbirth, 2010) and *Animal Crackers* (Scott Christian Sava, 2017) are two computer-animated films that involve human to non-human transformation, though these acts are framed by narratives of Native American folklore and the supernatural respectively. Reprising the physical capriciousness of Felix the Cat, Sandman from *Rise of the Guardians* also draws on visual metaphors and symbols summoned from his own revivifying and reanimating body (made of unstable particles. Sandman also evokes traditions of sand animation as pioneered by Caroline Leaf in the 1960s). However, computer-animated film bodies typically do not hold the same fluid and flexible properties that define other animated bodies. A demonstration of stability and immutability, computer-animated films fail to exhibit the hyperbolic and distorted representations characteristic of 'animated' behaviour in cartoons. As the eponymous elephant Horton from *Horton Hears a Who!* shrieks about his stretched trunk, 'it's not supposed to bend that way!'

As a consequence of this bodily sturdiness, computer-animated films have sidestepped animation's lengthy tradition in cartoons of dismemberment and the sensationalism of suffering bodies that Harry Ruskin suggests 'is nasty but unfortunately it is true' (1974: 48). Computer-animated films do not partake in the allure of injury, or the 'head and body blows' at the centre of animation's history of violence, and in the main avoid the physical comedy of stretching, splintering, crumpling, discoloration and squashing. This is not to say that computer-animated films do not contain the occasional violent element. But this is an alternate brand of brutality. Computer-animated film violence is closer to live-action cinema than cartoon violence, or even the body horror of *anime* (in which bodies are disfigured and refigured through transformation and invasion by foreign forces) (Napier 2005). Eric Lichtenfeld writes that 'Rather than mallets and meat cleavers [familiar from multiple *Tom and Jerry* narratives], the heroes of *The Incredibles* must evade machine gun fire and gasoline explosions – and the occasional laser beam and killer robot' (2004: 324). In *The Incredibles*, Elastigirl must remind her children that the 'bad guys' in the film 'won't exercise restraint'. Such an admission suggests that violence in the film's fictional world demarcates boundaries of good/bad, identifying the villain's malevolence and megalomania in ways that Jerry's relationship to Tom never did. Jerry is not positioned as a villain to Tom's hero, despite the 'painful indignity' (Palmer 1995: 162) he inflicts upon his feline nemesis. Computer-animated films, by comparison, frequently make spectators aware of the frailty and fragility of characters' bodies, revolting against the 'harmless vivisection' that leaves animated figures with 'no after-effects' (Leslie 2002: 6) of their violent escapades. Bodily mutilation and disfigurement are no longer implicated in a discourse of painless recovery and cartoon immortality. Characters bleed and break, lose their lower legs (*How to Train Your Dragon*), and suffer the heartbreak of being unable to bear children (*Up*). Actions hurt and characters suffer embarrassing 'growth spurts' (Balthazar Bratt in *Despicable Me 3*), both in individual films and across franchises, while superheroes are not immune to the perils of ageing. Even the *Toy Story* films implicate the rhetoric of a susceptible body within a discourse of disposability and diminishing value.

Computer-animated films have, on occasion, exploited their differences from live-action by nullifying the consequences of violent events, and have a character (impossibly) escape brutal tribulations unscathed. These exceptions to the rules of the genre may again be ameliorated by certain remarkable characters. Throughout *Wreck-It Ralph*, much is made of the regenerative possibilities of Fix-It Felix Jr., a video game avatar charged with the ability to 'respawn' (to become born again within a video game world) no matter how many times he is killed 'in-game'. Gaming practice involves the pleasures of 'rebirth, respawning, and reincarnation', and 'multiple selves and multiple lives are assumed in game construction'

(Detweiler 2010: 192–3). Death within a video game is a temporary setback, one that is easily rectified by the innate mechanisms of gameplay. Repeated comic spectacle is made out of Felix's intrinsic indestructibility, drawing him into the lineage of the hapless Wile E. Coyote and luckless Tom Cat. A short sequence has Felix wounded no less than nine times in quick succession. But after each injury, a musical melody cues his signature revival, and he returns as sprightly and jovial as before. The scene is played for its comedy to a watching audience whose laughter becomes instantly triggered ('We're killing them! Comedy gold!'). Fix-It Felix is certainly atypical of computer-animated films, and his durability is contextualised by the conditions of *Wreck-It Ralph*'s specific video game milieu.

Seeing the Funny Side

Computer-animated films have ushered in a new phase of funny faces, (re)staging the body as a comic spectacle in a variety of new ways. They exploit their capacity to convincingly animate physical traits and tics associated with laughter in the performance of individual characters, such as 'smiling, shaking of head or torso, crinkling of eyes' (Glenn 2003: 66–7). DreamWorks CG Supervisor Bert Poole suggests that 'comedy is one situation where a character's facial gestures are important', and thus high-key lighting techniques are employed to support the 'readability' of a computer-animated figure's expressive physiognomy (in Sullivan et al. 2013: 96). But the luminous properties of a Luxo world extend to the intelligibility of physical comedy and the articulation of animated slapstick. In the opening scene of *Kung Fu Panda 2*, Panda protagonist Po deploys increasingly unorthodox martial arts manoeuvres to protect the Valley of Peace community from encroaching Wolf Bandits. High-key lighting during this fight sequence enables spectators to see 'how the comedy plays out easily amongst a lot of action' (ibid.). Other formal techniques are employed across computer-animated films to augment the comic spectacle of the body in ways not typically thought of in relation to animation. As it does in live-action, editing can contribute to the expressiveness and comedy of a single or repeated gesture. The sequence from *Kung Fu Panda* depicting Po's failed entrance to the Dragon Warrior tournament, and Gru's attempts at gaining access to Vector's Fortress in *Despicable Me*, employs rapid-cutting and montage editing to underline the comedy of each character's physical actions. The excessive stylisation as they jump, climb and vault impenetrable walls amplifies the monotonous futility, but also the floundering comedy, of their repetitious actions.

Traditionally the reserve of action cinema and its highly stylised execution of violence, slow-motion techniques are another widespread feature of computer-animated films used to heighten audience suspense by elongating a shot's expected duration. Computer-animated films employ the stretched temporality of slow-motion sequences as a visual tactic intensifying the spectators' appreciation of their human and non-human characters, creating prolonged bursts of activity that do not delight in the animation of death, but find pleasure in animated life. The *Kung Fu Panda* films are well-versed in utilising slowed-down activity for its comedic potential, holding spectators' attention on Po's corpulent physique and ungainly movements. Bodies are also shown in excessive slow-motion in *The Magic Roundabout*, *Hoodwinked*, *Madagascar: Escape 2 Africa* (Eric Darnell and Tom McGrath, 2008), *Legend of the Guardians: The Owls of Ga'Hoole*, *Tangled*, *Brave* and *Trolls*, each disclosing and disintegrating computer-animated characters through their ulterior tempo. In one sequence from *Over the Hedge*, the abnormally vigorous squirrel Hammy gulps a sugar-loaded energy drink, prompting his pupils to dilate and his body to spasmodically gyrate. To visually convey Hammy's heightened hyperactivity, the film decelerates the surrounding action and affords the squirrel opportunity to wander impossibly – and at seemingly 'normal' speed – through the fictional world as it slowly unfolds (it is revealed that even the Earth has stopped spinning on its axis). Playing Hammy's caffeine-induced transcendence through the relativity of passing time, *Over the Hedge* reconfigures the character's sudden breakneck movement into a leisurely stroll through a world that appears to be moving in slow-motion.

The comic possibilities of slow-motion have also been mined by computer-animated films with a more self-conscious quality. The fight sequence between Princess Fiona and Robin Hood's Merry Men in *Shrek* parodies the visual spectacle of 'bullet-time' (or digital 'time-slice') technology: the digital turning inwards on itself to render its own visual capabilities. Popularised by *The Matrix* (The Wachowskis, 1999) as its signature style, bullet-time is a technology that brings the decelerated rhythms of slow-motion (as a device of duration) closer to the stillness of the freeze frame, whilst its conjoining of moving images with single photographs provides 'the illusion of movement in a comparable way to stop-motion animation' (Constandinides 2010: 83). Indeed, as Andrew Shail argues, bullet-time conflates live-action with animation in that it works to 'render real bodies as animated figures' (2005: 31), thereby allowing 'cinema' to take on the qualities of frame-by-frame animation through its use of multiple cameras to capture movement. Bullet-time is thus a highly animated temporality, and computer-animated films are able to easily recreate the visual effect of a process that conventionally involves virtual cinematography and digital compositing to achieve its spectacular effects. Although Michael North has argued that slow-motion has 'no real meaning in the context of animation' (2009: 59), the computer-animated film's simulation of the 'slo-mo' and bullet-time technique permits the physicality, mobility and animated acrobatics of its bodies to be played for laughs. The addition of slow-motion adds to the computer-animated film's comic arsenal by mimicking the technology used in live-action, enhancing through deceleration the humorous spectacle of bodily movement.

The solidity and volume to the computer-animated film's many bodies is supported by their construction as empathetic, engaging characters with strong personalities. Within cartoon comedy, Wells explains that the 'power of the personality' determines the impact and force of the animated gag, and it is therefore 'intrinsically funnier if a king slips on a banana skin than a child' (1998: 130). Computer-animated films have replaced animation's history of violence with a comedy of character, figuratively 'weighted' in favour of their distinctive temperaments and personalities. John and Kristin Kundert-Gibbs (2009) have looked specifically at how computer-animated characters are demonstrative of certain kinds of behavioural patterns by drawing on complex theories of character structure derived from twentieth-century psychiatric therapy and bioenergetics. They argue that many computer-animated films exhibit nuanced character types known by the labels *schizoid*, *oral*, *psychopath* (which can be further subdivided into *seducing* and *bullying* stereotypes), *masochist* and *rigid* (ibid.: 125). Anton Ego from *Ratatouille* displays *masochistic* body cues (hunched and compressed, contracted vertically), while *Toy Story*'s Buzz Lightyear 'is an excellent example of a *rigid* type' (ibid.: 130) on account of his hyper-narcissistic behaviour.

Beyond these pure categories, the antagonistic Bowler Hat Guy from *Meet the Robinsons* is further interpreted as a mix of the *masochist* and *psychopath* physicality, as his 'scheming desire' is reflected in his design ('overblown top half' and undersized legs) and self-sabotage tendencies (ibid.). Even the rare *oral* type, they suggest, is typified in the personality of Violet Parr from *The Incredibles*. Violet's superpowers of invisibility manifest several of her particular *oral* traits, such as an 'undercharged state', attempts at independency, underdeveloped physicality and whiny persona. According to Kundert-Gibbs, the *oral* character type 'develops an ego ideal that she is very charged and very energetic. [. . .] The world doesn't understand this energy, so others misunderstand all the energy the oral thinks she has' (ibid.). In *The Incredibles*, Violet's (normally latent) superhero capabilities for conjuring a protective force field visualise precisely this energy that both emerges from and defines elements of her *oral* character.

Computer-animated films can, however, mine the multi-faceted personalities of its complex characters for their comic potential. For example, *schizoid* personalities are traditionally defined according to abandonment and trauma. They are dissociative individuals who continually negotiate an anxious experience of feeling unwanted. Kundert-Gibbs argues that 'in dramatic work, schizoid characters are most often the comic sidekicks of the hero if they are 'good'. However, the *schizoid* also describes those characters in fictional works that 'snap' and become charged with cruelty and 'twisted morality' (ibid.: 123). What makes such character types funny, however, is the effortless attribution of them to computer-animated anthropomorphs. In *Antz*, Z admits that he had an anxious childhood (his father leaving when he was 'just a larva'). The *schizoid* personality also underscores the insecurity of *Toy Story*'s Rex ('I don't think I can take that kind of rejection!'). Humour emerges from the plastic dinosaur's preoccupation with his disproportioned body and lack of ferociousness. Other characters that might be identified as *schizoid* personalities include Melman the Giraffe in the *Madagascar* series ('You know how I have to get up every two hours because of my bladder infection') and the Donkey from *Shrek*, who confides in the eponymous ogre upon their first meeting that he 'don't have any friends'. But computer-animated films have also balanced the quirky, if slightly withdrawn, 'good' sidekick role with the hostile manifestation of the *schizoid* personality through their curiously retroactive depiction of its villains.

Computer-animated film characters are therefore increasingly imbued with developed personalities and a memory in ways that their unelastic, concrete bodies are not. Daniel Goldmark describes a climactic moment from *Ratatouille* in which food critic Anton Ego nostalgically 'recalls his mother effacing a boo-boo with a bowl of ratatouille' (2013: 213). Ego's first taste of the film's signature food dish cues a sudden flashback to a childhood memory of his mother's own cooking in their family kitchen (the bowl of ratatouille providing welcome distraction from the young Anton's grazed knee). It is the comical image of a pre-pubescent Anton gazing adoringly at his mother (and then down at his food) that undercuts his present-day arrogance by sympathetically portraying him as an innocent child. Several of the computer-animated film's primary antagonists, including Gru (*Despicable Me*), Megamind (*Megamind*), Bowler Hat Guy (*Meet the Robinsons*) and General Shankar (*Escape From Planet Earth*), are similarly demystified in humorous scenes of villainous youth that reveal them to be lonely, dissociative or unwanted children. They are each depicted as young, unappreciated dreamers who are the subject of parental hostility.

Such 'babyfication' or infantalising of animated characters often constitutes the inevitable nadir of a cartoon's life cycle, as studios attempt to revitalise waning interest through a 'childish' re-imagining of its primary cast. Examples include *Jim Henson's Muppet Babies* (1984–91), *The Flintstone Kids* (1986–8), *A Pup Named Scooby-Doo* (1988–91), *Tom & Jerry Kids* (1990–5), *Baby Looney Tunes* (2002) and *Pink Panther and Pals* (2010). But computer-animated films regressively age their characters to give motive to their avoidant behaviour. These revelatory comic sequences are designed to explicate the antagonist's later (misguided) aspirations of villainous superiority. They equally craft a space in which to laugh at their villainy by undercutting their cruelty and vindictive behaviour with the pleasure of their youthful re-design. Perhaps the greatest embodiment of the *schizoid* paradigm in the computer-animated film, however, occurs in *The Incredibles*. The film reveals that outcast and fantasist Buddy Pine's failed quest to become Mr Incredible's sidekick whilst still a child ('I am your ward, IncrediBoy!') leads him to develop his alternatively villainous persona, Syndrome, during adulthood (Figure 8.2). *The Incredibles* thus combines in its depiction of Buddy the two kinds of *schizoid* personalities typically found in the construction of fictional characters. The film suggests that to close off one manifestation of the *schizoid* personality (the 'sidekick' role) results in the other villainous behaviour 'snapping' into activation. In computer-animated films, then, villainous characters are particularly shown undergoing dramatic transformation and metamorphosis at the level of personalities, a change that is often read through their ascension to adulthood.

Figure 8.2 Frame grab from *The Incredibles* (2004) (Pixar Animation Studios). The youthful villainy of Buddy Pine/Syndrome.

As a funny old business, computer-animated films are predominantly a cinema of comedy, with their formal currency and versatility as a graphic art form designed to make audiences laugh and laugh again. The axiomatic partnership between computer-animated films and comedy is firmly entrenched in their development of more complex, nuanced characters, and the creation of an ensemble cast whose conflicting and complementary personalities support the genre's comic spirit of mockery and misrule. But the increasing depth and three-dimensionality of computer-animated film characters is also signalled by their unexpected and humorous mobility. Such characters may wrestle with conflicting emotions, develop feelings over time, or demonstrate a capacity to behave 'out of character', yet they are also charged with an ability to freely ascend from a Luxo world into the promotional spaces that surround them. As the next chapter argues, it is this freedom of movement through, into and across certain spaces that enhances their credibility, all the while raising to a higher pitch of emphasis their identity as fully-realised personalities.

CHAPTER 9

DreamWorks Animation, Metalepsis and Diegetic Deconstruction

The conjoining of animation with the narratological device of metalepsis has provided a more precise framework for analysing an extensive body of cartoons whose loose narrative structures lean heavily upon the contexts of their creation (Feyersinger 2010; Limoges 2011). For Gérard Genette, metalepsis within a literary context accounts for 'any intrusion by the extradiegetic narrator or narratee into the diegetic universe (or by the diegetic characters into a metadiegetic universe, etc.)' (1983: 235). Playing upon the 'double temporality of the story and the narrating', the impact of the metaleptic transgressions between narrative worlds – in any direction – occurs at the border or boundary between them; that is, the 'shifting but sacred frontier between two worlds, the world *in* which one tells, [and] the world *of* which one tells' (ibid.: 236). In the case of animation, the extradiegesis (metonymically symbolised by the animator's hand or animating instrument itself, though often both) intrudes or intervenes into the intradiegesis, to intimately and directly control the intradiegetic content and thereby dissolve fictional boundaries.

Computer-animated films are certainly not governed by the same logic of transgression and violation of borders that conventionally characterises this extensive lineage of 'deconstructive' animation, which commonly 'reveals the premises of its own construction for critical and comic effects' (Wells 2002a: 67). Animators do not physically intrude into the computer-animated fiction, nor is their offscreen presence visualised metonymically within the Luxo world through the 'hand of the artist' trope (Crafton 1979). In fact, these are films that have been identified for their strong resistance, rather than adherence, to the variations and modalities of metalepsis as a comedic device, cited as 'not part' (Power 2012: 46) of the kinds of self-reflexive animation that conventionally undertakes such disruptive operations. However, this chapter suggests the ways in which computer-animated films can be conceptualised according to a comedy of rhetorical metalepsis, identifying how metaleptic transgression plays a significant role in appreciating the complexity of their comedy. Computer-animated films certainly convey multiple strategies to achieve what Douglas Hofstadter has described as 'strange loops, or tangled hierarchies' (1979: 684) between the extradiegetic world of the author and the intradiegetic space of the fiction. Computer-animated characters can, for example, establish a degree of autonomy by communicating with their own extended extradiegetic world, from company logos to credits sequences and even the features of film form. This chapter argues that comedy arises at the junctures where spectators recognise the communication between the worlds as colliding fictions, where the conflict between the world of the framing and that which is framed is coerced into a comic spectacle.

Laughing at Logos

The creative re-design of corporate identities has been commonplace throughout cinema history, though such practices have proliferated in the contemporary Hollywood era. Paul Grainge points out that 'the early 1990s saw a flurry of modifications to studio logos in response to broad changes in corporate management and the launch of specific entertainment divisions' (2008: 69). Evolutions in the design of studio signification exploited technological developments in sound design and digital imagery, retaining the brand capital of the studio whilst affording a host of creative makeovers to the distinctive stamp of corporate authorship. One such refinement involved the adjustment and re-shaping of logos to accommodate particular blockbuster releases, tailoring the house style of corporate signatures in ways that reproduced the themes, aesthetics and mood of the film that was being introduced.

Computer-animated films have made significant contributions to this history, co-opting the topography of the logo within the film's habits and formal styles to craft a greater consistency between the text and the world of its promotion. In *Space Chimps*, the multi-coloured 'Vanguard' logo that opens the film is lowered by an intruding mechanical arm and dipped in metallic liquid Freznar (subsequently used in the main feature film by the film's villain, Zartog, to transform aliens into statues). For *Wreck-It Ralph*, the Walt Disney Animation Studios emblem is customised to reflect the film's retro-video game narrative. The black-and-white footage of *Steamboat Willie* (Walt Disney and Ub Iwerks, 1928) now incorporated into the Walt Disney Feature Animation logo design – first used in *Meet the Robinsons* – is pixelated in 8-bit computer graphics. Electronic arcade game style music also substitutes Mickey Mouse's tuneful whistling to fully envelop the company insignia into *Wreck-It Ralph*'s video game aesthetic. *The LEGO Movie* similarly personalises the opening Warner Animation Group and Village Roadshow logos, which appear as if expertly built from Lego bricks.

The disruption of these logos' visual integrity is typical of the new narrative meanings now attained by these corporate signatures. As Grainge puts it, 'Studio logos have come to play a more pronounced role in the formal, stylistic and thematic unfolding of Hollywood trailers and credit sequences, inviting questions not only about the nature of corporate branding in post-classical Hollywood, but also about how logos act upon, and can give meaning to, a film' (ibid. 71). The sustained customisation and increasing complexity of logos in the computer-animated film draws upon strategies of metalepsis to open up the paratextual space to invasion and corruption, creating logos that are not static and stable but moving and mobile. The sudden migration of computer-animated film characters that can effortlessly move from their original context into the world of branding material, corporate logos and company signs is a playful tangling of the world *of* which one tells and *in* which one tells. Computer-animated films use the infiltration of the intradiegesis into the extradiegesis to render its paratextual material highly unstable, making hospitable the material surrounding the fiction to the substance of the fiction itself. These are extradiegetic spaces, staged as equivalent to what Jean-Marc Limoges calls 'the present world of the spectator' (2011: 207), that is the reality of the extrafictional realm in which projection, reception and consumption take place. The logos have acquired their own storytelling functions, three-dimensional narrative spaces suddenly accessible and readily occupied by characters who can now enter into a dialogue with the paratextual world around them.

The introduction of animated characters into the paratextual material is, of course, a defining feature of the computer-animated films produced by Pixar. Beginning with *A Bug's Life*, each of Pixar's films open with the anthropomorphic star of *Luxo Jr.* entering into the 'PIXAR' logo and bouncing upon the 'I' until it comically deflates (prompting the lamp to turn sheepishly to the audience). This kind of comical intrusion has been prevalent across many other computer-animated films. At the start of *Escape From Planet Earth*, the Weinstein Company logo is abducted by one of the film's spaceships under a beam of luminous green light and dragged out beyond the frame, while in *Open Season 3* (Cody Cameron, 2010) an 'Open Season 2' logo is mistakenly presented, only to be hastily amended by the teeth of an attentive beaver that carves the correct title (the direct-to-video special *Open Season: Scared Silly* [David Feiss, 2015] even has its opening logo 'themed', tinted black and white to reflexively evoke its horror genre roots).

In their recourse to character movement across corporate and story worlds, computer-animated films offer up a highly creative set of para-textual media materials that fully exploit the possibilities of the studio logo. *Spirit of the Forest* depicts rodent protagonist Furi encased within the logo for Spanish film production company Dygra Films. Waving to the audience, Furi is unsettled from the safety of the crest by a dog, who chases him into the film's opening sequence. Both *Planes* (Klay Hall, 2013) and *Planes: Fire & Rescue* (Roberts Gannaway, 2014) similarly make the Disney Magic Castle and the DisneyToons logo respectively available to an aerobatic flyover routine by their main characters; in *Strange Magic*, the film's mischievous imp creature runs over, around and through the opening Lucasfilm company crest; and in *Air Bound*, the film's anthropomorphic cast piece together the 'Shirogumi Inc.' badge from its constituent parts.

Produced by the Malaysian KRU Studios, *Ribbit* (Chuck Powers, 2015) also exploits the storytelling possibilities of metaleptic intrusion to introduce its protagonists before the film's narrative properly begins. Amphibian protagonists Ribbit and Sandy are shown free to move within the three-dimensional architecture of the KRU Studios crest in a moment that, in many respects, becomes the film's first sequence. More recently, in *The Peanuts Movie* (Steve Martino, 2015), the precocious Schroeder sits at his iconic red toy piano in front of the golden Twentieth Century Fox logo and plays along with the orchestral fanfare, composed in 1933 by Alfred Newman, which traditionally accompanies the company's signature. In *Rio 2*, this fanfare is replaced with a Brazilian carnival drumbeat, while in *Minions*, *Trolls* and *Captain Underpants: The First Epic Movie*, the main characters are heard respectively humming along to the Universal fanfare (originally composed by James Horner) and John Powell and Harry Gregson-Williams's DreamWorks company music. Such devices of metalepsis intensify the 'highly self-conscious' and communicative raison d'être of the studio logo sequence (Bordwell et al. 1988: 25), re-making and ultimately narrativising these *sequences* as transitory and penetrable *spaces* through their invasion by computer-animated film characters (either visually or sonically). In so explicitly 'tailoring the form and appearance of logos for presentational ends' (Grainge 2008: 35), the extraneous intrusion into branding space by these unruly computer-animated bodies also reflexively acknowledges discourses of 'property' and 'protection' that traditionally comes with the territory of corporate branding.

A particularly regularised pattern of metalepsis has developed in this regard within the computer-animated features of one particular Hollywood studio. The Columbia Pictures logo, depicting an unidentified woman ('Lady Columbia') carrying a torch and draped in the American flag, has undergone only five stylistic revisions in design since 1924 (the most recent in August 1993 by artist Michael Deas). In October 1989, the famous logo was unofficially co-opted for the front cover of *Newsweek* following Japanese company Sony's acquisition of Columbia Pictures Entertainment the previous month. Laurie A. Freeman explains how 'the cover contained an illustration of the Columbia Pictures logo dressed in a kimono and the bold headline "Japan Invades Hollywood!"' (2002: 149). This satiric re-design of the Columbia logo reflects both its cultural recognisability, but also the novelty, spectacle and even controversy that can surround iconographic disruption. However, several computer-animated films have provided an alternate context in which the company's corporate identity has been refashioned, offering playful revisions of Columbia logo consistent with the films they preface.

In *Cloudy with a Chance of Meatballs*, an enlarged banana enters unexpectedly into the frame like a boomerang, easily toppling the Lady Columbia from her privileged position upon the carved plinth (Figure 9.1). In *Hotel Transylvania*, the authority of the female figure is similarly upturned, transformed into a bat that flaps towards the screen before lifting up the Columbia image to reveal another company identifier underneath (Sony Pictures Animation). Comical sound effects cue this disruption (including Lady's Columbia's shriek as she is flung from her position), matched to the unexpected fluidity of the typography as it succumbs to external intrusion. The joke of Lady Columbia is then repeated

Figure 9.1 Frame grab from *Cloudy with a Chance of Meatballs* (2009) (Sony Pictures Animation/Columbia Pictures). *Cloudy with a Chance of Meatballs* disrupts the stability and sanctity of its extradiegetic material.

in both sequels. Whereas the variant logo for *Hotel Transylvania 2* revisits the bat transformation, *Cloudy with a Chance of Meatballs 2* replays the banana gag but this time the fruit sprouts legs, and is joined by a similarly anthropomorphic strawberry carrying a torch as they run offscreen. Following this pattern, computer-animated film *Smurfs: The Lost Village* (Kelly Asbury, 2017) similarly chooses to replace Lady Columbia with a character from the main feature film. As the signature horn music reaches its climax, the iconic Torch Lady is once again toppled from her platform by Smurfette (in the process revealing Lady Columbia to be cardboard construction easily felled). It is now the blonde-haired Smurfette who willingly assumes the role of Torch Lady, momentarily replacing previous incumbent, newspaper artist Jenny Joseph, who had worn the star-spangled drape since 1992.

These logo variants and creative re-designs present a heavily stylised vision of metalepsis between the intra- and extradiegesis, a tangling of existents and events in what is a highly comic textual conflation. Indeed, as the latest Columbia logo that precedes *The Emoji Movie* (in which a human hand intrudes into the logo space and takes a photo of Torch Lady to send via a mobile phone) makes clear, the irreverence of metaleptic transgression remains a popular source of computer-animated film comedy. Jonathan Gray points out that it is not uncommon for paratexts to routinely 'take over the texts' (2010: 45) as a result of extreme merchandising strategies; a source of revenue particularly applicable to how computer-animated cinema has been historically packaged and sold to family audiences. However, the metaleptic crossings between intradiegesis and extradiegesis in computer-animated films serve to restate the value of the fiction. As the many Columbia variants illustrate, the computer-animated film text remains fully capable of claiming fleeting superiority over the paratext, 'taking over' the extradiegetic world by engaging and interacting with (and now even photographing) its content. The language of paratextuality, including images, signs and symbols, is thus implicated into the 'text' through a metaleptic arrangement that achieves its impact by blurring the distinction between narrative worlds.

Tangled Takeovers

Nowhere has this takeover been more in operation than across the cycle of feature-length computer-animated films produced by the DreamWorks Animation studio, which have exhibited an unprecedented fluidity between intradiegetic and extradiegetic worlds. Discussion of the DreamWorks logo treat the design of the emblem as a reflection of the creative visions of its founders Steven Spielberg, Jeffrey Katzenberg and David Geffen. For Chuck Robinson, the image of the 'half moon over water, with a small child cradled therein' (2009: 261) holds strong maternal undertones. Warren Buckland, on the other hand, claims the 'inspiring' image evokes facets of the American ideal, arguing that 'The emotional experience that DreamWorks is attempting to convey is an idyllic, idealistic, sentimental Norman Rockwell-type image of America – that is, another universal image of (lost) childhood innocence' (2003: 94). However, the decision to spin off the DreamWorks animation division into a separate company, 'DreamWorks Animation SKG', in 2004 ushered in a new direction for the company crest, extending the central feature of 'transformation' by introducing a strong comedic sensibility.

Released three weeks prior to the trading of the new division, *Shark Tale* added interest to the logo by appending an anthropomorphic worm to the end of the boy's fishing rod. The sudden amalgamation of fictional spaces in this way makes the Tom Sawyer-figure, who sits in the crescent moon and casts his fishing rod below, unexpectedly complicit with the activities of *Shark Tale*'s underwater ecology. With each of the studio's releases, the fishing boy has been subjected to a variety of tribulations that shatter the idyllic, sentimental connotations of the astral landscape. He has suffered an extraterrestrial abduction (*Monsters vs. Aliens, Home*); a violent bee attack prompting his fall from the moon (*Bee Movie*); and an assault and kidnapping by an army of military penguins (*Madagascar: Escape 2 Africa*). Replete with peach trees and lotus flower petals, the ornate 2D oriental stylings that accent the DreamWorks logos for their *Kung-Fu Panda* films (including the DVD bonus short *Secrets of the Furious Five* [Raman Hui, 2008]) replace the fishing boy altogether. For *Kung Fu Panda 3*, it is panda protagonist Po who vaults into the curve of the crescent moon, albeit ungainly, ascending a mountain pathway as he struggles to reach the lunar location ('Okay, guys. Just start without me'). In *Mr. Peabody & Sherman*, the young boy is again replaced by a character from the feature film, this time with seven-year-old Sherman, while in the DreamWorks computer-animated short *Rocky and Bullwinkle* (Gary Trousdale, 2014), the eponymous Rocket J. Squirrel and Bullwinkle Moose re-enact the fishing rod sequence in place of the logo's accepted inhabitant.

DreamWorks have continued to 'theme' the space of their logos and tailor them to the narratives of their feature films in a number of ways. For their more recent *The Boss Baby*, the words 'DreamWorks Animation' are suspended from wires as if hanging delicately from a baby's overhead mobile. In *Trolls*, the company name appears as a scrapbook with coloured felt pieces stuck together (anticipating the film's protagonist Poppy, who is an avid scrapbooker). Within DreamWorks' variant logo designs, metalepsis also explains the ways in which the studio's logo has been physically situated within the geography of the fictional world. During the opening to *Shrek the Third*, the virtual camera seamlessly descends from the production company logo down into the kingdom of Duloc. There is no visible partition designating the closure of the extradiegetic world, no fade-to-black cueing the conclusion of the logo space. A similarly fluid camera movement achieves the same effect in *Madagascar 3: Europe's Most Wanted* and *Turbo*. Werner Wolf suggests that the DreamWorks logo 'paradoxically leads directly into the intradiegetic world and thus plays with the border between reality and fiction' (2011: 13–14). No clear distinction exists between the world of the film and that of its promotion, and the blurring of spaces usually held distinct displaces the logo from its normal, recognisable style. In *The Croods*, for example, the DreamWorks logo forms out of dust collected on a rock buried deep among a series of prehistoric cave paintings that are etched onto the rock walls. For *Penguins of Madagascar*, the logo is similarly made part of the film's diegetic world, carved into a glacier that crashes into the Arctic seas and thereby seemingly open to the tumultuous conditions of the Luxo world.

Case Study: *Rise of the Guardians*

Richard Burt suggests that the animated logos that begin DreamWorks' animated features are 'film sequences in themselves' (2013: 181), playing at the start of the film rather than its end. In DreamWorks' *Rise of the Guardians*, the reconfiguration of the company logo is intended to fully exploit the narrative and visual possibilities of digital imagery to elaborately re-design the promotional space. It is protagonist Jack Frost who here assumes the position perched on the crescent moon: the fishing rod now substituted with Jack's frozen staff. The design of this logo makes clear use of the 'aerial panoramas and clean orchestral fanfares' (Grainge 2008: 76) that have come to characterise the newer styles of three-dimensional logo design and studio branding. The entire logo sequence that begins the film is re-animated to emphasise the visual effect of depth and dimension, with additional decor, new viewing angles and close-ups, an alternate musical score and sound effects that accompany the metaleptic intrusion of Jack into the sacrosanct space of the symbol.

Though lasting less than thirty seconds, *Rise of the Guardians* utilises metaleptic transgression within its logo sequence to 'explicitly mediate the spectator's access to the spatial and epistemic coordinates of the fictional world' (Purse 2013: 32). The sequence begins on a close-up of a floating snowflake, whose twisting path is followed down into Jack's hand as he sits perilously on the moon's edge. Jack bats the snowflake away with his staff, the camera tracking back to follow its momentum as it passes through the 'D' of the DreamWorks company name. As the remaining letters fall into place and the short sequence reaches its conclusion, the logo freezes as a result of Jack's involvement, next dissolving into a series of smaller snowflakes that scatter across the night sky. The traditionally 'gentle and romantic signification' of the DreamWorks logo (Brereton 2012: 163) is here accentuated by the range of digitally animated effects that foreshadow the film's icy themes and frosty motifs. The roving camerawork spatialises the DreamWorks logo by moving through and around the three-dimensional space, before the camera rests in its more familiar frontal position. It also draws attention to the 'threshold of embedding' (Genette 1988: 88) that characterises metalepsis as a rhetorical device, with Jack making a spectacle out of the violation of distinctions between diegetic space and the framing level of promotion. A paratext, in the words of Genette, constitutes a 'fringe' (1997: 2) that can control the reading of the text. But through metalepsis, *Rise of the Guardians* discloses how its computer-animated characters are able to reverse the power structures that support such an arrangement. It is now the text that can control and command the paratext.

Verbal Metalepsis and Comedic Credits

Few limits dictate the creative possibilities of metalepsis in computer-animated films, and the logos and branding spaces of the genre have expanded the creative scope given to studios as they play with their own corporate signatures. Indeed, by finding a place for corporate identities within the parameters of the fictional world, any separating boundary between framing extradiegesis and intradiegesis is progressively disintegrated. The opening to *Legend of the Guardians: The Owls of Ga'Hoole* employs swooping camerawork to pursue the airborne activity of protagonist Noctus the Owl. The owl's energetic movement is tracked as he flies impossibly through the letters of the Warner Brothers and Village Roadshow Pictures crests (that are seemingly suspended in mid-air). Following one final pass through the film's title, Noctus descends through the clouds into the film's Luxo world, the fictional forest kingdom of Tyto.

Both *Chicken Little* and, most notably, *The Wild* begin with what might be termed *verbal metalepsis*. Although *The Wild*'s father-and-son duo Samson and Ryan do not visually enter the logo space, the tangling effect is connoted by the staccato movements of the Walt Disney Pictures emblem that must pause, rewind and re-start to accommodate the demands of the dialogue ('Dad, I've heard this like a billion times'). The most sustained example of verbal metalepsis occurs in *The LEGO Batman Movie*, in which Batman narrates the film's entire opening sequence, including the logo, as if viewing the action live ('And logos. Really long and dramatic logos'). Conducting his voiceover offscreen throughout, Batman here does not directly impact or intrude upon the logo space. However the effect of the verbal commentary is metaleptic as it is rooted in the collapse of narrative spaces using held distinct. The collision between the contemporaneity of Batman's narrative voiceover and the ulterior temporality of unfolding onscreen events (as the object of Batman's verbal clarifications) results in the playful 'spilling over' of narrative material, one framed as a rhetorical flourish of radical disruption that connotes – and obtains its effect from – a porosity of boundaries.

Metalepsis in the computer-animated film can also be intertextual, removing not just the boundaries that separate a Luxo world from the world of studio branding, but those which separate individual Luxo worlds. Here, the spectator witnesses a particular kind of intertextual transgression in which the intradiegesis of one computer-animated film is comically tangled with the extradiegesis world of another. The newly revised Blue Sky Studios logo, which premiered with their computer-animated feature film *Epic*, now features the sabre-toothed squirrel Scrat from their *Ice Age* series. Scrat climbs the letters of the company crest in pursuit of his beloved acorn, only to fall off the side when the logo reaches its final upright position. The 'Illumination Entertainment' logo that is displayed at the start of *Despicable Me* also depicts one of the minions entering the frame, who reappear before the studio's computer-animated film *The Lorax*, where they attempt to fell a Truffula Tree now growing within the logo space. Since adopted as Illumination Entertainment's official mascots, the minions re-appear once more in yet another variant on the company emblem that opens *Despicable Me 2*, and (perhaps expectedly) appear again in the logo that begins their own spin-off feature film *Minions*. For *Sing*, four minions are shown enthusiastically humming the company name (although their high-pitch chant ultimately causes the lightbulbs that illuminate the logo to blow). Each of these metaleptic transgressions relies upon spectators' intertextual knowledge of the characters and their relationship to the studio. These opening logos operate serially: no two narratives are the same, but rather they work in accumulation to develop the supporting characters from *Despicable Me* across multiple computer-animated film texts.

With respect to devices of metalepsis, computer-animated films require spectators to not only consider what happens when two logically distinct worlds become contaminated, but also to consider the implication of an intradiegesis and extradiegesis as they intertextually combine. Computer-animated films utilise the space of the logo as a highly creative paratextual place, functioning as a gateway that provides access into the text. Metalepsis insinuates a Luxo world into the film's promotional diegesis, bringing spectators to the film (and introducing the characters) quicker by playing with the film's point of entry. The manipulation of the logo space also establishes the motifs of entering, leaving, crossing and traversing that are central to the computer-animated film's journey narratives. Just as Barry B. Benson and Jack Frost can move freely through and across the Luxo worlds of *Bee Movie* and *Rise of the Guardians* respectively, the journeys they embark upon can take them into the world of promotional material too.

Computer-animated films also regularly disturb the paratextual material that comprises its end. David Bordwell argues that while the studio era was characterised by a perfunctory 'The End' title, it was during the 1970s that 'closing credits swelled to several minutes, and filmmakers tried to energize them with a prolonged musical score and, occasionally, a continuing stream of footage' (2006: 47–8). No longer obligatory codas to the main feature, these credits (as extended epilogues) conventionally include the repetition of scenes (or entirely new ones), character backstories, or in some cases 'further bits of story action [that] may even be scattered among the final credits' (ibid: 48). Computer-animated films have continued this tradition in three main ways. Firstly, they tend to unfold their closing credits against the backdrop of decorative animated artwork. Burt argues that the closing titles of *Kung Fu Panda* 'unfold horizontally and continuously as a remarkably long Chinese scroll, recalling the scroll that is central to the plot of the film' (2013: 184). Further examples of this practice include the black and white etchings of artist Shiyoon Kim in *Tangled*; the images inspired by art history (Paleolithic, impressionist) that bring to a close *Wall-E*; and the custom typefaces and 2D artwork by Nate Wragg that decorate the closing credits of *Ratatouille*. *Alpha and Omega*, *A Monster in Paris* and *Ribbit* even close with original artwork, concept art and pencil sketches from their own production processes, while *Mars Needs Moms* achieves a similar effect by decorating its credits with behind-the-scenes motion capture footage.

Secondly, it is also not unusual for computer-animated films to include mid- or post-credits scenes as a way of providing additional narrative content, with integrated epilogue scenes a highly favoured resource that extends the boundaries of the Luxo world. *Happily N'Ever After, Rise of the Guardians, Zambezia, Penguins of Madagascar, Strange Magic, Spark: A Space Tail* (Aaron Woodley, 2016) and *The Emoji Movie* all have a mid-credits sequence, intercutting the names of cast and crew with bonus animated footage. *The Secret Life of Pets* even intersperses its closing credits with an extra scene that shows its canine cast attending a fancy dress party dressed as the minion characters from the studio's *Despicable Me* franchise. An impressive number of computer-animated films also include bonus postscripts that reward spectators' prolonged viewing after the final credits have rolled, such as *Shark Tale, Flushed Away, Kung Fu Panda, Happily N'Ever After, Rise of the Guardians, The Croods, Monsters University, Brave, Frozen, Finding Dory* and *The Boss Baby*. In *Ratchet & Clank* (Kevin Munroe, 2016), the post-credits scene reflexively acknowledges the audience's expectations around the persistence of this convention ('Move along, no extra little scene at the end of the movie. I said beat it'). A similar nod to cinema viewing accompanied the credits for theatrical screenings of *Chicken Little*, in which the young chicken is heard asking his father if they can 'get some popcorn on the way out' (this moment is significantly absent from the film's DVD release).

These supplementary post-credits sequences parallel the treatment of the opening logo spaces, and provide creative closing points that extend the pleasure of computer-animated film spectatorship. When the Disney logo is repeated at the climax of *Wreck-It Ralph*, for example, the pristine digital image pixelates, and the orchestral fanfare stutters to an abrupt halt. The malfunctioning image becomes, in video game terminology, a 'kill screen' (Wolf 2012b: 70), or a point in the game that randomly freezes and crashes as a result of a software bug, thus preventing the player's progress. But these kinds of cartoon codas may serve alternate purposes. They can award closure to individual and incomplete narrative arcs left unresolved (*Megamind, Frozen*); reiterate or expand upon motifs in the film (*Brave*), or simply add impressive visual decoration. For example, *Monsters, Inc.* includes an additional scene after its closing credits in which protagonists Mike and Sulley perform a musical based on the film's own narrative. *Happy Feet Two* concludes with the gradient circles familiar from the Looney Tunes logo, a design first premiered in the Friz Freleng cartoon *I Wanna Play House* (1936). The recollection of Golden Age-era artwork even extends to rehearsing the typography of 'That's All Folks!', the signature line (st)uttered by Porky Pig that is simultaneously written out in script at the end of most Warner Brothers cartoons.

The Big Finish

The third way that computer-animated films expand their closing credits is to draw once more on metalepsis to mingle the closing credits with the playful activity of characters. Closing credits become no longer just a list of involved personnel, or 'indispensable sources of information in historical and ethnographic research on the film industry and film production' (Kuhn and Westwell 2012: 100). In the computer-animated film, they function as continuations or extensions of the fictional world. Many of the genre's characters interact with the scrolling list of names: they hang off, dance around, through and on the credits, tilting, squeezing and pushing them to one side, or dragging them offscreen to provide space for their own performance. In the Spanish-Italian computer-animated film *Donkey Xote* (José Pozo, 2007), for example, the letters comprising the name of director José Pozo are scattered out of shot by a jousting horse who gallops unexpectedly into frame and headlong into the credited personal.

As the credits roll in *Madagascar*, *Flushed Away*, *Shrek the Third*, *Horton Hears a Who!*, *Igor*, *Chicken Little*, *Ice Age: Continental Drift*, *The Ugly Duckling and Me!*, *Rio*, *Happy Feet*, *Shrek Forever After* (Mike Mitchell, 2010), *Puss in Boots*, *Jungle Shuffle* (Taedong Park and Mauricio De la Orta, 2014) and *Sing*, additional musical accompaniment permits the characters to respond to an extradiegetic soundtrack, dancing and singing along to the music (often unsuccessfully) as they intermingle with the closing names. Danish computer-animated film *Ronal the Barbarian* achieves a similar effect, albeit with singing skeletons and then finally a series of flaming hands that enter from below and perform the hand gesture synonymous with heavy metal/rock music performances (known as the 'sign of the horns'). For *The Nut Job*, the entire animal cast 'break character' to dance as an ensemble to Korean-pop song 'Gangnam Style', while in the recent French-Canadian co-production *Sahara* (Pierre Coré, 2017) the film's cast of snakes and scorpions, including purple cobra Saladin, weave and scuttle around the scrolling list of names. Although computer-animated films are rarely musicals (though *Sing* and *Postman Pat: The Movie* [Mike Disa, 2014] are structured around a singing competition), these kinds of sequences are typically framed against the backdrop of an ensemble musical performance that provides a more self-conscious context for the metaleptic spectacle. As Elliot proclaims as the film's woodland creatures burst into rousing song in *Open Season 2*, 'big finish now!'

In his account of metalepsis in animation, Erwin Feyersinger is reluctant to call such acts of paratextual interaction metalepsis. He argues that the climax of *Finding Nemo*, in which the film's main aquatic cast swim around, hang from and stare longingly at the scrolling credits, is 'not proper metalepses' because there is 'no direct transgression of the diegetic border' (2010: 285). With minimal sense of invasion from one diegetic world to another and no perceivable 'edge' of the frame to cross, spectators 'are facing two separate, non-continuous versions of the characters, which may or may not have a metaleptic influence on each other' (ibid.). Although spectators are not placed as witness to the act of transgression, these closing credit sequences do have metaleptic qualities. Spectators assume a degree of continuity between the intra- and extradiegetic worlds having the move across these fictional frames made visible. In the case of *Finding Nemo*, the characters' recognition of the scrolling names provides a metaleptic bridge between the film's intra- and extradiegesis. When *Monsters, Inc.* and *Monsters University* protagonist Mike Wazowski briefly joins *Finding Nemo*'s aquatic cast in the closing credits, his intertextual presence reinforces the character's fluid movement across fictional frames. With each of these examples, the intradiegesis of the represented computer-animated storyworld emphatically collides with the framing corporate content. Much like Pat Sullivan and Otto Messmer's *Felix the Cat* cartoons, in which the eponymous hero could playfully entice the creative hand into the frame to graphically change the circumstances of the fiction, computer-animated film characters are able to communicate – albeit non-verbally – with their multiple creators. The flow between two narrative worlds also reflects how computer-animated films begin before the narration sets in, and continue long after their resolution. There is always more to see in a computer-animated film than that which can be contained by the text's running time, and characters are welcomed effortlessly into its paratextual fringes.

Computer-animated films play with where they begin and end, not just through the treatment of their own beginning and endings, but with the formal limits and threshold of the computer-animated image. Their narratives turn to metalepsis to engage with the parameters of 'film/not-film/not-yet-film/no-longer-film' (Elsaesser and Hagener 2010: 37), concerns that guided the development of classical film theory up to the Second World War (particularly in its grasp of film art and medium specificity), but which have been renewed again by live-action's increasing 'animation' through digital manipulation. In the final shot of *The Wild*, as Bridget the giraffe becomes trapped by the iris-in technique at the film's climax that constricts around her neck. Such surprising interactions with the traditional elements of film form implicate computer-animated film comedy within the lineage of Golden Age American cartoons. Throughout the Looney Tunes series, characters were able to quickly jump through the iris as it closed (as in Avery's 1938 short *Cinderella Meets Fella*); have it suddenly reopen to finish the story (*Ballot Box Bunny*, Freleng's 1951 Bugs Bunny cartoon) and even tear it to shreds if it was deemed to close too early (*Duck Amuck* [Chuck Jones 1953]).

In computer-animated films, other formal conceits set the stage for such comic interaction. These include the black matte bars that run horizontally along the top and bottom of the film image (defined as 'hard' mattes when achieved in filming and 'soft' mattes in projection), or in the 'letterboxing' process that involves adding masked black bars in home video transfer (as a product of conversion). Computer-animated films prime these mattes for comedy, absorbing the aspect ratios into their playspaces by fooling around with the symmetrical proportions of the widescreen format. The thick frame lines are co-opted through techniques of metalepsis into three-dimensional physical props. In the final shot of *Monsters vs. Aliens*, the hapless President Hathaway leans out of the black matte bars that frame him, gripping the lower bar of the widescreen effect as he unexpectedly addresses the spectator. The effect of this moment re-conjures something of Spanish artist Pere Borrell del Caso's *Escapism Criticism* (1874), a *trompe l'œil* painting that depicts a young boy mounting the (fictional) painted frame to (fictionally) burst the confines of the pictorial space. The construction of fictive frames has since been repeated in the recent teaser trailer for *Rio 2* in which bulldog Luiz (with a penchant for drooling) extends his neck and tongue beyond the matte bars.

Case Study: *Despicable Me 2 / Minions*

Just as *Duck Amuck* chronicles the futile attempts made by Daffy Duck to 'cope with the sheer weight of the black background scenery which falls upon him like a heavy awning' (Wells 2003: 218–19), both *Despicable Me 2* and *Minions* collapse the matte bars around the anarchic activity of the minions. In the former, the minions cut the black screen horizontally and prise open the heavy bars, reaching out towards the audience to trespass beyond the reality of their fiction and into the extradiegetic world of the videographic image (Figure 9.2). Teetering on the edge of the matte bars, the minions then fall out into the abyss, suddenly occupying a liminal space that is both 'film' and 'not film', supposedly beyond the reaches of the fictional world, but at the same time still somewhere between the world of the film and that of the spectator. *Minions* similarly places its characters in close proximity to the outer frame lines as a way of extending the boundaries of its fictional Luxo world. Reprising two visual jokes from *Despicable Me 2*, the minions are again able to clutch the matte bars

Figure 9.2 Frame grab from *Despicable Me 2* (2013) (Illumination Entertainment/ Universal Pictures). The matte bars are primed for comedy.

as if physical objects mounted somewhere within the diegesis, and blow bubbles that float out into the external space beyond. In one part of the credits sequence, a London beefeater appears beyond the rectangular mattes and blocks the view of the action as he moves right to left in front of the mattes.

Such ruptures in spatial continuity evidently maximise the effects of 3D, a staple of theatrical exhibition for computer-animated films since *Up* and *Monsters vs. Aliens* were the first to be authored in the stereoscopic format (using Autodesk Maya and Autodesk Lustre) rather than retrospectively converted. Barbara Klinger (2013: 2–3) argues that contemporary Hollywood cinema mobilises a regularised, 'codified repertoire' of stylistic elements designed to exploit 3D's signature effect, that of the illusion of depth along the Z-axis (an effect achieved through 'negative parallax'). Recent work on the depth and dimensions of groundbreaking 3D cinema (Elsaesser 2013; Ross 2015; Weetch 2016) has often cited computer-animated films to illustrate not only the application of digital 3D equipment, but the broader contribution of digital animation to the development of a discernible 3D style. In his analysis of the 3D visual strategies of Disney's short *Get a Horse!* (Lauren MacMullan, 2013) – that similarly manipulates the sanctity of film form, including shifting aspect ratios, rupturing screens and the illusion of space beyond (and behind) the frame – Owen Weetch argues that 'computer-generated animation' is 'particularly suited' (2016: 9) to the formal possibilities engendered by 3D cinema. Weetch notes that in the further case of *Frozen*, stereoscopy is put to 'use' and can 'work' (ibid.: 131) within its construction of the Anna/ Elsa relationship. *Frozen*'s rejection of planarity reflects how with the advent of 3D, diegetic space is becoming increasingly re-organised in the pursuit of new 'modes of spatiality' (Elsaesser 2013: 231) that fully exploit the attraction of 3D exhibition.

The treatment of the matte bars in *Despicable Me 2* and *Minions* is certainly devised with the visual splendour and excitement of stereoscopic 3D in mind, as characters reach or 'pop' out in ways that capitalise upon the extra dimensional volume of the diegetic world. The playing of foreground and background in this way spotlights the heightened 'spaciousness of space' (Klinger 2013: 2–3) afforded by 3D's accentuation of character protrusion or extension. However, the metalepsis central to this technique also offers a familiar rhythm to the computer-animated film in which nothing of the extradiegesis is safe or sacred. The threshold between audience and diegesis (as coexistent and connected, but separate spaces) is exploited in *Despicable Me 2* and *Minions* in ways that inter-rogate long-held theoretical questions concerning cinema as an entrance to and experience of another world.

De(con)structive Humour?

Metalepsis yields an unexpected spatial proximity between a computer-animated film's Luxo world and the framing world of corporate logos and film form, both staging and affirming the boundary that separates them whilst simultaneously articulating the very act of transgression. The frequent metaleptic interaction between computer-animated film characters and the paratextual world around them, and the subsequent collapsing of textual boundaries, draws upon and reworks conventions of the 'deconstructive' cartoon. Such cartoons encourage the spectator to laugh at the material components of the cartoon, unpicked, fragmented and exploded before their eyes. The grammar of cartoon syntax is reduced to its basic constituent parts, revealing the premises and processes of its construction. From Winsor McCay and J. Stuart Blackton, through to the deconstructive cartoon's maturity at the hands of Tex Avery, the world of the cartoon is regularly shown to be unstable. It can be rubbed out, erased, effaced and broken. In *Lucky Ducky* (Tex Avery, 1948), for example, a colour short in the late-1940s, two dogs chase a young duck past a signpost reading 'Technicolor Ends Here' into a sudden black and white landscape. The comedy lies in the sudden absence of animation, of space and (obviously) colour. The animated screen space of *Duck Amuck* is no less uncertain, and the offscreen animator (later revealed as Bugs

Bunny) not only removes the animated backdrop and its sound (prompting Daffy to fashion a 'Sound Please' sign), but also eliminates features of
Daffy himself, whether it is his beak or his entire body, leaving just a voice
(but no mouth).

Aylish Wood defines the cartoon space of *Duck Amuck* by its 'blank-
ness', a lack of space that prompts Daffy's inaction and inability to complete the demands of the "narrative situation' (2006: 135). By comparison,
the deconstructive elements of the computer-animated film contribute to
an intensification of presence rather than absence. These are films that use
up their screen spaces and more: nothing is a remainder, but everything
is potentially available. Metalepsis expands the computer-animated film's
fictional world, instead of abridging, restricting or confining it. Computer-
animated films continually incorporate their extradiegetic environments
into a Luxo world, turning them into extended performance spaces. The
events they reveal may not be intrinsically funny, but the characters' abilities to intrude and impress themselves onto another world holds distinct
comic possibilities. At these moments of metalepsis, computer-animated
films engage with the presence of screens and boundaries, partitions and
separations, and invite spectators to reflect upon the potential of the
characters to surmount such limitations. But the computer-animated film
further extends the parameters of the 'deconstructive' cartoon, playing
not only with the possibility of an extradiegetic or extra-filmic identity
for its characters, but as the next chapter argues, with the very illusionist
properties of the films themselves.

CHAPTER 10

The Mannerist Game

Approximately eight minutes into DreamWorks' computer-animated film *Monsters vs. Aliens*, a mysterious government van arrives at a Wedding Chapel to assess the crash site of an unidentified alien space-craft. Numerous operatives exit the vehicle, each one framed below the waist to preserve the faceless identity of the anonymous organisation. As the ominous doors of their van swing shut, and almost imperceptibly to the spectator, a film crew is briefly caught reflected in the vehicle's shiny black finish. A boom mic operator is crouched on his knees, behind which stands a row of figures observing the unfolding action. Designed to reward spectators' particularly attentive viewing, this discreet detail plays with the illusion that the digital veil has momentarily slipped to expose the concealed seams of the film's construction. Except, of course, the sudden visibility of recording equipment and crew plays no such role in any process of revelation and disclosure. *Monsters vs. Aliens* only purports to unpick the terms of its illusion, resisting the truthful reveal and instead playing with the common set of assumptions shared between spectator and animator around the production of computer-animated films.

The 'anti-illusionism' of this gesture is consciously staged, made contradictory or *allusive* in the sense that there is no real commitment to an anti-illusionist project. Norman Klein argues that 'for studying cartoons, anti-illusionism would include virtually every animated short, almost every gag, and so is not a very useful tool' (1993: 168). However, the computer-animated film frees anti-illusionism from any obligation to divulge the proper techniques of its image-making processes, instead aggregating and associating new meanings around the unique illusionary properties of the genre. Spectators, by extension, consent to this act, becoming party to tricks that depend on their knowingness for the comic function of the gag to be fulfilled. They remain entirely aware that the fictional world of *Monsters vs. Aliens* has not been produced by filmmaking equipment suddenly made visible in supposed error, and that the motion of exposing the illusion has been engineered for comic effect.

The post-cinema life of the computer-animated film normally schools spectators in its labour of manufacture, mainstreaming a 'vernacular knowledge' of digitally assisted filmmaking processes (Bode 2010: 69), and fuelling a desire to acquire a systematic appreciation of the work of animation that unfolds 'behind-the-scenes'. The camera apparatus and film crew spotted in *Monsters vs. Aliens* is thus a self-conscious moment that cultivates the artifice, adding humour and intrigue to a Luxo world by bringing out a comic contradiction between the grammar of the computer-animated film and the methods of live-action. Noël Carroll (1988: 299) argues that artwork classed as illusionist is never unmediated by its conventions. But computer-animated films stage their anti-illusionism as a comic flourish to keep spectators at a distance, preserving the disclosure of the illusion as itself an illusory act. This chapter builds the argument that such falsified or *allusive* anti-illusionism can be understood as a specifically Mannerist gesture.

Cinema Mannerism

Within the context of cinema, Mannerism has been employed as a useful descriptor to give shape and definition to a specific type of filmmaking practice in which style, as Adrian Martin argues, 'performs out of its own trajectories, no longer working unobtrusively at the behest of the fiction and its demands of meaningfulness' (1992: 91). If a classical film style is (historically) self-effacing and balanced in its construction of spatio-temporal continuity, then 'Mannerist' style is rooted in a love of complexity, confidently flaunting its restlessness and self-knowing skill in visually arresting ways. Embellishments and exaggerations are accented, style becomes substance.

Figured as an ahistorical or, perhaps, transhistorical term, Mannerism elucidates a seductive anti-naturalism within art and culture that contested theories of postmodernism and pastiche, as well as prefixes and hyphenations such as 'post-', 'retro-' and 'neo-', have all yearned to make increasing sense (see Straw 1987). Ginette Vincendeau points out that 'Mannerism is usually associated with more baroque film-makers' (1996: 50), and in the context of French cinema with the technical bravura and artistic virtuosity of filmmakers of the 'cinéma du look' movement. The stylistic decadence and flamboyancy of *Diva* (Jean-Jacques Beineix, 1981), *Subway* (Luc Besson, 1985) and later *Les Amants du Pont-Neuf* (Leos Carax, 1991) all celebrated the artifice of 'non-naturalistic self-conscious aesthetics' (ibid.). Evidence of cinema's Mannerist tendencies appears elsewhere in wider studies relating to specific genres and filmmaking practices, such as the rhizomatic mazelike narratives of film noir (Abrams 2007); the heritage drama and period film (Vidal 2012); the ostentatious authorial style of 'flashy, hyper-stylised directors' (Martin 2014); and the stylistic repertoire of contemporary Hollywood. Intensified continuity editing, as David Bordwell (2006: 189) puts it, functions in its formal hyperbole as a Mannerist revision of classic(al) continuity.

Derived from the Italian *maniera*, meaning idiosyncratic touch (borrowed from the French *manière* to define 'look' or *savour-faire*), the Mannerist style (*manierismo*) intervened between the classical antiquity of Renaissance artwork and the later Baroque period. Within the chronology of art history, Mannerism's main quality 'was less a single, coherent style than a new self-consciousness about style itself as a distinct and personal entity' (Kay 2010: 202–3), and was marked by a decline in the coherency and continuity of Renaissance perspective. Positioned within this historical lineage, the forthright self-conscious address adopted by the computer-animated film and its comedy of *allusive* anti-illusionism can therefore be considered highly 'Mannerist' in its invention. Speaking through knowing and self-conscious processes of 'stylish' stylisation, Mannerism's 'seduction of the fake and the [use of] artificial as basis' (Vidal 2012: 30) seems well-suited to the paradoxical, allusive gestures towards deconstruction made by several computer-animated films, which momentarily present animation production and live-action filmmaking practice as wholly inextricable.

The essence of Mannerism lies in a tense preservation of irreconcilable poles of 'classicism and anti-classicism, naturalism and formalism, rationalism and irrationalism' (Hauser 1986: 12). Maintaining the odd rhythms of these pairings produces a strange and stimulating paradox, a witty 'conjuring trick' performed by Mannerist artists. The wit of Mannerist play, and the odd appearances that such art produces, is a pairing of extremes without hierarchy, eliciting a feeling of estrangement in the viewer. Maria Rika Maniates suggests that as an aesthetic, style, theme, tone and ideology of distortion, 'Mannerism wants to startle' (1979: 5). The strangeness of Mannerist art perhaps explains why Mannerism in the context of animation has tended be associated with certain kinds of films and filmmakers, allied to the 'surrealist' credentials of Czech animator Jan Švankmajer (O'Pray 1995) and, more recently, the uncanny and unsettling screen worlds of the Quay Brothers (Buchan 2011). The Quays' stop-motion film *The Cabinet of Jan Švankmajer* (1984) is notably replete with Mannerist gestures, featuring a three-dimensional puppet version of

sixteenth-century Italian Mannerist artist Giuseppe Arcimboldo's painting *The Librarian* (1566) as its main protagonist. Arcimboldo's famous
composite heads certainly speak to this critical alliance of Mannerism with
more experimental, unorthodox animated forms. Produced during his
time at the Imperial Court in Prague, Arcimboldo's joke (*scherzi*) portraits
– that include *The Jurist* (1566), *Vertumnus* (1590) and the *Four Seasons*
series (1573) – are nightmarish collages depicting human physiognomies
through an assemblage of flora, fauna, fruits and vegetables, carefully
arranged into a playful, if monstrous, teratology (see Kaufmann 2009).
Despite the compositional chaos of Arcimboldo's quasi-human figures,
a playul reference to his Mannerist art can also be found within popular
computer-animated filmmaking. In *The Tale of Despereaux*, the body and
facial features of the film's mythical 'soup genie' (suggestively named
'Boldo') visually reprise Arcimboldo's palindrome works *The Vegetable
Gardener* (1590) and *Reversible Head with Basket of Fruit* (1590).

The unsettling effects of Arcimboldo's comical homunculi (and the
rhetorical schemes that structure his fascinating portrait paradoxes) help
illuminate the particular Mannerist register of computer-animated film
comedy. The genre's broader sense of humour can be conceptualised as a
playful *contaminatio* of live-action and animation, an exercise in rhetorical
excess that accumulates non-digital, analogue technology as a means of
presenting the terms of computer-animated film illusion. Italian Mannerist
contaminatio is a response to 'aesthetic belatedness' and a defence against
the Mannerist fear that 'all the good stories have been told already, and
told well' (Gross 2005: 20). *Contaminatio* works through degrees of invention and formal contrivance in pursuit of greater complexity and novelty
(as in Arcimboldo's paintings), using stylish technique and artful amalgam
to yield innovative combinations. Computer-animated films similarly
compromise any investment in authenticity through an 'excess of fidelity'
(Vidal 2012: 31) that seeks to rework and apply anti-illusionism as yet
another layer prohibiting full disclosure.

Mannerism in the computer-animated film therefore works in combination with metalepsis to extend the vocabulary of the deconstructive
cartoon, injecting new codes and conventions that play with the believ-
ability of its characters and the construction of its worlds. Indeed, Liliane
Louvel argues that 'As in narrative metalepsis, the *trompe-l'œil* produces
a discourse of interruption', whilst adding to its destabilising effects a
heightened self-reflexivity in that it functions 'as a veritable finger pointed
at itself' (2011: 65). Rooted in what Donald Crafton (1979) calls the
'hand of the artist' trope (*the finger that points at itself*), the deconstructive
cartoon normally attains its comic impact by self-consciously divulg-

ing its means of production, exploring the work of animation and the artifice of its invention. Computer-animated films craft a greater distance between deconstruction and deconstructed, not reflecting inwardly on its own animatedness but presenting itself openly as a constructed reality or simulacrum. But the revelation as an effect of *trompe l'œil* is itself a *trompe l'œil,* and it is this 'doubling' that is foundational to the computer-animated film's Mannerist 'tone'. Tone refers to the manner in which a film 'addresses its spectator and implicitly invites us to understand its attitude to its material and the stylistic register it employs' (Pye 2007: 7). The tone of the computer-animated film's Mannerism can be squared to its knowing appropriation of live-action epistemology as a way of supporting and challenging the 'true' principles or 'already known' of animated film production. Key to how the Mannerist style and tone of the computer-animated film is secured is through the specific treatment of its virtual camera.

The Mannerist Camera

Such have been the developments in virtual camera systems that 'perform' the conditions of the photographic image (motion blur, depth of field), animators now meet the demands of a role similar to a live-action director of photography. The involvement of renowned British cinematographer Roger Deakins as visual consultant on the computer-animated films *Rango, Wall-E, How to Train Your Dragon, Rise of the Guardians, The Croods* and *How to Train Your Dragon 2* was not only to contribute colour key reference points, check lighting effects and intensity within the film's luminous Luxo world, but also to coach animators in the fundamental principles of live-action cinematography. The computer-animated film's capacity to simulate photographic image-making processes, including features such as lens flare, implies that a mistake in a live-action film becomes a mark of credibility in a Luxo world. In the former, lens flare is an incidental property of filmmaking, produced in the act of recording due to reflections in the lens. In the latter, it is a simulated optical effect built into the computer software, designed to replicate the moment at which 'the virtually created "camera" turns towards the sun or other depicted light source' (Telotte 2008: 165). As an artefact of the analogue that signals and convincingly reconstructs the lens-based, indexical realism of live-action cinema, lens flare is an ocular trick in computer-animated films that solidifies the false impression of celluloid.

A lens flare nuances the very first shot of *A Bug's Life, Happy Feet Two, The Missing Lynx* and *Two by Two* (Toby Genkel and Sean McCormack,

2015), and appears in both the opening and closing shots of *Battle for Terra* as the virtual camera impossibly tracks back out from the ringed planet of Terra. It is also a moment of visual detail that adds further drama to the woodland animals' first glimpse of the gigantic foliage in *Over the Hedge*; Tintin and Snowy's visit to the library under the cover of darkness in *The Adventures of Tintin*; Mike Wazowski's momentous arrival on campus in *Monsters University*; and the penguins kinetic freefall from an aeroplane in *Penguins of Madagascar*. Lisa Purse suggests that the 'recent trend' for digitally-generated lens flare is not only a homage to celluloid cinema, but 'has the advantage of lending a photorealistic, illusory verisimilitude to digital effects shots' (2013: 41). Photorealism as a descriptor certainly attests to the technical virtuosity and innovation of computer software that has the capacity to (often flawlessly) simulate images that appear to be photographic. But it tells us nothing about the comic potential of such falsified imagery, and how the photographic qualities of the simulated film-based image (as filtered through a lens) have been exploited for their contribution to comedy.

The 'Mannerist' camera of the computer-animated film draws on the virtual apparatus' simulated properties for the specific purposes spectatorial amusement. Its (impossibly) flat, (fictionally) planar surface is employed to connote the presence of a camera situated within a Luxo world in the 'live' act of filming. Best remembered in this spirit is the twenty-five second epilogue to *Cars*, a sequence that exhibits the kind of self-consciousness of style at the cornerstone of Mannerist composition. The premise to this brief postscript is simple. An insect car flies unwittingly into the camera's lens, causing the anthropomorphic vehicle to recoil in dazed shock and a smudge from its blue paintwork to materialise on the apparatus' 'glass' front. The humour of this sequence is rooted in the seemingly erroneous error caused by a moment of unscripted action, which would otherwise corrupt the illusionist quality of the fiction, but which is here staged to enforce a (false) fidelity to live-action filmmaking. By opening out its virtual camera to unprecedented physical assault, *Cars* manipulates the fixed distance between diegesis and spectator, playing with the camera as a figure of separation that partitions them off from the fictional space.

Within the fictional worlds of the computer-animated film, the function of the Mannerist camera is predicated upon its abilities to withstand undue assault. A common feature is to contort characters against the camera's planar surface to further augment the comedy of their bodies. The final shots of *Over the Hedge* and *Open Season* both utilise this technique, with characters hitting the camera before slowly sliding down the lens and out of shot. The Wile E. Coyote/Road Runner computer-animated short *Coyote Falls* (Matthew O'Callaghan, 2010) also closes with this device. By squashing the Coyote up against its lens, the film appends the virtual camera to the wealth of malfunctioning ACME Company goods that are normally the cause of the coyote's physical pain. In a humorous account imagining a hypothetical court case between Wile E. Coyote and the ACME Company, Ian Frazier writes, 'Mr. Coyote states that on eighty-five occasions he has purchased of the Acme Company through that company's mail-order department, certain products which did cause him bodily injury due to defects in manufacture or improper cautionary labelling' (1990: 42–3). *Coyote Falls* adds its own virtual camera to this lengthy charge sheet.

The position of the virtual camera is also made increasingly perilous by those accidental, often spontaneous 'errors' that may occur within the hazardous environment of a film set. In two computer-animated films released in 2009, the Mannerist camera is again signalled by the unexpected acknowledgement of its diegetic presence. During *Ice Age: Dawn of the Dinosaurs*, spots of snow and mud are thrown against the camera's lens as Diego the sabre-toothed cat chases a gazelle, whilst in *Cloudy with a Chance of Meatballs*, a snowball fight (actually ice-cream) prompts a similar covering of the apparatus. The camera in *Cloudy with a Chance of Meatballs* does not belong to the diegetic camera crew who are filming the adverse weather conditions for a local television station Weather News Network. It is an objective camera located in the fictional town of Swallow Falls. The impenetrable lens of the Mannerist camera continues to be the ideal surface upon which to exhibit the viscosity of an array of products. The camera lens is obscured in *Over the Hedge* by a spray of whipped cream used to disguise Hammy the squirrel as rabid; in *Cars 2*, it is accidentally splashed with water by Red the fire truck; during the opening sequence to *Underdogs* falling rain collects on the camera's lens; and in *The Good Dinosaur*, when Arlo and Spot's fall into the ravine is refracted through water droplets that are propelled against the camera as they hit the water.

Blood also splatters onto the camera's lens during one of the frenzied attacks by the monstrous Grendel in *Beowulf*, and the final shot of *9* embellishes the computer-animated film screen with raindrops that perceptibly glow green to signify the bacteria that will hopefully return life to the film's devastated city. More recently, the underwater rescue of Duke by Max and Snowball in *The Secret Life of Pets* is similarly marked by an imperceptible water droplet as the water level rises inside a sinking animal control van, and in *Sausage Party* the fizzy fruit drink

Figure 10.1 Frame grab from *Sing* (2016) (Illumination Entertainment/Universal Pictures). *Sing* subjects its virtual camera to unexpected assault.

and red berry juice squirted on the lens during the aisle spill parodies the blood violently splashed onto the camera in war epic *Saving Private Ryan* (Steven Spielberg, 1998). Two sequences from *Despicable Me 3* – the frenetic boat heist by supervillain Balthazar Bratt that opens the film, and Gru and Lucy's failed deep-sea capture of Balthazar himself – each make use of 'accidental' ocean spray visible on the lens to show the occupational hazards of setting blockbuster action on water. However, the most sustained deployment of the Mannerist camera marks the climax of *Sing*. Several errant drops of water remain collected along the top edge of the frame during the sequence in which Buster Moon's family-run theatre crumbles under the weight of a flash flood. As the roving camera navigates the building's falling architecture, the water inadvertently splashed on the camera's lens draws attention to the diegetic presence of the apparatus (Figure 10.1). Adding to the immediacy to the events being depicted, *Sing* uses fleeting visual details to legitimise pro-filmic activity and denote the digital image as indexical artefact.

Case Study: *Surf's Up*

Surf's Up exploits the audiovisual rhetoric of the fly-on-the-wall documentary and the hallmarks of its observational *vérité* style to anchor the fragility of the film apparatus within the film's Luxo world. Following a group of documentary filmmakers as they record the fictitious 'Big Z Memorial' annual penguin surfing contest, the film is a parody of the wave of popular surfing documentaries *Thicker than Water* (Jack Johnson, Chris Malloy and Emmet Malloy, 2000), *Step into Liquid* (Dana Brown, 2003), *Billabong Odyssey* (Philip Boston, 2003), and *Riding Giants* (Stacey Peralta, 2004). Featuring talking head interviews, 1970s-style still photographs (Polaroid, instamatic), personal video diaries and found footage, *Surf's Up* crafts a visual style utilising temporal ellipses, hand-held camerawork, intermittent audio, oral testimony, and verbal interaction between anthropomorphic penguin characters and documentary crew (including the 'real' directing duo of Chris Buck and Ash Brannon). Indeed, the film substitutes the 'hand of the artist' trope foundational to animation's 'deconstructive' tradition for the 'voices of the film-makers' that are heard throughout, exchanging one offscreen authorial figure for another rooted in the familiar mechanisms of documentary filmmaking.

The unusual visual design of *Surf's Up* is intended to lend credibility to its events as if documented in real-time (*Surf's Up 2: Wavemania* adopts a similar formal style, and even opens with protagonist Cody Maverick splashing water on the camera lens). *Surf's Up*'s aesthetic was supported by innovative applications of motion-capture technology used to mimic the movements of a 'live' camera operator, rather than replicate the actions of its main star cast (including Jeff Bridges and Shia LaBoeuf). The 'HandyCam' system developed for the film 'allowed a live action camera to be used to "shoot" an animated scene' (Bredow et al. 2007: 11). During production, a camera operator would 'operate the physical camera and the capture system recorded those movements and used them to drive the virtual camera for the shot' (ibid.). Beginning with a close-up of a clapperboard, the film therefore interrogates what it means for an animated film to have a 'camera', specifically one with clear limitations as a recording apparatus that is frequently left to catch up with the unfolding action (Figure 10.2). *Surf's Up* therefore makes explicit the fictional use of editing as a production process, mining the visual currency of *cinéma-vérité* and fly-on-the-wall documentaries (film stock discoloration, scratching, strobing, negative and print dirt) to give weight to the illusion that pro-filmic events are cut from available audiovisual material.

While the animated documentary has become fertile critical terrain (Kriger 2012; Honess Roe 2013; Ehrlich 2013; Formenti 2014; Wells 2016), *Surf's Up* combines the non-fictional animated medium with the authenticity of the documentary aesthetic in ulterior ways. Animated documentaries are typically noted for their varied use of animation as a representational scheme implicated in strategies of reconstruction, resemblance, fabrication, substitution, expression and realisation, processes that are enabled by animation extending the boundaries of what is available in

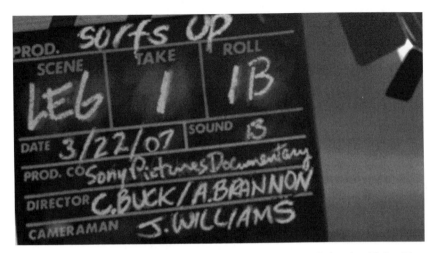

Figure 10.2 Frame grab from *Surf's Up* (2007) (Sony Pictures Animation/Columbia Pictures). Computer-animated filmmaking meets the 'mock documentary'.

live-action. In these terms, animation's fictionality is safely co-opted into the wider histories of the documentary that are no less tainted by the creatively false and the fictionally impure (what Annabelle Honess Roe calls the documentary's entirely illusory 'purist ideal' [2016: 22]). However, *Surf's Up* operates closer to an 'animated mockumentary' because it delights not in the recounting of fact but in the non-fictionalising of animation. The mockumentary is historically a rhetorical mode of address that both codifies and skews documentary conventions, often for political, satirical or purposes, but does so through the ironic substantiation of (often outlandish) subject matter by recognisable documentary discourse. *Surf's Up* is similarly conferred the appearance of a more factual artefact, approximating a mockumentary by combining animation and documentary to narrate a wholly fictional story.

Flawed Film and Fictive Frames

Numerous scholars have already looked to European art history for a vocabulary to discuss the camerawork of contemporary Hollywood cinema (Ndalianis 2004; Cubitt 2004, 2009). The visual pleasures afforded by digital technology have more than once been associated with a post-Mannerist, Baroque mode of address to account for a particular kind of post-classical, digitally-assisted formal mobility. Sean Cubitt describes 'neo-Baroque' mobile camerawork and digital compositing that promotes heightened 'vectorial movement' (2004: 228), which results in a decorative structuring of screen space. While this kind of fluid camerawork is both achievable and visible across the computer-animated film, there is a distinction to be made regarding its primary narrative function: one that offers an important corrective to the bypassing of Mannerism within these kinds of discussions of digital camerawork. The Mannerist camera of the computer-animated film is confined in its placement rather than in constant movement. It is not characterised by extreme travels through virtual space, but by stasis and stationary belonging. Its comic intentions are signalled through its virtual presence as a material camera, which inhabits the same intimate space as those objects and forces in the fictional world that can impact upon it. The 'neo-Baroque' and Mannerist styles can certainly coexist and share the same computer-animated film, as the examination of anthropomorphic camerawork in Chapter 4 demonstrated. But the Mannerist camera privileges surface over depth to secure its desired comic effects.

Another primary feature of the Mannerist camera is the stress that is placed on its unreliability as a recording instrument. Computer-animated films regularly spotlight the technological capabilities of the fictional apparatus, but do so by playing on the errors involved in their production, projection and exhibition. In at least two scenes of the French-Belgian-Swiss co-production *The True Story of Puss 'N Boots* (Jérôme Deschamps, 2009), the camera perceptibly wobbles as the eponymous Puss speeds past the frame, just as it does as a result of the thunderous speedway activity of passing vehicles in Pixar's *Cars* films. *Delgo* actually exploits the instability of a virtual camera to introduce main protagonists Delgo and Filo as they wander through the rock valleys of the planet Jhamora. Initially offscreen, the duo's arrival into the frame is signalled by the camera's sudden movement, reverberating with the characters' each encroaching step. In *The Wild*, the virtual camera even appears to slide from side to side during a climactic sequence set on a stolen tugboat, giving the impression that it is mounted on the deck, while as a story about a clumsy child, Danish computer-animated film *Albert* (Karsten Kiilerich, 2015) has several moments where the camera imperceptibly wobbles as a result of Albert's ungainly and unwieldy movements.

Stephen Prince has described the increasing sophistication of the virtual camera to convincingly replicate anamorphic lens defects and curvature, depth of field and focal lengths, as well as 'horizontally spiking lens flare' (2012: 97). However, the technical proficiency and credentials of digitally-created photorealism does more than simply affirm 'the simulacral nature of digital images' (Brown 2013: 27) in the post-photographic age, but rather allows for the qualities of analogue cinema to be played for laughs.

Twenty minutes into *Wall-E*, for example, the action becomes abruptly emancipated from conventional framing, and as the robot protagonist is chased by runaway shopping trolleys (whilst covertly spying on love interest EVE), the camera inexplicably loses its focus, before quickly readjusting and zooming into its mobile subject. At this moment, the virtual camera suddenly attains an operator, implying recording equipment mounted (and controlled) from a position somewhere from within the fiction. Spectators must therefore be attentive to the fictive and false exposures of filmmaking apparatus suggested in the computer-animated film's totally fictional reproductions.

Computer-animated film comedy has maintained one tradition germane to the earliest cel-animated shorts, pursuing the comic conceit of its own perishability, including the fallability of the film strip (particularly dominant in the 'deconstructive' cartoons of Tex Avery [see Wells 2002a: 67]). The opening shots of both *Monsters vs. Aliens* and *Surf's Up* depict the film jamming inside the projector, and as the action onscreen flickers the whirring sound of the film strip running through the machine's gate accompanies the intermittent image. In *Monsters vs. Aliens*, the film strip burns away completely to reveal the first image, just as it does in *Everyone's Hero* to mark an early scene transition. *Happily N'Ever After* also begins in this disruptive way, though the celluloid's slipping (to reveal the sprocket holes running along the side) is far from accidental. The film is paused, rewound and replayed at the behest of an omniscient narrator Rick ('let's go back a little'), so that it appears as if events are unfolding live in projection. A similar trick is used in *Igor*, as the eponymous ogre narrates the onscreen action whilst pausing the film to introduce the footage of himself. The closing credits of *Despicable Me* add more to the illusion by firing the minions from a rocket within the diegesis out of the film screen, to impossibly enter the projection room and burn away the filmstrip. The situation is salvaged as the bright white light provides the ideal backdrop for the minions' spontaneous shadow puppet show.

Such comic flourishes that explore the limitations of the film cel can be viewed through the lens of Mannerism. They share with an older period of Mannerism a predilection for *trompe l'œil* illusion effects and, in particular, the 'animation' of real space through persuasive architectural illusion. Describing painter Giulio Romano's fresco *Sala dei Giganti* (1524–34) on the Romano-designed Palazzo de Tè villa in Mantua, Italy, art critic Linda Murray (1977) explains how it depicts figures apparently struggling to hold up the pillars that support the surrounding Palazzo, creating the illusion that the structure is in the process of collapse. Their bodies are positioned in convoluted, spiral poses, twisted into exaggerated and unnatural configurations. Murray describes the *Sala dei Giganti* as the 'the epitome of Mannerist decoration – this blend of the real and the false, of the witty, sophisticated and amusing in the imagery [. . .] the contrast between the consciousness of the solidity of reality and the imaginativeness of the terrifying carnage on the walls' (ibid.: 130). The crumbling masonry, falling keystones and slipping triglyphs portrayed in the *Sala dei Giganti* establishes a contradiction between the disingenuous façade and the structural integrity of the building. Computer-animated films create their own comic 'carnage' by setting up an opposition between what they show (mechanical errors) and the truthfulness of their production. These strategies of imitation charm the spectator's eye by visually corrupting the computer-animated film's pristine surface: *trompe l'œil* errors announce the genre's artifice, and invite spectators' appreciation of the means of representation itself.

False Starts and Missed Openings

The 'carnage' of the Mannerist camera marks a nostalgia for the imperfect. Finding a place for 'celluloid' within contemporary digital imagery, computer-animated films impersonate indexical conditions through an emphasis on the fragility of the illusion upon which cinema depends. While the less sensationalist rhetoric of recent digital theory views photographic simulation within an ongoing continuum of filmic illusionism present 'since the dawn of cinema' (Purse 2013: 5), the increased folding of cinematographic notions of realism into discourses of humour by the computer-animated film situates indexicality within a new comic register. The excess of obedience to the photochemical processes of live-action cinema are wholly decorative and openly duplicitous gestures, a Mannerist manipulation of the armoury of reality effects that are increasingly available in persuasive computer graphics. Mannerist art has been defined as a 'phenomenon of conscious self-deception' (Hauser 2002: 52), and computer-animated films are notably invested in the playful tricks of 'photographic' illusion. However, the *trompe l'œil* details lacing the genre, particularly those localised around photorealism and virtual camera, begin to suggest another common heritage between Mannerism and animation.

Hand-drawn animation traditionally relies upon significant spatial cues, and the convincing creation of depth through forced perspective, planes of composition, horizon lines, and vanishing points, to enable spectators to attribute dimension to flat cel-animated worlds. This 'fool-the-eye' work of animated aesthetics and their fundamental *trompe l'œil* effects were famously invoked in a gag that emerged as a staple of the Wile E. Coyote and Road Runner cartoons, and featured in the duo's very first short directed by Chuck Jones. In *Fast and Furry-ous* (1949), the hapless Coyote paints a convincing cartoon tunnel on a sheer rock face, hoping to entice the Road Runner to run headlong into the solid wall, only for the intended victim to impossibly cross the threshold and enter without hesitation into the image to safety. Wile E. Coyote is a skilled artist, a master of pictorial illusion whose phony tunnels painted on the rocky canyon walls are an achievement of verisimilitude. It is the Road Runner who confuses the terms under which spectators are to understand the illusion, defying naturalistic laws by exchanging a flat image for a three-dimensional space that the character can seamlessly hurtle into (the Coyote's own attempts at passing into the image prove hilariously futile). Computer-animated films are complicit in the same kinds of strangeness engendered in these cartoons. Though altogether less anarchic, they no less source their comedy from the volumetric depth of its illusionistic worlds, and the rich three-dimensionality of its spaces, by disclosing the terms of the illusion at the same time as such conditions are persistently withheld. Mannerism, as Barbara Bond suggests, 'employs contraries' (2004: 274) and the computer-animated film's predilection for systematically dismantling the convincing illusion of its images through non-animated, typically live-action, means only cultivates the genre's artifice, rather than punctures it. As with the Coyote standing perplexed at the Road Runner's seemingly impossible entrance into his own animated image, the puzzled spectator delights at the accomplishments of computer-animated film worlds, all the while still left wondering with increasing fascination as to how it was all really done.

A common narratological device of deception employed in this respect is that which Werner Wolf has defined as the 'missing opening frame' (2006: 188), a fooling technique employed to mark the beginning of a fiction as a temporal and spatial false start. The initial and supposedly fictional reality is belatedly exposed as an 'embedded' framing device, which soon gives way to the 'truthful' (and thus correct) level of fiction. The technique's intention to deceive is rooted in the scope it creates for a spectatorial 'misreading', which is fuelled by an illogical and often abrupt shift in spectator position as they come to terms with an act of deception. Animation works particularly well in service of this metareferential technique given that it is fundamentally a technology of illusion, and so any withholding of a framing story, or the delayed reveal of the fictional world's 'authentic' conditions, can be further folded into the animated medium's own illusion of 'perspective'.

Multiple computer-animated films make use of such false openings as a storytelling device to self-consciously disassemble their digital illusion, whilst simultaneously feigning a clash between computer-animation and the construction of its images. The opening action sequences *Toy Story 3*, *Tad: The Lost Explorer*, *Underdogs* and *The Boss Baby*, for example, all take place inside the imagination of their respective child protagonists. A cut from one fictional reality to another often signals the disjuncture between the captivating energy of the imagined spaces and the drabness of the 'real'. In both *Planet 51* and *A Monster in Paris*, however, it is traditions of the cinema and cinema-going that provide each film with their respective false openings. The frenetic action of an 'alien' attack that begins Jorge Blanco's film is nothing more than a scene from the fictional disaster film 'Humaniacs' (albeit one enjoyed by an increasingly hysterical movie audience). Set in the early-1900s French capital, *A Monster in Paris* similarly begins inside the cinephilic imagination of shy movie projectionist Emile, who daydreams his fantasy of a relationship with love interest Maud into a screening of black-and-white romantic drama 'Spring Romance'. However, it is the 'missing opening frame' utilised in Disney's third computer-animated feature *Bolt* that directly (if falsely) demystifies the aesthetics of the computer-animated film as a product of elaborate audiovisual façade, this time in keeping with the production of high-budget quality television.

Case Study: *Bolt*

Following a short prologue establishing the adoptive relationship between seven-year-old Penny and her new White Shepherd puppy Bolt, *Bolt* begins with an opening action sequence set five years on. Working together to fight crime, not only are the duo shown making full use a range of weaponry as they give chase to Dr Calico (who has kidnapped Penny's scientist father), but Bolt has been genetically modified for additional speed and superheroic agility. However, Penny and Bolt's high-octane pursuit of the villainous Calico is abruptly cut short by the piercing ring of an alarm bell, which cues both the end of the frenetic onscreen action and the appearance of the surrounding crew previously out of shot. The computer-animated film illusion is suddenly exposed as a series of perspectival backdrops, props and actors. Even the vast urban landscape is revealed to be a convincingly painted set drawn to scale, which is then slowly raised to reveal the walls of a studio: an interior space merely doubling as exterior (Figure 10.3). Flatness and depth are folded in together, bringing the capabilities of digital perspective and three-dimensional action into unexpected alignment with the ornate glass painted mattes of the Hollywood studio era (rather than more contemporary green/blue screen technologies). As the

Figure 10.3 Frame grab from *Bolt* (2008) (Walt Disney Animation Studios).
Bolt dismantles the visual credibility of digital imagery as a technology of persuasive
realistic representation.

eponymous 'star' of the series, Bolt is then returned to his trailer, while
the television production team watch back the film's opening sequence to
check the quality of the footage (one member of the team admits 'we gotta
boom mic').

The *allusive* anti-illusionism that supports *Bolt*'s alleged discourse of
revelation is predicated on impressing impossible fictional junctions and
margins of manufacture onto the computer-animated film illusion. For
Chris Pallant, '*Bolt* features a number of shots that could not have been
done in a live-action film' (2011: 141), and yet the stridently reflexive
disclosure of film practices seems designed to suggest that this is *exactly*
how such effects were achieved. Given the spectacular vistas, mobile
camerawork and exciting visual effects that comprise *Bolt*'s opening, it
is unlikely that the action could have taken place 'diegetically' within
the confines of a studio space, however impressive or expansive the set's
dimensions. The film's accomplishments of deception deliberately catches
spectators up in its own simulacrum effect. Furthermore, it is *Bolt*'s use of
the 'missing opening frame' that permits it to make false claims towards its
similarities with live-action cinema, and to align the unity and coherency
of its digital illusion with an ulterior set of visual effects.

Bolt's manipulation of filmic illusion, and the discord and estrangement felt within its 'missing opening', additionally connects the film to
a Mannerism paradigm. Wolf suggests the 'missing opening' technique
of narration generally 'has a startling, disorientating or metatextual

effect' (2006: 188). Mannerist art similarly 'holds everything in a state of dissonance, dissociation and doubt', served by 'clashing impulses' that self-consciously disturb 'balance' and agitate style (Maquerlot 1995: 17). The effect of *Bolt*'s excess of anti-illusionism is likewise highly performative, in that it attains its impact from a momentary lack of narrative clarity. The film intrigues because the rhetoric of 'seems' like that has historically accompanied persuasive digital imagery is here substituted with the 'seams' of artificial construction, in what is a highly Mannerist dismantling of the film illusion that only adds to the misapprehension.

Outtakes and Bloopers

The inclusion of feigned blooper reels and outtake material within computer-animated films maintain the Mannerist masquerade through a rhetoric of deception that is again highly illusory. Beginning with *A Bug's Life*, and continuing in *Toy Story 2*, *Final Fantasy: The Spirits Within*, *Monsters, Inc.*, *Jonah: A Veggietales Movie* and *Barbie in a Mermaid Tale* (Adam L. Wood, 2010) – as well as the Indian-American co-production *Roadside Romeo* (Jugal Hansraj, 2008) and the Danish feature *Terkel in Trouble* (Kresten Vestbjerg Andersen, Thorbjørn Christoffersen and Stefan Fjeldmark, 2004) – many computer-animated films have utilised fictional behind-the-scenes exposés to place spectators as supposed witness to the logistics of computer-animated film production. More recently, *The LEGO Movie*, *Storks* and *The LEGO Batman Movie* have all produced separate blooper material to accompany their respective DVD releases. Frank Eugene Beaver argues the particular fascination of blooper or 'gag' reels lies in 'what it can reveal about actors and the filmmaking process, often in very human or humorous ways' (2007: 184). Computer-animated films extend the limits of such fascination through the humour of false disclosure, and the discrepancies innate to this *trompe l'œil* device. Constructed sets, artificial lighting rigs, and camera set-ups are all comic tools building the computer-animated film's intention to deceive. Ornate painted matte backdrops glimpsed in the outtake material further sustain the fooling encounter. Recalling the Coyote's pictorial illusions, flatness and depth are bound together through the illogical alignment of two-dimensional and three-dimensional worlds. The computer-animated film world is staged as fragile and fallible, prone to mishap. It is an unflattering space where 'actors' embarrassingly extemporise and require rehearsal time, and directors lament the danger of losing the light.

Computer-animated film bloopers substitute for the types of real technological faults and graphical errors that can arise in the 'real-life' production resulting in, for instance, the separation of characters from their clothes, over-extension of body parts, or a grotesque curvature and monstrous contortion in the faces. Such technical bloopers are typically included on the DVD releases, as with *Shrek* and *Shrek 2*'s 'technical goofs'; the 'incredi-blunders' in *The Incredibles*; the 'wee blunders' of *Brave*; and the 'gag animation' of *Big Hero 6* that disclose technical glitches that can occur during the animation of progression reels. But the fictional 'live-action' outtakes and bloopers also introduce new concerns, such as the ineptitude and amateurism of the animated actors, including their inability to deliver lines of dialogue, uncontrollable laughter or a general clumsiness that belies their usually refined movement. David Bell argues that 'Special effects don't make mistakes, but can be made to make mistakes' (2001: 61), and a computer-animated film world is a space where bad (and over-) acting is deliberately allowed to occur.

The upshot of the computer-animated film's blooper reel, and the surplus material allegedly excised from the final cut, is the impression of a character's existence outside the narrative world. Within computer-animated film comedy, there is a new emphasis on *selves* and *persons* rather than *cels* or *pixels* as the source of computer-animated film illusion. There are two strategies used to achieve such an effect. Firstly, bloopers function as a site of 'horizontal' (Fiske 1987) intertextuality insofar as they pertain to relations between texts that are traditionally linked along the axis of character, content and genre. Computer-animated characters freely trespass from one film to another. Woody appears during the outtakes in *A Bug's Life*, while Flik and Heimlich return the favour in *Toy Story 2*, reappearing under the (wrong) assumption that they are starring in 'A Bug's Life 2'. *Toy Story*'s Rex the Dinosaur also appears in the outtake material of *Monsters, Inc.* auditioning for a role as one of the film's monstrous characters (enquiring 'do I get the part?' when the scene is finally cut. He doesn't).

Computer-animated films also play with the possibility that their characters possess a consciousness in advance of their screen role, and that they are capable of independent thought and behaviour. For example, the blooper reel that closes *Toy Story 2* crafts a particular kind of working relationship between Woody and Buzz that is absent from their onscreen, diegetic pairing. Multiple 'takes' are ruined by Woody's mischievous behaviour, as he terrorises Buzz using a series of increasingly outlandish practical jokes (pulling faces during a scene, drawing 'This Space For Rent' on Buzz's plastic wings). While the neurotic personality of Rex is sustained in the *Monsters, Inc.* bloopers, the outtake material of *Toy Story 2* shows spectators a Woody unlike the heroic persona he otherwise

embodies onscreen. Even the anxieties about toy disposability and obsolescence that are central to *Toy Story 2*'s narrative are (re)played for laughs
in the bloopers, as Woody's pull-string snaps from his body during one
take of a scene (prompting Jessie the Cowgirl's uncontrollable laughter).

In this way, bloopers can be viewed as part of a broader strategy – also
part of the promotion of computer-animated films – to establish a greater
divide between 'character' and 'actor'. Within the extradiegetic world
of computer-animated films, actors are subject to casting calls and audi-
tions (as with Lots-O'-Huggin' Bear and Ken's try-out for *Toy Story 3*)
or, in the case of the very first French computer-animated film *Kaena:
The Prophecy*, 'interviewed' to discuss the demands of screen acting. In
a hidden bonus feature contained on its DVD release, the computer-
animated cast of *Final Fantasy: The Spirits Within* are even depicted in a
choreographed dance routine to Michael Jackson's 1983 song 'Thriller'.
This musical sequence contributes to the playful fiction that these are
actors able at any moment to play 'against type'.

At the core of the blooper compilation, then, is an emphasis upon disparate conceptions of multiplicity: the many performative spaces and sets
(including a division between offscreen and onscreen spaces within a Luxo
world), the numerous filmmaking personnel usually veiled from view but
suddenly revealed, and of various 'takes' ruined by malapropisms, laughter, injury and accident. Computer-animated films invert the principles of
'deconstructive' animation by playing with the terms of their origination,
dismantling their illusionist activity by making false claims about their
relation to live-action cinema. Marie-Laure Ryan suggests that beyond the
postmodern fascination with self-reflexivity, self-reflexive devices 'could
also be a response to the curiosity aroused by the development of a new
medium' (2007: 269). To affirm the terms of its difference, the computer-
animated film is involved, as this chapter has argued, in a highly creative
play with the novelty of its screen spaces, employing a type of comedy that
constantly turns back on itself to contemplate the new computer-animated
worlds that have been created.

Conclusion:
Satisfying a Spirit of Adventure

Given that generic systems are an evolving, fluid grouping of elements governed by broader patterns of sameness and difference, reiteration and variance, it is not possible to predict the scope or lifespan of any film genre. The formal features presented in this book certainly do not exhaust the description and theorisation of the computer-animated film's own lively generic repertoire. If animation is a global business then computer-animated films are an international genre, and as more films are cumulatively added (and as the technology of digital animation is subject to refinement), their textual vocabulary is more than likely to mutate rather than obtain greater stability. The generic features of future computer-animated films may no longer be derived from those examples that preceded them, but instead deviate in the way that film genres have historically leaned towards hybridisation and hyphenation. However, it has not been the purpose of this book to predict the future of computer-animated films, or to ascribe them dramatic points of departure ahead of time. Rather, the features presented across each chapter account for the computer-animated film's 'story so far'. By reflecting back upon a group of popular films that have yet to be quantified or qualified as a film genre, this book has sought to demonstrate that 'computer-animated film' is a name that can be assigned to a specific type of film.

This book has therefore attempted to open up computer-animated films to greater contact with one another to become more alert to their repeating narrative structures and the specificity of their fictional worlds. But the attraction of computer-animated films lies in their employment of diverse modes of address and appeal to different types of spectatorial knowledge. Rick Altman argues that genres are historically grounded in that they 'serve diverse groups diversely' and 'have multiple conflicting audiences' (1999: 207–8). Computer-animated films certainly provide multiple viewers with shifting categories of interpretation. Spectators schooled in the broader machinations of the computer-animated film may prove better equipped to judge how/if/whether certain criteria are (to be) fulfilled. In other cases, new generic allegiances may be forged based upon pleasures located in the simple repetition, consistency and variation of formal features within and without the genre.

Despite genre criticism's abilities to afford greater intelligibility to the computer-animated film, their generic classification and the desire to identify them according to a fixed generic category should also not be viewed as the end point of critical discussion. It ought, rather, to pave the way for closer, more rigorously formalist approaches that are receptive to instances when computer-animated films deviate from, or simply push at the boundaries of, their generic contract. The contact between a single computer-animated film and the computer-animated film genre is far from uniform, but is instead fluctuating as each computer-animated film takes what it needs from the genre's codes and conventions. The treatment of computer-animated films as a genre also interrogates the wider practices and processes of genre criticism that have been historically tailored to the live-action cinema. Genre analysis positions the institutionally defined corpus of 'computer-animated films' to further analysis at the level of formal structure. To examine the genericity of computer-animated films is to position industry, technology and textuality in relation to each other, guiding us towards what filmmakers may conceive of when they set out to produce a computer-animated film, *and* what audiences might expect of computer-animated films more broadly.

Genre criticism also operates as a complement and counterpoint to analysis of the signature style of individual studios, including those smaller cycles and franchises associated with particular animation facilities. Altman argues that part of the 'easily exploitable' industry of Hollywood genres has involved 'studio-specific resources (contract actors, proprietary characters, recognizable styles)' alongside 'common features that can be imitated by other studios (subject matter, character types, plot patterns)' (1998: 15). However, within the industrial system of Hollywood computer-animated filmmaking and its dominant 'Big Five', the proprietary textual features of individual companies are not the only explanation for the existence of commonalities between computer-animated films. The wider genericity can be identified *across* the rich diversity of companies and facilities, despite evident distinctions between them with regards to design policies, formal preferences and ideological positions. The examination of computer-animated films as a genre identifies and preserves such studio specificities, without assuming in advance how they contribute to the critical and popular formulation of common meanings. This is particularly significant given that the familiar studio name and textual features of the film itself may not always coincide with expectations held by critics and audiences. Genre criticism enables an investigation into the kinds of relationships that exist between individual studios and broader generic criteria. The focus on the institutional context of computer-animated film production foregrounds connections with and between surrounding texts, adding another important point of engagement with how computer-animated films – and their dense network of meanings – interact with their all-digital neighbours.

In the case of *Wreck-It Ralph*, for example, the film is simultaneously the fifty-second entry in Walt Disney's animated feature-film canon *and* a computer-animated film. On the one hand, the film promotes the standardised Disney values of innocence and optimism, offering audiences escapist fantasy through an enchanting magical narrative. However, a critical approach to *Wreck-It Ralph* that examines the film as belonging to a wider computer-animated film genre allows its narrative, characters, and other formal features to be seen in more complex ways. The relationship between child protagonist (and video game 'glitch') Vanellope von Schweetz and the lonely Ralph himself is sharply defined as one of surrogate father/daughter. Ralph's parenthood-by-proxy in *Wreck-It Ralph* exhibits the computer-animated film genre's lack of investment in the conventional structure of the nuclear family (as discussed in Chapter 2). Yet childhood experience is also the common ground between Vanellope and Ralph, who is no less childlike than his surrogate daughter, despite his seemingly advanced age and imposing, impossible physical appearance. Ralph is determined, enthusiastic, exuberant, immature and tempestuous, trading childish insults with Vanellope (such as 'Booger Brain' and 'Fart Feathers') as part of their growing rapport and mutual respect. In *Wreck-It Ralph*, Ralph's erratic, juvenile behaviour stretches the terms of the adult/child distinction. As Vanellope comments when goading her sulking father figure, 'Enjoy your little tantrum, diaper baby?' *Wreck-It Ralph* thus becomes less recognisable as a familiar Disney film when analysed through its membership to a computer-animated film genre. In this way, the relationship between Vanellope and Ralph, which lies at the heart of the film, is aligned with what computer-animated film narratives more generally have to say about the culture of childhood.

Animating Childhood

> Goodnight Agnes. Never get older.
> (Gru, *Despicable Me 2*)

Computer-animated films convey a notable fascination with the vicissitudes and values of childhood. There has been a spate of recent film scholarship interested in bringing into greater relief the multiple functions of the child within the context of cinema. These have ranged from investments in the child as pedagogical subjects primed to be socialised (Doherty 2002); the figure of the child as a potent and powerful narrative agent (Wilson 2003); the rise of the 'teenpic' genre (Lebeau 2008); and the wider politics underlying their ambiguous status as performers (Lury 2010). However, the narratives of computer-animated films also invite a consideration of what it means to be a child. Judith Halberstam has argued that contemporary animation narratives are intended to closely match the new rhythms of childishness by celebrating those values associated with childlike activity. In the late 1970s, critics lamented such 'juvenilization' of Hollywood cinema, a tendency attributed to a cycle of blockbuster films that included *Jaws* and *Star Wars* (George Lucas, 1977). The criticisms levelled at these films emerged from how, as James Chapman puts it, 'narrative complexity and psychological depth are sacrificed for size, spectacle and special effects' (2003: 142). More recently, British-born director Danny Boyle (in Sciretta 2013) has described with some disdain the 'Pixarification' of contemporary cinema, suggesting that Pixar, like *Star Wars*, is closing off challenging adult movies that address adult violence, sexuality and dilemmas.

Computer-animated films do not retreat from things that matter. Their narratives engage with contemporary culture by speaking to the real world experience of a child. Children, Halberstam writes, 'stumble, bumble, fail, fall, hurt; they are mired in difference, not in control of their bodies, not in charge of their lives' (2011: 47). Each of this book's chapters lays the groundwork for thinking about how computer-animated films trade in a host of playfully childlike things. Chapter 5 registers these connections through how computer-animated films cater to the child's faculties of imagination in their treatment of junk, rubbish and discarded objects. But childlike themes, behaviours and pleasures are encountered at various other interstices across the genre. The journey narrative, the enlivened anthropomorph and the metaleptic transgressions of diegetic worlds normally held distinct, all appeal to a childlike 'spirit of adventure', to quote the name of Charles Muntz's airship in *Up*. Children love to explore (their spaces, their bodies, their boundaries), and as they grow, perhaps to escape parental control, enforced duty and regulated behaviour. Exploration in the computer-animated film is about going along for the experience, and surmounting injury or obstacle, rather than becoming preoccupied with the certainty of glory or success. Kate Crawford has, however, raised questions about the treatment of normative adulthood offered in Halberstam's account of animated features, and in particular the *prizing* of childishness by *prising* it from those values associated with being an 'adult'. Crawford argues that the separation of adolescents and adults from children remains far from secure, and that we should not accept 'too readily this child/adult distinction' (2012: 145). Portmanteau terms such as 'kidult', 'manchild' and 'adultescents' all point to a degree of cross-generational pollination and age inversion (ibid.: 146). Such shifts in socially prescribed roles are not irrefutable signs of a culture in crisis through the collapse of orthodox adulthood. Rather, the new childishness of adults expresses the relocation (rather than diminishment) of certain adultlike aspirations, and to upturn 'traditional temporalities of adulthood' (ibid.). Computer-animated films emerge as a particular kind of response to such moments of social and cultural change. They are attuned to shifting notions of the child by consciously straining the boundaries of normative adulthood.

Computer-animated films are replete with adult figures increasingly amenable to forms of childlike conduct. Narratives reveal their fallibilities and frailties, anxieties and weaknesses in ways that indicate adults have not (fully) set aside their childish ways. Silly and idiotic, puerile and preposterous, irresponsible and immature, the conventional shape and definition of adult characters is washed away 'in a flood of childlike jubilation' (Langford 2010: 250). Parents are loving and protective but impatient and irritable. As Louis Rothschild states, Marlin (*Finding Nemo*) is a father 'who like a child, continues to encounter opportunities to develop and grow' (2009: 224). Adults are shown to be openly technophobic and humorously inept when working contemporary technology (*Cloudy with a Chance of Meatballs*). They may resort to childish pranks and games (*Hotel Transylvania*, *Despicable Me 3*), or display awkward behaviour when confronted with a love interest (*Ratatouille*, *Rio*). Extended families are often bizarrely impulsive and eccentric too (*Meet the Robinsons*), and adult humans, more generally, are distinguished by their laughable shape and ungainly movements (*Wall-E*), diminutive stature (Lord Farquaad in *Shrek*) or as being selfish, vain and in childlike thrall to a doting mother (*Shrek 2*'s Prince Charming). Even superheroes are lazy and languid (*Megamind*), often excitable but petulant in their childish rivalries (*Despicable Me*), and in some cases appear insecure and socially stunted (*The Incredibles*). Other adults are destructively mischievous, preferring to destroy rather than create by smashing and tearing their way through the world (*Wreck-It Ralph*). Even the elderly Granny Puckett in *Hoodwinked* is revealed as a young-at-heart extreme sports enthusiast who engages in the danger of thrilling, if risky, recreational activities. Furthermore, multiple computer-animated films (*Monsters, Inc.*, *Chicken Little*, *Surf's*

Up, *Despicable Me*, *Wreck-It Ralph* and *Up*) are centred upon child/adult interaction, playing with divisions of 'young' and 'old' to suggest not their autonomy from each other, but their connectedness and interchangeable nature.

Childlikeness can also be positively re-discovered by adults in acts of narrative redemption. When acerbic food critic Anton Ego (*Ratatouille*) samples the film's eponymous culinary dish, a childhood flashback – portrayed in warm, comforting hues – disarms his otherwise uncompromising demeanour. His skeletal body softens, his stern and morbidly pale face suddenly relaxes. Childlikeness for Anton marks a return to life, a nostalgic state permitting his salvation and reformation from villainy. He even relinquishes his pen, shedding his prior vocation as critic, as he is caught up in the rush of childhood memories. For those youthful characters that ascend to adulthood, the retention of the inner child is paramount to the prolonging of childlike attitudes into adult years. Toy owner Andy cannot resist the lure of childlike activity during the climax of *Toy Story 3*. Andy's sudden re-engagement of his childish ways invigorates both the sentient toys' true function and highest point of living, and his own childlike exuberance (which he will reluctantly leave behind at the film's conclusion). Finally in *Frozen*, the celebration of sisterhood between infant siblings Elsa and Anna is replaced by a more 'frosty' kinship as the characters reach the cusp of adulthood. Wrestling with their traumatic upbringing – in which Elsa's cryokinetic powers accidentally wound the young Anna – the teenage sisters progressively lose their childish enthusiasms. Anna has her childhood memories magically wiped while Elsa becomes a recluse. The drama of *Frozen*'s narrative trajectory hinges upon whether or not the playfulness of the sisters' childhood relationship will finally be rediscovered. Elsa's adage to 'Conceal it, don't feel it. Don't let it show' therefore refers to more than just her clandestine sorcery but to her prior childish energies, which have similarly become hidden from her sister and the townsfolk of Arendelle.

In computer-animated films, the child/adult distinction is thus not fixed or 'frozen' but flowing; figuring, instead, as generational continuity offering new possibilities for their collision. In *Robots*, the identities of child/adult become even more interchangeable through the body parts used by the humanoids that instantly 'age' the wearer. In contemporary animated feature films, gender is, as Halberstam points out, often fluid and amorphous. But age is no less ambiguous, and can be emptied of its meaningful content within the construction of what she calls an 'assembled self' (2011: 46). The brief sequence in *Robots* when a young Rodney Copperbottom struggles to adjust to his oversized 'big boy' metallic torso

– despite retaining his same youthful face and legs – places the child/adult distinction in more visually comic terms. Like Andy's childish exploits in *Toy Story 3*, *Robots* informs spectators that to be (or to embody) an adult is to engage in a culturally-determined act of improvisation, and that an outwardly adult body may conceal a more childlike disposition.

Computer-animated films offer future opportunity to examine how, as a genre, they mobilise questions about the cultural experience and significance of childhood, and their redefinition of adulthood. For adult spectators, the childlike behaviour of adult figures (and, by extension, child characters that are increasingly precocious, assertive and adept) may not seem obviously and immediately attractive. Nevertheless, computer-animated films embrace such personality disorders, invested in the joy of youthful pleasures by encouraging adults to accept their childlike ways. Computer-animated film narratives judge only those elder states-men who take it all too seriously and who, unlike Anton Ego, are not softened by contact with childlike feelings. In fact, Anton's return to childhood in *Ratatouille* may function as a model for the nostalgic attrac-tion of computer-animated films for the adult spectator more generally. Rothschild describes experiencing a 'transgenerational moment of remem-bering as a son while simultaneously acting and feeling as a father' (2009: 240) when watching *Finding Nemo*. Spectatorial pleasure lies, then, in the sudden, momentary confusion of child and adult identities. Moreover, as the child/adult hybrid figure of Rodney in *Robots* makes clear, learning lessons of self-change always involves the necessary 'juggling' of child/adult attributes as part of growing up. Philosopher Paolo Virno (2005) has suggested that it is time to 'reactivate childhood', to be subversive and playful and go beyond the imperious adult figure. Computer-animated films perform such actions, drawing upon a generational continuity to carve a space for the contemporary cultural figure of the childlike adult. By prolonging childhood by restoring it to adults, these films stage a meeting of adult and child that inscribes adulthood with the positivity of youth.

Far from simply reproducing outworn family values, computer-animated films challenge normative conceptions of ossified, uninspired adulthood. These are narratives that illuminate the precarious path marking the ascension from childhood to adulthood today, but they do so via the contribution of a series of repeating formal features that this book has worked towards defining. The treatment of computer-animated films *as a genre*, and the attributes identified in each of the preceding chapters, therefore demonstrates a model of analysis that invites a more focused examination of their familiar pleasures. It has been the purpose of this book to make the case for the complexities of computer-animated films (and their often vexed historical and theoretical connections to animation's own filmmaking traditions) to be understood as a function of genre. Through its many illustrative examples, this book has invoked genre as a way of 'coming to terms' with the computer-animated film's prominence within both global animation and digital media contexts, and their place across contemporary moving image culture.

Bibliography

Abrams, Jerold J. (2007), 'From Sherlock Holmes to the hard-boiled detective in film noir', in Mark T. Conrad and Robert Porfirio (eds), *The Philosophy of Film Noir*, Lexington: University Press of Kentucky, pp. 69–88.

Aita, Sean (2012), 'Dance of the Übermarionettes: toward a contemporary screen actor training', in Aaron Taylor (ed.), *Theorizing Film Acting*, London: Routledge, pp. 256–70.

Aldred, Jessica (2006), 'All aboard *The Polar Express*: a 'playful' change of address in the computer-generated blockbuster', *animation: an interdisciplinary journal*, 1: 2 (November), 153–72.

Allen, Steven (2009), 'Audio-Avery: sound in Tex Avery's MGM cartoons', *Animation Journal*, 17: 7–22.

Alloway, Lawrence (1971), *Violent America: The Movies 1946–1964*, New York: Museum of Modern Art.

Alloway, Lawrence (2006), *Imagining the Present: Context, Content, and the Role of the Critic: Essays by Lawrence Alloway*, edited by Richard Kalina, London and New York: Routledge.

Altman, Rick (1984), 'A semantic/syntactic approach to film genre', *Cinema Journal*, 23: 3 (Spring), 6–18.

Altman, Rick (1998), 'Reusable packaging: generic products and the recycling process', in Nick Browne (ed.), *Refiguring American Film Genres: History and Theory*, Berkeley: University of California Press, pp. 1–41.

Altman, Rick (1999), *Film/Genre*, London: BFI Publishing.

Altman, Rick (2008), *A Theory of Narrative*, New York: Columbia University Press.

Andrew, Dudley (1984), *Concepts in Film Theory*, New York: Oxford University Press.

Apodaca, Anthony A. and Larry Gritz (2000), *Advanced RenderMan: Creating CGI for Motion Pictures*, San Diego, CA: Academic Press.

Armitage, John (2000), 'The Kosovo War took place in orbital space: Paul Virilio in conversation', *CTheory*, 18 October, <http://www.ctheory.net/articles. aspx?id=132> (accessed 30 June 2017).

Asherie, Rebecca (2012), 'Heavenly voices and bestial bodies: issues of performance and representation in celebrity voice-acting', *Animation Practice, Process and Production*, 1: 2, 229–48.

Bachelard, Gaston (1994), *The Poetics of Space*, translated by Maria Jolas, Boston, MA: Beacon Press.

Baker, Simon (2001), *Picturing the Beast: Animals, Identity, and Representation*, Champaign, IL: University of Illinois Press.

Bal, Mieke (1985), *Narratology: Introduction to the Theory of Narrative*, translated by Christine van Boheemen, Toronto: University of Toronto Press.

Barker, Jennifer M (2009), *The Tactile Eye: Touch and the Cinematic Experience*, Berkeley: University of California Press.

Barker, Martin and Thomas Austin (2000), *From Antz to Titanic: Reinventing Film Analysis*, London: Pluto Press.

Barnes, Brooks (2009), 'Animation upstarts are joining the fray', *The New York Times*, 2 June, <https://mobile.nytimes.com/2009/06/03/movies/03anim.html> (accessed 30 June 2017).

Barrier, Michael (1999), *Hollywood Cartoons: American Animation in its Golden Age*, Oxford: Oxford University Press.

Barrier, Michael (2007), 'Ed Hooks on *Ratatouille*', *Michael Barrier.Com*, August, <www.michaelbarrier.com/Home%20Page/WhatsNewArchivesAugust07.htm#hooks> (accessed 30 June 2017).

Barthes, Roland (1985), *The Responsibility of Forms: Critical Essays on Music, Art and Representation*, translated by Richard Howard, New York: Hill and Wang.

Beaver, Frank Eugene (2007), *Dictionary of Film Terms: The Aesthetic Companion to Film Art*, New York: Peter Lang.

Beeton, Sue (2005), *Film-Induced Tourism*, Clevedon: Channel View Publications.

Beiman, Nancy (2010), *Animated Performance: Bringing Imaginary Animal, Human and Fantasy*, London: Thames and Hudson.

Bell, David (2001), *An Introduction to Cybercultures*, London: Routledge.

Bell, John (2008), *American Puppet Modernism: Essays on the Material World in Performance*, New York: Palgrave Macmillan.

Bergson, Henri [1911] (2005), *Laughter: An Essay on the Meaning of the Comic*, Mineola, NY: Dover Publications.

Berleant, Arnold (1991), *Art and Engagement*, Philadelphia: Temple University.

Betz, Frederick (2001), *Executive Strategy: Strategic Management and Information Technology*, New York: John Wiley and Sons.

Bevilacqua, Joe (1999), 'Celebrity voice actors: the new sound of animation', *Animation World Magazine*, 4: 1 (April), <http://www.awn.com/mag/issue4.01/4.01pages/bevilacquaceleb.php3> (accessed 30 June 2017).

Bode, Lisa (2010), 'No longer themselves? Framing digitally enabled posthumous "performance"', *Cinema Journal*, 49: 4 (Summer), 46–70.

Bond, Barbara (2004), 'Postmodern Mannerism: an examination of Robert Coover's Pinocchio in Venice', *Critique: Studies in Contemporary Fiction*, 45: 3, 273–92.

Bondanella, Peter (2006), *Hollywood Italians: Dagos, Palookas, Romeos, Wise Guys, and Sopranos*, New York and London: Continuum.

Booker, M. Keith (2010), *Disney, Pixar, and the Hidden Messages of Children's Films*, Santa Barbara, CA: Greenwood Press.

Booker, M. Keith (2011), *Historical Dictionary of American Cinema*, Lanham, MD: Scarecrow Press.

Bordwell, David (1989), *Making Meaning: Inference and Rhetoric in the Interpretation of Cinema*, Cambridge, MA: Harvard University Press.

Bordwell, David (1997), *Narration in the Film*, London: Routledge.

Bordwell, David (2002), 'Film futures', *SubStance*, 31: 1, 88–104.

Bordwell, David (2006), *The Way Hollywood Tells It: Story and Style in Modern Movies*, Berkeley: University of California Press.

Bordwell, David [2007] (2011), 'Rat rapture', in David Bordwell and Kristin Thompson, *Minding Movies*, Chicago: University of Chicago Press, pp. 229–34.

Bordwell, David and Kristin Thompson (2011), *Minding Movies: Observations on the Art, Craft, and Business of Filmmaking*, Chicago: University of Chicago Press.

Bordwell, David, Janet Staiger and Kristin Thompson (1988), *The Classical Hollywood Cinema: Film Style and Mode of Production to 1960*, London: Routledge.

Boscagli, Maurizia (2014), *Stuff Theory: Everyday Objects, Radical Materialism*, London and New York: Bloomsbury.

Botting, Frank and Scott Wilson (2004), 'Toy law, toy joy and *Toy Story 2*', in Leslie J. Moran, Emma Sandon, Elena Loizidou and Ian Christie (eds), *Law's Moving Image*, London: Cavendish Publishing, pp. 61–73.

Boulter, Jay (2005), 'Transference and transparency: digital technology and the remediation of cinema', *Intermédialités*, 6: (Autumn), 13–26.

Boulter, Jay and Richard Grusin (2000), *Remediation: Understanding New Media*, Cambridge, MA: MIT Press.

Bowers, Maggie Ann (2004), *Magic(al) Realism*, New York: Routledge.

Brabham, Daren C. (2006), 'Animated blackness in Shrek', *Rocky Mountain Communication Review*, 3: 1 (Summer), 64–71.

Brand, Stewart (1989), *The Media Lab: Inventing the Future at MIT*, New York: Penguin Books.

Branigan, Edward (1984), *Point of View in the Cinema: A Theory of Narration and Subjectivity in Classical Film*, New York: Mouton.

Branigan, Edward (2002), 'Nearly true: forking plots, forking interpretations: a response to David Bordwell's "Film Futures"', *SubStance* 31: 1, 105–14.

Bredow, Rob, David Schaub, Daniel Kramer, Matthew Hausman, Danny Dimian and R. Stirling Duguid (2007), 'Surf's Up: the making of an animated documentary', *SIGGRAPH 2007*, <http://library.imageworks.com/pdfs/imageworks-library-Surfs-Up-the-making-of-an-animated-documentary.pdf> (accessed 30 June 2017).

Brereton, Pat (2012), *Smart Cinema, DVD Add-Ons and New Audience Pleasures*, New York: Palgrave Macmillan.

Brodesser, Claude and Ben Fritz (2005), 'Hollywood hearing voices', *Variety*, 398: 1 (16 May–22 May), 68.

Brophy, Philip (2003) 'The animation of sound', in Kay Dickinson (ed.), *Movie Music: A Film Reader*, London: Routledge, pp. 133–42.

Brown, Bill (2001), 'Thing theory', *Critical Inquiry*, 28: 1 (Autumn), 1–22.

Brown, Noel (2012), *The Hollywood Family Film: A History, from Shirley Temple to Harry Potter*, New York: I. B. Tauris.

Brown, Noel (2017), *The Children's Film – Genre, Nation, and Narrative*, London: Wallflower Press.

Brown, Noel and Bruce Babbington (eds) (2015), *Family Films in Global Cinema: The World Beyond Disney*, London: I. B. Tauris.

Brown, William (2012), '*Avatar*: stereoscopic cinema, gaseous perception and darkness', *animation: an interdisciplinary journal*, 7: 3 (November), 259–71.

Brown, William (2013), *Supercinema: Film Philosophy for the Digital Age*, New York: Berghahn.

Browne, Nick (1998), *Refiguring American Film Genres*, Berkeley and Los Angeles: University of California Press.

Bruno, Giuliana (2002), *Atlas of Emotion: Journeys in Art, Architecture and Film*, New York: Verso.

Brydon, Suzan G. (2009), 'Men at the heart of mothering: finding mother in *Finding Nemo*', *Journal of Gender Studies*, 18: 2 (June), 131–46.

Brzeski, Patrick (2016), 'China box office: "Kung Fu Panda 3" earns impressive $6.4m in previews', *The Hollywood Reporter*, 25 January, <http://www.hollywoodreporter.com/news/china-box-office-kung-fu-858877> (accessed 30 June 2017).

Buchan, Suzanne (2006), 'The animated spectator: watching the Quay Brothers' "Worlds"', in Suzanne Buchan (ed.), *Animated Worlds*, Eastleigh: John Libbey Publishing, pp. 17–40.

Buchan, Suzanne (2011), *The Quay Brothers: Into a Metaphysical Playroom*, Minneapolis: University of Minnesota Press.

Buchan, Suzanne (2013), 'Theatrical cartoon comedy: from animated portmanteau to the *Risus Purus*', in Andrew Horton and Joanna E. Rapf (eds), *A Companion to Film Comedy*, Chichester: Wiley-Blackwell, pp. 521–43.

Buckland, Warren (2003), 'The role of the auteur in the age of the blockbuster: Steven Spielberg and DreamWorks', in Julian Stringer (ed.), *Movie Blockbusters*, London: Routledge, pp. 84–98.

Buckland, Warren (2014), 'Introduction', in Warren Buckland (ed.), *Hollywood Puzzle Films*, New York: Routledge, pp. 1–14.

Bugrimenko, Elena and Elena Smirnova (1994), 'Paradoxes of children's play in Vygotsky's theory', in Gerald C. Cupchick and Janos László (eds), *Emerging Visions of the Aesthetic Process*, Cambridge: Cambridge University Press, pp. 286–99.

Bukatman, Scott (2012), *The Poetics of Slumberland: Animated Spirits and the Animating Spirit*, Berkeley: University of California Press.

Bull, Michael and Les Back (2003), 'Introduction: into sound', in Michael Bull and Les Back (eds), *The Auditory Culture Reader*, Oxford, New York: Berg, pp. 1–17.

Burt, Richard (2013), 'Writing the ends of cinema: saving film authorship in the cinematic paratexts of *Prospero's Books*, Taymor's *The Tempest* and *The Secret of Kells*', in Judith Buchanan (ed.), *The Writer on Film: Screening Literary Authorship*, Basingstoke: Palgrave Macmillan, pp. 178–92.

Buscombe, Ed (1970), 'The idea of genre in the American cinema', *Screen*, 11: 2 (March–April), 33–45.

Cameron, Warren (2008), *Modular Narratives in Contemporary Cinema*, Basingstoke, New York: Palgrave Macmillan.

Campbell, Joseph (1998), *The Hero with a Thousand Faces*, 3rd edn, Novato, CA: New World Library.

Canemaker, John (2005), 'Disney erases hand-drawn animation', *Wall Street Journal*, 9 August, <http://www.opinionjournal.com/la/?id=110007081> (accessed 30 June 2017).

Carroll, Bret E. (ed.) (2003), *American Masculinities: A Historical Encyclopedia*, New York: Sage Publications.

Carroll, Jane Suzanne (2011), *Landscape in Children's Literature*, New York: Routledge.

Carroll, Noël (1998), 'Anti-illusionism in modern and postmodern art', *Leonardo*, 21: 3, 297–304.

Carson, Anne (1998), *Autobiography of Red*, New York: Vintage.

Cavell, Stanley (1979), *The World Viewed: Reflections on the Ontology of Film*, enlarged edn, Cambridge, MA: Harvard University Press.

Cegielski, Scott (2006), 'Character splash system', *Computer Graphics World*, 29: 10 (October), <http://www.cgw.com/Publications/CGW/2006/Volume-29-Issue-10-Oct-2006-/Character-Splash-System.aspx> (accessed 30 June 2017).

Chapman, James (2003), *Cinemas of the World: Film and Society from 1895 to the Present*, London: Reaktion.

Chatman, Seymour (1980), *Story and Discourse: Narrative Structure in Fiction and Film*, New York: Cornell University Press.

Chatman, Seymour (1990), *Coming to Terms: The Rhetoric of Narrative in Fiction and Film*, Ithaca, NY: Cornell University Press.

Cheu, Johnson (ed.) (2013), *Diversity in Disney Films: Critical Essays on Race, Ethnicity, Gender, Sexuality and Disability*, Jefferson, NC: McFarland and Company.

Chion, Michel (1994), *Audio-Vision: Sound on Screen*, translated by Claudia Gorbman, New York: Columbia University Press.

Chion, Michel (1999), *The Voice in Cinema*, translated by Claudia Gorbman, New York: Columbia University Press.

Chion, Michel (2000), 'Audio-vision and sound', in Patricia Kruth and Henry Stobart (eds), *Sound*, Cambridge: Cambridge University Press, pp. 201–21.

Cholodenko, Alan (1991), 'Who Framed Roger Rabbit, or the framing of animation', in Alan Cholodenko (ed.), *The Illusion of Life: Essays on Animation*, Power Publications in association with the Australian Film Commission, Sydney, pp. 209–42.

Cholodenko, Alan (2008), 'The animation of cinema', *Semiotic Review of Books*, 18: 2, <http://projects.chass.utoronto.ca/semiotics/vol18.2.pdf> (accessed 30 June 2017).

Christensen, Jerome (2012), *America's Corporate Art: The Studio Authorship of Hollywood Motion Pictures*, Stanford, CA: Stanford University Press.

Clayton, Alex (2010), 'Performance, with strings attached: *Team America*'s snub to the actor', in Tom Brown and James Walters (eds), *Film Moments: Criticism, History, Theory*, London: BFI Publishing, pp. 127–30.

Cohan, Steven and Ina Rae Hark (eds) (1997), *The Road Movie Book*, London: Routledge.

Cohen, Karl F. (1997), *Forbidden Animation: Censored Cartoons and Blacklisted Animators in America*, Jefferson, NC: McFarland and Company.

Combs, Steven C. (2002), 'The Dao of communication criticism: insects, individuals, and mass society', *Social Semiotics*, 12: 2 (August), 183–99.

Comolli, Jean-Louis and Jean Narboni (1977), 'Cinema/ideology/criticism (1)', in John Ellis (ed.), *Screen Reader 1: Cinema/Ideology/Politics*, London: Society for Education in Film and Television, pp. 2–11.

Constandinides, Costas (2010), *From Film Adaptation to Post-Celluloid Adaptation*, New York: Continuum.

Cook, Malcolm (2015), 'Pixar, "The Road to Point Reyes", and the long history of landscapes in new visual technologies', in Chris Pallant (ed.), *Animated Landscapes: History, Form and Function*, London: Bloomsbury, pp. 51–72.

Cornea, Christine (2007), *Science Fiction Cinema: Between Fantasy and Reality*, Edinburgh: Edinburgh University Press.

Corrigan, Timothy (2012), 'Introduction: movies and the 2000s', in Timothy Corrigan (ed.), *American Cinema of the 2000s: Themes and Variations*, New Brunswick, NJ: Rutgers University Press, pp. 1–18.

Costello, Martin (2006), 'Stop motion puppets in CG', *SIGGRAPH 2006*, <http://staffwww.itn.liu.se/~andyn/courses/tncg08/sketches06/sketches/0660-costello.pdf> (accessed 30 June 2017).

Cotta Vaz, Mark (1999), '*A Bug's Life*: an entomological epic', *Cinefex*, 76: (January), 41–50, 133–40.

Coyle, Rebecca (2010), 'Introduction', in Rebecca Coyle (ed.), *Drawn to Sound: Animation Film Music and Sonicity*, London: Equinox Publishing, pp. 1–22.

Crafton, Donald (1979), 'Animation iconography: the "Hand of the Artist"', *Quarterly Review of Film Studies*, 4: 4 (Fall), 409–28.

Crafton, Donald (2013), *Shadow of a Mouse: Performance, Belief, and World-Making in Animation*, Berkeley: University of California Press.

Crawford, Kate (2012), 'Re-animating adulthood', in Kerry H. Robinson and Cristyn Davies (eds), *Queer and Subjugated Knowledges: Generating Subversive Imaginaries*, Oak Park, IL: Bentham Books, pp. 140–56.

Creekmur, Corey K. (1997), 'On the run and on the road: fame and the outlaw couple in American cinema', in Steven Cohan and Ina Rae Hark (eds), *The Road Movie Book*, London: Routledge, pp. 90–112.

Crockett, Tobey (2009), 'The '*Camera* as Camera:' how CGI changes the world as we know it', in Scott Balcerzak and Jason Sperb (eds), *Cinephilia in the Age of Digital Reproduction: Film, Pleasure and Digital Culture*, vol. 1, London: Wallflower Press, pp. 117–39.

Cubitt, Sean (2004), *The Cinema Effect*, Cambridge, MA: MIT Press.

Cubitt, Sean (2009), 'The supernatural in neo-baroque Hollywood', in Warren Buckland (ed.), *Film Theory and Contemporary Hollywood Movies*, New York: Routledge, pp. 47–65.

Curtis, Scott (1992), 'The sound of the early Warner Bros. cartoons', in Rick Altman, *Sound Theory, Sound Practice*, London: Routledge, pp. 191–203.

Darley, Andrew (1990), 'From abstraction to simulation: notes on the history of computer imaging', in Philip Hayward (ed.), *Culture, Technology, and Creativity in the Late Twentieth Century*, London: John Libbey Publishing, pp. 339–64.

Darley, Andrew (1997), 'Second-order realism and post-modernist aesthetics in computer animation', in Jayne Pilling (ed.), *A Reader in Animation Studies*, London: John Libbey Publishing, pp. 16–24.

Darley, Andrew (2000), *Visual Digital Culture: Surface Play and Spectacle in New Media Genres*, London: Routledge.

Davis, Nick (2009), 'The Incredibles', in John White and Sabine Haenni (eds), *Fifty Key American Films*, New York: Routledge, pp. 244–49.

Deleuze, Gilles (1986), *Cinema 1: The Movement-Image*, translated by Hugh Tomlinson and Barbara Habberjam, London: Athlone Press.

Deleuze, Gilles and Felix Guattari (1987), *A Thousand Plateaus: Capitalism and Schizophrenia*, translated by Brian Massumi, London: Athlone Press.

Denby, David (1998), 'Ants in their pants: *Antz* movie review', *New York Magazine*, 12 October, <http://nymag.com/nymetro/movies/reviews/2848/> (accessed 30 June 2017).

Denison, Rayna (2008), 'Star-spangled Ghibli: star voices in the American versions of Hayao Miyazaki's films', *animation: an interdisciplinary journal*, 3: 2 (July), 129–46.

Denison, Rayna (2017), 'Anime's star voices: voice actor (Seiyū) performance and stardom in Japan', in Tom Whittaker and Sarah Wright (eds), *Locating the Voice in Film: Critical Approaches and Global Practices*, New York: Oxford University Press, pp. 101–18.

Detweiler, Craig (2010), 'Conclusion: born to play', in Craig Detweiler (ed.), *Halos and Avatars: Playing Video Games with God*, Louisville, KY: Westminster John Knox Press, pp. 190–6.

Dobson, Nichola (2009), *The A to Z of Animation and Cartoons*, Lanham, MD: Scarecrow Press.

Doherty, Thomas Patrick (2002), *Teenagers and Teenpics: Juvenilization of American Movies*, Philadelphia, PA: Temple University Press.

Drake, Philip (2004), 'Jim Carrey: the cultural politics of dumbing down', in Andrew Willis (ed.), *Film Stars: Hollywood and Beyond*, Manchester: Manchester University Press, pp. 71–88.

Dunn, David Hastings (2006), '*The Incredibles*: an ordinary day tale of a superpower in the post 9/11 world', *Millennium – Journal of International Studies*, 34: 2 (February), 559–62.

Dunne, Michael (2001), *Intertextual Encounters in American Fiction, Film, and Popular Culture*, Bowling Green, OH: Bowling Green State University Popular Press.

Durgnat, Raymond (1969), *The Crazy Mirror: Hollywood Comedy and The American Image*, New York: Horizon Press.

Dyer, Richard (1979), *Stars*, London: BFI Publishing.

Ehlrich, Nea (2013), 'Animated documentaries: aesthetics, politics and viewer engagement', in Suzanne Buchan (ed.), *Pervasive Animation*, New York: Routledge, pp. 248–71.

Eisenstein, Sergei (1986), *Eisenstein on Disney*, translated by Jay Leyda, London: Methuen.

Eleftheriotis, Dimitrios (2010), *Cinematic Journeys: Film and Movement*, Edinburgh: Edinburgh University Press.

Elsaesser, Thomas (2009), 'The mind-game film', in Warren Buckland (ed.), *Puzzle Films: Complex Storytelling in Contemporary Hollywood Cinema*, Oxford: Wiley-Blackwell, pp. 13–41.

Elsaesser, Thomas (2013), 'The "return" of 3-D: on some of the logics and gene-alogies of the image in the twenty-first century', *Critical Inquiry*, 39 (Winter), 217–46.

Elsaesser, Thomas and Malte Hagener (2010), *Film Theory: An Introduction Through the Senses*, New York: Routledge.

Falzon, Christopher (2005), *Philosophy Goes to the Movies: An Introduction to Philosophy*, London: Routledge.

Falzon, Christopher (2007), *Philosophy goes to the Movies: An Introduction to Philosophy*. London: Routledge.

Feeney, Mark (2009), 'Back to the future', *Boston Globe*, 7 June, <http://archive. boston.com/ae/movies/articles/2009/06/07/pixars_success_is_an_up_to_the_minute_throwback/> (accessed 30 June 2017).

Ferrari, Chiara Francesca (2010), *Since When Is Fran Drescher Jewish?: Dubbing Stereotypes in The Nanny, The Simpsons, and The Sopranos*, Austin: University of Texas Press.

Feyersinger, Erwin (2010), 'Diegetic short circuits: metalepsis in animation', *animation: an interdisciplinary journal*, 5: 3 (November), 279–94.

Finklea, Bruce W. (2017), 'Nurturing new men and polishing imperfect fathers via hetero- and homosocial relationships in Pixar films', in Rebecca Ann Lind (ed.), *Race and Gender in Electronic Media: Content, Context, Culture*, London and New York: Routledge, pp. 89–104.

Fiske, John (1987), *Television Culture*, London: Methuen.

Formenti, Cristina (2014), 'The sincerest form of docudrama: re-framing the animated documentary', *Studies in Documentary Film*, 8: 2, 101–15.

Frazier, Ian (1990), 'Coyote vs. Acme', *The New Yorker*, 26 February, 42–3.

Freedman, Yacov (2012), 'Is it real . . . or is it motion capture?: the battle to redefine animation in the age of digital performance', *The Velvet Light Trap*, 69 (Spring), 38–49.

Freeman, Laurie A. (2002), 'Media', in Steven Kent Vogel (ed.), *US-Japan Relations in a Changing World*, Arlington, VA: Oakland Street Publishing, pp. 125–59.

Frelik, Pawel (2014), 'Digital film and audiences', in Sonja Fritzsche (ed.), *The Liverpool Companion to World Science Fiction Film*, Liverpool: Liverpool University Press, pp. 247–64.

Fritz, Ben (2004), 'CGI toons: is there more "Shrek" green?' *Variety*, 31 October, <http://variety.com/2004/film/news/cgi-toons-is-there-more-shrek-green-1117912709/> (accessed 30 June 2017).

Fritz, Ben and Dave McNary (2006), 'Critter jitters', *Variety*, 402: 7 (3 April–9 April), 1.

Furniss, Maureen (1999), 'Animation literature review', *Animation Journal* (Spring), <http://www.animationjournal.com/books/reviews/litrev.html> (accessed 30 June 2017).

Furniss, Maureen (2000), 'Motion capture: an overview', *Animation Journal*, 8: 2 (Spring), 68–82.

Gadassik, Alla (2010), 'Ghosts in the machine: the body in digital animation', in María del Pilar Blanco and Esther Peeren (eds), *Popular Ghosts: The Haunted Spaces of Everyday Culture*, London: Continuum International Publishing Group, pp. 225–38.

Genette, Gérard (1983), *Narrative Discourse: An Essay in Method*, translated by Jane E. Lewin, New York: Cornell University Press.

Genette, Gérard (1988), *Narrative Discourse Revisited*, translated by Jane E. Lewin, New York: Cornell University Press.

Genette, Gérard (1997), *Paratexts: Thresholds of Interpretation*, translated by Jane E. Lewin, Cambridge: Cambridge University Press.

Ghez, Didier (2010), *Walt's People: Talking Disney With the Artists Who Knew Him*, vol. 9, Bloomington, IN: Xlibris.

Ghez, Didier (2011), *Walt's People: Talking Disney With the Artists Who Knew Him*, vol. 11, Bloomington, IN: Xlibris.

Glenn, Phillip J. (2003), *Laughter in Interaction*, Cambridge: Cambridge University Press.

Goble, Mark (2010), *Beautiful Circuits: Modernism and the Mediated Life*, Columbia: Columbia University Press.

Godfrey, Alex (2011), Johnny Depp's a chameleon and Justin Timberlake's a bear', *The Guardian*, 5 March, <http://www.guardian.co.uk/film/2011/mar/05/johnny-depp-rango-caine-gnomeo> (accessed 30 June, 2017).

Goldmark, Daniel (2005), *Tunes for 'toons: Music and the Hollywood Cartoon*, Berkeley: University of California Press.

Goldmark, Daniel (2013), 'Pixar and the animated soundtrack', in John Richardson, Claudia Gorbman and Carol Vernallis (eds), *The Oxford Handbook of New Audiovisual Aesthetics*, New York: Oxford University Press, pp. 213–26.

Goldmark, Daniel and Charlie Keil (2011), *Funny Pictures: Animation and Comedy in Studio-Era Hollywood*, Berkeley, Los Angeles: University of California Press.

Goldmark, Daniel and Yuval Taylor (eds) (2002), *The Cartoon Music Book*, Chicago: A Capella Books.

Gould, Steven Jay (1987), 'A biological homage to Mickey', in Nancy R. Comley, David Hamilton, Carl H. Klaus, Robert Scholes, Nancy Sommers and Jason Tougaw (eds), *Fields of Writing: Motives of Writing*, New York: St Martin's Press, pp. 500–8.

Grainge, Paul (2008), *Brand Hollywood: Selling Entertainment in a Global Media Age*, London: Routledge.

Grant, Barry Keith (2007), *Film Genre: From Iconography to Ideology*, London: Wallflower Press.

Gray, Jonathan (2006), *Watching with The Simpsons: Television, Parody, and Intertextuality*, New York: Routledge.

Gray, Jonathan (2010), *Show Sold Separately: Promos, Spoilers, and other Media Paratexts*. New York: New York University Press.

Greven, David (2016), *Ghost Faces: Hollywood and Post-Millennial Masculinity*, Albany: State University of New York Press.

Grodal, Torben (1997), *Moving Pictures: A New Theory of Film Genres, Feelings, and Cognition*, New York: Oxford University Press.

Gross, Kenneth (2011), *Puppet: An Essay on Uncanny Life*, Chicago: University of Chicago Press.

Gross, Robert F. (2005), 'Mannerist noir: *Malice*', in Thomas Richard Fahy (ed.), *Considering Aaron Sorkin: Essays on the Politics, Poetics, and Sleight of Hand in the Films and Television Series*, Jefferson, NC: McFarland and Company, pp. 19–35.

Halberstam, Judith (2011), *The Queer Art of Failure*, Durham, NC: Duke University Press.

Hamilton, Cliff (1983), 'Anthropomorphism: you should know what it is', *Rangelands*, 5: 4, 166.

Hansen-Miller, David and Rosalind Gill (2011), '"Lad flicks": discursive reconstructions of masculinity in popular film', in Hilary Radner and Rebecca Stringer (eds), *Feminism at the Movies*, London and New York: Routledge, pp. 36–50.

Hardy, Jonathan (2010), *Cross-Media Promotion*, New York: Peter Lang.

Harries, Dan (2000), *Film Parody*, London: BFI Publishing.

Harries, Dan (2002), 'Film parody and the resuscitation of genre', in Steve Neale (ed.), *Genre and Contemporary Hollywood*, London: BFI Publishing, pp. 281–93.

Haswell, Helen (2014), 'To infinity and back again: handdrawn aesthetic and affection for the past in Pixar's pioneering animation', *Alphaville: Journal of Film and Screen Media*, 8 (Winter), Web. ISSN: 2009-4078.

Hauser, Arnold (1986), *Mannerism: The Crisis of the Renaissance and the Origin of Modern Art*, vol. 1, Cambridge, MA: Harvard University Press.

Hauser, Arnold (2002), *The Social History of Art, Vol. 2: Renaissance, Mannerism, Baroque*, London: Routledge.

Hayes, Derek and Chris Webster (2013), *Acting and Performance for Animation*, Burlington, MA: Focal Press.

Hayles, Katherine N. and Nicholas Gessler (2004), 'The splitstream of mixed reality: unstable ontologies and semiotic markers in "The Thirteenth Floor", "Dark City", and "Mulholland Drive"', *PMLA*, 119: 3, 428–99.

Hayward, Philip (2010), 'Polar grooves: dance, music and musicality in *Happy Feet*', in *Drawn to Sound*, 90–103.

Heath, Stephen (1981), *Questions of Cinema*, Bloomington: Indiana University Press.

Henderson, Stuart (2014), *The Hollywood Sequel: History and Form, 1971–2010*, London: BFI Publishing.

Herhuth, Eric (2017), *Pixar and the Aesthetic Imagination: Animation, Storytelling, and Digital Culture*, Berkeley: University of California Press.

Hofstadter, Douglas R. (1979), *Gödel, Escher, Bach: An Eternal Golden Braid*, Hassocks: Harvester Press.

Holian, Heather (2015), 'Animators as professional masqueraders: thoughts on Pixar', in Deborah Bell (ed.), *Masquerade: Essays on Tradition and Innovation Worldwide*, Jefferson, NC: McFarland and Company, 2015), pp. 231–40.

Holliday, Christopher (2012), 'Emotion capture: vocal performances by children in the computer-animated film', *Alphaville: Journal of Film and Screen Media*, 3 (Summer), ISSN: 2009-4078.

Holliday, Christopher (2016), 'Carl's moving castle: "animated" houses and the renovation of play in *Up* (2009)', in Eleanor Andrews and Stella Hockenhull (eds), *Spaces of the Cinematic Home: Behind the Screen Door*, London: Routledge, pp. 19–31.

Holson, Laura M. (2006), 'Animation films slip as viewers see reruns', The New York Times, 2 October, <http://www.nytimes.com/2006/10/02/business/worldbusiness/02iht-animation.3003482.html> (accessed 30 June 2017).

Honess Roe, Annabelle (2013), *Animated Documentary*, Basingstoke: Palgrave Macmillan.

Honess Roe, Annabelle (2016), 'Animated documentary', in Daniel Marcus and Selmin Kara (eds), *Contemporary Documentary*, London: Routledge, pp. 42–56.

Hooks, Ed (2011), *Acting for Animators*, London: Routledge.

Hooks, Ed (2012), 'The significance of *Rango*', *Animation World Network*, 28 February, <http://www.awn.com/blogs/ed-hooks-acting-animators/significance-rango> (accessed 30 June 2017).

Hopewell, John (2015), 'AFM: Grindstone takes North America on "Wicked Flying Monkeys", *Variety*, 5 November, <http://variety.com/2015/film/festivals/afm-grindstone-wicked-flying-monkeys-1201633494/> (accessed 30 June 2017).

Hubley, John and Zachary Schwartz (1946), 'Animation learns a new language', *Hollywood Quarterly*, 1: 4 (July), 63–8.

Hutchings, Peter (1995), 'Genre theory and criticism', in Joanne Hollows and Mark Jancovich (eds), *Approaches to Popular Film*, Manchester: Manchester University Press, pp. 59–77.

Iampolski, Mikhail (1998), *The Memory of Tiresias: Intertextuality and Film*, Berkeley: University of California Press.

Jameson, Frederic (1986), 'On magic realism in film', *Critical Inquiry*, 12: 2 (Winter), 301–25

Jenkins, Henry (2004), 'The work of theory in the age of digital transformation', in Toby Miller and Robert Stam (eds), *A Companion to Film Theory*, Oxford: Blackwell Publishing, pp. 234–61.

Jenkins, Henry (2006), *Convergence Culture: Where Old and New Media Collide*, New York: New York University Press.

Jess-Cooke, Carolyne (2009), *Film Sequels: Theory and Practice from Hollywood to Bollywood*, Edinburgh: Edinburgh University Press.

Jess-Cooke, Carolyn and Constantine Verevis (eds) (2010), *Second Takes: Critical Approaches to the Film Sequel*, Albany: State University of New York Press.

Jin, Dai (2016), *New Korean Wave: Transnational Cultural Power in the Age of Social Media*, Chicago: University of Illinois Press.

Johnston, Neala (2011), 'Australian animator Marek Kochout packs a punch in *Kung Fu Panda 2*', *Herald Sun*, 30 June, <http://www.heraldsun.com.au/entertainment/movies/australian-animator-marek-kochout-packs-a-punch-in-kung-fu-panda-2/story-e6frf9h6-1226084643165#content> (accessed 30 June 2017).

Jones, Mike (2007), 'Vanishing point: spatial composition and the virtual camera', *animation: an interdisciplinary journal*, 2: 3 (November), 225–43.

Jurkowski, Henryk (1983), 'Transcodification of the signs systems of puppets', *Semiotica*, 47: 1–4, 123–46.

Karon, Paul (2001), 'Beastly battle brewing', *Variety*, 385: 6 (2 December 2001 – 6 January 2002), 36.

Karpf, Anne (2006), *The Human Voice: The Story of a Remarkable Talent*, London: Bloomsbury Publishing.

Kaufmann, Thomas DaCosta (2009), *Arcimboldo: Visual Jokes, Natural History, and Still-Life Painting*, London: University of Chicago Press.

Kay, Ann (2010), 'Mannerism', in Stephen Farthing (ed.), *Art: The Whole Story*, London: Thames and Hudson, pp. 202–3.

Keeton, William (1967), *Biological Science*, New York: W. W. Norton.

Keil, Charlie and Kristen Whissel (eds) (2016), *Editing and Special/Visual Effects*, New Brunswick, NJ: Rutgers University Press.

Kennedy, John (1992), *The New Anthropomorphism*, New York: University of Cambridge Press.

Kerlow, Isaac (2004), *The Art of 3D: Computer Animation and Effects*, 3rd edn, Hoboken: NJ: John Wiley and Sons.

Kinder, Marsha (2002), 'Hot spots, avatars, and narrative fields forever: Buñuel's legacy for new digital media and interactive database narrative', *Film Quarterly*, 55: 4, 2–15.

King, Barry (2012), 'Articulating digital stardom', in Aaron Taylor (ed.), *Theorizing Film Acting*, London: Routledge, pp. 271–85.

King C. Richard, Carmen R. Lugo-Lugo and Mary K. Bloodsworth-Lugo (2010), *Animating Difference: Race, Gender and Sexuality in Contemporary Films for Children*, New York: Rowman and Littlefield Publishers.

King, Geoff (2002a), *New Hollywood Cinema: An Introduction*, London: I. B. Tauris.

King, Geoff (2002b), *Film Comedy*, London: Wallflower Press.

Kirsner, Scott (2008), Inventing *the Movies: Hollywood's Epic Battle Between Innovation and the Status Quo, from Thomas Edison to Steve Jobs*, Boston, MA: CinemaTech Books.

Kisacikoglu, Gokhan (2006), 'Directing plant interactions for over the hedge', *SIGGRAPH 2006*, <http://dl.acm.org/citation.cfm?id=1179909> (accessed 30 June 2017).

Kitses, Jim (1969), *Horizons West: Anthony Mann, Budd Boetticher, Sam Peckinpah: Studies of Authorship within the Western*, Bloomington: Indiana University Press.

Klein, Amanda Ann and R. Barton Palmer (2016), *Cycles, Sequels, Spin-offs, Remakes, and Reboots: Multiplicities in Film and Television*, Austin: University of Texas Press.

Klein, Norman (1993), *Seven Minutes: The Life and Death of the American Cartoon*, London: Verso.

Klein, Norman (1998), 'Hybrid cinema: *The Mask*, masques, and Tex Avery', in Kevin S. Sandler, *Reading the Rabbit: Explorations in Warner Bros. Animation*, New Brunswick, NJ: Rutgers University Press, pp. 209–20.

Klevan, Andrew (2005), *Film Performance: From Achievement to Appreciation*, London: Wallflower Press.

Klinger, Barbara (1984), '"Cinema/Ideology/Criticism" revisited: the progressive text', *Screen*, 25: 1 (January–February), 30–44.

Klinger, Barbara (2013), 'Three-dimensional cinema: the new normal', *Convergence: The International Journal of Research into New Media Technologies* (July), 1–9.

Knight, Damon (1967), *In Search of Wonder: Essays on Modern Science Fiction*, Chicago: Advent Publishers.

Knox, Israel (1957), 'Comedy and the category of exaggeration', *Journal of Philosophy*, 54: 25 (December), 801–12.

Kozloff, Sarah (1989), *Invisible Storytellers: Voiceover Narration in American Fiction Film*, Berkeley: University of California Press.

Krämer, Peter (2006), 'Steven Spielberg', in Linda Ruth Williams and Michael Hammond (eds), *Contemporary American Cinema*, Maidenhead: Open University Press), pp. 166–9.

Kriger, Judith (2012), *Animated Realism: A Behind-the-Scenes Look at the Animated Documentary Genre*, Oxford: Focal Press.

Krzywinska, Tanya (2006), 'Blood scythes, festivals, quests, and backstories: world creation and rhetorics of myth in world of Warcraft', *Games and Culture*, 1: 4, 383–96.

Kuhn, Annette and Guy Westwell (2012), *A Dictionary of Film Studies*, Oxford: Oxford University Press.

Kundert-Gibbs, John and Kristin Kundert-Gibbs (2009), *Action!: Acting Lessons for CG Animators*, Indianapolis: Wiley Publishing.

Lamarre, Thomas (2006), 'New media worlds', in Suzanne Buchan (ed.), *Animated Worlds*, Eastleigh: John Libbey Publishing, pp. 131–50.

Langford, Barry (2005), *Film Genre: Hollywood and Beyond*, Edinburgh: Edinburgh University Press.

Langford, Barry (2010), *Post-Classical Hollywood: Film Industry, Style and Ideology since 1945*, Edinburgh: Edinburgh University Press.

Lanier Jr, Clinton D., Aubrey R. Fowler III and C. Scott Rader (2014), 'What are you looking at, ya hockey puck?!' Anthropomorphizing brand relationships in the *Toy Story* trilogy', in Stephen Brown and Sharon Ponsonby-McCabe (eds), *Brand Mascots: And Other Marketing Animals*, New York and London: Routledge, pp. 35–54.

Lasseter, John (1987), 'Principles of traditional animation applied to 3D computer animation', *Computer Graphics*, 21: 4 (July), 35–44.

Lawson, Tim and Alisa Persons (2004), *The Magic Behind the Voices: A Who's Who of Cartoon Voice Actors*, Jackson: University Press of Mississippi.

Lebeau, Vicky (2008), *Childhood and Cinema*, London: Reaktion Books.

Lee, Nora (1989), 'Computer animation comes of age', *American Cinematographer*, 70: 10 (October), 78–87.

Lehman, Christopher (2007), *American Animated Cartoons of the Vietnam Era*, Jefferson, NC: McFarland and Company.

Leitch, Thomas M. (2002), *Crime Films*, Cambridge: Cambridge University Press.

Leslie, Esther (2002), *Hollywood Flatlands: Animation, Critical Theory and the Avant-Garde*, London: Verso.

Lichtenfeld, Eric (2004), *Action Speaks Louder: Violence, Spectacle, and the American Action Movie*, Westport, CT: Praeger.

Limoges, Jean-Marc (2011), 'Metalepsis according to Tex Avery: pushing back the frontiers of transgression (an extended definition of metalepsis)', in Karin Kukkonen and Sonja Klimek (eds), *Metalepsis in Popular Culture*, Berlin: de Gruyter, pp. 196–212.

Lister, Martin, Jon Dovey, Seth Giddings, Iain Grant and Kieran Kelly (2009), *New Media: A Critical Introduction*, London: Routledge.

Lodge, Guy (2014), 'Film review: "The House of Magic"', *Variety*, 21 July, <http://variety.com/2014/film/global/film-review-the-house-of-magic-1201264637/> (accessed 30 June 2017).

Louvel, Liliane (2011), *Poetics of the Iconotext*, Burlington, VT: Ashgate Publishing Company.

Lukas, Scott (2013), *The Immersive Worlds Handbook: Designing Theme Parks and Consumer Spaces*, Burlington, MA: Focal Press.

Lury, Karen (2010), *The Child in Film: Tears, Fears and Fairy Tales*, London: I. B. Tauris.

Lusinsky, Adolph, Paul Felix, Ernie Petti, Sean Jenkins, Adrienne Othon, Patrick Dalton, Hank Driskill and John Murrah (2009), 'Applying painterly concepts in a CG film – *Bolt*', *SIGGRAPH 2009*, <http://dl.acm.org/citation.cfm?id=1598011> (accessed 30 June 2017).

Macallan, Helen and Andrew Plain (2010), 'Filmic voices', in Norie Neumark et al. (eds), *Voice: Vocal Aesthetics in Digital Arts and Media*, Cambridge, MA: MIT Press, pp. 243–66.

McArthur, Colin (1972), *Underworld USA*, New York: Viking Press.

McClean, Shilo T. (2007), *Digital Storytelling: The Narrative Power of Visual Effects in Film*, Cambridge, MA: MIT Press.

McDonald, Paul (2000), *The Star System: Hollywood's Production of Popular Identities*, London: Wallflower Press.

McDonald, Paul (2012) 'Story and show: the basic contradiction of film star acting', in Aaron Taylor (ed.), *Theorizing Film Acting*, London: Routledge, pp. 169–83.

MacDonald, Sean (2016), *Animation in China: History, Aesthetics, Media*, New York: Routledge.

McDonnell, Kathleen (2005), *Honey, We Lost the Kids: Re-Thinking Childhood in the Multimedia Age*, Toronto: Second Story Press.

Mandelbrot, Benoît (1983), *The Fractal Geometry of Nature*, San Francisco: W. H. Freeman and Company.

Maniates, Maria Rika (1979), *Mannerism in Italian Music and Culture 1530–1630*, Manchester: Manchester University Press.

Manovich, Lev (2001), *The Language of New Media*, London: MIT Press.

Manovich, Lev (2005), 'Cinema and digital media', in Andrew Utterson (ed.), *Technology and Culture, The Film Reader*, New York: Taylor and Francis, pp. 27–31.

Maquerlot, Jean-Pierre (1995), *Shakespeare and the Mannerist tradition: a reading of five problem plays*, Northamptonshire: Woolnough Bookbinding Limited.

Marcello, Starr A. (2006), 'Performance design: an analysis of film acting and sound design', *Journal of Film and Video*, 58: 1–2 (Spring), 59–70.

Margolin, Uri (2010), 'From predicates to people like us: kinds of readerly engagement with literary characters', in Jens Eder, Fotis Jannidis and Ralf Schneider (eds), *Characters in Fictional Worlds: Understanding Imaginary Beings in Literature, Film, and Other Media*, Berlin: Walter de Gruyter, pp. 400–15.

Marks, Laura U. (2000), *The Skin of the Film: Intercultural Cinema, Embodiment, and the Senses*, Durham, NC: Duke University Press.

Marshall, Elizabeth and Özlem Sensoy (2009), 'The same old hocus-pocus: pedagogies of gender and sexuality in *Shrek 2*', *Discourse: Studies in the Cultural Politics of Education*, 30: 2 (June), 154–61.

Martin, Adrian (1992), '*MISE EN SCENE* IS DEAD, or the expressive, the excessive, the technical and the stylish', *Continuum*, 5: 2, 87–140.

Martin, Adrian (2014), *Mise en Scène and Film Style: From Classical Hollywood to New Media Art*, London: Palgrave Macmillan.

Mast, Gerald (1976), *The Comic Mind: Comedy and the Movies*, New York: Random House.

Mathijs, Ernest (2013), 'Cronenberg connected: cameo acting, cult stardom and supertexts', in Kate Egan and Sarah Thomas (eds), *Cult Film Stardom: Offbeat Attractions and Processes of Cultification*, London: Palgrave Macmillan.

Mealing, Stuart (1998), *The Art and Science of Computer Animation*, Exeter: Intellect Books.

Meinel, Dietmar (2014), 'The garden in the machine: myth and symbol in the digital age', in Eric Erbacher, Nicole Maruo-Schröder and Florian Sedlmeier (eds), *Rereading the Machine in the Garden: Nature and Technology in American Culture*, Frankfurt am Main: Campus-Verlag, pp. 190–210.

Meinel, Dietmar (2016), *Pixar's America: The Re-Animation of Amreican Myths and Symbols*, London: Palgrave Macmillan.

Mitchell, Peter (2003), 'Nemo-led recovery hope', *The Age*, 4 June, <http://www.theage.com.au/articles/2003/06/03/1054406187273.html> (accessed 30 June 2017).

Mittell, Jason (2014), *Genre and Television: From Cop Shows to Cartoons in American Culture*, New York and London: Routledge.

Moine, Raphaëlle (2008), *Cinema Genre*, Oxford: Blackwell Publishing.

Montgomery, Colleen (2016), 'Pixarticulation vocal performance in Pixar animation', *Music, Sound, and the Moving Image*, 10: 1, 1–23.

Montgomery, Colleen (2017), '*Double Doublage*: vocal performance in the French-dubbed versions of Pixar's *Toy Story* and *Cars*', in Tom Whittaker and Sarah Wright (eds), *Locating the Voice in Film: Critical Approaches and Global Practices*, New York: Oxford University Press, pp. 83–100.

Mortimer, Claire (2010), *Romantic Comedy*, London: Routledge.

Moskowicz, Julia (2002), 'To infinity and beyond: assessing the technological imperative in computer animation', *Screen*, 43: 3 (Autumn), 293–314.

Moxey, Keith (2008), 'Visual studies and the iconic turn', *Journal of Visual Culture*, 7: 2 (August), 131–46.

Mulvey, Laura (2007), 'A clumsy sublime', *Film Quarterly*, 60: 3 (Spring), 3.

Murch, Walter (1994), 'Foreword', in Michel Chion, *Audio-Vision: Sound on Screen*, translated by Claudia Gorbman, New York: Columbia University Press, pp. vii–xxiv.

Murray, Linda (1977), *The High Renaissance and Mannerism: Italy, The North and Spain 1500–1600*, London: Thames and Hudson.

Murray, Robin L. and Joseph K. Heumann (2011), *That's All Folks?: Ecocritical Readings of American Animated Features*, Lincoln: University of Nebraska Press.

Naficy, Hamid (2001), *An Accented Cinema: Exilic and Diasporic Filmmaking*, Princeton, NJ and Oxford: Princeton University Press.

Napier, Susan J. (2005), *Anime: From Akira to Howl's Moving Castle: Experiencing Contemporary Japanese Animation*, New York: Palgrave Macmillan.

Ndalianis, Angela (2004), *Neo-Baroque Aesthetics and Contemporary Entertainment*, Cambridge, MA: MIT Press.

Neale, Steve (1980), *Genre*, London: BFI Publishing.

Neale, Steve (2000), *Genre and Hollywood*, London: Routledge.

Neale, Steve (2002), 'Introduction', in Steve Neale (ed.), *Genre and Contemporary Hollywood*, London: BFI Publishing, pp. 1–7.

Neale, Steve (2012), 'Questions of Genre', in Barry Keith Grant (ed.), *Film Genre Reader IV*, Austin: University of Texas Press, pp. 178–202.

Neale, Steve and Frank Krutnik (1990), *Popular Film and Television Comedy*, London: Routledge.

Neumark, Norie, Ross Gibson and Theo Van Leeuwen (eds) (2010), *Voice: Vocal Aesthetics in Digital Arts and Media*, Cambridge, MA: MIT Press.

Neupert, Richard (2011), *French Animation History*, Chichester: John Wiley and Sons.

Neupert, Richard (2015), 'French animated cinema, 1999 to present', in Alistair Fox, Michel Marie and Raphaëlle Moine, *A Companion to Contemporary French Cinema*, Chichester: John Wiley and Sons, pp. 333–55.

Neupert, Richard (2016), *John Lasseter (Contemporary Film Directors)*, Urbana: University of Illinois Press.

Ngai, Sianne (2005), *Ugly Feelings*, Cambridge, MA: Harvard University Press.

North, Dan (2008), *Performing Illusions: Cinema, Special Effects and the Virtual Actor*, London: Wallflower Press.

North, Dan, Bob Rehak and Michael S. Duffy (eds) (2015), *Special Effects: New Histories, Theories, Contexts*, London: BFI/Palgrave.

North, Michael (2009), *Machine-Age Comedy*, New York: Oxford University Press.

O'Pray, Michael (1995), 'A Mannerist surrealist', in Peter Hames (ed.), *Dark Alchemy: The Films of Jan Švankmajer*, Westport, CT: Greenwood Press, pp. 48–77.

Osmond, Andrew (2007), 'Ratatouille' review, *Sight and Sound*, 17: 10 (October), 66.

Paik, Karen (2007), *To Infinity and Beyond! The Story of Pixar Animation Studios*, London: Random House.

Pallant, Chris (2011), *Demystifying Disney: A History of Disney Feature Animation*, London: Bloomsbury.

Pallant, Chris (2012), 'Digital dimensions in actorly performance: the aesthetic potential of performance capture', *Film International*, 10: 3 (August), 37–49.

Palmer, Jerry (1995), *Taking Humour Seriously*, London: Routledge.

Parkin, Lin (2011), 'Voice over community petitions the Oscars', *VoiceOverTimes*, 8 April, <http://www.voiceovertimes.com/2011/04/08/voiceover-community-petitions-the-oscars/> (accessed 30 June 2017).

Pavis, Patrice (1998), *Dictionary of the Theatre: Terms, Concepts and Analysis*, Toronto and Buffalo: University of Toronto Press.

Perkins, V. F. (1993), *Film as Film: Understanding and Judging Movies*, New York: Da Capo Press.

Perkins, V. F. (2005), 'Where is the world? The horizon of events in movie fiction', in John Gibbs and Douglas Pye (eds), *Style and Meaning: Studies in the Detailed Analysis of Film*, Manchester: Manchester University Press, pp. 16–41.

Peterson, Mark Allen (2005), *Anthropology and Mass Communication: Media and Myth in the New Millennium*, New York: Bergahn Books.

Pimentel, Octavio and Paul Velázquez (2009), '*Shrek 2*: an appraisal of mainstream animation's influence on identity', *Journal of Latinos and Education*, 8: 1, 5–21.

Power, Patrick (2008), 'Character animation and the embodied mind–brain', *animation: an interdisciplinary journal*, 3: 1 (March), 25–48.

Power, Patrick (2009), 'Animated expression: expressive style in 3D computer graphic narrative animation', *animation: an interdisciplinary journal*, 4: 2 (July), 107–29.

Power, Patrick (2012), 'Ludic Toons: the dynamics of creative play in studio animation', *American Journal of Play*, 5: 1 (Fall), 22–54.

Prell, Karen (2012), 'From puppets to pixels and portals', *Karen Prell* website, <http://www.karenprell.com/Karen_Prell_Home.html> (accessed 30 June 2017).

Price, David A. (2009), *The Pixar Touch: The Making of a Company*, New York: Vintage.

Prince, Stephen (1996), 'True Lies: perceptual realism, digital images, and film theory', *Film Quarterly*, 49: 3, 27–37.

Prince, Stephen (1997), *Movies and Meaning: An Introduction to Film*, 2nd edn, Boston: Allyn and Bacon.

Prince, Stephen (2012), *Digital Visual Effects in Cinema: The Seduction of Reality*, New Brunswick, NJ: Rutgers University Press.

Pringle, Hamish (2004), *Celebrity Sells*, Chichester: John Wiley and Sons.

Proschan, Frank (1981), 'Puppet voices and interlocutors: language in folk puppetry', *Journal of American Folklore*, 94: 374 (October–December), 527–55.

Proschan, Frank (1983), 'The semiotic study of puppets, masks, and performing objects', *Semiotica*, 47: 1–4, 3–44.

Purse, Lisa (2013), *Digital Imaging in Popular Cinema*, Edinburgh: Edinburgh University Press.

Pye, Douglas (2007), 'Movies and tone', in John Gibbs and Douglas Pye (eds), *Close-Up 02: Movies and Tone/Reading Rohmer/Voices in Film*, London: Wallflower Press, pp. 1–80.

Riffel, Casey (2012), 'Dissecting Bambi: multiplanar photography, the cel technique, and the flowering of full animation', *The Velvet Light Trap*, 69 (Spring), 3–16.

Robertson, Barbara (1998), 'Meet Geri: the new face of animation', *Computer Graphics World*, 21: 2 (February), 20–24, 28.

Robertson, Barbara (2006), 'Flushed with success', *Computer Graphics World*, 29: 10 (October), <http://www.cgw.com/Publications/CGW/2006/Volume-29-Issue-10-Oct-2006-/Flushed-with-Success.aspx> (accessed 30 June 2017).

Robertson, Pamela (1997), 'Home and away: friends of Dorothy on the road in Oz', in Steven Cohan and Ina Rae Hark (eds), *The Road Movie Book*, London: Routledge, pp. 271–86.

Robinson, Chuck (2009), 'The technological chain letter and the nuclear family in *The Ring*', in Lisa DeTora (ed.), *Heroes of Film, Comics and American Culture: Essays on Real and Fictional*, Jefferson, NC: McFarland and Company, pp. 253–67.

Rösing, Lilian Munk (2016), *Pixar with Lacan: The Hysteric's Guide to Animation*. London: Bloomsbury.

Ross, Miriam (2015), *3D Cinema: Optical Illusions and Tactile Experiences*, London: Palgrave Macmillan.

Rothschild, Louis (2009), 'Finding a father: repetition, difference, and fantasy in *Finding Nemo*', in Bruce Reiss and Robert Grossmark (eds), *Heterosexual Masculinities: Contemporary Perspectives from Psychoanalytic Gender Theory*, London: Routledge, pp. 217–30.

Ruskin, Harry (1974), *Comedy is a Serious Business*, Woodstock, IL: Dramatic Publishing Company.

Ryan, Marie-Laure (2007), 'Looking through the computer screen: self-reflexivity in net.art', in Winfried Nöth and Nina Bishara (eds), *Self-Reference in the Media*, Berlin: Walter de Gruyter, pp. 269–89.

Ryu, David and Paul Kanyuk (2007), 'Rivers of rodents: an animation-centric crowds pipeline for *Ratatouille*', *Pixar Technical #07-02* (May), <http://graphics.pixar.com/library/RiversOfRodents/paper.pdf> (accessed 30 June 2017).

Sandler, Kevin S. (1997), 'Pogs, dogs or ferrets: anthropomorphism and animaniacs', *Animation Journal*, 6: 1, 44–53.

Sandler, Kevin S. (1998), 'Gender evasion: Bugs Bunny in drag', in Kevin S. Sandler, *Reading the Rabbit: Explorations in Warner Bros. Animation*, New Brunswick, NJ: Rutgers University Press, pp. 154–71.

Sarafian, Katherine (2003), 'Flashing digital animations: Pixar's digital aesthetic', in Anna Everett and John T. Caldwell (eds), *New Media: Theories and Practices of Digitextuality*, New York and London: Routledge, pp. 209–23.

Satz, Aura and Jon Wood (2009), 'Introduction', in Aura Satz and Jon Wood (eds), *Articulate Objects: Voice, Sculpture and Performance*, Bern: Peter Lang, pp. 15–27.

Schaffer, William (2004), 'The importance of being plastic: the feel of Pixar', *Animation Journal*, 12: 72–95.

Schatz, Thomas (2009), 'New Hollywood, new millennium', in Warren Buckland (ed.), *Film Theory and Contemporary Hollywood Movies*, New York: Routledge, pp. 19–46.

Sciretta, Peter (2013), 'Video: Danny Boyle says we're in danger of losing adult movies due to "the Pixarification of movies"', *SlashFilm*, <http://www.slash-film.com/video-danny-boyle-says-were-in-danger-of-losing-adult-movies-because-of-the-pixarification-of-movies/> (accessed 30 June 2017).

Scott, Allen John (2005), *On Hollywood: The Place, The Industry*, Princeton, NJ: Princeton University Press.

Seidman, Steve (1981), *Comedian Comedy*, Ann Arbor, MI: UMI Research Press.

Serritella, Vincent, Hosuk Change, Leon J. W. Park, Ferdi Scheepers and Brett Levin (2016), 'Lapping water effects in *Piper*', *SIGGRAPH 2016*, <http://dl.acm.org/citation.cfm?id=2927457> (accessed 30 June 2017).

Shail, Andrew (2005), '"You hear about them all the time": a genealogy of the sentient program', in Stacy Gillis (ed.), *The Matrix Trilogy: Cyberpunk Reloaded*, London: Wallflower Press, pp. 23–35.

Shaw, Ian Graham Ronald (2010), 'Wall-E's world: animating Badiou's philosophy', *Cultural Geographies*, 17: 3, 391–405.

Shershow, Scott Cutler (1995), *Puppets and 'Popular' Culture*, Ithaca, NY: Cornell University.

Shull, Michael S. and David E. Wilt (2004), *Doing Their Bit: Wartime American Animated Short Films 1939–1945*, 2nd edn, Jefferson, NC: McFarland and Company.

Sickels, Robert (2011), *American Film in the Digital Age*, Santa Barbara, CA: Praeger.

Siegel, Lewis N. (2014), 'Frozen on ice: rendering frost and ice on Frozen', *SIGGRAPH 2014*, <http://dl.acm.org/citation.cfm?id=2614137> (accessed 30 June 2017).

Siegel, Tatiana, Scott Roxborough, Rhonda Richford and Clarence Tsui (2013), 'Inside the weird world of international dubbing', *The Hollywood Reporter Magazine*, 14 March, <http://www.hollywoodreporter.com/news/argo-django-unchained-inside-weird-427453> (accessed 30 June 2017).

Sito, Tom (2006), *Drawing the Line: The Untold Story of the Animation Unions from Bosko to Bart Simpson*, Lexington: University Press of Kentucky.

Sito, Tom (2013), *Moving Innovation: A History of Computer Animation*, Cambridge, MA: MIT Press.

Smith, Jacob (2008), *Vocal Tracks: Performance and Sound Media*, Berkeley: University of California Press.

Snider, Burr (1995), 'The Toy Story story: how Lasseter cam to make the first 100-percent computer-generated theatrical motion picture', *WIRED* 3: 12 (December), <http://www.wired.com/wired/archive/3.12/toy.story_pr.html> (accessed 30 June 2017).

Sobchack, Vivian (2004), *Carnal Thoughts: Embodiment and Moving Image Culture*, Berkeley: University of California Press.

Sobchack, Vivian (2006), 'Final fantasies: computer graphic animation and the [dis]illusion of life', in Suzanne Buchan (ed.), *Animated Worlds*, Eastleigh: John Libbey Publishing, pp. 171–82.

Sobchack, Vivian (2008), 'The line and the animorph or "travel is more than just A to B"', *animation: an interdisciplinary journal*, 3: 3 (November), 251–65

Sobchack, Vivian (2009), 'Animation and automation, or, the incredible effortfulness of being', *Screen*, 50: 4 (Winter), 375–91.

Sperb, Jason (2016), *Flickers of Film: Nostalgia in the Time of Digital Cinema*, New Brunswick, NJ: Rutgers University Press.

Staiger, Janet (2006), 'Complex narratives: an introduction', *Film Criticism*, 31: 1–2, 2–4.

Stam, Robert (1992), *Reflexivity in Film and Literature from Don Quixote to Jean-Luc Godard*, New York: Columbia University Press.

Stam, Robert, Robert Burgoyne and Sandy Flitterman-Lewis (eds) (2005), *New Vocabularies in Film Semiotics: Structuralism, Post-Structuralism and Beyond*, London: Routledge.

Stamp, Richard (2004), 'We scare because we care.™ How monsters make friends in animated feature films', in Paul L. Yoder and Peter Mario Kreuter (eds), *Monsters and the Monstrous: Myths and Metaphors of Enduring Evil*, Oxford: Inter-Disciplinary Press, pp. 69–79.

Stewart, Garrett (1999), *Between Film and Screen: Modernism's Photo Synthesis*, Chicago: University of Chicago Press.

Stewart, Susan (2003), *On Longing: Narratives of the Miniature, the Gigantic, the Souvenir, the Collection*, 8th edn, Durham, NC, and London: Duke University Press.

Stokes, Brian (2003), 'A brave new world of puppetry: Part 1: Introduction to virtual puppets', *Puppetry Journal*, 55: 2 (Winter), 22–3.

Stout, Janis P. (1983), *The Journey Narrative in American Literature: Patterns and Departures*, Westport, CT: Greenwood Press.

Straw, Will (1987), 'The discipline of forms: Mannerism in recent cinema', *Cultural Studies*, 1: 3, 361–75.

Street, Rita (1998), *Computer Animation: A Whole New World*, Rockport, MA: Rockport Publishers.

Strzelczyk, Florentine (2008), 'Fascism and family entertainment', *Quarterly Review of Film and Video*, 25: 3, 196–211.

Sullivan, Karen, Gary Schumer and Kate Alexander (2013), *Ideas for the Animated Short: Finding and Building Stories*, 2nd edn, Burlington, MA: Focal Press.

Szalai, Georg (2013), 'South African animation studio Triggerfish gets funding, plans action-comedy "Seal Team"', *The Hollywood Reporter*, 15 November, <http://www.hollywoodreporter.com/news/south-african-animation-studio-triggerfish-656331 (accessed 30 June 2017).

Tapley, Kristopher (2016), '"Sausage Party": Seth Rogen's "R-rated Pixar movie" devours Comic-Con', *Variety*, 22 July, <http://variety.com/2016/

film/news/sausage-party-seth-rogens-r-rated-pixar-movie-devours-comic-con-1201820574/> (accessed 30 June 2017).

Tasker, Yvonne (1998), *Working Girls: Gender and Sexuality in Popular Cinema*, London: Routledge.

Teevan, Matthew (2011), 'Animating by numbers: workflow issues in Shane Acker's *9*', *Animation Practice, Process and Production*, 1: 1, 83–96.

Telotte, J. P. (2008), *The Mouse Machine: Disney and Technology*, Chicago: University of Illinois Press.

Telotte, J. P. (2010), *Animating Space: From Mickey to Wall-E*, Lexington: University Press of Kentucky.

Thompson, Kirsten (2005), 'Animation', in Maurice Charney (ed.), *Comedy: A Geographic and Historical Guide*, vol. 1, London: Praeger, pp. 135–52.

Thompson, Kristin (1980), 'Implications of the cel animation technique', in Teresa De Lauretis and Stephen Heath (eds), *The Cinematic Apparatus: Technology as Historical and Cultural Form*, New York: St Martin's Press, pp. 106–20.

Thompson, Kristin [2006] (2011), 'By Annie standards', in David Bordwell and Kristin Thompson, *Minding Movies*, Chicago: University of Chicago Press, pp. 159–66.

Tiffin, Jessica (2009), *Marvelous Geometry: Narrative and Metafiction in Modern Fairytale*, Detroit: Wayne State University Press.

Tillis, Steve (1992), *Towards an Aesthetics of the Puppet: Puppetry as a Theatrical Art*, Westport, CT: Greenwood Press.

Tillis, Steve (1996), 'The actor occluded: puppet theatre and acting theory', *Theatre Topics*, 6: 2, 109–19.

Tillis, Steve (1999), 'The art of puppetry in the age of media production', *Drama Review*, 43: 3 (Fall), 182–95.

Todorov, Tzvetan (1990), *Genres in Discourse*, New York: Cambridge University Press.

Tranter, Paul J. and Scott Sharpe (2008), 'Escaping Monstropolis: child-friendly cities, peak oil and *Monsters, Inc.*', *Children's Geographies*, 6: 3 (August), 295–308.

Tudor, Andrew (1973), *Theories of Film*, New York: Viking Press.

Tudor, Andrew (2002), 'From paranoia to postmodernism: the horror movie in late modern society', in Steve Neale (ed.), *Genre and Contemporary Hollywood*, London: BFI Publishing, pp. 105–16.

Tudor, Deborah (2008), 'The eye of the frog: questions of space in films using digital processes', *Cinema Journal*, 48: 1 (Fall), 90–110.

Turner, Chris (2004), *Planet Simpson: How a Cartoon Masterpiece Documented an Era and Defined a Generation*, New York: Random House.

Turnock, Julie A. (2015), *Plastic Reality: Special Effects, Technology, and the Emergence of 1970s Blockbuster Aesthetics*, New York: Columbia University Press.

Tyler, Dennis (2013), 'Home is where the heart is: Pixar's *Up*', in Johnson Cheu (ed.), *Diversity in Disney Films: Critical Essays on Race, Ethnicity, Gender, Sexuality and Disability*, Jefferson, NC: McFarland and Company, pp. 268–83.

Tyler, Tom (2003), 'If horses had hands...', *Society and Animals*, 11: 3, 267–81.

Ulin, Jeff (2010), *The Business of Media Distribution: Monetizing Film, TV and Video Content in an Online World*, Burlington, MA: Focal Press.

Velarde, Robert (2010), *The Wisdom of Pixar: An Animated Look at Virtue*, Westmont, IL: InterVarsity Press.

Verrier, Richard (2013), 'Out of toon with the times?', *The Star*, 2 September, <http://www.thestar.com.my/lifestyle/entertainment/movies/news/2013/09/02/out-of-toon-with-the-times/> (accessed 30 June 2017).

Vidal, Belén (2012), *Figuring the Past: Period Film and the Mannerist Aesthetic*, Amsterdam: Amsterdam University Press.

Vincendeau, Ginette (1996), *The Companion to French Cinema*, London: BFI Publishing.

Virilio, Paul (1991), *The Lost Dimension*, New York: Semiotext(e).

Virno, Paolo (2005), 'Childhood and critical thought', *Grey Room*, 21 (Fall), 6–12.

von Borries, Friedrich, Steffen P. Walz and Matthias Bottger (eds) (2007), *Space Time Play: Computer Games, Architecture and Urbanism: The Next Level*, Berlin: Berkenhäuser Verlag.

Walters, James. *Alternative Worlds in Hollywood Cinema: Resonance Between Realms*. Bristol: Intellect, 2008.

Ward, Paul (2002), 'Computer games as remediated animation', in Geoff King and Tanya Krzywinska (eds), *ScreenPlay: Cinema/Videogames/Interfaces*, London: Wallflower Press, pp. 122–35.

Wasko, Janet (2001), *Understanding Disney: The Manufacture of Fantasy*, Cambridge: Polity.

Watson, Paul (2003), 'Critical approaches to Hollywood cinema: authorship, genre and stars', in Jill Nelmes (ed.), *An Introduction to Film Studies*, 3rd edn, London and New York: Routledge, pp. 129–58.

Weaver, Tyler (2013), *Comics for Film, Games, and Animation: Using Comics to Construct Your Transmedia Storyworld*, Burlington, MA: Focal Press.

Weetch, Owen (2016), *Expressive Spaces in Digital 3D Cinema*, London: Palgrave Macmillan.

Wells, Paul (1998), *Understanding Animation*, London: Routledge.

Wells, Paul (2002a), *Animation: Genre and Authorship*, London: Wallflower Press.

Wells, Paul (2002b), *Animation and America*, Edinburgh: Edinburgh University Press.

Wells, Paul (2003), 'To affinity and beyond: Woody, Buzz and the new authenticity', in Thomas Austin and Martin Barker (eds), *Contemporary Hollywood Stardom*, New York: Oxford University Press, pp. 90–102.

Wells, Paul (2009a), 'To sonicity and beyond! Gary Rydstrom and quilting the Pixar sound', *Animation Journal*, 17: 23–35.

Wells, Paul (2009b), *The Animated Bestiary*, London: Rutgers University Press.

Wells, Paul (2011), 'Shane Acker: big worlds, little stories – counting up to 9', *Animation Practice, Process and Production*, 1: 1, 97–105.

Wells, Paul (2013), 'Laughter is ten times more powerful than a scream: the case of animated comedy', in Andrew Horton and Joanna E. Rapf (eds), *A Companion to Film Comedy*, Chichester: Wiley-Blackwell, pp. 497–520.

Wells, Paul (2016), 'Writing animated documentary: a theory of practice', *International Journal of Film and Media Arts*, 1: 1, <http://revistas.ulusofona. pt/index.php/ijfma/article/view/5432> (accessed 30 June 2017).

West, Elliot (2012), *The Essential West: Collected Essays*, Norman, OK: University of Oklahoma Press.

Whissel, Kristen (2014), *Spectacular Digital Effects: CGI and Contemporary Cinema*, Durham, NC and London: Duke University Press.

Whiteley, Gillian (2011), *Junk: Art and the Politics of Trash*, London: I. B. Tauris.

Whitley, David (2012), *The Idea of Nature in Disney Animation: From Snow White to WALL-E*, Burlington, VT: Ashgate Publishing Company.

Whittington, William (2012), 'The sonic playpen: sound design and technology in Pixar's animated shorts', in Trevor Pinch and Karin Bijsterveld (eds), *The Oxford Handbook of Sound Studies*, New York: Oxford University Press, pp. 367–86.

Williams, Linda (1991), 'Film bodies: gender, genre, and excess', *Film Quarterly*, 44: 4 (Summer), 2–13.

Willis, Sharon (2008), 'Movies and wayward images', in Chris Holmund (ed.), *American Cinema of the 1990s: Themes and Variations*, New Brunswick, NJ: Rutgers University Press, pp. 45–69.

Wilson, Emma (2003), *Cinema's Missing Children*, London: Wallflower Press.

Wisnovsky, Robert (2005), 'Avicenna and the Avicennian tradition', in Peter Adamson and Richard C. Taylor (eds), *The Cambridge Companion to Arabic Philosophy*, New York: Cambridge University Press, pp. 92–136.

Wojcik, Pamela Robertson (2006), 'The sound of film acting', *Journal of Film and Video*, 58: 1–2 (Spring/Summer), 71–83.

Wolf, Mark J. P. (2012a), *Building Imaginary Worlds: The Theory and History of Subcreation*, New York: Routledge.

Wolf, Mark J. P. (2012b), *Encyclopedia of Video Games: The Culture, Technology, and Art of Gaming*, vol. 1, Santa Barbara, CA: Greenwood Press.

Wolf, Werner (2006), 'Defamiliarized initial framings in fiction', in Werner Wolf and Walter Bernhart (eds), *Framing Borders in Literature and in Other Media*, Amsterdam: Editions Rodopi, pp. 295–328.

Wolf, Werner (2011), 'Is there a metareferential turn, and if so, how can it be explained?', in Werner Wolf (ed.), *The Metareferential Turn in Contemporary Arts and Media: Forms, Functions, Attempts at Explanation*, New York: Editions Rodopi, pp. 1–49.

Wolff, Ellen (2007), 'Animated performance', *Millimeter – The Magazine of Motion Picture and Television Production*, 35: 6 (November–December), 24, 26–27.

Wood, Aylish (2006), 'Re-animating Space', *animation: an interdisciplinary journal*, 1: 2 (November), 133–52.

Wood, Aylish (2007), *Digital Encounters*, New York: Routledge.

Wood, Aylish (2015), *Software, Animation and the Moving Image: What's in the Box?*, London: Palgrave Macmillan.

Wooden, Shannon R. and Ken Gillam (2014), *Pixar's Boy Stories: Masculinity in a Postmodern Age*, Lanham, MD: Rowman and Littlefield.

Wright, Jean Ann (2005), *Animation Writing and Development: From Script Development to Pitch*, Burlington, MA: Focal Press.

Zusne, Leonard, and Warren H. Jones (2014), *Anomalistic Psychology: A Study of Magical Thinking*, New York: Psychology Press.

Index